The Law of Succession: '

Roger Kerridge

School of Law, University of Bristol, BS8 1RJ

Europa Law Publishing, Groningen 2011

The Law of Succession: Testamentary Freedom

European Perspectives

Edited by Miriam Anderson and Esther Arroyo i Amayuelas

European Studies in Private Law (5)

Europa Law Publishing is a publishing company
specializing in European Union law, international trade
law, public international law, environmental law and
comparative national law.
For further information please contact Europa Law
Publishing via email: info@europalawpublishing.com
or visit our website at: www.europalawpublishing.com.

Typeset in Scala and Scala Sans, Graphic design by
G2K Designers, Groningen/Amsterdam

NUR 828; ISBN 978-90-8952-087-6

Preface

In most jurisdictions, both legal operators and those unversed in law consider the law of succession to be one of the most technically complicated legal areas.

The solutions offered by the law of succession often require the application of ancient principles and rules, the meaning of which remains obscure to the general public. The overall result is that the idiosyncrasies of each system are attributed to the peculiar characteristics of the country or region where that particular law of succession applies. Complexity leads to different results, and then these different results are linked to a particular tradition or culture. This is clearly a simplification, since there is no doubt that family law is determined by cultural, religious and social values, and the law of succession needs to take those values into account. But recent comparative studies show that the differences are by no means insurmountable. Hopefully this book will contribute to this realization.

On April 30, 2010 a conference was held in Barcelona, under the auspices of the Spanish presidency of the European Union. It was organized by the University of Barcelona and the Catalan Government, within the commemorative acts for the 50th anniversary of the first Catalan civil law Compilation. The new Catalan regulation on succession had only come into force on January 1, 2009, but the conference aimed to analyse the reform and its goals from a European perspective. The chosen topic was freedom of testation, to be dealt with from a threefold perspective: the limitations imposed by human rights; the restraints deriving from the regulation on forced share, and the possibility to plan one's succession by means of an inheritance agreement. The surviving spouse or cohabitant's position was also scrutinized, since the forced share granted to issue (and maybe also to parents and further ascendants) equals limiting the testator's freedom to benefit his or her partner, and, on the other hand, the lack of conformity with the rules on intestacy may lead more people to execute wills.

This book presents the proceedings of the conference, addressing the above mentioned issues, but has a much broader approach, covering English common law, two examples of Eastern European systems and one from Scandinavia. The first chapter, by Professor Pintens, gives a general overview of the different solutions to be found in Europe, while evaluating the need and opportunity of harmonization in this area. The second contribution, by Professor Bonomi, addresses the Proposal for a Regulation of the European Parliament and of the Council on jurisdiction, applicable law, recognition and enforcement of decisions and authentic instruments in matters of succession and the creation of a European Certificate of Succession, focusing on the implications that the adoption of this instrument would have on freedom of testation; the mere existence of this proposal proves that the European Union feels the need to intervene in this area, due to the increase in the number of international successions during the last decades.

The second part of this book is dedicated to the reforms that have taken place in Catalonia. An initial chapter provides an overview of the succession system in force, designed to guide readers through the following chapters (Professors Arroyo Amayuelas and Anderson), which address restraints on testamentary freedom (Professor Bosch Capdevila), new grounds for disinheritance (Professor Vaquer) and inheritance agreements (Professor Navas Navarro) in this particular jurisdiction.

The third part of the book contains papers from different professors addressing the key topics in their jurisdictions: England and Wales (Professor Kerridge); Germany (Professor Röthel); Hungary (Professor Csehi); Italy (Professor Fusaro); The Netherlands (Professor Milo); Norway (Professor Hambro); Scotland (Professor Clive); Slovenia (Professor Kraljić); Spain (Professor Cámara Lapuente).

The editors wish to thank all contributors for their cooperation throughout the process of producing this book, which has been financed by the Spanish Ministry of Science and Innovation (DER 2008-03992/JURI (MICINN) and by the Generalitat de Catalunya (2009 SGR 221)).

We cannot end this preface without expressing our deep sorrow at the loss of Professor Peter Lødrup, who had initially undertaken to produce the Norwegian report for this book with enthusiasm and who found time, even when his health problems were beginning to prevent him from working, to recommend his colleague Professor Peter Hambro to take on this task at short notice.

Barcelona, 2 February 2011.
Miriam Anderson/Esther Arroyo i Amayuelas

Contents

	Preface	v
	Contents	vii
	Abbreviations	xviii
	Authors	xxvi

PART	I	**Harmonization of Succession Law in Europe: The Current Debate**	
CHAPTER I		**Need and Opportunity of Convergence in European Succession Laws**	
		Walter Pintens	3
	I	Introduction	5
	2	Need for Convergence in European Substantive Succession Laws	6
	3	Opportunity of Convergence in European Substantive Succession Laws	8
	3.1	Spontaneous Harmonisation	8
	3.1.1	The Statutory Portion of the Surviving Spouse	8
	3.1.2	Compulsory Portion of Children	12
	3.1.3	Conclusion	17
	3.2	Institutional Unification	19
	3.2.1	Achievements	19
	3.2.2	Promotion of What We Have	21
	3.3	Legal Scholarship	21
	4	Conclusions	22
CHAPTER 2		**Testamentary Freedom or Forced Heirship? Balancing Party Autonomy and the Protection of Family Members**	
		Andrea Bonomi	25
	I	Introductory Remarks	27
	2	The Connecting Factor of the Last Habitual Residence of the Deceased	29
	3	The Choice of Applicable Law	31
	4	Agreements as to Succession	34
	5	The Public Policy Exception	36
	6	Final Remarks	38

PART   II   **New Trends in Catalan Succession Law**

CHAPTER 3   **Between Tradition and Modernisation: A General**
             Overview of the Catalan Succession Law Reform
             Esther Arroyo i Amayuelas – Miriam Anderson   41

       1   Introduction   43
       1.1   The Diversity of Private Law Systems in Spain   43
       1.2   Catalonia: From the 1960 Compilation to a Civil Code 44
       2   An Overview of the Law of Succession in Book IV of
             the Catalan Civil Code   45
       3   The Law of Succession and Legal Tradition: New Rules
             for Old Principles   48
       3.1   The Appointment of an Heir Is a Prerequisite for the
             Validity of a Will   49
       3.2   The Heir As a Universal Successor   51
       3.3   *Nemo Pro Parte Testatus, Pro Parte Intestatus Decedere Potest* 51
       3.4   *Semel Heres, Semper Heres*   52
       4   The Impact of Social and Economic Changes on the Law of
             Succession   54
       4.1   Freedom of Testation and Respect for the Testator's Wishes 54
       4.1.1 New Grounds for Unworthiness and a Longer List of
             Victims of Reprehensible Conduct   55
       4.1.2 A New Ground for Disinheritance: The Lack of
             Normal Family Interaction Attributable to the Forced Heir 56
       4.1.3 The Protection of the Elderly Testator   57
       4.2   The Adaptation of the Law of Succession to
             New Family Models   58
       4.2.1 The Equalization of Spouses and Cohabitants   58
       4.2.2 Improvements in the Position of the Surviving Spouse or
             Cohabitant   60
       4.3   Succession within the Family Business: The Modernization
             of Inheritance Agreements   65
       5   Changes within Tradition: The Incomplete Reform of the
             Forced Share   68
       6   Conclusions   71

CHAPTER 4   **Testamentary Freedom and Its Limits**
             Esteve Bosch Capdevila   73

       1   Introduction   75
       1.1   The Testator's Will as the Supreme Law of Succession 75
       1.2   Protecting Testamentary Freedom   75
       1.3   The Types of Limits to Testamentary Freedom   75

2	Limits Derived from the Testator's Wishes	77
2.1	Provisions in a Will Aiming to Prevent Future Testamentary Modification or Revocation	77
2.2	*Ad Cautelam* Clauses: Do They Protect or Limit Testamentary Freedom?	77
2.2.1	The Admission of *Ad Cautelam* Clauses in the Catalan Legal Tradition and in the Precedents of Book IV of the CC Cat	78
2.2.2	The Silence of Book IV of the CC Cat Regarding the *Ad Cautelam* Clauses	79
3	The Limits Imposed by a Third Party: The Problems Caused by *Captatorias Institutiones*	80
4	The Legal Limits to the Content of Testamentary Provisions	82
4.1	Limits that Affect the Conditions that a Testator Can Impose	82
4.1.1	Limits Deriving from the Principle *Semel Heres Semper Heres*	82
4.1.2	Limits Derived from Certain Conditions Being Unlawful	84
4.2	Limits Affecting Specific Clauses	85
4.2.1	The Incompatibility between Testate and Intestate Heirs and Testamentary Freedom	86
4.2.2	The Limits Imposed on Fideicommissum	86
4.3	The Lineage Principle	87
4.4	Discriminatory Clauses	87
CHAPTER 5	**Freedom of Testation, Compulsory Share and Disinheritance Based on Lack of Family Relationship** Antoni Vaquer Aloy	89
1	Preliminary Remarks	91
2	Reforms of the Compulsory Share in European Laws of Succession: No Abrogation, Only Reduction	92
3	A Weaker Compulsory Share in Catalonia	93
4	The New Gorund for Disinheritance in Art. 451-7.2 e of the Catalan Civil Code	95
4.1	Subsistence of the Compulsory Share, with Widening Grounds for Disinheritance	95
4.2	Behaviour-Based Succession Systems	95
4.3	Compulsory Share, Disinheritance and Descendants' Behaviour in Catalan Law	98
5	Concluding Remarks	103

CHAPTER 6   **Freedom of Testation Versus Freedom to Enter Into Succession Agreements and Transaction Costs**
Susana Navas Navarro   105

1   Introduction   107
2   The Legislator's Choice: An Inheritance Agreement Prevails
Over and Is Sometimes Incompatible With a Will   109
3   The Deceased's Choice: Succession Within the
Family Business   112
3.1   Preliminary Remarks   112
3.2   The Family Estate: From "Homestead" to "Business"?   115
3.3   Economic Costs Derived from Entering into Succession
Agreements   117
3.3.1   Transaction Costs and the Choice of the Successor   118
3.3.2   Economic Costs Derived from the Deceased's Change
of Mind   120
3.4   Possible "Efficient" Instruments for Succession Within the
Family Business   123
4   Final Conclusions   125

PART   III   **National Perspectives on the Law of Succession in the 21st Century**

CHAPTER 7   **Freedom of Testation in England and Wales**
Roger Kerridge   129

1   Introduction   131
2   History   131
3   Trusts as a Restraint on Freedom of Testation   134
4   The Mortmain Act   136
5   The 'Construction' (or Interpretation) of Wills   137
6   The *Pla and Puncernau* Case Viewed from England   139
7   Contracts to Leave Property by Will, Proprietary Estoppel
and Mutual Wills   142
7.1   Validity of a Contract to Leave Property by Will   142
7.2   Proprietary Estoppel   142
7.3   Mutual Wills   143
8   Freedom of Testation in England in the Twentieth and
Twenty First Centuries   145
9   What Problems Are There Under the 1975 Act?   148
10   Particular Problems with Children and Step-children   151
11   Reform of the 1975 Act   151

CHAPTER 8	**Law of Succession and Testamentary Freedom in Germany** A. Röthel	155

1	Introduction	157
2	Testamentary Freedom and Public Policy (§ 138 BGB)	157
2.1	Conditional Inheritance: "Undue Influence" on Heirs?	158
2.2	Wills in Favour of Disabled People or of People in Need versus Social Welfare	159
2.3	The "Rule Against Perpetuities"	159
2.4	Particular Testamentary Prohibitions	161
3	Testamentary Freedom and the Compulsory Portion (§§ 2303 ff. BGB)	162
3.1	Overview of the Basic Concept	163
3.2	Reforms in the Law on Compulsory Portion (2009)	164
3.2.1	Increase of Compulsory Portions Due to *Inter Vivos* Donations (§ 2325 BGB latest amendment)	164
3.2.2	Deferment (§ 2331a BGB latest amendment)	164
3.2.3	Deprivation of the Compulsory Portion (§ 2333 BGB)	164
4	Testamentary Freedom and Inheritance Agreements	165
4.1	Overview of the Applicable Law	165
4.2	Reform Debate	165
5	Summary: Requirements of Freedom of Testation Fit for the Present Day	166

CHAPTER 9	**The Law of Succession in Hungary** Zoltán Csehi	167

1	Introduction	169
2	Freedom of Testation versus *Ordre Public*	170
2.1	Restrictions Imposed by Human Rights and Fundamental Rights	171
2.1.1	Preliminaries on Human Rights	171
2.1.2	The Modern Hungarian Constitution	172
2.1.3	The Practice of the Constitutional Court Concerning Succession	173
2.2	Public Law Restrictions	175
2.3	Private Law Restrictions	175
3	Freedom of Testation versus Legally Granted Hereditary Rights	177
3.1	Preliminaries on Compulsory Share	177
3.2	Functions of the Compulsory Share	177
3.3	The Rules on Compulsory Share	180
3.3.1	Beneficiaries	180
3.3.2	Extent	182

3.3.3	Basis	182
3.3.4	Facts Affecting the Allocated Share	183
3.3.5	Payment	183
3.3.6	Obligor	183
3.3.7	Collisions with Other Rights	184
3.3.8	The Future of the Compulsory Share	184
4	Freedom of Testation versus Freedom to Enter into Inheritance Agreements	184
4.1	Contracts Regulated Outside the Law of Succession	185
4.1.1	Support Contract	185
4.1.2	Life Insurance	185
4.1.3	Savings Deposits	185
4.1.4	Copyright	186
4.2	Contracts Within the Law of Succession	186
4.2.1	Inheritance Contracts	186
4.2.2	*Donatio Mortis Causa*	188
4.2.3	Contract Among Descendants on Anticipated Inheritance	189
5	*De Lege Ferenda*	190

CHAPTER 10   **Freedom of Testation in Italy**
Andrea Fusaro

		191
1	Freedom of Testation and *Ordre Public*	193
1.1	Freedom To Make a Will: Different Types of Wills	193
1.2	*Ordre Public*	193
1.2.1	The Prohibition of Indefinite Settlements	193
1.2.2	Conditions Imposed on the Heir	194
2	Intestacy	194
3	Freedom of Testation and Hereditary Rights Legally Granted	195
3.1	Forced Share	195
3.2	Subjects	196
3.3	Quotas and Rights	196
3.4	Calculation of the Forced Share	197
3.5	The Reduction of Testamentary Dispositions and Donations	197
3.6	The Circulation of Assets	197
4	Freedom of Testation versus Freedom to Enter into Inheritance Agreements	198
	Annex: Draft of a Family Agreement	200

CHAPTER 11   **Acquisition of Property by Succession in Dutch Law. Tradition between Autonomy and Solidarity in a Changing Society**
J. Michael Milo   203

1   Introduction   205
2   Principles and Developments in Dutch Succession Law   205
2.1   Principles and Other Determining Factors   205
2.2   Developments in Precodified Dutch Law   208
2.3   From the First Codification Onwards   211
3   Contemporary Succession Law in General   214
3.1   Succession and Matrimonial Property Law   214
3.2   Succession, Systematization, and Acquisition of Property   215
3.3   Intestate Succession   217
3.4   Testamentary Dispositions and Restrictions   218
4   Position of the Spouse and the Children   223
4.1   Intestate Positions of Spouse and Children   223
4.2   Testate Position of Spouse and Children   225
4.3   Forced Heirship   226
5   Concluding Remarks   226

CHAPTER 12   **The Norwegian Approach to Forced Share, the Surviving Spouse's Position and Irrevocable Wills**
Peter Hambro   229

1   Introduction   231
2   The Forced Share Inheritance   231
3   The Contents of Wills   234
4   The Position of the Surviving Spouse   235
5   Irrevocable Wills   238
6   Other Irrevocable Instruments   239
6.1   Insurance Policies   239
6.2   Pre- and Postnuptial Agreements   240

CHAPTER 13   **Restraints on Freedom of Testation in Scottish Succession Law**
Eric Clive   241

1   Underlying Values   243
2   Freedom of Testation and Protection of Certain Claimants   245
2.1   Fixed Share for Spouse or Civil Partner   246
2.2   Fixed Share for Issue   249
2.3   Protection of Cohabitants   251
3   Other Restraints on Freedom of Testation   253

3.1   Inheritance Tax   253
3.2   Limitations on Accumulation of Income   254
3.3   Limitations on Future Liferents   255
3.4   Purposes Otherwise Contrary to Public Policy   256

CHAPTER 14   **Freedom of Testation in Slovenia**
              Suzana Kraljić   257

1   Introduction   259
2   Freedom of Testation   260
2.1   *Ordre public*   260
2.2   Forced Share and *Exheredatio*   260
3   Especial Limitations for Agricultural Holdings   265
4   Inheritance Agreements   267

CHAPTER 15   **Freedom of Testation, Legal Inheritance Rights and**
              Public Order under Spanish Law
              Sergio Cámara Lapuente   269

1   Overview   271
2   Limits on the Freedom to Dispose *Mortis Causa* in the
        Spanish Civil Code and in the Autonomous Communities   271
2.1   Legal Frame   271
2.2   Description of the *ex lege* Rights in Favour of the
        Deceased's Family   272
2.3   Assessment of the Main Legislative Trends   278
2.3.1   Strengthening the Legal Position of Surviving Spouses   278
2.3.2   Legal Rights in Favour of a Cohabitant   279
2.3.3   Scarce Enlargement of the Grounds of Disinheritance
        and Unworthiness   281
2.3.4   Special Protection for Certain Social Groups   282
3   Material Freedom of Testation   283
3.1   The Current Debate Regarding the Suppression or
        Modification of the Forced Share ('Legítima')   283
3.1.1   Arguments in Favour of Forced Shares ('Legítimas')   284
3.1.2   Arguments in Favour of Testamentary Freedom   285
3.2   Proposed Solutions   286
3.3   Channels for Relaxation without Eliminating the
        Forced Share   289
3.3.1   Reforms Already Implemented in the Spanish Civil Code   289
3.3.2   Other Reforms that Might be Suitable in View of
        Comparative Law (Both Interregional and International)   290
3.4   Other Possible Enlargements of Material Freedom
        of Testation   293

4	Formal Freedom of Testation	293
4.1	Testamentary Forms	293
4.2	Inheritance Agreements, Joint Wills and Other *Mortis Causa* Instruments	294
4.3	Delegation of the Power to Make a Will, Appointment of Representatives with the Power to Choose Beneficiaries or to Distribute the Estate, or Appointment of Trustees ('fiducia sucesoria')	296
4.4	Notaries' Plea for Further Reforms	299
5	Freedom of Testation and Public Order	299
5.1	Is the Forced Share a Matter of Public Order?	299
5.2	Does the Spanish Constitution Guarantee the Forced Share?	300
5.3	Scope of Spanish Public Order in International Succession	301
5.4	Public Order and Fraud to the Law of Succession	303
	Bibliography	308

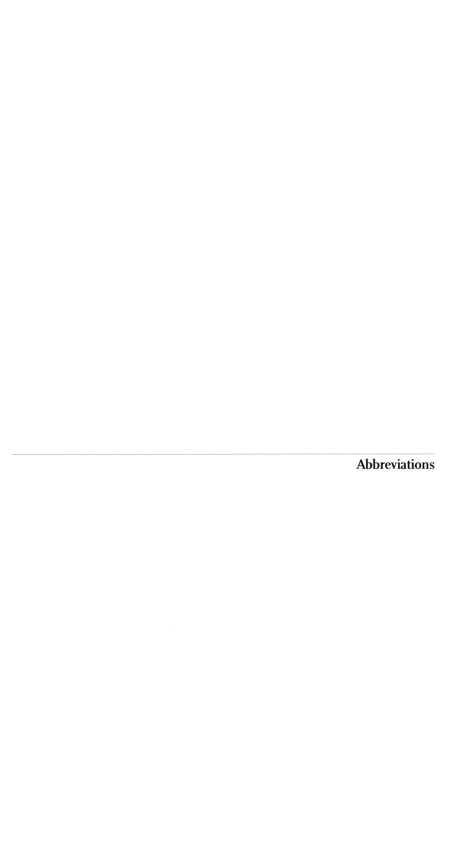

Abbreviations

AAMN	Anales de la Academia Matritense del Notariado
AC	The Law Reports, Appeal Cases (from 1891 to the present)
ACiv.	Actualidad Civil
AcP	Archiv für die civilistische Praxis
ADC	Anuario de Derecho civil
AFDUDC	Anuario da Facultade de Dereito da Universidade da Coruña
AJA	Actualidad Jurídica Aranzadi
AJ Famille	Actualité Juridique Famille
All ER	All England Law Reports
All ER Annual Rev.	All England Law Reports. Annual Review
Am. J. Comp. L.	American Journal of Comparative Law
AnuarioDGRN	Anuario de la Dirección General de los Registros y del Notariado
ARACRTPR	Act on Restablishment of Agricultural Communities and Restitution of Their Property and Rights (Slovenia)
ArCiv.	Aranzadi Civil
Arizona Law Rev	Arizona Law Review
Art./art.	Article
AS	Act of Succession (Norway).
ATF	Arrêt Tribunal Federal (Suisse) (Ruling by the Swiss Federal Court)
ATSJC	Auto Tribunal Superior de Justicia de Cataluña (Catalan Supreme Court Decision)
BayGVBl.	Bayerisches Gesetz- und Verordnungsblatt (Law and Ordinance Gazette for Bavaria)
BayObLG	Bayerisches Oberstes Landesgericht (Bavarian Higher Regional Court; Bavarian appellate court until 2006)
BDT	Bírósági Döntések Tára (Monthly review of the rulings of the Court of Appeals of Hungary)
BGB	Bürgerliches Gesetzbuch (German Civil Code)
BGBl	Bundesgesetzblatt (German Federal Law Gazette)
BGH	Bundesgerichtshof (German Federal Court of Justice)
BGHZ	Entscheidungen des BGH in Zivilsachen (Decisions of the Federal Court of Justice on civil matters, Germany)
BH	Bírósági Határozatok (Monthly review of rulings of the Supreme Court of Hungary)
BIMJ	Boletín de Información del Ministerio de Justicia
BOA	Boletín Oficial de Aragón (Aragón Official Gazette)
BOE	Boletín Oficial del Estado (Spanish Official Gazette)
BOPC	Butlletí Oficial del Parlament de Catalunya (Official Gazette of the Catalan Parliament)
Brandeis LJ	Brandeis Law Journal
BVerfG	Bundesverfassungsgericht (Federal Constitutional Court, Germany)

BVerfGE	Entscheidungen des BVerfG (Decisions of the Federal Constitutional Court, Germany)
BW	Burgerlijk Wetboek (Dutch Civil Code)
Camb Law J	Cambridge Law Journal
c.	Chapter
Car.	Carolus
Cass. civ.	Cassazione civile/Cassation civile
CC	Civil Code
CC Cat	Catalan Civil Code
CCJC	Cuadernos Civitas de Jurisprudencia Civil
CDCC	Catalan Civil Law Compilation
Cf.	Compare
CE	Constitución Española (Spanish Constitution)
CF	Codi de Família (Catalan Code on Family Law)
Ch. Cas	Selected Cases in Chancery 1681-1698
Ch.	The Law Reports, Chancery Division (from 1891 to the present)
Ch. D.	The Law Reports, Chancery Division (from 1875 60 1890)
Cl. & F	Clark & Finnelly's House of Lords Cases
CLR	Commonwealth Law Reports
Cmnd.	Command Paper (Paper presented to the UK Parliament by the Government, 1956-1986)
CO	Code of Obligations (Slovenia)
CoA	Companies Act (Slovenia)
Coord.	Coordinator
CRRA	Copyright and Related Rights Act (Slovenia)
CRS	Constitution of the Republic of Slovenia
CS	Codi de Succesions (Catalan Code on Succession)
Curt, Moo PC.	Curteis' Eccelsiastical Reports, Moore's Privy Council Cases
DA	Denationalization Act (Slovenia)
DCFR	Draft Common Frame of Reference
DGRN	Dirección General de los Registros y del Notariado (Directorate General for Registries and Notary Services, Spain)
DNotZ	Deutsche Notar-Zeitschrift
DOGC	Diari Oficial Generalitat de Catalunya (Catalan Official Gazette)
DP	Discussion Paper
DPyC	Derecho Privado y Constitución
DSPC	Diari de Sessions del Parlament de Catalunya (Official Publication of the Catalan Parliamentary Sittings)
EC	European Community
ECHR	European Court/Convention on Human Rights
ECJ	European Court of Justice
ECR	European Courts Reports
Ed(s).	Editor(s)
edn	edition

e.g.	exempli gratia
EGBGB	Einführungsgesetz zum Bürgerlichen Gesetzbuch
	(Preliminary Provisions to the German Civil Code)
EJCL	Electronic Journal of Comparative Law
ErbR	Zeitschrift für die gesamte erbrechtliche Praxis
ERPL	European Review of Private Law
ET&P	Entrepreneurial Theory and Practice
EU	European Union
f(f).	following (one or more elements)
F.C.R.	Family Court
Fam	The Law Reports, Family Division
Fam Bus Rev	Family Business Review
FamPra.ch	Die Praxis des Familienrechts
FamRZ	Zeitschrift für das gesamte Familienrecht
FLR	Family Law Reports
fn.	Footnote
GBl. BW	Gesetzblatt für Baden-Württemberg
	(Official Gazette for Baden-Württemberg)
GG	Grundgesetz (German Constitution)
DNotI	Deutsches Notar Institut (German Notary Institute)
GOM	Groninger Opmerkingen en Mededelingen
GVBl. NW	Gesetz- und Verordnungsblatt für das Land
	Nordrhein-Westfalen (Official Gazette for North Rhine-Westphalia)
GW	Grondwet (Dutch Constitution)
Harv Law Rev	Harvard Law Review
Hastings Law J	Hastings Law Journal
HL Cas	Clark & Finnelly's House of Lords Reports New Series
HR	Hoge Raad (The Netherlands Supreme Court)
IA	Inheritance Act (Slovenia)
IAHA	Inheritance of Agricultural Holdings Act (Slovenia)
ICLQ	International and Comparative Law Quarterly
IGTA	Inheritance and Gift Tax Act (Slovenia)
i.e.	id est
INE	Instituto Nacional de Estadística (National Institute of Statistics)
Innst. O.	Proposition to Parliament (Norway)
Int. Leg. Mat.	International Legal Materials
IPRax	Praxis des Internationalen Privat- und Verfahrensrechts
JDI	Journal de droit international
J Leg Stud	Journal of Legal Studies
J Bus Vent	Journal of Business Venturing
J Polit Econ	Journal of Political Economy
JO	Journal Officiel (French Official Gazette)
J Organ Behav	Journal of Organizational Behaviour
J Small Bus Manag	Journal of Small Business Management

JUR	Citation from the Westlaw-Aranzadi database
JurisPR-FamR	Juris PraxisReport Familienrecht
JCP	Jurisclasseur Périodique
JZ	Juristenzeitung
KG	Kammergericht, Superior Court of Justice in Berlin, equivalent to a Higher Regional Court (Oberlandesgericht, OLG) in other areas
La Law Rev	Lousiana Law Review
LandesheimG	Landesheim Gesetz (Law on retirement homes and asylums in Baden-Württemberg, Germany)
LASCM	Ley de Aragón de sucesiones por causa de muerte (Succession Law in Aragon, Spain)
Law Com	Law Commission
LD	Legislative Decree
LEC	Ley de Enjuiciamiento Civil (Spanish Law on Civil Procedure)
LG	Landgericht (Regional Court, Germany)
LPartG	Lebenspartnerschaftsgesetz (Civil Partnership Act, Germany)
LQR	Law Quarterly Review
LR P&D	Law Reports, Probate and Divorce Cases (from 1866 to 1875)
Mich Law Rev	Michigan Law Review
MFRA	Marriage and Family Relations Act (Slovenia)
MJ	Maastricht Journal of European and Comparative Law
MLR	Modern Law Review
No./no(s).	Number/number(s)
NJ	Nederlandse Jurisprudentie
NJW	Neue Juristische Wochenschrift
NTBR	Nederlands Tijdschrift voor Burgerlijk Recht
OCV	Official Consolidated Version
OJ	Official Journal of the European Communities
OLG	Oberlandesgericht (Higher Regional Court, Germany)
Ohio N Univ Law Rev	Ohio Northern University Law Review
OW	Overgangswet (Transition Law, The Netherlands)
P	Law Reports, Probate
p(p).	Page(s)
P. & C.R.	Property, Planning and Compensation Reports
PG	Parlementaire Geschiedenis
PIL	Private International Law
PJ	Poder Judicial
PK	Polgári Kollégium állásfoglalása (Opinion of the college of the judges of the Supreme Court of Hungary)
RabelsZ	Rabels Zeitschrift für ausländisches und internationales Privatrecht
Rb	Rechtbank
RCDI	Revista Crítica de Derecho Inmobiliario
RCDIP	Revue Critique de Droit International Privé

RCDP	Revista Catalana de Dret Privat
RDGDEJ	Resolució de la Direcció General de Dret i Entitats Jurídiques
	(Resolution of the Directorate General for Law and
	Legal Entities, Catalan Governement)
RDM	Revista de Derecho Mercantil
RDP	Revista de Derecho Privado
RDPat	Revista de Derecho Patrimonial
REDI	Revista Española de Derecho Internacional
RESL	Review of Economic Studies Limited
RTDC	Revue Trimestrielle de Droit Civil
RGD	Revue Générale de Droit
RGZ	Entscheidungen des Reichsgerichts in Zivilsachen
	(Decisions of the Supreme Court of the German Reich)
RJC	Revista Jurídica de Catalunya
RJCLM	Revista Jurídica de Castilla-La Mancha
RJNavarra	Revista Jurídica de Navarra
RJN	Revista Jurídica del Notariado
RNotZ	Rheinischen Notar-Zeitschrift
RS	Republic of Slovenia
RSSCPA	Registration of Same-Sex Parternships Act (Slovenia)
Rt	Norsk Retstidende
RTDF	Revue Trimestrielle de Droit Familial
SAP	Sentencia Audiencia Provincial
	(Spanish Provincial Court of Appeal Judgment)
SC	Session Cases
Scot Law Com	Scottish Law Commission
SG	Sozialgericht (German Social Welfare Court)
SLT	Scots Law Times
STC	Sentència del Tribunal Constitucional
	(Spanish Constitutional Court Judgment)
Stellenbosch LR	Stellenbosch Law Review
STS/SSTS	Sentencia/s del Tribunal Supremo
	(Spanish Supreme Court Judgment(s))
STSJC	Sentència del Tribunal Superior de Justícia de Catalunya
	(Catalan Supreme Court Judgment)
TFEU	Treaty on the Functioning of the European Union
TfR	Tidsskrift for rettsvitenskap
Tulane LR	Tulane Law Review
U. Cal. D. LR	University of California Davis Law Review
UNTS	United Nations Treaty Series
Univ Chicago Law Rev	University of Chicago Law Review
Univ Penn Law Rev	University of Pennsylvania Law Review
Utah Law Rev	Utah Law Review
Ves Jun	Cases in the Court of Chancery from 1789 to 1817
	reported by Francis Vesey Junior

VG	Verwaltungsgericht (German Administrative Court)
Vid./vid.	Videtur
VSH	Vrhovno sodišče Hrvaške (Supreme Court of Croatia)
VSK	Višje sodišče v Kopru (High Court of Koper)
VSL	Višje sodišče v Ljubljani (High Court of Ljubljana)
Wisconsin LR	Wisconsin Law Review
W.L.R	Weekly Law Reports
WNa	Wet op het Notarisambt (Notary Act, The Netherlands)
WNH	Wetboek Napoleon, ingerigt voor het Koningrijk Holland (Code Napoléon, adapted for the kingdom of Holland)
WoqG	Pflege- und Wohnqualitätsgesetz (Law on the regulation of assistance, care and housing quality of the elderly and disabled, Germany)
WPNR	Weekblad voor Privaatrecht, Notariaat en Registratie
WSNP	Wet Schuldsanering Natuurlijke Personen (Rules on debt relief of natural persons – incorporated in the insolvency act, art. 284-362 FW, The Netherlands)
WTG	Wohn- und Teilhabegesetz (Law on home assistance and care, Germany)
WTLR	Wills and Trusts Law Reports
ZErb	Zeitschrift für die Steuer- und Erbrechtspraxis
ZEuP	Zeitschrift für Europäisches Recht
ZEV	Zeitschrift für Erbrecht und Vermögensnachfolge

Authors

Miriam Anderson is Senior Lecturer of Private Law at the University of Barcelona.

Esther Arroyo i Amayuelas is Senior Lecturer of Private Law at the University of Barcelona.

Andrea Bonomi is Professor at the University of Lausanne, Switzerland. Director of the Center of Comparative, European and International Law of the University of Lausanne.

Esteve Bosch Capdevila is Professor of Private Law at the University Rovira i Virgili (Tarragona).

Sergio Cámara Lapuente is Professor of Private Law at the University of La Rioja (Spain).

Eric Clive is Visiting Professor at the School of Law of the Edinburgh University. Former member of the Scottish Law Commission.

Zoltán Csehi is Professor of Law at ELTE Faculty of Law (Budapest) and holds the Chair of Commercial Law at Pázmány Péter Catholic University, Faculty of Law (Budapest).

Andrea Fusaro is Professor of Comparative Legal Systems in the Faculty of Law at the University of Genova. He is also Pubblic Notary in Genova (Italy).

Peter Hambro is Assistant Professor at the Law Faculty of the University of Oslo (Norway).

Roger Kerridge M.A., LL.B. (Cantab.) is Professor of Law at the University of Bristol. Solicitor.

Suzana Kraljić is Assistant Professor at the Faculty of Law of the University of Maribor (Slovenia).

J. *Michael Milo* is Associate Professor at the Molengraaff Institute for Private Law, Utrecht University.

Susana Navas Navarro is Professor of Civil Law at the University Autònoma de Barcelona.

Walter Pintens is Professor at the University of Leuven (Belgium) and Honorary Professor at Saarland University (Germany).

Anne Röthel holds the Chair for Civil Law, European and International Private Law at Bucerius Law School (Hamburg).

Antoni Vaquer Aloy is Professor of Private Law at the University of Lleida.

PART I

Harmonization of Succession Law in Europe: The Current Debate

CHAPTER I

Need and Opportunity of Convergence in European Succession Laws

Walter Pintens

I Introduction

In the past the impact of succession law and especially international succession law was rather small. Earnings were modest. Real wealth was for the happy few. Property in foreign countries was seldom owned.

Times have changed. Succession law has grown in importance. During the course of the next decades transmission of wealth through inheritance will be very important throughout the whole of Europe. Estates have increased. In Germany for example the average value of an inheritance in 2010 has increased to 287,000 EUR, representing a fifty percent increase on the average 1998 value.[1] There are a number of reasons for this capital growth. The revenue of elderly people has increased due to the revalorisation of pensions in the seventies and eighties.[2] Consequently, elderly people dispose of a regular and stable income and often do not need to use their assets for their maintenance and care. In times of increasing economic activity stock exchange profits have led to considerable capital gains.

It is not uncommon for this capital to be invested transnationally. More and more people acquire property abroad or have a bank account in a foreign country, leading to an increase in cross-border succession cases.[3]

The Proposal of 14 October 2009 for a Regulation of the European Parliament and the Council on jurisdiction, applicable law, recognition and enforcement of decisions and authentic instruments in matters of succession and the creation of a European Certificate of Succession[4] was accompanied by an impact assessment giving more detailed information on the magnitude of international successions and wills.[5] In the European Union 4.5 million people die each year. The impact assessment study estimates that 10% of all those successions have an international dimension. This may be due to the existence of movable or immovable assets in another Member State, to the deceased having a nationality other than that of the Member State in which he or she was resident or due to the fact that potential heirs live in another Member State than the last habitual residence of the deceased.[6] The international dimension of the inheritance also has implications for the value of the estate since a wealthier person is likely to have property in a foreign country. In successions without any cross-border dimension, the average value of the estate is estimated to be 137,000 EUR whereas the study estimates that in successions with a cross-border dimension

---

[1] Branchereport Erbschaften, BBE-Unternehmensberatung, Cologne 1999. Cf. Nave-Herz (2009) 202 ff.

[2] Pestiau (1994) 9. Although in some European countries pensions are still modest.

[3] See also Terner (2007) 149.

[4] COM (2009) 154 final. Hereto Dörner (2010) 221 ff.; *Max Planck Institute for Comparative and International Private Law* (2010) 522 ff.; Schurig (2010) 343 ff.; Kohler and Pintens (2010) 1483 ff. Concerning the preparatory work see Dutta (2009) 547 ff.; Harris (2008) 181 ff.; Kohler and Pintens (2009) 1531 ff.; Lehmann (2006); Lokin (2009) 54 ff.; Terner (2007) 147 ff.

[5] SEC (2009) 410 of 14 October 2009, 18 ff. and 53 ff. (annex).

[6] SEC (2009) 410 of 14 October 2009, 18.

the value of the estate is around double that figure, i.e. 274,000 EUR. The value of all cross-border successions in Europe is therefore an estimated 123.3 billion EUR per year.[7]

Those cross-border cases allow international succession law to come to the fore. The most important example is of course the above mentioned proposal for an EU-Regulation.

2 Need for Convergence in European Substantive Succession Laws

Many authors are rather sceptical about the possibility of substantive family and succession law unification. For them, unification in this field is complicated, delicate and therefore not feasible. They believe that the need for harmonisation can be satisfied by unification of private international law and especially by unification of conflict of law rules and that this approach has the advantage that the cultural and historical diversity of substantive law could be preserved.[8] Of course, the contribution of private international law has been very important during the last decades and will continue to be important in the future. The Hague Convention of 5 October 1961 on the Conflicts of Laws Relating to the Form of Testamentary Dispositions was very successful,[9] the other Hague conventions on international succession law less so.[10] An EU-Regulation on matters of succession law will be an important step forwards. A uniform conflict of laws rule based on the last residence of the deceased will set an end to the divide between those legal systems having a uniform rule and those making a distinction between movable and immovable assets. To a certain extent it will also remove the need for domestic courts to apply foreign law. But the Regulation will not set an end to the application of foreign law since for example domestic courts will have to apply foreign law chosen by *professio iuris*.

But the primary question is whether conflict of law rules are able to solve all the problems caused by the diversity of substantive succession law. If the possibility of a choice of law is not available or has not been used, the outcome of an international succession case is completely dependent upon the law of the country of last residence. A change of residence can provoke a loss of inheritance rights for certain heirs, since the shares inherited by family members vary depending on which national law is applicable.[11] Legal certainty, predictability

---

[7] SEC (2009) 410 of 14 October 2009, 18.

[8] See e.g. Spellenberg (2005) No. 47.

[9] 510 UNTS 175.

[10] E.g. the Hague Convention of 1 August 1989 on the Law Applicable to Succession to the Estates of Deceased Persons (28 Int. Leg. Mat. 150) was only ratified by the Netherlands. See Cámara Lapuente (2008) 1193 ff.

[11] Cf. Dethloff, Arguments for the unification and harmonisation of family law in Europe, in: Boele-Woelki (2003) 39 ff.; Dethloff (2004) 553 ff.

and expectations are severely undermined and a feeling of injustice is created. Only harmonisation of substantive succession law can completely prevent this. It is therefore advisable to accompany the unification of private international law with some harmonisation of substantive law.[12]

Some legal scholars reject unification and even harmonisation on the ground that it will lead to a loss of culture. But for many this cultural restraint loses importance. For Prof. Leipold it is an empty slogan.[13] As family law, succession law has undergone major changes in all legal systems and as Prof. Langbein already stated in 1984: 'over the course of the twentieth century, persistent tides of change have been lapping at the once quiet shores of the law of succession'.[14] Succession law is indeed less static than it is thought to be.[15] National succession laws have not proven to be resistant to reforms and to the reception of foreign law. In most European legal systems succession law has undergone many reforms, often inspired by the law of their neighbouring countries, to the degree that much national individuality and culture have already been lost.[16] Therefore, large parts of succession law are no longer deeply rooted in national traditions.

We have not lost a part of our culture through all of these reforms. Cultural embedment does not mean that we are embedded in a culture to such an extent that we give up our identity when cultural changes occur. If this were so, we would not only have legal rigidity but also cultural rigidity. One has to be able to go beyond his or her culture.[17] Europe's splendour and attractiveness springs from its cultural diversity,[18] but this splendour is better served with diversity in language and art rather than by legal diversity. Diversity is indeed not a value in itself.[19] Cherishing legal diversity denies the fact that law, even though embedded in our culture, is primarily an instrument to regulate human relationships and is not an end in itself. In the words of the French lawyer René Demogue: 'Le droit n'est pas fait pour soi-même, mais pour le besoin de l'homme'.[20] Cherishing law as a symbol of culture, whatever the circumstances, will inevitably isolate us from the benefits of comparative law and from the benefits of harmonisation and unification of law as well.

---

[12]   Cf. Dethloff (2004) 544.

[13]   Leipold (2000) 650.

[14]   Langbein (1984) 1108.

[15]   Zimmermann (2009) 510.

[16]   Pintens (2003) 8.

[17]   See also Antokolskaia (2002) 268 ff.

[18]   Collins (2008) 124.

[19]   Contra: Legrand (1999).

[20]   Law is not made for itself but for the needs of mankind.

3 Opportunity of Convergence in European Substantive Succession Laws

Opportunities of convergence in European substantive succession laws lie in spontaneous harmonisation, institutional unification and legal scholarship.

3.1 Spontaneous Harmonisation

If despite the diversity of European succession laws a certain European consensus is reached, in the form of a relatively moderate approximation of the legal systems, then this is not the consequence of a deliberate and promoted policy of national legislators, but rather primarily the result of sociological developments as well as of developments in family law. The reinforcement of solidarity between husband and wife during the marriage due to the introduction of egalitarian matrimonial property regimes in the sixties and seventies has also influenced the law of succession and has led to solidarity beyond death in that field. Vertical inheritance where children are the favoured heirs has changed in favour of a horizontal order which subordinates the claims of children in favour of the surviving spouse. Further, the equality of all children in family law has not gone without notice in succession law. Following the 1979 decision of the European Court of Human Rights (ECHR) in *Marckx* the demise of discrimination in the law of succession began,[21] concluding, it seems, with the decision in *Mazurek* in 2002 and *Merger and Cross* in 2004.[22] In other fields, such as the compulsory portion of children, the impact of sociological changes has been rather limited.

It is possible to illustrate divergence and convergence of national substantive succession laws with two examples: the statutory portion of the surviving spouse and the compulsory portion of children.[23] Furthermore, from these examples one can draw a conclusion regarding the degree of harmonisation and Europeanization of succession law.

3.1.1 The Statutory Portion of the Surviving Spouse

The surviving spouse's right to succession is fashioned in a number of different ways. In some legal systems the surviving spouse's position is rather weak and he or she does not obtain full ownership, his or her rights

---

[21] ECHR (*Marckx v Belgium*), Series A, No. 31.

[22] ECHR (*Mazurek v France*), No. 34406/97, 2000 ECHR II, 1, 2000 D. 332, note Thierry 2000 Dr.fam. 20, note Lamy, 2000 FamRZ 1077, note Vanwinckelen, 2000 JCP II 102861, note Sudré and Gouttenoire-Cornu; (*Merger and Cross v France*) No. 68864/01, 2005 JCP I 103, note Sudré, 2008 RTDF 1063, note Demart. For an overview see Pintens (2005) 1074.

[23] For overviews see Cámara Lapuente (2008) 1199 ff.; De Waal (2006) 1071 ff; De Waal (2007) 1 ff.; Heggen (2007) 1 ff.; Henrich and Schwab (2001); Pintens (2001) 628 ff.

being limited instead to a life interest. A leading example of this approach is French law. In the original version of the *Code Napoléon* the surviving spouse hardly had any rights to succession: he or she only inherited when there were no relatives up to the twelfth degree. The *ratio legis* of this weak position lied in the foundations of the devolution of property on death. The first foundation was the family duty of maintenance (*le devoir de famille*). This duty did not allow for the surviving spouse to be classed as an heir due to the family being viewed as an entity based entirely on blood relationship. The second foundation was the maintenance of the heritage within the family. A stronger position of the surviving spouse would have, in absence of common children, meant the loss of the estates for the family. It was not until the end of the nineteenth century that a reform was implemented in France, whereby the surviving spouse attained inheritance rights in the form of a life interest (usufruct). The scope of this life interest increased the more distant the remaining heirs were. This reform was prompted by sociological developments. The family was no longer seen as a blood relationship, but rather as a community of life, to which the spouse belonged by nature. Moreover the composition of the inheritance had changed. An inheritance, more often than not, no longer had a family character: it was no longer composed of family heirlooms, but of assets that the testator had acquired through labour. With the reform a compromise was reached: the life interest guaranteed on the one hand the improvement of the surviving spouse's legal position, on the other hand the allocation of the residue (*nuda proprietas*)[24] to relatives meant that assets remained within the family. Even when the French legislature later awarded the surviving spouse full ownership, if the deceased left non-privileged collateral heirs, his or her position remained weak. Even until recently the surviving spouse only inherited a quarter of the inheritance in usufruct when the deceased left issue, which had the consequence that he or she was often unable to continue the matrimonial standard of living. A 2001 reform improved the position of the surviving spouse.[25] If the deceased left issue, the surviving spouse now has an option: he or she can choose between either the life interest of the whole inheritance or a quarter in full property (art. 757).[26] If the deceased left other relatives, the surviving spouse inherits full property (art. 757-1).

These developments in French law show that the confinement to a life interest is losing ground. In 1981 Belgian law also distanced itself from French law, significantly improving the position of the surviving spouse.[27] The right to succession in the form of a life interest has been partially abandoned. If the deceased left children, the surviving spouse continues to inherit a life interest, but now of the whole estate (art. 745 bis § 1 para. 1). If there is no issue, a distinction on the basis of the matrimonial property regime has to be drawn. Where

---

[24] Nuda proprietà or nue-propriété means the residuary property after deduction of the usufruct.

[25] See Beignier (2002) 41 ff.

[26] Articles without further reference refer to the civil code of the legal system concerned.

[27] Pintens *et al.* (2010) 763 ff.

the spouses married under the default regime of the community of acquests or under any other community system adopted by marital agreement, the surviving spouse inherits the whole community in full property and a life interest over the personal assets of the deceased (art. 745 bis § 1 para. 2). Where they married under separation of property, the inheritance rights of the surviving spouse are restricted to a life interest of the whole estate. Spanish law still limits the spouse's statutory portion to a life interest in a part of the succession where there are descendants and ascendants (art. 834 and 837). However, since 1981, if the deceased left other relatives, the spouse inherits the whole estate in full property (art. 944). The new Catalan succession law also maintains a universal usufruct for the surviving spouse when the deceased left descendants but offers an option for the attribution of one fourth of the inheritance in full property and the usufruct of the family home (art. 442-3 para. 1 and 442-5). If the deceased leaves no issue, the surviving spouse inherits the whole estate in full property but the parents have a right to a compulsory portion (art. 442-3 para. 2). In Hungarian law the surviving spouse inherits a life interest if the deceased leaves descendants (§ 615). If there are no issue, the surviving spouse inherits the whole estate (art. 607).[28]

In comparison to a right of succession in the form of full ownership, the split of property into a life interest and *nuda proprietas* has the advantage that issue or other heirs do not irrevocably lose their entitlement to the property. The split reconciles the interests of the family with those of the surviving spouse, who is able to continue his or her standard of living. Especially in the case of a small estate, the life interest protects the surviving spouse better than a share in full property.

The split is not always reconcilable with an appropriate administration of assets. It is therefore more common that legal systems award the surviving spouse a statutory portion in full property. This is, inter alia, the case in Austria (art. 757), Germany (§ 1931), Greece (art. 1820-1821), Italy (art. 581-582), Poland (§ 931), Portugal (art. 1239) and Switzerland (art. 462), where the statutory portion increases according to the order of the other heirs.

In all those systems a trend to restrict or to strike out the right of succession of distant relatives, or even of the children, in favour of the surviving spouse exists. The reason behind this development can be found in the solidarity between spouses beyond death, but also in the demographic developments and in the building-up of an estate. Examples can be found in most Nordic jurisdictions such as Denmark, where the surviving spouse inherits one-half of the estate, if the deceased left descendants; if there are no descendants then the spouse bars further relatives and inherits the whole estate (§ 9 Inheritance Act).

Since the Administration of Estates Act 1925, English law has also seen some development of the restriction of the rights of heirs, even where those heirs are the children, in favour of the surviving spouse. This tendency has been consolidated by several amendments, the last one being the Law Reform (Succession)

---

[28] Nevertheless the ascendants have certain rights concerning family property.

Act 1995.[29] The surviving spouse receives the personal chattels absolutely.[30] This means that he or she is entitled to the household assets, which have to be understood in the broadest sense; it includes all articles of personal and ornamental use and all of the contents of the home even, for example, the deceased's riding horse. Moreover, where the deceased leaves issue, the surviving spouse receives the fixed net sum with interest of £ 250,000.[31] In addition he or she receives a life interest in one-half of the balance of the residual estate, i.e. the balance after deduction of the personal chattels and the fixed net sum with interest. Where the deceased leaves no issue but certain specified relatives as parents or their descendants, the fixed net sum with interest increases to £ 450,000. In addition the surviving spouse receives one-half of the balance absolutely. Where the deceased leaves no issue and no specified relatives the surviving spouse inherits the entire residual estate absolutely. In practice this rule means that the spouse is the sole heir in smaller or medium sized estates.

In Sweden the spouse inherits the entire estate, even where children exist. However he or she may not dispose of it by will as it should be passed to the heirs of the previously deceased on his or her own death (s. 3 Inheritance Act). The surviving spouse is to be regarded as a preliminary heir, the children as reversionary heirs.[32] An exponent of this development is Dutch law. The old civil code awarded the spouse a child's statutory portion in full ownership where children were present. The more children, the smaller the spouse's portion became or, as it was sometimes expressed, the law of succession became a punishment for fertility. If other relatives survived, the spouse had a very strong position. As heir of the first successoral order he or she excluded all relatives. The revised succession law that entered into force as book 4 of the new civil code on 1 January 2003, departs from this model and grants the spouse full ownership of the entire property even if there are children. The children are only entitled to a pecuniary claim. This claim is only enforceable after the death of the surviving spouse, in case of his or her bankruptcy or private insolvency or in the cases detailed in the deceased's will (art. 4:13). If the surviving spouse has the intention to remarry, the children have a discretionary power to claim the property of the assets, subject to a life interest for the surviving spouse (art. 4:19).[33]

The tendencies that emerge – a shift from life interest to full property; an increase of the statutory portion – undoubtedly favour the surviving spouse to the detriment of the children and, to an even greater extent, distant relatives. They accommodate the wish of most spouses that the legal position of the surviving spouse should be strengthened, at least where small and medium

---

[29] S. 46 ff. Administration of Estates Act 1925. See Parry and Kerridge (2009) 8 ff.

[30] S. 55 (1) Administration of Estates Act 1925. See Parry and Kerridge (2009) 10 f.

[31] Family Provision (Intestate Succession) Order 2009 made by the Lord Chancellor under s. 8 Family Provision Act 1966.

[32] Only a child of the deceased, who is not a child of the surviving spouse, may claim his or her share after the death of the first spouse.

[33] See Van Erp (2007) 196 ff.

inheritances are concerned. In weaker systems the surviving spouse's position will often be safeguarded by a prenuptial agreement (assignment of the community property, *institution contractuelle*) and by the making of a will.

3.1.2 Compulsory Portion of Children

In almost all civil law jurisdictions children enjoy a compulsory portion.[34] In most of those systems such as in Austria (§ 765), the Czech Republic (art. 479), Germany (§ 2303 para. 1), Greece (art. 1825), Hungary (art. 665) and Switzerland (art. 471) the child's compulsory portion is fixed at one half of the statutory portion,[35] in Catalonia (art. 451-5) and Denmark (§ 5 para. 1 Inheritance Act), where more emphasis is put on private autonomy and freedom of testation, at only one-fourth of the estate (art. 451-5). In others such as in Belgium and France the portion depends upon the number of children: One-half if the deceased has left one child, two-thirds if he or she has left two children and three-quarters if he or she has left three or more children (art. 913). In Portugal the portion is fixed at one-half, when there is one child and at two-thirds, when there are two or more children (art. 2159). In both models however the compulsory portion is independent from the size of the estate. Only in Norway and recently also in Denmark a limitation has been introduced. Already in 1918 the Norwegian *Lex Michelsen* restricted the compulsory portion, which is two-thirds of the estate, to 1 million Kroner per child (§ 29 Inheritance Act).[36] In Denmark, where the compulsory portion is only one-fourth of the estate, the testator can restrict it to 1 million Kroner per child (§ 5 Inheritance Act).[37] In Spain the compulsory portion (*legítima*) is fixed at two-thirds of the estate, but the testator can differentiate between his or her children.[38] The children are entitled to one-third in equal shares (*legítima estricta*), but the testator can freely dispose of the other third in favour of some of them (*mejora*) (art. 806).

The compulsory portion traditionally found its roots in the solidarity between generations. This solidarity implied that specific heirs had the right not to be left uncared for. The compulsory portion performed a maintenance function. It provided the heir with a certain standard of living. Increases in life expectancy have vitiated these rationales. Today children inherit at a later age, at a time when they have achieved an elevated standard of living and have often accumulated assets through their own labour. However one must not overlook that in times of bad economy children may also be in a difficult position; they may face a reduction in purchasing power, high social dues and taxes or even unemployment. But, viewed in general, the law of succession no longer provides

---

[34] One of the very few exceptions is Navarra. See the report by S. Cámara Lapuente in this book.

[35] In Sweden too it is fixed at one-half of the statutory portion, but the children are only entitled to this share after the death of the surviving spouse.

[36] Ca. 120,000 EUR. See Lødrup (2007) 237. See also the contribution by Hambro in this book.

[37] Ca. 135,000 EUR. See Ring and Olsen-Ring (2008) 451.

[38] See Arroyo i Amayuelas (2007) 262 ff. See the report by S. Cámara Lapuente in this book.

a standard of living, but rather at most improves the standard at a time when it is no longer really necessary. The compulsory portion therefore no longer has a maintenance function and can thus no longer be viewed as an extension of the parental obligation to provide for their children. Parents accomplish their obligations to provide for their children through the financing of their education. The wealth of these children therefore no longer lies in their future inheritance, but rather in their academic or other achievements.

In view of these sociological developments the question of whether or not a testator, who was able to deal freely with his or her estate during his or her lifetime, should face restrictions in the freedom to make a will is being debated in many European legal systems. If there are dependent heirs at the time of the testator's death, who have to rely on the inheritance for support, then a compulsory portion is not necessary to solve this problem, but a maintenance claim could provide a remedy. An example of this solution is found in English law. Towards the end of the seventeenth century the development of the freedom to make a will led to the demise of the customary compulsory portion.[39] However, during the twentieth century, Parliament reinstated the restriction upon the freedom to make a will in favour of dependent relatives through the introduction of family provisions. The Inheritance (Family Provision) Act 1938 and the Inheritance (Provision for Family and Dependants) Act 1975 gave the courts judicial discretion to alter the content of the disinheriting will and to assign a reasonable financial provision to persons in need listed by the statute. Claimants are the spouse or civil partner, a former spouse or former civil partner who has not entered into a subsequent marriage or civil partnership, cohabitees having lived together with the deceased as spouses or civil partners for two years immediately preceding the death of the deceased, children, persons treated as children of the family and dependants.[40] Provision can be made in the form of periodical payments, a lump sum, a transfer of property, a settlement of property, an acquisition of property or variation of a marital agreement.[41] In some civil law jurisdictions need plays a role to a certain extent. In Polish law where the compulsory portion is fixed at one half of the statutory portion, the compulsory portion increases to two thirds of the statutory portion, if the children are minors or permanently unable to work (art. 999 § 1).

Even in civil law systems where the compulsory portion is firmly rooted in legal traditions and legal culture, the question whether it is still a justifiable infringement of the freedom to make a will has been discussed. It was one of the most important issues in discussions about the introduction of a new succession law in the Netherlands. Many leading authors have, in vain, solicited

---

[39] Cf. Borkowski (2002) 258 ff.

[40] S. 1 Inheritance (Provision for Family and Dependants) Act 1975. See Parry and Kerridge (2009) 164 ff. and the contribution by Kerridge in this book.

[41] S. 2 Inheritance (Provision for Family and Dependants) Act 1975. See Borkowski (2002) 287 ff.; Parry and Kerridge (2009) 202 ff.

the abolition of the compulsory portion.[42] Simplification of the law of succession and testamentary freedom were leading motifs, whereby the latter was the focus of the discussions. Legal doctrine was firstly of the opinion that the child's upbringing and care gave that child an adequate social start such that the rights of that child were thereafter exhausted. The child had received that to which it had a right, so that there was no reason to award the child an inviolable right to the estate of its parents. Moreover such a right leads to the situation where spouses try everything to circumvent the compulsory portion with the purpose of improving the position of the surviving spouse. Secondly, legal doctrine points out that the institution of a compulsory portion patronises the testator. Why shouldn't a person dispose of his or her assets as that person pleases? That may be by favouring the surviving spouse to the detriment of the children, or by favouring one child above the others. One will have one's reasons. Most testators know what they are doing and normally act fairly.

Increasing wealth has fuelled discussions about the compulsory portion even more. A discussion even took place in Germany, where the constitution protects both testamentary freedom *(Testierfreiheit)* and the family character of succession *(Verwandtenerbrecht)* as fundamental elements of the law of succession.[43] Protection of the former is the result of the right of ownership as guaranteed by the constitution (art. 14 para, 1 GG), and protection of the latter is the result of the protection of marriage and family (art. 6 para. 1 GG), from which it is derived that the next of kin are entitled to claim an inviolable right upon a part of the estate of their relative. Consequently, the legal order needs to observe this constitutional compromise between testamentary freedom and family succession. The family character of the law of succession implies more than a claim to maintenance by the heir in need. It means that the freedom to dispose by will needs to be restricted by a compulsory portion allocated to the descendants, the parents, the spouse and the registered partner. The way the legislator needs to organise the compulsory portion cannot be derived from the constitution. It is open to the legislator to grant the forced heir a compulsory portion in kind or only one in value. The extent of the compulsory portion has not been laid down in the Constitution. Nevertheless, the legislator's duty to warrant forced heirs an appropriate share in the estate can be derived from the Constitution.

In 2000 the *Bundesverfassungsgericht* (German Constitutional Court) confirmed the traditional view that the compulsory portion is based on the solidarity among generations.[44] However, the Court pointed out that the Constitutional Courts' judgments have not completely clarified the relationship between testamentary freedom and compulsory portion, and whether or not the Constitution makes provision for the granting of a minimum portion of the estate to close family members even if this is against the will of the testator. The *Bundesverfassungsgericht* seized the opportunity to emphasise that this relation-

---

[42] Van Mourik (1991) No. 6018.

[43] See Badura (2007) 151 ff.; Pintens and Seyns (2009) 169 ff.

[44] BVerfG 30 August 2000, 2000 FamRZ 1563, 2001 NJW 141, 2000 ZEV 339, note Mayer.

ship might be reviewed on the basis of the last will of the testator in which he or she firmly expressed the wish to exclude the holder of a compulsory portion (e.g. due to the estrangement of the two parties) or in situations where the statutory provisions on the compulsory portion would lead to a disproportionate limitation of the freedom to dispose of the assets in that particular case. Consequently, a large part of the doctrine had the impression that an absolute right to a compulsory portion would not survive, but that it would be necessary to review whether the compulsory portion and limitations that it brings about were still adequate and whether or not the principle of proportionality had been violated.

In a decision of 19 April 2005 the *Bundesverfassungsgericht* took a more restricted view and underlined that the compulsory portion has, in principle, an irrevocable and family character and that it is independent of any need or circumstances.[45] The Constitutional Court seized the opportunity to elaborate on the constitutional principles governing testamentary freedom and the compulsory portion. With respect to the latter, the Court clearly adheres to the doctrine's majority opinion and invokes both art. 14 and 6 GG. The guarantee of art. 14 safeguards the rights of children to an irrevocable participation in the inheritance of their parents, independent of need. The compulsory portion is part of the successoral guarantee of art. 14 GG as an element passed down through the ages. The Court strongly emphasised this historical argument. Moreover, the compulsory portion is the expression of family solidarity. Art. 6 GG guarantees the relationship between the testator and his children as a long life community, with the right and obligation to take responsibility for each other. This obligation justifies guaranteeing the children an economic basis with the compulsory portion. Especially in cases of estrangement between the parent and children the compulsory portion sets forth limitations to testamentary freedom and the possibility of punishing a child with deprivation.

The rules of the BGB on the compulsory portion of children (§ 2303 par. 1) were declared to be in accordance with the Constitution. On the one hand they guarantee children an appropriate participation in the inheritance of their parents, on the other hand they leave the testator enough freedom to realise his or her ideas about the devolution and division of the estate.

From this case we can conclude that the *Bundesverfassungsgericht* clearly declared the law on the *Pflichtteil* constitutional and gave a crushing reply to the compulsory portion's critics.[46] The decision of the *Bundesverfassungsgericht* was criticised by some legal scholars on the basis that the historical argumentation was rather weak and the court did not discuss the argument that the compulsory portion is a product of its time and is now outdated.[47]

The 2005 decision of the *Bundesverfassungsgericht* closed the door on the abolition of the compulsory portion or for a reform prescribing need as a

---

[45] BVerfG 19 April 2005, 112 BVerfGE 332, 2005 FamRZ 872, 1441, note Mayer, 2005 JZ, 1007, note Otte, 2005 NJW, 1561, 2005 ZErb 169, 2005 ZEV 301.

[46] Gaier (2007) 164.

[47] Mayer, note on BVerfG 19 April 2005, 2005 FamRZ 1442.

preliminary condition. The main principles governing the compulsory portion have been declared part of the *Institutsgarantie*, making reform impossible without a previous constitutional amendment. However, the door was not completely closed. The Court clearly left a margin of appreciation to the legislature by admitting that certain elements of the compulsory portion are not part of the *Institutsgarantie*.[48] The legislature will therefore be able to decide on, for example, the proportion between testamentary freedom and compulsory portion and will be able to diminish this portion or vary the portion in relation to the value of the estate.[49] The Minister of Justice made a reform proposal but immediately declared that the amount of the portion as such would not be touched. The area of reform is very limited and primarily concerns the deprivation grounds, which have been enlarged by an Act of 24 September 2009, in force since 1 January 2010.

All of these developments indicate that, although there is discussion, the compulsory portion prevails across almost all European civil law jurisdictions. Even today continuation of the estate in the family is being used as justification to maintain the compulsory portion albeit that equality of all children is being used even more. Ethical, natural law and philosophical reasons are called upon, so that everywhere in Europe – with the exception of the common law – the compulsory portion is retained. However the significance of the compulsory portion should not be overstated. The general trend, to extend the inheritance rights to the surviving spouse, even to award him or her a compulsory portion, narrows the compulsory portion of the children.

But this does not mean that there is no convergence at all. The trend from a compulsory portion in kind, which is a *pars hereditatis* of assets *in natura*, to a monetary claim is remarkable. This development should be welcomed because it takes new social realities into consideration. During the drafting of the BGB it was already pointed out that the testator usually had valid reasons for disinheriting his or her child. If the legislature nevertheless wanted to include the child in the inheritance, then it was not appropriate, under the circumstances, to award him or her a compulsory portion in kind. In this situation it would be better to award the child a mere value right. Furthermore, a compulsory portion in kind is also an obstacle to the circulation of goods, especially immovable property. In the case of donations or bequests there is always a risk that a forced heir has a claim on the asset itself, when the gift supersedes the available part of the estate and violates the compulsory portion.[50] Legal systems that traditionally award a compulsory portion in kind are developing in this direction. Even French law, which was always viewed as the exponent of a compulsory portion in kind, has been drastically altered through Acts in 1938, 1971 and 2006, and has developed towards a monetary claim. Also the new Dutch civil code follows German law. The person with a right to a compulsory portion is not an heir any

---

[48] Badura (2007) 155.

[49] Gaier (2007) 163.

[50] Fusaro (2009) 755.

more but a creditor with a monetary claim. Other examples are found in Austria (§ 775), Catalonia (art. 451-11 and 451-22 para. 4), Hungary (§ 672)[51] and Poland (art. 991). But some legal systems, such as Belgium (art. 920 ff.), Estonia (§ 106 Inheritance Act), Greece (art. 1825), Italy[52] and Spain (art. 806) with some exceptions (art. 841 and 1057)[53] maintain the compulsory portion in kind.

The significance of the compulsory portion is generally moderated, especially in the Germanic legal family, by the rule that declares a gift to be inviolable, if at the time of succession an ascertained period since receiving the donation has elapsed. In Catalonia (art. 451-5 b) and Germany this period is ten years,[54] in other systems such as in Austria and Lichtenstein (§ 785 para. 3), the period is much shorter and fixed at two years. The reason for defining such a time period lies mainly in the fact that it becomes more difficult to prove the gift through passage of time, but it is also justified by not wanting to expect the testator to spend his or her life preserving the estate for the benefit of the forced heirs.

Lastly it must be pointed out that in many legal systems the compulsory portion does not have the inviolable character that it has in some legal systems of the Romanic legal family such as in Belgian or Spanish law, where a deprivation is only possible on the rather restrictive grounds of intestate unworthiness. In most legal systems of the Germanic legal family, as well as the Nordic countries and even some systems of the Romanic legal family, there are wider possibilities to withhold the compulsory portion. Catalan law is also an example of this tendency (art. 451-17).

All these elements narrow the significance of the compulsory portion. However the starting points, especially between common and continental law, remain very different. It is clear that the compulsory portion will remain a part of continental succession law for a long time, but reform attempts will aim to restructure the compulsory portion through a compulsory portion in value and an extension of the deprivation grounds. Both reforms seem to be sufficient to relax the relationship between testamentary freedom and the family's right to succession.

3.1.3   Conclusion

Analysis of these the two topics reveals a very different result. As for the statutory portion of the surviving spouse, solutions remain quite different in their final results and even more different in their details but in all the jurisdictions surveyed there is a strong tendency to fortify the position of the surviving spouse and to increase his or her statutory portion, mostly in full property. If the deceased leaves issue, the solutions vary from one quarter

---

[51]   See Csehi (2007) 278 and also in his contribution to this book.

[52]   Cubeddu-Wiedemann (2008) 853.

[53]   See Arroyo i Amayuelas (2007) 260 ff.

[54]   But in Germany a reduction of 10% *per annum* is taken into account (§ 2325).

of the estate to the whole estate. The final solution is not always reached in the same way. In some jurisdictions such as the Dutch and Swedish, the statutory portion is always equal to the whole estate, regardless of its size, but with certain measures protecting the children. In English law the size of the estate is taken into account with the result that in the case of a small or medium sized estate the surviving spouse inherits the whole estate. If the deceased leaves no issue, the tendency is even clearer. In some legal systems the spouse has to share the estate with the parents of the deceased, but siblings are increasingly excluded. This example illustrates that legal systems undergo a comparable evolution due to the same social changes resulting in a spontaneous approximation and harmonisation.

As for the compulsory portion there is a certain approximation among the civil law systems but the difference in approach between the civil and common law systems is undeniable.

These are not the only examples upon which one can draw to illustrate a certain spontaneous harmonisation of European succession laws. In other areas, that have not been discussed here, there are also certain, but still very moderate, correlations, for example, the form of a will. The strict provisions as to form in the Romanic legal family are relaxed slightly by case-law, so that there is a shift towards the more lenient approach found in the Germanic legal family. Contracts on an inheritance are generally forbidden in the Romanic family of law, but all legal systems recognise many exceptions to this general rule. In France the recent reform of 23 June 2006 maintained the prohibition but allows future heirs to waive the right to claim the recovery of gifts (art. 929) and opens a possibility for family arrangements. In Italy the introduction of the *patto di famiglia* is also a step forwards. In the Germanic legal family such contracts are widely used. English law has comparable legal formations, like the 'contract to leave a gift' and 'contract not to revoke a will'.[55] In the first case the beneficiary becomes a creditor to the estate. In the latter the beneficiary is not able to prevent the revoking of the will, as wills are generally revocable. He or she can however claim for compensation. In legal systems prohibiting or restricting contracts on an inheritance more and more scholars advocate them as an instrument for effective estate planning. Catalan law could serve as a source of inspiration (art. 431-1 ff.).

In other areas differences between jurisdictions run deeper and are difficult to reconcile. An important example is the transfer of inheritance from the deceased to the heirs. Here, very different transfer methods exist: transfer *ipso iure* as in France and Germany, transfer through acceptance as in Italy and Spain (*aditio hereditatis*), transfer through judicial decision as in Austria and Lichtenstein (*Einantwortung*) and transfer through an intermediate, the *personal representative* of the *common law*.[56] Here spontaneous legal assimilation is not likely. Instead a concept needs to be developed, on the basis of a better law

---

[55] See Kerridge in this book.

[56] Y.H. Leleu (1996).

approach. That this is not to be seen as a utopian idea is shown by the *Uniform Probate Code* in the USA.

3.2   Institutional Unification

The example of the statutory portion of the surviving spouse has shown that spontaneous convergence has occurred in succession law, but even then this convergence is restricted to broad tendencies and fine details remain different. The examples of the compulsory portion and the transfer of the inheritance have indicated that in certain other fields spontaneous convergence cannot be expected. Here the legal systems are deeply divided and only a more institutional approach can be of any help.

3.2.1   Achievements

Institutional achievements have been realised trough case law of the European Courts and by European and international instruments.

a) Case law

Some judgments of the European Court of Justice (ECJ) and the European Court of Human Rights (ECHR) have erased major discriminations. However, the contribution of the ECJ does not lead to a unification of substantive succession law but rather has been restricted to procedural questions as can be seen in the case of *Hubbard* concerning the *cautio judicatum solvi* for an executor of a will[57] or to inheritance tax as in *Barbier*.[58] The freedoms of the Treaty or the citizenship of the Union will not easily lead to a unification of substantive law.

The ECHR has made a major contribution concerning the successoral position of children born out of wedlock with its judgments in *Marckx, Inze, Mazurek* and others.[59] In *Pla and Puncernau* the Court even went too far in rejecting an interpretation of a will by the courts of Andorra and holding that the will did not make a distinction between biological and adopted children and that therefore no interpretation was necessary.[60] The judgment denied the interpretation problems and the available interpretation methods. It is indeed a surpassed point of view that a clear last will does not require interpretation. In a peculiar way, the Court distinguished the intention of the testator from the interpretation of the last will. Every interpretation needs to appoint a central role to the intention of the testator and needs to search for this intention. In his dissenting opinion, Judge Bratza justly points out that the ECHR cannot prevent a testator

---

57 ECJ *Hubbard v Hamburger* No. C-20/92 [1993] ECR I-3777, 1994 RCDIP 83, note Droz.

58 ECJ *Barbier* C-364/01 [2003] ECR I-15013.

59 See Pintens (2005) 1048 ff.; Pintens and Pignolet (2005) 22 ff.

60 ECHR (*Pla and Puncernau v Andorra*) No. 69498/01, 2004 Reports VIII, 2004 FamRZ 1467, note Pintens, 2005 ZEV 162. See Arroyo i Amayuelas and Bondia García (2004) 7 ff.; Pintens (2005) 1056 ff.; Staudinger, 2005 ZEV 140 ff. See also the contribution by Kerridge in this book.

from discriminating between his or her children, regardless of their descent, nor can the effect of fundamental rights concerning family relations prevent or limit testamentary freedom. The intention of the testator and his or her testamentary freedom hold a key position in the testamentary succession. Only the compulsory portion can limit this testamentary freedom.

However in general the Court's contribution to the abolition of discriminations in succession law has been of major importance although further impetus cannot be expected from the Court. The Court can only contribute where discriminations lay at hand. Those discriminations are not present in fields as compulsory portion or transfer of the inheritance. In these fields convergence can only be reached trough institutional unification with European and international instruments.

b) European and International Instruments

The European Union has no general competence for the unification of national substantive law. Article 65 EC and the new article 81 TFEU are primarily restricted to private international law. But this article also opens up the possibility of unifying substantive law in cross border-cases.

The only achievement of the Council of Europe in the field of succession law is the Basle Convention of 16 May 1972 on the Establishment of a Scheme of Registration of Wills.[61] According to Article 1, the Convention does not establish an international registry but only a scheme of registration of wills with a view of facilitating, after the death of the testator, the discovery of the existence of the will. Each Contracting State has to follow the scheme and appoint a national body responsible for the registration and for answering, after the death of the testator, requests for information. Registration is not subject to conditions of nationality or residence of the testator, which means that a will can be registered in any State party to the Convention.

A major initiative on an international level has been undertaken by UNIDROIT, resulting in the Washington Convention of 26 October 1973 providing a Uniform Law on the Form of an International Will.[62] This Convention deals with substantive law providing a uniform law on an additional will which is a compromise between the secret will (*testament mystique*) of the civil law and the witnessed will of the common law. The will made according to the provisions of the Convention and the Uniform law is valid and enforceable in the

---

[61] The Convention has been ratified by Belgium, Cyprus, Estonia, France, Italy, Lithuania, Luxemburg, The Netherlands, Portugal, Spain and Turkey. In England and Wales the Administration of Justice Act 1982 contains provisions for a registry of wills in view of the ratification of the Convention (s 24). See Brandon (1982) 742. But the provision never came into force.

[62] The Convention was ratified by Belgium, Canada (for Manitoba, Newfoundland, Ontario, Alberta, Saskatchewan, Prince Edward Island, New Brunswick, Nova Scotia), Cyprus, Ecuador, France, Italy, Libya, Niger, Portugal and Slovenia. The United Kingdom has not ratified the Convention but it was incorporated in England and Wales by s. 27 of the Administration of Justice Act 1982. See Brandon (1983). This section is not yet in force.

Contracting States, regardless of the place where it was made, of the location of assets and of the nationality, domicile or residence of the testator (art. 1 Uniform Law). The advantage of this system lies in the avoidance of any probate procedure.

3.2.2   Promotion of What We Have

A first step towards unification could lie in the promotion of both Conventions. A system of registration of wills was ultimately not included in the Proposal for a Regulation on succession law but will be dealt with as part of a future Community initiative.[63] Is it really necessary to establish a new system, given that the Basle Convention is already in force in ten Member States?[64] Two solutions are possible: the creation of national registers or the creation of a European register. If one opts for the first solution, then the new system should be compatible with the Basle Convention. Otherwise those ten Member States will have to change their registration system. Therefore, there is no reason to deviate from the Basle Convention and establish a new system. The European Union cannot accede to the Convention since it is only open to States. A special Protocol could be a solution. Otherwise every Member State has to take an initiative. The second solution consisting in the creation of a central European register therefore seems perhaps desirable at first sight. However this could be excessive since only a minority of the wills in the European Union are related to a cross-border context.

In its opinion on the Green Paper on succession law the European Economic and Social Committee called for further harmonisation and specifically mentioned testate succession.[65] It is clear that a proposal for unification of substantive law on wills exceeds the competence of the Union. EU activities will be restricted to international succession law as the Proposal for a regulation in this field shows. But a proposal for a European will in cross-border cases could be based on art. 81 TFEU. The Washington convention could serve as a model for such a European will. A further step is the proposed European Certificate of Inheritance which is on the interface between private international and substantive law (art. 36 ff. Proposal).

Further unification of substantive succession law by international conventions or European regulations cannot be expected in the near future.

3.3   Legal Scholarship

If one wants to move forward, the solution lies in comparative legal scholarship. Although much has been done to ensure better information and understanding of national substantive succession laws with encyclopaedias

---

[63] Explanatory memorandum, COM (2009) 154 final, p. 2.

[64] Cf. Terner (2007) 169.

[65] OJ 2006 C 28/1.

and overviews,[66] interest in real comparative work has been rather weak. Historically succession law has rarely been the subject of profound comparative legal
studies. This is quite understandable since it is a difficult, technical and particular field, where a mixture of Roman, customary and common law leads to very
diverse regulation.[67] Prof. Zimmermann even calls it virgin territory, which has
been neglected by modern scholarship.[68] However, there has recently been an
awakening interest in comparative succession law. Differences between the legal
systems are seen as obstacles to the circulation of capital and to the acquisition
of foreign property, with the result that legal writers are searching for a common
core, preparing the way for a careful and prudent harmonisation. Already at the
turn of the century even those who seek to limit a European civil code to the law
of obligations and contracts in order to preserve national civil codes, can still
accept the codification of a few common general principles of family and succession law.[69]

Nowadays more and more scholars advocate the inclusion of succession law
in the search for a *ius commune* preparing the way for a careful harmonisation.
Some authors have pleaded for the establishment of a Commission on European Succession Law following the example of the Commission on European
Family Law,[70] which published principles on divorce and maintenance and on
parental responsibility and is now working in the field of matrimonial property
law. Recently an initiative was taken by Prof. Zimmermann and others leading
to the establishment of an international research group on succession law. The
group is not restricted to European succession lawyers but also includes legal
historians and scholars of non-European jurisdictions. As its first project the
group will focus upon legal formalities which are imposed in order for a person
to make an effective testamentary disposal of his or her property. The account
of the national succession laws should be analytical and critical, highlighting
successes and failures, whether in doctrine or policy, and discussing proposals for reform. This initiative will perhaps provoke discussion but could also be
an impetus for further research in comparative succession law. The example of
the Commission on European Family Law illustrates that such an initiative can
bring a neglected field to the fore.

4   Conclusions

In 2004 the author had the honour to be invited to the Catalan
Juridical Days in Tossa de Mar and to speak about the harmonisation of family

---

[66]   See Pintens (1997 ff), Ferid *et al* (2010), Garb and Wood (2010), Hayton (2002), Süß (2008).

[67]   Hereto Neumayer (1978 and 1990).

[68]   Zimmermann (2009) 504.

[69]   See Schwintowski (2002) 210.

[70]   Terner (2007) 77.

law.[71] The conclusion on this topic was that (i) an institutional unification of substantive family law still had a long way to go and that such an institutional unification was at that time not advisable, (ii) at first a long phase of spontaneous approximation of laws was necessary and (iii) this harmonisation of family law would in its first stage be a task for research and education. Those conclusions are applicable to succession law too. An intense scientific discussion is also necessary in this field. Harmonisation of law will only be successful once emphasis is placed upon what is common to the European legal systems and when differences are placed in perspective rather than denied, thus creating a European consciousness. This can only be reached through education and the evolution of legal science. Discussing a modern codification such as the Catalan model from a comparative perspective is an important contribution to this idea.

---

[71] Pintens (2005) 21 ff.

CHAPTER 2

Testamentary Freedom or Forced Heirship?

Balancing Party Autonomy and the Protection of Family Members

Andrea Bonomi

1 Introductory Remarks

Balancing party autonomy and the protection of family members has always been one of the crucial problems of the law of succession. The solutions adopted in the individual national legal systems vary greatly, and the dividing line runs through the heart of Europe.

In the civil law tradition, forced heirship rights play a very central role in the regulation of successions. In common law jurisdictions the emphasis is more on testamentary freedom, whereas the protection of some family members (and sometimes other dependants) is normally assured through less rigid mechanisms. Dispositions upon death also take different forms from one jurisdiction to the other. Wills are generally recognized; however some legal systems offer a wider range of tools for the exercise of party autonomy, including agreements as to successions, mutual wills, trusts and other will substitutes.[1]

The harmonization of the substantive laws of succession of the Member States would be an immense task, which the European Union cannot undertake. It is therefore not surprising that the problems arising out of the vast disparities of domestic legislations have been tackled from the perspective of conflict of laws and jurisdictions.

On the basis of the competence that was attributed to it by the Treaty of Amsterdam,[2] and within the framework of the plan for regional unification of private international law rules that it conceived on that basis,[3] the European Commission has elaborated a very broad and detailed Proposal for a regulation concerning private international law aspects of succession.

Backed by an important study drafted by the German Notary Institute (DNotI), in collaboration with professors Heinrich Dörner and Paul Lagarde,[4] and by the responses to a Green Paper presented in 2005,[5] the Commission Proposal was presented on 14 October 2009.[6] It will then be submitted to the

---

[*]   This texts reflects the ideas expressed in an article written for the Nederlands Internationaal Privatrecht (2010) 605-610.

[1]   See above, W. Pintens in this same book, 3.1.3.

[2]   See articles 61 and 65, Title IV of the EC Treaty, as introduced by the Treaty of Amsterdam.

[3]   Council and Commission Action Plan Implementing the Hague Programme, Document of the Council of the European Union No. 9778/2/05 REV 2 JAI 207. Since the entry into force of the Treaty of Amsterdam, 13 European regulations in private international law have been promulgated.

[4]   German Notary Institute (2004).

[5]   Green paper on successions and wills, of 1 March 2005, COM(2005) 65 final. The responses of the States, as well as those of several private associations and individuals, to the questions posed in this text indicated a strong interest for this project, notwithstanding certain reservations.

[6]   Proposal for a Regulation of the European Parliament and of the Council on jurisdiction, applicable law, recognition and enforcement of decisions and authentic instruments in matters of succession and the creation of a European Certificate of Succession, COM (2009) 0157 final. For comments, see Kindler (2010) 44 ff.; Lein (2010) 107 ff.; Bonomi (2010) 47 ff.

Council of the European Union and the European Parliament within the framework of the co-decision procedure of Art. 251 of the EC Treaty.[7]

Although very broad and ambitious, the Proposal mainly[8] concerns private international law issues, i.e. jurisdiction, choice of law and recognition and enforcement of decisions. This does not, however, mean that it has no potential impact on substantive law aspects.

At least since the so called "conflict-of-laws Revolution", which challenged the traditional conception of private international law, it is well known and generally accepted that the solutions of conflict of laws problems are not neutral, but often reflect specific State interests and substantive law policies adopted at the domestic level. The problem with the European project, as with all undertakings of unification of private international law at the international level, is that the drafter of the uniform rules cannot rely on a base of unified substantive law. This is quite clear in the field of succession, where the underlying substantive policies widely diverge among the Member States. As previously mentioned, the disparities go to the roots of succession law and directly touch the dilemma between testamentary freedom (and more generally party autonomy) and the protection of family members.

In the absence of unified substantive EC law on succession and of uniform directives coming from the legislation of the Members States, the drafters of the Proposal were required nevertheless to make important policy choices. The result is a text that clearly reflects a rather "liberal" approach to the problems of international succession. It is submitted that the solutions envisaged by the Commission to the most important issues dealt with in the Proposal clearly foster testamentary freedom and, more generally, party autonomy. At the same time, they tend to weaken national forced heirship rights and reduce their effectiveness, at least in transnational situations.

The most obvious expression of this liberal approach is the admission of the testator's choice of the applicable law in art. 17 of the Proposal. But this is not the only aspect. Other elements to the same effect are the shift from stable connecting factors, such as nationality and *situs*, to a rather unstable one such as habitual residence, the very favourable treatment provided for agreements as to succession, and the restricted role assigned to the public policy exception.

We do not intend to criticize this result. We agree on many aspects of the proposed regulation and even where we disagree, we understand perfectly and respect the reasons behind the proposed solutions. The purpose of this paper is simply to show that the future Regulation, although mainly concerned with private international law, is not neutral with regard to such a crucial substantive law issue as the balance between party autonomy and the protection of family members.

---

[7] As provided in art. 67 par. 5 of the EC Treaty.

[8] The only substantive law issue that is directly dealt with in the Proposal is the creation of a European Certificate of Succession (Chapter VI of the Proposal, arts. 36 to 44).

2   The Connecting Factor of the Last Habitual Residence of the Deceased

The first expression of the liberal approach lies, in our opinion, in the choice of the habitual residence as the principal connecting factor, both for jurisdictional purposes and for the selection of applicable law. According to art. 4 of the Proposal, "[...] the courts of the Member States on whose territory the deceased had habitual residence at the time of their death shall be competent to rule in succession matters." According to art. 16, "[u]nless otherwise provided for in this Regulation, the law applicable to the succession will be that of the State in which the deceased had their last habitual residence at the time of their death."

From the point of view of many Member States, this solution constitutes a fundamental change from their national conflict solutions. A majority of the Member States currently submits successions to the law of the deceased's last nationality.[9] Other Member States follow a dualist (or "scissionist") approach: they submit both intestate and testamentary succession of immovables to the law of the *situs*, whereas succession to movables is governed either by the law of the domicile, by the law of the habitual residence, or by the national law of the deceased.[10] Only a few countries submit the entire succession to the law of the last domicile or the last habitual residence of the deceased.[11] Similar solutions are often used in the field of jurisdiction.

The shift from nationality and *lex situs* towards habitual residence is due to several reasons, of both political and technical nature, which we will not analyze here.[12] What we would like to stress is that this change, if compared with the current situation, represents an important factor of flexibility, which will further testamentary freedom and reduce the effectiveness of forced heirship rights.

One should first consider that, in each Member State, the great majority of succession cases concerns citizens of the relevant State and property situated on its territory. In the present situation, the national private international law rules grant, in most of these cases, that the local courts have jurisdiction and can apply their domestic law. Therefore, if the *lex fori* provides for forced heirship rights, these will be enforced.

---

[9]   This is the case, *inter alia*, of Austria, Germany, Greece, Hungary, Italy, Poland, Portugal, Slovenia, Spain and Sweden.

[10]   Domicile is used in France, Luxembourg, Ireland and the United Kingdom (but of course, the meaning of domicile is not the same in all these countries!). Habitual residence has been adopted in Belgium since 2004. Romanian law submits movables to the national law of the deceased.

[11]   Domicile is used in Denmark (which however is not concerned by the proposed regulation). The Netherlands apply the complex system of the 1989 Hague Convention (based on a compromise between the criteria of nationality and habitual residence, see art. 3 of the Convention) and Finland has adopted a similar approach.

[12]   See Bonomi (2010) 52 ff.

In some Member States, the testator has no serious possibility of escaping the local mandatory rules. This is the case in most nationality-based systems. German citizens, for instance, cannot avoid the application of German forced heirship rules ("Pflichtteil"). Even if the deceased moves his or her domicile abroad, German courts will have jurisdiction over a dispute concerning the succession and will apply German law, in principle to the whole of the estate.[13] The same is also true in most systems based on nationality.[14]

In scissionist systems based on the application of the *lex situs* for immovables and the law of domicile (or of habitual residence) for movables, there is greater flexibility. A change of domicile (or habitual residence) can lead to a change of the law applicable to the movable part of the estate and thus permit the evasion of local forced heirship provisions. The application of local law is nevertheless granted for immovable property situated in the State concerned.[15] Thus a French citizen, who owns movable and immovable property in France, can escape the French law *réserve* with respect to the movable assets of his or her estate, but not for the immovables situated in France.[16]

In the proposed regulation, the law of the last habitual residence of the deceased will apply to the whole of the estate, without any distinction between movables and immovables. This means that a person can determine the law applicable to his or her succession by simply moving his or her habitual residence abroad. No special protection is provided for family members; the forced heirship provisions of the former habitual residence will be excluded and

---

[13] The only restriction results from art. 3(3) EGBGB with respect to immovables situated in a country where they are submitted to the law of the *situs* by virtue of "special provisions" (as is the case in "dualist" systems); Dörner (2007) art. 25, No. 570 ff. By acquiring an immovable in such a country, a German citizen can partially avoid the application of German law.

[14] Italian law is a little more flexible, due to the admission of the choice of law: the testator has the right to submit his or her succession to the law of his or her State of habitual residence. However, this choice cannot deprive the heirs resident in Italy of the forced heirship rights granted to them by Italian law (Art. 46(2) of the Italian PIL statute). In Spain, there is no possibility to escape from the application of Spanish law. However, a certain degree of flexibility results, at the domestic law level, from the existence of regional legal systems ("derechos forales"), which are often less protective of family members than the Spanish Civil Code: see Cámara Lapuente (2007) 29 ff., as well as in this same book, section 2.

[15] In certain systems, however, immovables can be "converted" into movables. In France, this can be done by transferring them to a company ("société civile immobilière"), provided that the transfer was not motivated only by the purpose of avoiding forced heirship rights or other mandatory provisions. See the recent decision: Cass. 20 octobre 2010, *Petites affiches*, 23 novembre 2010, No. 233, p. 4, and the *Caron* case: Cass., 20 March 1985, *RCDIP*, 1986, p. 66, note Y. Lequette and *JDI*, 1987, p. 81, note M. L. Niboyet-Hoegi. In common law systems, the doctrine of "equitable conversion" may apply under certain circumstances.

[16] Furthermore, the so called "droit de prélèvement" will protect the French heirs, who will be able to obtain compensation out of the property situated in France (not only immovable, but also movable property) for the losses resulting from the application of a foreign law to the part of the estate situated abroad.

possibly replaced by those of the new habitual residence (if they exist). Thus, a German or French citizen, who intends to disinherit his or her children can move to London; the whole of the estate will then be governed by English law, irrespective of the nature of the assets and their situation. Under English law, the children are not entitled to a reserved portion of the estate; they only have the possibility of applying for "family provision" under the 1975 Inheritance (Family and Dependants Provision) Act, but the limited protection they are afforded by this statute will entirely depend on the circumstances of the case.

No doubt that the proposed solution constitutes the expression of a liberal approach. It favours testamentary freedom and reduces the effectiveness of domestic forced heirship provisions. It can be used (and possibly abused) for informed estate planning purposes. *Mutatis mutandis*, there is an analogy between the approach envisaged for international successions and the free movement of companies resulting from the European Court of Justice case law.[17] The change of the habitual residence will allow for the exclusion of forced heirship rights as the establishment of the company abroad allows for the exclusion of local mandatory provisions of company law. Strictly speaking, this is not party autonomy, but it is a *de facto* freedom which entails important legal consequences: as it is sometimes said, people can "choose with their feet".

Of course, a change of the habitual residence does not necessarily favour testamentary freedom, but can also lead to the opposite results, i.e. to the application of a law which is more protective to family members. In this case, forced heirship rights and other restrictions of testamentary freedom can come into play which were unknown to the law of the previous residence. Thus if an English citizen moves to France or Germany, some of his or her family members will benefit from reserved rights unknown under English law. It would however be wrong to infer from this that the proposed regulation is "neutral". In fact, if the law of the habitual residence is perceived as too restrictive, the testator will have the right to submit the estate to the law of his or her nationality under the proposed art. 17.

3 The Choice of Applicable Law

According to art. 17 of the Proposal, "[a] person may choose as the law to govern the succession as a whole the law of the State whose nationality they possess". The right of the testator to choose the law applicable to his or her succession is the most clear and evident expression of the liberal approach of the Proposal.

This will probably be one of the most innovative features of the future Regulation. At present, the freedom of choice is still the exception in the field

---

17   ECJ, 9 March 1999, C-127/97, *Centros*, ECR, 1999, p. I-1459 ; 5 November 2002, C-208/00, *Überseering*, ECR, 2002, p. I-9919 ; 30 September 2003, C-167/01, *Inspire Art*, ECR, 2003, p. I-10155 ; 16 December 2008, C-210/06, *Cartesio*, ECR, 2008, p. I-9641.

of successions, since only a limited number of private international law systems allow it. This is the case in Switzerland, where the deceased's choice of the applicable law has existed since the end of the 19th century and was reaffirmed in the Private International Law Act of 1987.[18] Under the influence of the Hague Convention of 1989,[19] the freedom of choice was also recognized, to a greater or lesser extent, in the legislations of certain Member States of the EU (such as Belgium,[20] Estonia,[21] Finland,[22] Italy,[23] The Netherlands,[24] Romania[25] and, in a much more restrictive way, Germany).[26] In the majority of the Member States, however, the freedom of choice is presently excluded in the area of succession.

The admission of the choice of the applicable law represents in itself an enlargement of testamentary freedom. By such a choice, the testator can escape from the mandatory provisions of the law applicable to the succession and profit from the more liberal approach of the law he or she has chosen.

The main objection against the admission of the choice of law in the field of succession has traditionally been the need to protect the expectations of family members.[27] This is the main reason why the choice is presently still excluded in many countries. Even in some of the private international systems in which the freedom of choice has been admitted, it is subject to significant restrictions. In Germany, for instance, the only admissible choice is that of German law for immovables situated in Germany; the danger of evasion of local forced heir-ship rights is thus completely excluded.[28] In other countries, it is accepted that a foreign law can be designated, but the choice cannot deprive forced heirs of the rights that are granted to them by the law of the forum (Italy),[29] or by the law that would govern the succession in the absence of choice (Belgium, Romania).[30] Only few countries have followed the very liberal approach which characterises

---

[18] See arts. 87(2), 90(2) and 95(2) of the Swiss Private International Law Act of 18 December 1987.

[19] See art. 5 of the 1989 Hague Convention.

[20] Art. 79 of the Private International Law Code of 2004.

[21] § 25 of the Private International Law Act of 27 March 2002.

[22] Art. 26(6) of the Law on Succession.

[23] Art. 46(2) of the Private International Law Act of 1995.

[24] In The Netherlands the freedom of choice results from arts. 5 and 6 of the Hague Convention of 1989, which is applicable in this country.

[25] Art. 68(1) of the Private International Law Act of 1992.

[26] According to art. 25(2) EGBGB, a person can only choose German law for immovable property located in Germany.

[27] Among the opposers, see Goré (1994) 193 ff.; Ferid (1996) 93 ff.

[28] Dörner (2007) Art. 25, No. 497.

[29] See above, fn. 23.

[30] See above, fn. 20 and 25. The same solution prevails in Quebec: art. 3098 al. 2 of the Civil Code.

Swiss law[31] and the 1989 Hague Convention (this is the case of the The Netherlands, Finland and Estonia).[32]

Following this model, the Commission's Proposal tends to allow the choice of law regardless of its impact on forced heirship rights, i.e. even if it leads to the application of a national law that ignores such rights, or recognizes them only in a more restricted way than the law applicable in the absence of choice. This liberal solution substantially enhances the practical utility of the choice of law and meets with the approval of professionals active in the field of estate planning.

The choice of this liberal solution is counterbalanced by the more restrictive options taken in the Proposal with respect to other regulatory issues related to the freedom of choice.

The most important restriction is that a person only has the right to choose his or her national law as applicable to the estate. The choice available is thus more restricted than that provided for under Belgian, Dutch, Estonian and Finnish law, as well as under the Hague Convention of 1989.[33]

Contrary to such texts, the Proposal does not allow the choice of the law of the State of a person's habitual residence at the time of the choice, a possibility that can be useful to 'fix' the applicable law (and thus ensure the perpetuity of an estate plan) in view of a future change of residence. The reason for the exclusion of this option is probably twofold. On the one hand, since the choice of law has been conceived as a means of reconciling national systems based on domicile and nationality, only the choice of national law was perceived to be consistent with this purpose. On the other hand, the right to choose the law of the habitual residence at the time of the choice was considered to be more easily abused for the purpose of avoiding the mandatory provisions of the otherwise applicable law. As an example, a person could easily transfer his or her habitual residence abroad for a short period, just for the purpose of choosing the law of a specific country for estate planning purposes (e.g. the law of a country without forced heirship rules) and then come back to his or her country of origin while continuing to benefit from the foreign, more favourable succession law. This kind of manipulation is more difficult if the choice is limited to a person's national law.

Notwithstanding this and other restrictions,[34] the recognition of party autonomy is a clear expression of the liberal approach of the proposed Regulation.

---

[31] In the well-known *Hirsch v Cohen* case of 1976 (ATF 102 II 136), the Swiss Federal Court decided that the choice by the testator of his or her national law is not abusive and does not contradict public policy, even if the chosen law does not provide for forced heirship rights.

[32] See above, fn. 21, 22 and 24.

[33] All these texts permit the choice of the national law or of the law of the habitual residence of the deceased, both at the time of the designation and at the time of death.

[34] According to art. 17(1) and (2) of the Proposal, the choice of law must concern the estate "as a whole", it must be "expressly determined" and "included in a declaration in the form of a disposition of property upon death".

Persons living in a country other that their country of origin will have the option to choose between their national law and the law of their habitual residence. If they possess two or more nationalities, they will be able to choose among several national laws.[35] As mentioned before, they could also envisage moving their habitual residence abroad. Because of this plurality of options, the expectations of family members will certainly be weaker than in the present situation.

4   Agreements as to Succession

Art. 18 of the Proposal contains special rules concerning agreements as to succession which are very favourable to the validity of such acts.

Agreements as to succession are a very useful tool for estate planning purposes. At present, there exists a split in Europe between the countries which admit and favour such acts and those who prohibit them, although with some exceptions. Because of these disparities, the validity of these agreements depends on the law applicable to the succession, and this creates a situation of uncertainty which is an obstacle to their use.

The impact of agreements as to succession on testamentary freedom and forced heirship rights is not unequivocal. Some types of agreements (such as *pactes successoraux d'attribution*) can be considered a restriction (albeit self-imposed) of testamentary freedom. As a matter of fact, such agreements include contractual dispositions upon death, which are in principle irrevocable; therefore they limit the freedom of the testator to change his or her will until the very last moment of life. This is the reason why such agreements were traditionally prohibited by Roman law and are still prohibited in many countries. By contrast, other types of agreement (such as *pactes de renonciation*) contain an anticipated waiver of forced heirship rights and constitute therefore a means for expanding testamentary freedom. They can be regarded as a consensual restriction of forced heirship rights. In any case, all agreements as to succession constitute an expression of party autonomy, since they enlarge the range of tools by which the transmission of the estate can be organized.

The provisions of the proposed Regulation, which are largely inspired by the 1989 Hague Convention, clearly tend to favour the validity of such agreements (*favor validitatis*). Three rules included in art. 18 are designed to this effect:

1) According to art. 18(1), the agreement shall be governed by the law which would be applicable to the succession on the day when the agreement was concluded. If the agreement is not valid pursuant to that law, it will nevertheless be valid if this is the case under the law applicable to the succession at the time of death. This provision is clearly designed to uphold the validity of the agreement in the case of "conflit mobile", i.e. when the law applicable to the succes-

---

[35]   This is not clearly stated in the Proposal, but it results, by way of interpretation, from the case law of the European Court of Justice concerning multiple nationalities: see in particular ECJ 16 July 2009, C-168/08, *Hadadi*.

sion changes between the moment of the agreement and the moment of death. This is in particular the case when the person whose succession is concerned has changed his or her habitual residence after the agreement. The technique used is that of "alternative" connections. This rule is inspired by art. 9 of the 1989 Hague Convention; it already exists under some national private international law systems,[36] but is new for others.[37]

2) Where the agreement concerns the succession of a plurality of persons ("bilateral" or "plurilateral" agreements)[38], it will be valid if it is accepted by the law applicable to the succession of at least one of them (art. 18(2) of the Proposal). This rule, which also uses alternative connections, is much more innovative than the previous one: the solutions presently adopted in national and international texts are based either on a cumulative or on a distributive application of the law governing the succession of all the persons whose successions are concerned.[39]

3) The parties may submit the agreement to the national law of the person or one of the persons whose succession is involved. Contrary to the choice of law under art. 17, this choice only concerns "the agreement" (which probably means the validity and the effects of the agreement) and not the succession as a whole.

It should be noted that the inclusion of these special rules on the validity of agreements as to succession imposes the recognition of such agreements even in those Member States that presently prohibit them. Therefore, the provisions of art. 18 can also be considered to be an expression of the overall approach of the proposed Regulation in favour of party autonomy. Do they also affect forced heirship rights?

In general, agreements as to succession do not deprive forced heirs of their rights without their consent. To that extent, they are neutral with regard to the protection of family members. This is also accepted in private international law. According to art. 18(4) of the Proposal, the application of the law provided for in this article "shall not prejudice the rights of any person who is not a party to the agreement and who, in accordance with the law determined in article 16 or 17, has an indefeasible interest or another right of which it cannot be deprived by

---

[36] Such as Germany (art. 26(5) EGBGB), Spain (art. 9.8 Civil Code) and Switzerland (art. 95(1) PIL statute).

[37] In most countries, the validity of all dispositions upon death is governed by the law applicable to the succession, which is determined at the moment of death.

[38] This is, for instance, the case when husband and wife enter into an agreement as to their successions, by including reciprocal dispositions, or dispositions in favour of their children.

[39] The method of cumulative application is adopted by art. 10 of the 1989 Hague Convention ("Where the agreement involves the estates of more than one person, the agreement is materially valid only if it is so valid under all the laws which [...] would have governed the succession to the estates of all those persons"). It is also followed in art. 95(3) of the Swiss PIL Act. By contrast, a part of the German doctrine favours a "distributive" approach (i.e. the validity and effects of agreements are governed with respect to each succession by the law applicable to the estate of each of the persons concerned); H. Dörner (2007) Art. 25, No. 363.

the person whose succession is involved". In other words, forced heirship rights are determined by the law applicable to the succession (which is determined at the moment of death) and they cannot be affected by an agreement, even if it is valid under art. 18.

However, this neutrality of the agreement obviously does not benefit the heirs who are party to it and have agreed to waive, entirely or in part, their indefeasible rights. This concerns *pactes de renonciation*; the parties to such agreements cannot challenge their validity or effects by invoking forced heirship rights under the law applicable to the succession at the moment of death. Let's assume that a son has waived his forced heirship rights by an agreement concluded with his mother at a time when the latter had her habitual residence in Germany. The agreement is valid under German law, which is applicable under art. 18(1) of the future Regulation. Subsequently, the mother moves to Italy, where she dies. Under Italian law, applicable to the succession under art. 16 of the future Regulation, the son would have the right to a reserved portion and the anticipated waiver of such right would be void. Nevertheless, the agreement is still valid under art. 18(1) and the son, who was a party to it, cannot assert his forced heirship rights under Italian law (art. 18(4)).

In these cases, the validity of the agreement (and the validating rules of art. 18) implies a restriction of the effectiveness of forced heirship provisions of certain Member States in international situations. This solution, although perfectly justified, is further evidence of the non-neutrality of the future Regulation.

5 The Public Policy Exception

The choice of law rules of the Regulation can lead to the applicability of a law which does not grant sufficient protection to the rights of family members. Can the public policy exception be of any help?

It is useful first to better define the situations in which this question can arise.

This is obviously not the case when the court of competent jurisdiction applies its own domestic law. Thus, in the system of the future Regulation, public policy will play no role in the case of a change of the habitual residence from one Member State to another. In such a case, the court of the new habitual residence will be competent for the succession (art. 4) and will apply (in the absence of a choice) its internal law (art. 16). Forced heirship provision of the law of a previous residence cannot come into play through the public policy exception.

It is also submitted that public policy cannot be invoked by a party to an agreement as to succession that is valid under art. 18 to enforce his or her forced heirship rights against that agreement. Thus, in our previous example, since the waiver agreement is valid under German law (designated by art. 18(1) of the Proposal), Italian courts of the place of the last habitual residence of the deceased cannot rely on the Italian public policy to reject the effects of the agreement. To do so would run counter to the rationale of art. 18 and limit the *"effet utile"* of the Regulation.

The question of public policy arises when the competent court must apply a foreign law which is less protective of the family members than the law of the forum. Under the Proposal, this will be the case in two situations:

1) the deceased had his or her last habitual residence in a Member States but has designated his or her national law as applicable to the succession (art. 17);[40]

2) the deceased had his or her last habitual residence in a State which is not a Member of the European Union, but the courts of a Member State have "residual jurisdiction" under art. 6 of the Proposal.[41]

In such cases, art. 27 of the Proposal will come into play. This provision takes a very restrictive approach to public policy. In particular, art. 27(2) indicates that the application of the law designated by the Regulation "may not be considered to be contrary to the public policy of the forum on the sole ground that its clauses regarding the reserved portion of an estate differ from those in force in the forum".

From the wording of this provision, it seems clear that mere disparities in the amount or the nature of forced heirship rights cannot be regarded as incompatible with the public policy of the forum. If this is true, no violation of public policy can be seen in the fact that, under the foreign applicable law, a family member of the deceased is entitled to a smaller portion of the estate than under the *lex fori*, that he or she is granted only a claim against the estate and not all the rights and duties of an heir, that he or she can claim only a sum of money and not a right to the assets *in natura*, that only some *inter vivos* gifts are taken into account to calculate the forced heirship rights and are subject to claw-back, etc.

---

40 Provided that the case is not referred to the court of the State of the nationality under art. 5 of the Proposal (according to art. 5: "[w]here the law of a member State was chosen by the deceased to govern their succession in accordance with article 17, the court seised in accordance with article 4 may, at the request of one of the parties, and if it considers that the courts of the Member States whose law has been chosen are better placed to rule on the succession, stay proceedings and invite the parties to seise the courts in that Member State with the application".)

41 Art. 6 of the Proposal provides for "residual jurisdiction": "Where the habitual residence of the deceased at the time of death is not located in a Member State, the courts of a Member State shall nevertheless be competent on the basis of the fact that succession property is located in that Member State and that: (a) the deceased had their previous habitual residence in that Member State, provided that such residence did not come to an end more than five years before the court was deemed to be seised: or, failing that, (b) the deceased had the nationality of that Member State at the time of their death; or, failing that, (c) an heir or legatee has their habitual residence in the Member State; or failing that, (d) the application relates only to this property."

This does not however mean that differences in the protection of family members can never justify the application of the public policy exception. Thus, it is clear that discriminations between the heirs because of birth, sex, nationality or religion, can be contrary to public policy.

The most difficult question is whether public policy can play a role when the foreign law does not provide for protection at all, or protects certain family members but not others (the surviving spouse or the children), or makes the protection depend on the existence of a (maintenance) need. It is submitted that art. 27(2) does not exclude the use of public policy in these cases: therefore, the answer will depend on the courts of the Member States. Although in some European countries courts have refused to make use of the public policy exceptions to protect forced heirship rights,[42] the question is still open.

6 Final Remarks

Although targeting private international law issues, the proposed Regulation can be regarded as the expression of a quite liberal approach to successions.

It is submitted that the choice of this approach for international cases can also, in the long term, have an indirect impact on crucial aspects of the domestic law of succession. Thus, the adoption of conflict rules favouring agreements as to succession will probably reinforce the opinion that the prohibition of such agreements, which still exists in several Member States, has been outlived and favour substantive law reform. *Mutatis mutandis*, the adoption of conflict rules that reduce the effectiveness of forced heirship rights in international situations may also stimulate the existing debate on possibly rendering more flexible these traditional protection mechanisms in purely internal situations.[43]

As already noted in other areas of law, the European Union could, through the unification of the private international law of succession, have an influence on the development of the substantive laws of the Member States.

---

[42] This is the case in Spain. See STS 15 novembre 1996, *Lowenthal*. See comments by Rodríguez Pineau (1998) 135, and by Borrás 227.

[43] For Spain, see Cámara Lapuente (2007) 31 ff., and in this same book (section 3.1). For Hungary, Csehi, in this book (section 3.3.8). For The Netherlands, Milo, in this book (section 4.3). For Scotland, Clive, in this book (section 2).

PART II

New Trends in Catalan Succession Law

CHAPTER 3

Between Tradition and Modernisation

A General Overview of the Catalan Succession Law Reform

Esther Arroyo i Amayuelas – Miriam Anderson

1 Introduction

The 1991 Code on Succession (CS), in force until 1 January 2009, has been replaced by the Catalan Act 10/2008, 10 July, by which Book IV of the Catalan Civil Code (CC Cat) was promulgated. It updates and reforms the law of succession, within the context of a process of modernization of Catalan private law that can be traced back to the 1980s, but has acquired a new dimension during the last decade, when successive governments, with different political ideologies, have promoted the codification of private law.

The following pages include a general presentation of the law of succession in force in Catalonia. The main changes introduced by the 2008 reform are highlighted, but, although there are relevant innovations, the past is by no means abandoned. Probably this is a rational response to the need to gradually adapt to the new family models as well as to the different mechanisms for the transfer of assets that the Catalan society has absorbed.

Prior to addressing these issues, the paper briefly presents the historic and constitutional backgrounds that encompass the development of private law in the Autonomous Communities in Spain and, therefore, also of Catalan private law, thus allowing the coexistence of different systems within the State.[1]

1.1 The Diversity of Private Law Systems in Spain

The 1978 Spanish Constitution (CE) recognizes the existence of "nationalities" and "regions" and their right to attain different levels of autonomy within the unity of the State (art. 2 CE), thus breaking a long centralist tradition which lasted until relatively recent times (i.e. when Franco's dictatorship came to an end in 1975). Previous attempts at decentralization (such as the 1873 bill for a federal constitution or the 1931 Republican Constitution) were short lived. At present, decentralization is political and administrative, but some territories have also been singled out by the Constitution due to factors like language, law, history or insularity. These differentiating factors explain why some territories maintain their own private law systems (i.e. civil law systems, excluding commercial law). Art. 149.1.8 CE provides that only those regions that already had separate legislation in 1978 would be able to preserve, modify and develop their civil law systems. Aragon, Catalonia, Navarre, The Basque Country, Galicia and the Balearic Islands filled this prerequisite and this is the reason why civil law is not uniform throughout Spain. However, it must be noted that because the Spanish Parliament is not always agile enough to adapt to social needs, some Autonomous Communities that, according to the Constitution,

---

*   This study falls within the scope of the research projects DER 2008-03992/JURI (MICINN) and 2009 SGR 221 (Generalitat de Catalunya).

[1]   In depth, *inter alia*, Vaquer Aloy (2006a) 1 ff., (2006b) 672 ff., (2008) 69 ff.; Arroyo Amayuelas – González Beilfuss (1995) 564 ff.; Arroyo Amayuelas (1998) 411 ff. From a historic perspective, Scholz (1982) 577-582; Gacto Fernández (1981) 219-266; Badosa Coll (2003) 136 ff.

cannot enact civil law norms have gone ahead and done it anyway. Notwithstanding, this is the exception rather than the rule. For the purposes of this paper, it is sufficient to bear in mind that some regional regulations survived the enactment of the Spanish Civil Code (1888-1889) and that from 1978 onwards the Constitution allows the Autonomous Parliaments to preserve, modify and develop these provisions.

1.2 Catalonia: From the 1960 Compilation to a Civil Code

The first modern compilation of Catalan civil law dates back to 1960, although it was promulgated as a Spanish act, since under the dictatorship there were no regional legislative bodies. With democracy reinstated, once the Constitution (1978) and the Statute of Autonomy of Catalonia (1979) were in force, the text of the Compilation was adapted to the constitutional principles (for instance, differences among issue were eradicated) and translated officially into Catalan in 1984. But the origins of the Compilation still marked its limitations. In 1960, the guiding principle was to lay down only those Catalan traditional institutions that differed from those contained in the Spanish Civil Code. This is why the 569 articles of the 1955 Draft Compilation where reduced to only 344 in the definitive text, which focused on family law (95 articles) and the law of succession (180 articles). The influence of Roman law was clear, and reference to the Spanish Civil Code frequent.[2]

The pre-constitutional Compilation was designed to be an intermediate step towards the goal of a unified civil law for the whole of Spain. Signs of this goal being abandoned are shown by a 1974 reform of the Spanish Civil Code, which no longer considered regional civil legislations to be provisional. Since 1979 Catalan civil law has developed way beyond the most optimistic expectations.

This has been attained by means of different techniques, such as amendments to the Compilation, separate statutes and partial codes. In the 1990s two partial codes were enacted, in order to present a complete regulation of Catalan family and succession law, thus avoiding the frequent (and quite often undue) subsidiary application of the Spanish CC. There is no need for it if the Autonomous system is complete, but legal operators can be trapped by the inertia of a time when this was not the case. These ideas are still in the background of the vindication of a Catalan Civil Code,[3] although there are other reasons for it too;

---

[2]   For a general perspective, see Roca Sastre (1981) 101 ff.

[3]   Of course there is a link between nationalism and codification that the new 2006 Catalan Statute of Autonomy enhanced. However, the Constitutional Court judgment 31/2010, 28 June, declared a number of articles of the Statute unconstitutional and laid down a strict construction of others; this tempers the gist of the 2006 Statute of Autonomy. Regarding civil law, the Court gave a restrictive interpretation to art. 129 of the Statute, in accordance with the doctrine it had maintained in 1993. Although Catalan civil law has evolved much further than the 1993 judgments would have allowed, the Constitutional Court still clings to this obsolete construction of the constitutional distribution of powers between the State and the Autonomous Communities. Therefore, nothing has really changed, except for the fact that

as already mentioned, the slow capacity of reaction shown by the Spanish legislature encourages the Autonomous Communities to develop their own systems as demanded by social changes, and codification entails technical improvements, since it brings about simplification and makes the law more accessible.

The Catalan Act 29/2002 set forth the structure of the Catalan Civil Code: it was to contain six books as well as additional, transitional, and final provisions (art. 2). Five of those books have already been enacted and have come into force; only the book on contracts is pending.

2   An Overview of the Law of Succession in Book IV of the Catalan Civil Code

Book IV CC Cat came into force on January 1, 2009. It is structured in six different parts: following the general provisions (part I), testamentary succession is granted a relevant position (part II), preceding the regulation of inheritance agreements (part III, which somewhat arguably includes the regulation of *donationes mortis causa*) and that of intestacy (part IV). Part V deals with inheritance rights granted by the law (forced share and the so-called "widow's quarter" or *quarta uxoris*) and Part VI is dedicated to the rules on acquisition of assets *mortis causa* (formalities and effects of acceptance and disclaimer, plurality of heirs, collation or hotch-pot rules and protection of the heir's position).

The immediate precedent of the provisions in force is the Code on Succession 1991 (CS), although they do deviate from its rules in quite a few aspects,[4] as shown in the following paragraphs.

The CS incorporated important reforms that had been enacted before, especially regarding intestacy (1987),[5] reserves or legal reversion (1987)[6] and

---

the political climate is more hostile at the moment, so it is to be expected that the Constitutional Court is asked to decide on the constitutional adequacy of new Catalan statutes (we must bear in mind that most of the Constitutional Court's judgements are promoted by parliamentary political groups). On this issue, see, Badosa Coll, Egea Fernández, Roca Trías, in: http://www10.gencat.net/eapc_revistadret/recursos_interes/especial%20estatut/ca_ese/ca.

[4]   A general perspective in Lamarca Marquès (2008) 906 ff; Ferrer Riba (2009) 15 ff.

[5]   Act 9/1987, 25 May (DOGC No. 850, 20 June 1987). This act was an important step towards improving the surviving spouse's position: he or she succeeds in second place, immediately after the decedent's issue, and even if the latter take in first place, the surviving spouse has the usufruct over the entire estate, although up until the CC Cat it could not encumber the issue's forced share (see below section 4.2.2 a). See Casanovas Mussons (1987) 297 ff.

[6]   Act 11/1987, 25 May (DOCG No. 851, 12 June), which derogated the legal reversion of patrimonial assets that art. 271 of the Compilation accepted, albeit with some variations, by referring to art. 811 of the Spanish CC. See Roca Sastre (1981) 118.

forced share (1990)[7] and it modernized – to an extent – the regulation contained in the Compilation; for instance, it systematized the grounds for unworthiness, it regulated the administration of assets acquired by minors and it updated the rules on the *quarta uxoris*. However, the 1991 CS was very influenced by the 1955 Draft Compilation. This had the advantage of allowing the legislature to produce a very high quality regulation in a relatively short span of time, but it also presented an important drawback: it hampered the development of the Catalan law of succession. Namely, the traditional principles were maintained and the regulation on inheritance agreements remained linked to marriage and to family economy; also, it contained a very detailed regulation on fideicommissum, although it was generally admitted that the practice of appointing successive heirs was in clear decline. The historical importance of fideicommissum seemed sufficient to justify the legislature's option, and the same applied to the possibility of making a will before the local priest, which had obviously not been used for years.[8]

Book IV CC Cat eliminates some of these anachronisms and its provisions are specifically designed for the urban and industrialized Catalan society, where new family structures have emerged (cohabitation, same-sex partnerships, single-parent families, couples living with children from previous relationships, etc.) and the model of various generations living together has been abandoned in favour of the nuclear family. Although there are many family businesses, the succession of which presents specific problems that Book IV tries to address, the assets of most families are the home and movables, and the woman contributes actively towards their acquisition thanks to having accessed the work market. It is also relevant to stress the increase in the number of youngsters and elderly people who are dependent on their parents or children, respectively, for very long periods of time.[9] All of these factors have an influence in the distribution of estates. Therefore, the new provisions on succession promote full equality of children (in those few areas where some form of discrimination could still be found; i.e. adoptive children are no longer deprived of collateral relatives – uncles and aunts – within the adoptive family); they improve the surviving spouse's position; they grant the surviving cohabitant the same status as the spouse, and the forced share is weakened. The number of articles dedicated to

---

[7] Act 8/1990, 9 April (DOGC No. 1280, 18 April). The most outstanding reforms were the design of the forced share as a *ius in personam* (i.e. not a charge over the estate), the reduction of the period of time during which it could be claimed (from 30 to 15 years) and the limitation of the right to the forced share in the ascendant line to parents, excluding further removed ancestors.

[8] Instead, it repealed the so-called sacramental will and the testament *parentum inter liberos*, which had always been the typical holographic Catalan testament. On this and on the introduction of the Spanish holographic will in Catalonia, Marsal Guillamet (1994) 459 ff.

[9] A sociological analysis of Spanish families from the 17th century onwards in Reher (1996). More recent data in: Facal Fondo – Torrens Calle (2010) 43 ff. On the impact of new tendencies on estate planning, De Waal (2007) 6-10; Cámara Lapuente (2007) 22 ff.; Kroppenberg (2009) 1484; Castelein (2009) 34-37.

the construction of fideicommissa is drastically reduced (although the regulation is still long and detailed) and there are new limits on the duration of the settlement. Together with the elimination of the obligation to reserve assets inherited by one parent from the other in favour of their issue ("binuptial reservation"), these rules show that the principle of maintenance of assets within the family has eroded. Freedom of testation has been enhanced thanks to the introduction of new grounds for unworthiness and disinheritance and rules aiming to avoid undue influence on elderly testators. Finally, the procedure to ensure that the heir is only liable for the decedent's debts up to the value of the inherited assets has been simplified; although it is still not the default rule, it operates as such in practice.

It is obvious that a new regulation will not satisfy the interests of all parties and, in some instances, the evaluation of the reform will depend on what perspective is adopted, i.e. whether it is analysed from the point of view of a testator or a surviving spouse/cohabitant, or the beneficiary of the forced share. But some aspects of the new law of succession are technically deficient from all perspectives and it is often difficult to construe the norms in order to obtain an efficient solution, because the 2008 Act was not preceded by public debates or massive academic discussion and it is not clear where the legislature drew from, since no preliminary reports are available.[10] At a late stage during the parliamentary proceedings, in order to reach "a greater consensus", an *ad hoc* committee was appointed to draft a new bill, which explains why it is almost impossible to find out where the modifications come from and what was the reasoning behind them.[11] The following lines present just a few of these technical flaws.

The legislature aimed for certain uniformity in the time limitations applicable within the law of succession. The text is an improvement in this respect, but inconsistencies can still be detected. As in most continental systems, the heir is central for any type of succession (testate, intestate or contractual). If the heir has not accepted while the decedent was still alive (contractual succession), he or she must do so after the estate is devolved at death; the title does not pass automatically.[12] Art. 461-12.1 CC Cat provides that the heir has 30 years from the demise to accept or disclaim,[13] but this is inconsistent with the fact that if the

---

[10] This is in clear contrast with the process followed in France, where a survey completed by over 3,500 notaries was carried out before embarking on the reform that lead to the French Act 728/2006, 23 June. See Ginisty (2010). One would have thought this kind of preparation would be more feasible the smaller the territory and the population.

[11] Some information can be found in Ferrer Riba (2009) 15-16; Vaquer Aloy (2008) 84-85. There were two bills, one in 2006 (BOPC No. 353, 15 June) and the other in 2007 (BOPC No. 33, 19 February), with identical content. This was due to the anticipated dissolution of Parliament and the resubmission of the same text after the new Parliament had been elected.

[12] For a general perspective of other systems, De Waal (2007) 22-25; Leleu (2004) 338-340; Kroppenberg (2009) 1561-1562; Cavanillas Mújica (2004) 1003 ff.

[13] Although this is affected by the fact that inheritance tax must be paid within six months and the same applies to the possibility of limiting the heir's liability to the value of the inherited assets (art. 461-15-1

heir is subject to a condition precedent, the condition may be also be fulfilled during 30 years since the demise (art. 423-15.3 CC Cat). Therefore, the conditional heir may acquire the right to inherit and lose it at the same time. On the other hand, for connected matters, there are norms that take into account, as the starting date for the limitation period they provide, the moment when the heir knew or could have reasonably known that he or she had the right to accept or disclaim (for instance, art. 461-15.1 CC Cat),[14] instead of the time of death.

Another example of lack of uniformity can be found in art. 412-6.2 and 422-3.1 CC Cat. According to the former, only those who would *immediately* benefit from the declaration of unworthiness of an heir or legatee may initiate proceedings to obtain such declaration. By contrast, anyone who would benefit (immediately or not) from successfully challenging a will may do so. Therefore, the potential beneficiaries under the rules on intestacy cannot pursue a declaration of unworthiness of a testamentary heir if the will also provided for a substitutional heir, yet they could challenge the will or a provision thereof even if others (such as the substitutional heir) precede them in the order of potential beneficiaries.

It has also been noted that it does not make much sense to allow the so-called closed or secret notarized will[15] to be drafted using any durable technical means (art. 421-14.2 CC Cat) and yet forbidding blind people to use this form of will. Notwithstanding, the additional provision 2 of Book IV shows that the Catalan legislature would be open to allow the use of Braille. However, this would require the public notaries' regulations to be changed, but the Catalan parliament is constitutionally barred from carrying out this type of reform. On the other hand, notaries are already warning against the risk of fraud and obsolescence if electronic signatures and other technical devices are used, which renders reform in this direction pointless.[16]

3 The Law of Succession and Legal Tradition: New Rules for Old Principles

Book IV aims to balance tradition and modernity by implementing as many changes as needed – and as few as possible. The idea is not to upturn the system, as shown by the fact that the principles of the Catalan law

---

CC Cat). On the other hand, those interested in the inheritance, including creditors, may force the potential heir to decide (art. 461-12.2 CC Cat).

[14] Casanovas Mussons (2009) 1492.

[15] Where the testator hands the notary a sealed envelope and states that the envelope contains his or her last will and testament.

[16] Jou Mirabent (2009) 214; Mezquita García-Granero (2009) 102-104, 110, who is even more critical with the admission of this kind of techniques in informal documents left by the deceased to complement a will and which can contain, among other provisions, legacies the value of which does not exceed 10% of the estate (art. 421-21 CC Cat), since the notary does not intervene in their drafting (art. 421-21 CC Cat).

of succession, first formulated by J. Martí i Miralles,[17] have been maintained, in spite of being severely criticized in contemporary legal writing.[18]

Under Catalan succession the appointment of an heir, whose acquisition is qualified as universal (art. 411-1, 423-2, 462-1 CC Cat), is essential (art. 423-1.1, 431-18.1, 441-2.1, CC Cat). Although in practice testate succession plays a preeminent role,[19] inheritance agreements prevail over testaments and these are preferent to intestacy. These three different types of succession are incompatible among each other (as expressed for the incompatibility between testate and intestate heirs by the rule *nemo pro parte testatus, pro parte intestatus decedere potest*, art. 411-3.2 and 3, 423-3 CC Cat). Therefore, an heir cannot lose his or her status once accepted (*semel heres, semper heres*, art. 423-12.1 CC Cat).

Together with the reduced forced share in Catalonia (a quarter of the augmented estate), which leaves a good share of the estate to be disposed of freely, these principles (*nemo pro parte* and *semel heres*) also contribute to explaining why in Catalonia only a quarter of the successions accepted before a notary are intestate.[20] As will be shown below, these principles lead to forcing or expanding the testator's express will. Also, we must not forget that this preference for wills may reflect a dislike for the rules on intestacy; it remains to be seen whether the new regulation will alter this tendency.

3.1   The Appointment of an Heir Is a Prerequisite for the Validity of a Will

Unlike the Spanish CC (art. 764), the Catalan CC requires the appointment of an heir and if there is a will, it is a condition for the validity thereof (art. 423-1.1, 422-1.3 CC Cat). The only exceptions to this rule are the appointment of a universal executor (art. 423-1.3, 429-7.2 CC Cat) or, for testa-

---

[17] Martí i Miralles (1925).

[18] Puig Ferriol (1984) 39 ff.; Ferrer Riba (2009) 19; Garrido Melero (2008) 11, 31, 78.

[19] As shown by the following data: in 2009, for a population where 6,355,569 inhabitants had reached the age to make a will, 109,071 wills and other *mortis causa* acts were drafted, i.e. a will for every 58 Catalans that are 14 or older [*Anuario DGRN* (2009/III)]. Lamarca Marquès (2010) 1171-1172 presents similar, but not identical figures (probably because only wills are taken into account); data referring to the Catalan census are taken from there. For global evaluations on the number of wills executed in Spain, see Delgado Echeverría (2006) 103 ff.; Cámara Lapuente (2007) 6-7 and in this book (section 4.1).

[20] Statistic data in Lamarca Marquès (2010) 1172, although the figures differ slightly from those officially given in the *Anuario*. According to the *Anuario DGRN* (2009/III), 61,454 deeds on succession were executed, that is about 20,000 more than the author mentions, using data from the Association of Catalan Notaries. In any case, there is a marked difference in the number of intestate successions compared with testamentary ones: it seems that 11,427 declarations of intestate heirs were made, of which 10,304 were authorized by notaries and 1,123 by a judge (for more remote relatives). It must be noted that not all the deeds that appear in the statistics include acceptance and that the data does not allow to differentiate between acceptance by heirs and by legatees (so more than one deed may be drafted for each succession).

tors subject to the local norms of Tortosa, the distribution of the entire estate through legacies (art. 423-1.2 CC Cat). If the will is void, the rules on intestacy will apply, but the testator's wishes will be respected, to a point, by means of the conversion of the will into a codicil (art. 422-6.1 CC Cat). For some, this proves that it is absurd to require the appointment of an heir for the validity of the testament:[21] succession will be intestate, but the beneficiaries will be burdened with the legacies contained in the testament, now called codicil. However, although the formalities of a testament and those required for a codicil are the same (art. 421-20.3 CC Cat), the content is not: a codicil cannot contain provisions that affect the heir's position (art. 421-20.2 CC Cat), so if the conversion operates, these will be lost. Also, the testator's will is not fully respected because codicils are incapable of revoking a previous testament; this means that the conversion does not necessarily lead to intestacy: this will only be the case when there is no previous testament that revives due to the latest one (the one that did not include the appointment of an heir) being null and void, and its provisions remaining only as the content of a codicil. Probably the testator never envisaged the revival of the previous will, which shows how distorting it is to maintain these old principles.

Under the CS, it was very problematic to decide on the validity of wills where the testator only excluded certain intestate beneficiaries, without actually naming an heir. Following some case law in this line,[22] art. 423-10.1 CC Cat considers these wills valid insofar as they in fact reveal the testator's preference for the non-excluded heirs. This rule makes sense, since if it were held that the will is void and that it is converted into a codicil, the testator's will would be ineffective because heirs cannot be excluded by means of a codicil (art. 421-10.2 CC Cat), and therefore all the beneficiaries under intestacy would maintain their rights over the estate.

Similar problems arose when the only content of the testament was to revoke a previous testament.[23] Under the CS, it was unclear whether such a testament could be considered valid or not. Art. 422-9.5 CC Cat expressly provides that these wills are valid, but there are still unsolved questions. First, is there in such a will an implicit appointment of the list of intestate beneficiaries or is the testator simply expressing that he or she wants to die intestate?[24] The answer to this

---

[21] Ferrer Riba (2009) 19; Cf. Puig Ferriol – Roca Trias (2009) 45.

[22] See STSJC 23 April 1998 (RJ 10053), with a comment by Cámara Lapuente (2000a) 743 ff.; Marsal Guillamet (2000) 61; Garrido Melero (2008) 89; Puig Ferriol-Roca Trías (2010) 510. Criticizing it, Ferrer Riba (2009) 20. See Cámara Lapuente (2000b) 46-49, where the author goes into great detail on the various situations that may arise, both under the Spanish CC (for which he proposes a different solution to that explained in the text, pp. 62-69) and in a comparative perspective.

[23] On the limited acceptance of the merely revocatory will in the Catalan legal tradition, Marsal Guillamet (2000) 56-60; Anderson (2009a) 300-301.

[24] Del Pozo Carrascosa – Vaquer Aloy – Bosch Capdevila (2009) 91-92 defend the first solution. In favour of the second, Puig Ferriol – Roca Trias (2009) 194; Anderson (2009a) 301; Lamarca Marquès (2010) 1182-1183.

question is by no means irrelevant: if the testament is considered to contain a mere reference to the list of intestate beneficiaries, but not to the other provisions on intestacy, then, for instance, the surviving spouse would not have the right to the usufruct over the entire estate if the testator left issue.[25] On the other hand, the wording of art. 422-9.5 CC Cat is misleading, since it refers to a testament that is "merely revocatory"; this may be taken to mean that for a will to be valid without the appointment of an heir it cannot contain any other provision, such as a legacy, because in this case it would be converted into a codicil and therefore it would not have the power to revoke a previous will if there was one. This interpretation would clearly be at odds with the testator's will. Finally, the new regulation does not take into account the possibility that the testator has executed two "merely revocatory" wills in a row; although this is certainly not a usual occurrence, it seems clear that in this case the testator does not want the rules on intestacy to apply, but the revival of the first, non revocatory, will.[26]

All these problems, which are technical but have important practical consequences, are the result of preserving principles that can end up having numerous exceptions but, more importantly, add complexity to the law of succession.

3.2   The Heir As a Universal Successor

By accepting the inheritance, the heir takes on the decedent's position in all aspects that are transferrable *mortis causa* and acquires the entire estate or a share thereof. Some assets may be excluded from the estate if the title passes directly to a legatee upon the decedent's demise.[27] The heir is also liable for the decedent's debts; even with his or her personal assets, unless he or she has protected them by making an inventory of the estate within six months from the time when the heir knew or could reasonably know that the he or she had the right to accept or disclaim the inheritance (art. 461-14, 461-15, 461-17 CC Cat).

The heir is therefore a universal successor. But the heir's title is also expansive, especially due to the effect of the next principle we will be dealing with: the incompatibility between testate and intestate succession.

3.3   *Nemo Pro Parte Testatus, Pro Parte Intestatus Decedere Potest*

The Latin aphorism conveys the idea that partial intestacy, as far as the heir's title is concerned, is not possible.[28] This incompatibility between

---

[25] See section 4.2.2. b) for the rules on intestacy.

[26] Anderson (2009a) 300-301.

[27] Catalan civil law allows both obligatory and proprietary legacies, i.e. legacies that impose an obligation on the heir, and legacies of assets that belong to the testator and pass directly to the legatee upon death, respectively (art. 427-10 CC Cat).

[28] Although it is possible to burden the intestate heirs with legacies and devises contained in a codicil (art. 421-20.1 CC Cat), so that it can be said that there is partial intestacy regarding the estate, but there cannot be a testamentary and an intestate heir in the same succession.

testate and intestate hereditary titles is exceptional in the European legal context.[29] The consequences of this principle are multifold; to a large extent, the law has to force the construction of the testator's will in order to preserve it.

For instance, even when the testator has expressly stated that the vacant share left by one of the appointed heirs is not to be distributed among the rest, this will be the result provided by the law (art. 462-1 CC),[30] unless the vacant share is to follow another course due to the existence of a substitutional heir (*substitution vulgaris*) or the applicability of the right of representation or the *ius transmissionis*.[31]

Another example of the way in which the law expands the testator's will concerns the case where the testator has provided that an heir is to receive just one, or only certain assets, that belong to the estate. Art. 423-4 CC Cat provides that if this is the only heir appointed in the will, he or she becomes the universal successor, i.e. the heir receives the entire estate. If there is another testamentary heir, then the one who was left only with certain assets is considered a legatee. Probably this would be the best solution also in the first case: the testamentary heir could be considered a legatee named in a codicil (the converted testament) and the rest of the estate (and the hereditary title) would pass under the rules on intestacy. This would be more in line with the testator's will and, moreover, it would not infringe the *nemo pro parte* rule.[32]

This principle also has another implication: the heir cannot hold this position for a certain amount of time only, i.e. testate and intestate succession cannot operate successively. Hence the rule *semel heres, semper heres*.

3.4   Semel Heres, Semper Heres

This principle could be translated as "once an heir, always an heir". It entails that the appointment of an heir cannot be subject to an initial or a final term of time or to a condition subsequent; if the testator has provided such terms or conditions, the law deprives them of any effect (art. 423-12.1 CC Cat). On the contrary, conditions precedent are admitted (art. 411-4.2, 423-12.2, 461-2.2 CC Cat). The dogmatic explanation for this different treatment is that both initial and final terms are not retroactive, which means that the intestate beneficiaries should take before or after the testamentary heir succeeds (art.

---

[29] Pérez Simeón (1999) 15 ff. On the meaning of the rule and the evolution thereof in Castile and in Catalonia, Bosch Capdevila (2006). On the expansion of hereditary shares to cover vacant shares under the CS, Bosch Capdevila (2002).

[30] Criticism, for the old law, in Pérez Simeón (1999) 15 ff.; for the law in force, see Del Pozo Carrascosa – Vaquer Aloy – Bosch Capdevila (2009) 506; Ferrer Riba (2008) 21. In favour of the solution in force, Lamarca Marquès (2010) 1181.

[31] I.e. the transmission of the right to accept or disclaim the inheritance to the heir's successors when the former has died before accepting or disclaiming (art. 461-13 CC Cat).

[32] Del Pozo Carrascosa – Vaquer Aloy – Bosch Capdevila (2009) 52; Garrido Melero (2008) 81.

805.2 Spanish CC).[33] An heir subject to a condition subsequent would also lose his or her position if the condition were fulfilled; in this case, even accepting that conditions have retroactive effects when established in a *mortis causa* act (*ex* art. 1120 Spanish CC), which is arguable, the law seems to be protecting the permanence of the testamentary entitlement, rather than the *semel heres, semper heres* principle as such. Since a condition subsequent does not prevent the heir's acceptance and acquisition of the estate, probably a better solution would have been for the law to imply a fideicommissum in favour of the intestate heirs.[34] On the other hand, if conditions precedent are considered acceptable (art. 423-14 CC Cat), the same should apply to initial terms; the estate could be provisionally administered by the appointed heir, thus avoiding the presence of temporary intestate heirs.[35] The current solution conflicts with the testator's will and this is especially absurd if we bear in mind that the testator has other ways of attaining the same result (for instance, by appointing an executor for the administration of the estate for a certain period of time – art. 429-7.1, 429-8.1 and 429-13.4 CC Cat –, by granting the usufruct to an ascendant so that the estate passes to an heir that is not even conceived at the time of death – art. 423-7.3 and 4 CC Cat –, by delegating the choice of heirs in another person (art. 424-1 ff. CC Cat) or by means of a successive appointment of heirs, i.e. a fideicommissum).[36] If the testator chooses a fideicommissum, the subsequent heir or fideicommissary heir is subject to an initial term or to a condition precedent, but also the prior or fiduciary heir is subject to a final term or to a condition subsequent. Therefore, the rule should not be so strict when the testator decides to establish these terms and conditions in a more straightforward manner.

The *semel heres, semper heres* principle also bars the possibility of appointing an heir for life, which would amount to appointing this heir for an (uncertain) period of time. Therefore, the law intervenes once more to preserve the traditional principles. If the testator has appointed a subsequent heir, there will be a fideicommissum. But if there is no subsequent heir, the heir for life is considered a universal heir with all its consequences (art. 423-4 CC Cat), i.e. he or she can dispose *inter vivos* and *mortis causa* of the estate, as if the testator had not limited the appointment to the heir's lifetime.

In the same line of safeguarding the *semel heres, semper heres* principle and, through this, preserving the *nemo pro parte* rule, art. 423-5 CC Cat deals with the case where the testator has granted someone the universal usufruct over the estate. According to this provision, the usufruct holder is treated in the same way as an heir to whom only certain assets are left (art. 423-3 CC Cat); therefore, if there is another heir appointed in the will, the usufruct holder is considered a legatee. If the testator has not appointed another heir but has foreseen who is to receive the estate when the usufruct holder dies, the latter is considered a fiduci-

---

33 Marsal Guillamet (2003) 689, 690.

34 Calatayud Sierra (1994) 604; Garrido Melero (2008) 92-93.

35 Calatayud Sierra (1994) 603.

36 Ferrer Riba (2009) 22.

ary heir and the former a fideicommissary heir. Finally, if the testator has only granted the usufruct and made no further arrangement, the usufruct holder is considered a fiduciary heir, and the intestate heirs are treated like fideicommissary heirs. The justification of this solution is dubious: the usufruct holder could simply be treated as a legatee appointed in a codicil and the intestate heirs would receive the encumbered estate with no breach of the *nemo pro parte* principle.[37] And why the solution differs from that given for the heir for life is a mystery.[38]

4 The Impact of Social and Economic Changes on the Law of Succession

The social changes that have taken place during the last 20 years have made it necessary to revise the law of succession. The main reforms focus on three areas: there is the aim to further extend the freedom of testation and respect the testator's wishes by introducing new grounds for disinheritance and unworthiness and prohibitions to succeed; on the other hand, changing family models need to be taken into account; and, finally, efficient mechanisms need to be in place for succession within the family business.

4.1 Freedom of Testation and Respect for the Testator's Wishes

Testate succession is governed by the testator's will, as expressed following the formalities provided by the law (art. 421-1 CC Cat). Freedom of testation is, therefore, the basic principle. The new grounds for disinheritance, as well as the reform of the grounds for unworthiness (which, of course, also apply under intestacy) and the regulation of prohibitions to succeed, that aim at ensuring that the testator is not unduly influenced when drafting the will, tend to reinforce freedom of testation.

An unworthy beneficiary can be excluded from the inheritance because of reprehensible actions against the decedent or his or her next of kin, which are often also criminal offences or deserve a private law sanction.[39] Under Catalan law, unworthiness is not the same as disinheritance; the latter refers only to deprivation of the forced share if the testator decides to do so and as long as there is a valid reason for disinheritance, whilst the former affects the capacity to receive any type of benefit from the decedent's estate. All grounds for unworthiness are also valid reasons to disinherit (art. 451-17.2 a CC Cat), but not the other way around. On the other hand, prohibitions to succeed have nothing to do with the beneficiary's conduct; the mere fact of being the notary

---

[37] Ferrer Riba (2009) 22; cf. Puig Ferriol – Roca Trías (2009) 60.

[38] Ferrer Riba (2009) 23.

[39] For a comparative analysis of this and other issues, comprising Catalan law, see Zimmermann (2009) 505-508. More detail in Zimmermann (2010) 463 ff.

who drafted the testator's will or the testator's guardian (unless the guardian is also a close family member), for instance, is sufficient for the law to consider that the testator's will has been influenced, thus rendering any gift to these people ineffective. This legal presumption is not rebuttable. Although they are regulated among the general provisions (Part I of Book IV), it seems natural to understand, as shown by their justification, that these prohibitions do not apply to intestate beneficiaries or to those who have the right to a forced share.[40] Both prohibitions and unworthiness render gifts ineffective, but not automatically: the persons who would take if the unworthy beneficiary or the person included in a prohibition were excluded from the inheritance will have to obtain a judicial declaration to this effect, even if there is a previous verdict or judgment condemning the reprehensible conduct.[41] By contrast, it is left to the testator whether he or she wants to disinherit a person who would otherwise be entitled to a forced share and to do so the prerequisites provided in art. 451-18 CC Cat must be fulfilled.

4.1.1 New Grounds for Unworthiness and a Longer List of Victims of Reprehensible Conduct

New grounds for unworthiness include wilful criminal offences such as grievous bodily harm, torture, offences against personal freedom, moral and sexual integrity (art. 412-3 b CC Cat), thus covering gender based violence.[42] The victim may be the decedent, his or her surviving spouse or cohabitant or any ascendant or descendant. It is surprising that the rule does not include the children of the surviving spouse or cohabitant, at least if they were living with the decedent.[43] When the offender and the victim are spouses or cohabitants, this ground for unworthiness may not be required, since *de facto* separation excludes the surviving spouse or cohabitant from the succession anyway (art. 422-13, 442-6, 452-2 CC Cat). Also, unworthiness may have been forgiven by the decedent (art. 412-4 a and b CC Cat). Bearing in mind that quite often gender based violence does not lead to the couple separating completely or it generates situations where cohabitation ceases and is later reinstated, the real question is whether cohabitation can be considered an act of reconciliation that excludes unworthiness. The solution will be down to the courts; it will depend

---

[40] Gómez Pomar (2009) 103, 121-122. Under the CS, prohibitions to succeed were provided for in art. 147, in the chapter dedicated to the appointment of heirs, within the Part dealing with testate succession.

[41] Against this solution, see Ollé Favaró (2010) 452; indirectly, Garrido Melero (2008) 27.

[42] Regarding the lack of consistency of these norms with the Criminal Code, see Ferrer Riba (2009) 32; Gómez Pomar (2009) 109. On gender based violence, critical with the Catalan regulation, García Rubio – Herrero Oviedo (2009) 479-480.

[43] The same applies when the unworthy conduct amounts to murder (art. 412-3 a CC Cat) and in the case of disinheritance under art. 457-17.2 b, c CC Cat.

on the concept of unworthiness that they uphold: Should the decedent's presumed will prevail? Or should the offender be punished in any case?[44]

As well as generalizing the inclusion of criminal offences against family obligations, the other innovation in the field of unworthiness is the wording of art. 412-3 f CC Cat, which considers parents unworthy if they have been suspended or deprived of custody on grounds attributable to them. This last provision is very difficult to apply, since judicial decisions on parental rights very rarely state who the situation is attributable to. Since the goal is to protect the minor involved, not to punish the guilty party, the question now is whether, for instance, a drug addict mother who has not taken care of her child since birth is unworthy to succeed if this child dies before her. It is very complicated to decide who's "fault" it is that she was unable to look after her child.

4.1.2   A New Ground for Disinheritance: The Lack of Normal Family Interaction Attributable to the Forced Heir

The regulation of disinheritance in the CC Cat presents two innovations. The first one is the extension of the reason for disinheritance that consists of ill-treating or failing to comply with maintenance obligations towards the decedent's cohabitant (art. 451-17 b, c CC Cat). This can be relevant regarding ill-treatment, and also if a common descendent has failed to provide for his or her parent (the decedent's cohabitant), but not among cohabitants themselves, since there are no maintenance obligations between cohabitants, according to the new regulation on cohabitation in Book II. Probably this is due to the different perspective on cohabitation adopted in the book dedicated to family law and the book dedicated to succession; we will address this issue in section 4.2.1.

The second relevant reform is the inclusion of continuous and obvious lack of family relationship between the decedent and the forced heir, insofar as it is attributable to the latter. Therefore the mere fact that communication is less frequent than usual or even nonexistent is not enough to disinherit. The idea is to protect children from previous marriages or relationships. The burden of proving that the lack of family interaction was attributable to the forced heir will lie on the heir (who would benefit from just disinheritance, since he or she would not have to pay the forced share, art. 451-20.1 CC Cat). The new Catalan provision has already been criticized; for some, this ground for disinheritance is too vague and may allow allegation of facts that are very difficult to prove;[45] according to another opinion, this is positive since it enhances testamentary

---

[44]   In a case subject to the Compilation, concerning unworthiness to claim the *quarta uxoris* (on which, see section 4.2.2. c) of this paper), the STJC 8 June 1993 (RJ 6325) found that reconciliation could be deduced from the fact that although the husband had been expelled from the family home, he was later readmitted. This does not solve all the problems that may arise, since in many domestic violence situations cohabitation never ceases.

[45]   Lamarca Marquès (2009a) 293-294.

freedom to the detriment of family solidarity.[46] It does seem clear that it will lead to more litigation.[47] For example, if the forced heir is homosexual and that causes a breakdown in the relation with his or her father, is there a valid ground for disinheritance?

4.1.3   The Protection of the Elderly Testator

When a will is drafted by or executed with the notary's partici-pation, the notary appreciates whether the testator is capable of making a will (art. 421-7, 421-9 CC Cat).[48] This applies to all testators, although obviously old age will be an element for the notary to take into account and he or she may ask for the assistance of medical professionals if in doubt. But art. 412-5 CC Cat introduces a further mechanism designed to safeguard the elderly testator's freedom of testation, by providing that for gifts to those who have cared for the testator (such as home-helps, hospitals or elderly people's homes) to be consid-ered effective they have to be contained in a testament drafted by a notary (i.e. the so called *open* will, where the notary drafts the text following the testator's instructions). The only alternative is an inheritance agreement, where a public notarized deed is also required (art. 431-7.1 CC Cat).

Probably this norm should not be included in the article dedicated to prohi-bitions to succeed, since these beneficiaries are able to succeed, albeit only if certain formalities are complied with.[49] However, the main criticism stems from the fact that the only beneficiaries affected by this limitation are those who had been looking after the testator as a result of a contract entered into to that effect. Therefore, it does not cover public institutions or charities,[50] when the reasons to suspect that the testator may have been unduly influenced seem to be the same.

Finally, yet another inconsistency can be highlighted. A 2000 Catalan Act[51] that regulates a kind of maintenance contract, where a person or a couple undertake to look after another person or couple who are over 65, or disabled in some way, provides inheritance rights for the carers, as long as they have

---

[46]   Vaquer Aloy, in this book (section 4.3). In favour of the introduction of a similar ground for disinherit-ance in Dutch law, Van Mourik (2009) 121.

[47]   Ferrer Riba (2009) 25; Ribot Igualada (2009) 1401-1402; Ollé Favaró (2010) 453. Even the legislature is aware of this: see DSPC Serie P, No. 54, 18 June 2008, 9. Preamble to Act 10/2008, VI. 5.

[48]   Jou Mirabent (2009) 177-180; Anderson (2009b) 1 ff. Under the Spanish CC, see Rodríguez Guitián (2007) 115 ss.

[49]   Del Pozo Carrascosao – Vaquer Aloy – Bosch Capdevila (2009) 447-448. According to Garrido Melero (2008) 25-26, it is a "formal" incapacity. On this practical problem in other countries and, particularly, in common law systems, Sonnekus (2007) 88-91. For Germany and The Netherlands, see Röthel and Milo, in this book (sections 2.4 and 3.4, respectively). Under the Spanish CC, contrary to redirect the issue to the doctrine of fraud, Rodríguez Guitián (2006) 90-99.

[50]   Gómez Pomar (2009) 124; Garrido Melero (2008) 26.

[51]   Act 22/2000, 29 December (DOGC No. 3304, 12 January 2001).

lived with the decedent for the four years prior to his or her death. In general terms, these rights amount to a quarter of the estate if the decedent left a will and, if the rules on intestacy apply, the carers take the entire estate prevailing over collateral relatives other than siblings and the issue thereof. This has been criticized, since the contract is not gratuitous but for consideration, so the carers have been paid for their services,[52] although probably the legislature wanted to benefit these people (who will have lived through the decedent's last years) to the detriment of those who, in spite of being related to the decedent, did not look after him or her for whatever reason. Family solidarity would be thus replaced by bonds formed at a later stage in life. Whatever side is taken in this debate, it does not make any sense to grant legal rights to the carers on the one hand and, on the other, to suspect them of unduly influencing the testator's will, which, from another point of view, may even be considered paternalistic and an unnecessary restriction on the testator's right to not disclose the content of his or her will to anyone.

4.2 The Adaptation of the Law of Succession to New Family Models

Unlike the Spanish CC, which, leaving aside some minor reforms,[53] bases the law of succession on the same family model as when it was enacted at the end of the 19th century, Catalan law has been gradually adapting to new family structures and relations. Book II CC Cat, which came into force on 1 January 2011, contains the new family law and is an example of this modernization of the system, although its spirit is slightly different to that inspiring the earlier Book IV on succession, as will be noted in the following lines.

4.2.1 The Equalization of Spouses and Cohabitants

This is one of the innovations with greatest social impact. The Act on cohabitation dates back to 1998 and it only granted rights in intestacy to same-sex partners, although not even these were at the same level as the surviving spouse's.[54] The discrimination towards heterosexual cohabitants was justified by the fact that these could choose to marry if they wished to, but even

---

[52] Ribalta Haro – Arroyo Amayuelas (2001) 80.

[53] Rebolledo Varela (2010) 25 ff.

[54] Art. 34 Act 10/1998, 15 July (DOGC No. 2687, 23 July 1998) and STSJC 9 March 2009 (JUR 2009/3273). Catalonia was the first autonomous community to regulate cohabitation, providing for the partner's rights and duties. Currently most territories have their own acts on cohabitation (albeit some contain public law rules only), but those subject to the Spanish CC law of succession are not granted any rights whatsoever, since there is not a Spanish regulation. A comparative perspective in Ginebra Molins (2006) 95 ff.; Arroyo Amayuelas (2005) 397 ff. See also, Cámara Lapuente, in this book (section 2.2, Tables 3-4 and section 2.3.2).

this arguable justification disappeared when the Spanish Parliament allowed same-sex marriages in 2005.[55] In this new context, the alternatives were to either repeal the rights granted to cohabitants in their partner's succession or to improve the position of both heterosexual and homosexual cohabitants. The latter was the preferred option, thus confirming the trend towards the so-called *horizontalization* of succession. According to the recent Book II CC Cat, the legal effects of cohabitation require either the couple to have lived together for two years or the execution of a deed expressing the will to form a unmarried couple or that they have common issue while living together (art. 234-1 CC Cat). If either of these conditions is fulfilled, the surviving cohabitant has exactly the same rights (and treatment in general)[56] as the surviving spouse; see art. 441-2 and 442-3 ff. CC Cat for intestacy and art. 452-1 ff. CC Cat for the *quarta uxoris*.[57] It must be noted that these rights are granted regardless of how long the cohabitation has lasted, as with marriage, although in the case of unmarried couples without children who have not executed the above mentioned deed it may be more difficult to prove the situation that gives rise to legally granted rights (i.e. cohabitation for at least two years).

Finally, we cannot end this brief presentation on the cohabitant's position without highlighting that there seems to be a grave inconsistency between the approach taken in Book II and in Book IV CC Cat. In 2008, when the latter was enacted, the principle of full equalization to the surviving spouse was implemented throughout the text, with no restrictions whatsoever. By contrast, the preamble to the 2010 act containing Book II states, very arguably, that in contemporary Catalan society partnerships are conceived as a "test marriage", destined to become a marriage or dissolve. Although this could be the result of having maintained the wording of previous draft bills, the actual provisions seem to confirm the view held in the preamble. There are no duties and obligations (not even the basic maintenance and support standards) between cohabitants while they are living together (art. 234-3 CC Cat) and only when the relationship ends some maintenance and compensation claims arise (art. 234-9 ff. CC Cat). Whilst the principle of solidarity derived from cohabitation seems to have inspired the norms on succession, this is not the case as far as family law is concerned. So the obvious question is whether it is coherent to grant full succession rights to what is considered a mere "test marriage".

---

[55] Act 13/2005, 1 July 2005 (BOE No. 157, 2 July 2005).

[56] For instance, the surviving cohabitant of an incapacitated person who cannot make a will can be appointed *substitutum exemplaris* (art. 425-12 CC Cat) and there are no limitations for cohabitants to enter into inheritance agreements (art. 431-12 a, b CC Cat). On the other hand, the cohabitant will be excluded from succession, as will the surviving spouse, if he or she had ceased to live with the decedent at the time of death (art. 422.13, 442-6, 452-2 CC Cat).

[57] On which, see below section 4.2.2. c).

4.2.2 Improvements in the Position of the Surviving Spouse or Cohabitant

One of the main reforms concerns the position of the surviving spouse or cohabitant in cases of intestacy, in the line of securing it. However, and in spite of the fact that in most wills the main beneficiary is the surviving spouse (or cohabitant),[58] under the rules on intestacy he or she only takes when the decedent leaves no issue (as provided by the 1987 reform), but is preferred to the decedent's parents (who retain the right to the forced share) and collateral relatives (art. 442-3.2 CC Cat). If the decedent leaves issue, the surviving spouse or cohabitant is not totally destitute, since he or she has a usufruct over the entire estate (art. 442-3.1 CC Cat). The main innovations are the possibility to commute this usufruct for a share of the estate and the rule providing that if all the decedent's children disclaim, the right to inherit will not pass to further removed descendants (i.e. grandchildren), but to the surviving spouse or cohabitant (art. 442-2.2 CC Cat). We will deal with these and other modifications improving the spouse or cohabitant's position in this section.

a) The Strengthening of the Universal Usufruct

As already mentioned, if the intestate decedent leaves descendants, the surviving spouse or cohabitant has the usufruct over the entire estate. This may seen insufficient if we bare in mind that the default rule under Catalan law is that no matrimonial community property system is in place during marriage. Yet in other jurisdictions where marriage entails a community property system the surviving spouse is granted a share of the estate depending on what other relatives the decedent leaves.[59] It is impossible to decide on the best solution

---

[58] Spouses tend to execute wills in favour of each other. See Vaquer Aloy (2009) 1263; with further precisions, previously (2007) 16. The same tendency to benefit the surviving spouse can be found in England, according to Matthews (2009) 113.

[59] In The Netherlands a community property system is the default rule and yet, the surviving spouse takes first under intestacy, together with the issue, who cannot claim their share immediately. See Van Erp (2007) 194-195; Verbeke-Leleu (2004) 341; Castelein (2009) 13; Van Mourik (2009) 108-109; Milo, in this book (section 4.1). In Germany, where there is no community property as such, although the spouse who has gained more during the marriage will have to share this increase in wealth when the marriage comes to an end, the surviving spouse always takes together with other relatives (issue, ascendants or collateral relatives); depending on how close these relative were to the decedent, the spouse's share varies (§ 1931-1932 BGB). If the decedent leaves issue, the spouse takes a quarter of the estate. § 1931.4 BGB provides that if the default matrimonial property system does not apply, so that there is neither a community nor the possibility to participate in the spouse's increase in wealth, if the decedent left one or two children and a surviving spouse, they take in equal shares (including other descendants by right of representation). In Italy, where community property is the default system (art. 159; 177 ff. Italian CC) the surviving spouse takes together with the decedent's descendants, ascendants or collateral relatives, and the former's share varies depending on how close these relatives were to the decedent and, if applicable, how many children he or she left (if the decedent only left one child, the spouse takes

without taking into account the circumstances of the case, i.e. the value of the usufruct compared with the value of the share granted to the surviving spouse, the composition of the estate (big or small, rural or urban, including productive assets or not) and its manageability, the surviving spouse or cohabitant's age (sometimes he or she may be as young as the decedent's children) or the relation between the surviving spouse or cohabitant and the decedent's children who are to inherit (especially if they are not also the survivor's children).

The Catalan legislature decided to maintain the universal usufruct, but strengthening it in different ways. First, the usufruct encumbers the descendant's forced share (art. 442-4.1 CC Cat), as opposed to what art. 331.2 CS provided.[60] Still certain interpretation problems arise. For some, it is not clear whether a descendant can disclaim his or her share under intestacy and then claim an unencumbered forced share, as would be the case if the usufruct were voluntary (art. 427-34.2, 451-9 CC Cat),[61] but certainly the goal of the reform would not be attained if this possibility were admitted, since it leads directly to a reduction of the usufruct. The only case where the descendants would retain the right to their forced share would be if they all disclaimed the inheritance, since then the surviving spouse would be the sole heir in full ownership.[62]

Another innovation is that the universal usufruct is not terminated when the surviving spouse or cohabitant remarries or enters into another relationship (art. 442-4.3 CC Cat), as is still the case for other legally granted benefits (such as the right to live in the family home and be maintained by the estate during the year following the spouse or cohabitant's death: art. 231-31.2 CC Cat). Thus the usufruct is no longer linked to the spouse or cohabitant's future needs (it is not maintenance based), but rather it aims to compensate for the contributions to the family's wealth and care made while the decedent was alive.

Finally, the law allows the surviving spouse or cohabitant to commute the usufruct for a quarter of the estate in full ownership and the usufruct over the

---

half the estate; if the decedent left more than one child, the spouse takes a third, art. 581 Italian CC). In France, where the default system is also community property (art. 1400 French CC), a similar rule applies; if the decedent left issue and a surviving spouse, the latter takes a quarter of the estate, but he or she can commute it for a usufruct over the entire estate if all the decedent's issue are also the surviving spouse's (art. 756 ff. French CC). For a comparative perspective, see Pintens, in this book (section 3.1.1). Regarding the surviving spouse's rights in Spain, Pérez Escolar (2003); Corral García (2007); Cámara Lapuente (2007) 17-18 and annex 2; the same author, in this book (section 2.2, table 2).

[60] There have been cases where the courts applied the current rule, contradicting the legal provision in force under art. 331.2 CS. *In extenso*, on the repealed rule, Espiau Espiau (1996) 629 ff., 641-642. On the reform, see Lamarca Marquès (2010) 1203; Vaquer Aloy (2009) 1268-1270; Del Pozo Carrascosa – Vaquer Aloy – Bosch Capdevila (2009) 374-375.

[61] Gete-Alonso (2009) 235-236 considers that the reform excludes this possibility; Ollé Favaró (2009) 462-463 and Vaquer Aloy (2009) 1270 hold the contrary.

[62] See section 4.2.2. b).

family home (art. 442-4 CC Cat).[63] This possibility is especially useful for the average estate that includes the family home and maybe some savings, since otherwise the surviving spouse or cohabitant can find it impossible to maintain unproductive assets, especially if the relationship with the heirs (the decedent's children) is not that good. However, the fact that it is up to the surviving spouse or cohabitant only to commute can generate problems when the estate comprises a business.

If the surviving spouse or cohabitant decides to commute, this removes the assets thus received completely from the family estate.[64] This system is reminiscent of that provided by art. 757 of the French CC, although in France the general rule is that the surviving spouse takes a quarter of the estate as an heir, unless he or she decides to commute this title for the usufruct over the entire estate; this option is only available if the other heirs are children of both the decedent and the surviving spouse.[65] It would seem that the Catalan rules are better for the surviving spouse or cohabitant, since the usufruct over the family home is maintained even if the right to commute is enforced. However, art. 764 of the French CC grants the surviving spouse the right to dwell in the family home (that the decedent can exclude by means of a notarized testament) and to use the chattels thereof. This right counts towards the spouse's share (art. 765 French CC), in the same way as in Catalonia the value of the usufruct over the family home is deducted from the value of the estate to calculate the right to a quarter of the estate, as already mentioned (art. 442-5.4 CC Cat).

b) Exceptions to successio graduum et ordinum

Following the Roman tradition, intestacy in Catalonia adheres to the principle of *succession graduum et ordinum*. The list of intestate heirs is: 1) descendants; 2) surviving spouse or cohabitant; 3) ascendants; 4) siblings and their issue; 5) carers (art. 8 Act 22/2000, as mentioned above in section 4.1.3); 6) other collateral relatives (up to the fourth degree; i.e. cousins); 7) the Catalan Generalitat. According to the general principle, the estate is offered in the first place to the decedent's children; only if there are no children or if they will not or cannot inherit,[66] the estate will be offered to the decedent's grandchildren. If there are no descendants, the surviving spouse or cohabitant may take the entire estate and thus successively until the estate is devolved to the Generalitat, which cannot disclaim. The new art. 442-2.2 CC Cat provides an important exception to this system: if all the decedent's children disclaim, as long as certain condi-

---

[63] Although the value of the usufruct over the family home is taken into account in order to reduce the right to a quarter of the estate.

[64] Lamarca Marquès (2010) 1207.

[65] Corpart (2002) 2952 ff.; Pereña Vicente (2003) 7 ff.; Bellivier-Rochfeld (2002) 156 ff.; Grimaldi (2002) 48 ff.; Ferrand (2009) 191-192.

[66] It must be noted that in some cases the right of representation will allow grandchildren to take in their parent's place (art. 441-7 CC Cat).

tions are fulfilled, the estate will not be offered to the grandchildren, but to the surviving spouse or cohabitant.

This exceptional rule is to be welcomed, since it gives a solution to a frequent occurrence which would otherwise be technically more complicated and expensive from a tax point of view. Namely, quite often the decedent's children feel that the rules on intestacy are not fair, so they are happy to disclaim their right to inherit in favour of the surviving spouse or cohabitant, especially if it is their father or mother. Under the old law, if they were to barely disclaim, the rules on intestacy would direct the estate towards the grandchildren, not towards the surviving spouse, so their objective would be defeated. On the other hand, if they disclaimed *in favour of* the surviving spouse (or cohabitant), their acts would amount to implicit acceptance of the inheritance (art. 461.5 b CC Cat) and subsequent transfer to the surviving spouse or cohabitant. Two transmissions, which would entail, among other consequences, double taxation.

Art. 442-2.2 CC Cat aims to solve these problems, but it does not address the main issue, which is lack of conformity with the position of the surviving spouse or cohabitant in intestacy.[67] Moreover, the provision contains certain restrictions that are difficult to justify. For instance, it only applies when all the issue disclaim; the question is why it should not apply partially when only one or more children wish to benefit the surviving spouse or cohabitant. On the other hand, and this is even more difficult to explain, the exception does not apply if there are children of the decedent only; again, if they get on well with their step mother or father or with their parent's partner and wish to disclaim in his or her favour, why not allow them to do so?

Finally, it must be noted that quite often the surviving spouse or cohabitant will be the guardian and legal representative of the decedent's minor children; disclaimer in their name requires a court's authorization (art. 461-9.2 CC Cat), which may be problematic to obtain, given the clear conflict of interests arising in this case.[68]

c) Modification of the quarta uxoris

In Catalonia, the surviving spouse or cohabitant is not a forced heir (art. 452-5.2 CC Cat),[69] but, as a *post mortem* effect of marriage, he or she has the right to receive up to a quarter of the estate when, taking into account his or her own assets and those that he or she receives as a result of the division of matrimonial property, when applicable, or in the decedent's succession, the surviving spouse or cohabitant is unable to provide for his or her own maintenance. This right

---

[67] *In extenso*, Beckert (2008) 52, 83 ff. An outline in Castelet (2009) 23-24; Milo, in this book (section 3.2).

[68] On this matter, before Book IV CC Cat came into force, see RDGEJD 19 October 2009 (DOGC No. 5516, 30 November 2009); RDGEJD 20 October 2009 (DOGC No. 5520, 4 December 2009). Academic opinion on the reform, Ginebra Molins (2009) 1241-1242; Lamarca Marquès (2010) 1196; Ollé Favaró (2010) 464; Del Pozo Carrascosa – Vaquer Aloy – Bosch Capdevila (2009) 368, 375; Gete-Alonso (2009) 226-227.

[69] Preamble to Act 10/2008, VI 8.

is no longer conditioned by the number of children that the decedent leaves, it applies in both testate and intestate succession and it is much clearer now that it is totally maintenance focused, which has lead to the modification of the rules to calculate it (they are now similar to the rules to calculate the force share). This new *quarta uxoris* is determined following the criteria that would have been applied if the marriage (or cohabitation) had ended by divorce (or termination of the cohabitation) (art. 452-1 CC Cat),[70] so that the surviving spouse or cohabitant is not left in a worse position than if that were the case.

d) The Effect of Death on Matrimonial Proceedings (Separation, Divorce and Nullity)

All rights and claims that the surviving spouse may have against the estate disappear if at the time of death the spouses were divorced or legally or *de facto* separated, as well as if at that time divorce, separation or nullity proceedings had been initiated (art. 442-6, 452-6 CC Cat).[71] The same applies to the surviving cohabitant if at the time of death they had ceased to live together. *De facto* separation may be difficult to prove, but what mostly draws one's attention is the fact that the mere initiation of divorce, separation or nullity proceedings determines the loss of rights, instead of allowing the heirs to continue the proceedings, as was the case under the CS (art. 335, 381.1, II CS). As far as divorce and separation are concerned, the modification is justified, not just because the action is personal (art. 88 Spanish CC), but mainly because the court will necessarily grant the separation or divorce as long as some minimum requirements have been complied with (namely, that the marriage has lasted three months: art. 81 Spanish CC).[72] However, the same does not apply to nullity, and yet the Catalan law treats all three cases equally. On the other hand, although the surviving spouse (or cohabitant) loses *mortis causa* rights, he or she can still claim for different forms of compensation linked to the matrimonial proceeding (or cohabitation breakdown), within the time limits set forth by Book II, on family law (art. 232-5.5, 232-11.2, 233-14.2, 234-10.3, 234-14 CC Cat).

e) The Elimination of the Legal Reservation in Favour of Children from a Previous Marriage

Book IV does away with the so-called "binuptial reservation" (art. 411-8 CC Cat).[73] Previously, art. 387 CS imposed on the surviving spouse the obligation to reserve for the children he or she had had with the decedent the assets inherited

---

[70] Espiau Espiau (2009) 639-678; Lamarca Marquès (2009a) 300-307; Ferrer Riba (2009) 30-31.

[71] A similar provision can be found in § 1933 BGB, which also allows the surviving spouse to claim maintenance. By contrast, in Italy if the divorce proceedings are still pending the spouse is not considered divorced (art. 585 Italian CC). In France, only divorce (not separation) excludes succession rights (art. 301, 702 CC). On the regulation in Germany, see Röthel in this book (section 3.1).

[72] Puig Ferriol – Roca Trías (2009) 522; Del Pozo Carrascosa – Vaquer Aloy – Bosch Capdevila (2009) 367; Gete-Alonso (2009) 231.

[73] For the old law, RDGEJ 12 June 2007 (JUR 146969); STJC 8 June 2009 (JUR 4297); STSJC 31 May 2010 (JUR 5129). On transitional provisions, Del Pozo Carrascosa – Vaquer Aloy – Bosch Capdevila (2009)

from the latter (or as an intestate heir of a common child) if he or she remarried or had more children or adopted them. It would have been anachronistic to preserve this institution in a society where the number of second or third marriages, of extra-matrimonial families and of adoptions has grown massively. The alternative would have been to extend the obligation to ex-cohabitants and also for cases when the survivor finds a new partner, which would have benefitted the decedent's children. This has not been the chosen solution, so that currently rules to preserve patrimonial assets within the family are very limited; they only apply to the intestate succession of a person who dies before reaching the age of 14 (when testamentary capacity is recognized) and to the mechanism to avoid it, *substitutio pupilaris* (art. 444-1 and 425-7.1 CC Cat, respectively).[74] If the testator wishes to maintain assets within the family, this can be attained by means of a fideicommissum, where the surviving spouse or cohabitant is the prior or fiduciary heir and the decedent's children, the fideicommissary heirs.

4.3   Succession within the Family Business: The Modernization of Inheritance Agreements

Unlike the Spanish CC, that forbids inheritance agreements (art. 1271: agreements on a future inheritance are banned), on the grounds that their irrevocability hinders testamentary freedom, that the suspicion of undue influence is powerful or that they encourage the desire for the decedent to pass, Catalonia has always favoured them, by means of the contractual appointment of an heir, sometimes including an immediate transfer of assets.[75]

Nevertheless, traditional inheritance agreements were linked to marriage and, in fact, they had to be included in a marriage settlement (art. 63.1, 340.2 CDCC; art. 67.1 CS, art. 15.1 CF) intended to organize the family's economy: in the settlement, the father appointed an heir among his children (usually, the elder son) when the latter married, in exchange for the dowry that the bride's father would contribute (art. 23 CF); this couple and their issue were to take over the homestead.[76] The estate or a share thereof could be conveyed immediately to the sole heir. This was possible thanks to the fact that the forced share reserved to the father's issue was (and is) only a quarter of the augmented estate, which could be paid out in money, even if there was none in the estate. This is how the homestead could pass from generation to generation without being divided. Both in the Compilation and in the CS the regulation of inheritance agreements was based on this rural model, which nowadays has been completely abandoned,

---

39-40. Critical of the reform, Garrido Melero (2008) 13-14; Salvador Coderch – López Burniol (2009) 87-88.

[74] Lamarca Marquès (2010) 1210-1213; Gete-Alonso (2009) 256-257.

[75] Egea Fernández (2009) 28, fn. 31. On the situation under the Spanish CC and reform proposals, Sánchez Aristi (2006) 477 ff.; Álvarez Lata (2009) 555 ff.

[76] Egea Fernández (2009) 18.

as the farming economy has dwindled, the importance of extended families has diminished, marriages break up and non-matrimonial families are usual.[77]

Marriage settlements have been in decline for decades and, together with them, so have inheritance agreements. The statistics do not reveal how many marriage settlements contain inheritance agreements, but notaries state that the former usually only decide on the organization of the economy of the marriage or on the consequences of separation or divorce.[78] Notwithstanding, the 1991 CS, following the Compilation, still contemplated the possibility of an agreement on *economic family unity* (which previously was implicit in any inheritance agreement: art. 71 CDCC), where both the decedent and the heir undertook to work for the benefit of the family and to sustain its members (art. 75 CS); it also regulated a *usufruct for family governance,* which ensured that the decedent or, after his (or her) death, the surviving spouse, would retain control over the family (art. 69 CS), and it dedicated around 30 articles to different types of inheritance agreements, classified basically depending on whether the designated heir was a party to the contract or not (art. 71-100 CS). Cases where the heir was a party to the contract included those where the parent or parents unilaterally designated one of their children to be their heir, which the latter accepted, and inheritance agreements where the spouses reciprocally appointed each other as heirs. A typical case where the heir would not be a party to the agreement was that where the spouses designated their common issue as heirs.[79]

Taking into account the criticism against this regulation and some academic proposals for reform,[80] the CC Cat admits inheritance agreements whether they are included in a marriage settlement or not (although they always have to be executed in a notarized deed: art. 431-7.1 CC Cat) and inheritance agreements concerning only certain assets or a share of the estate (art. 431-29 CC Cat).[81] The innovation lies in the fact that as well as family and marriage based inheritance agreements, unmarried couples and other relatives may now enter into inheritance agreements (art. 431-2 CC Cat) and, on the other hand, no consideration is required, either from the heir or from the other spouse's family, where applicable.[82] The parties to the agreement can be reciprocal beneficiaries or – and this is another novelty – the beneficiary can be someone who is not a party to the agreement, with no family links with the parties, thus including legal entities.[83] The distinguishing note in this case is that the beneficiary does not acquire any rights, does not become heir, until the decedent dies.[84] The grounds of nullity,

---

[77] López Burniol (1994) 329; González Bou (2005) 738-743; Jou Mirabent (2005) 362.

[78] González Bou (2005) 745-746. Data for 1990-1991, in López Burniol (1994) 330; for 2007, Navas Navarro, in this book (section 2).

[79] González Bou (2005) 752-753; Jou Mirabent (2005) 365-368.

[80] *Inter alia*, González Bou (2005) 760-761; Jou Mirabent (2005) 370 ff.

[81] Navas Navarro (2009) 1 ff.

[82] Egea Fernández (2009) 18.

[83] Del Pozo Carrascosa – Vaquer Aloy – Bosch Capdevila (2009) 307.

[84] Critical considerations in García Rubio – Herrero Oviedo (2009) 469-472.

modification and revocation are also provided for (431-9 a 16 CC Cat) in quite a broad manner, so that the irrevocability of the agreement is by no means absolute. In conclusion, inheritance agreements are not linked to a marriage and, as already mentioned, they need not include the entire estate.

The reform aims to facilitate succession within the family business, but now in the context of a capitalist urban society (art. 431-6.2 CC Cat). As this also entails decisions concerning how the family members or other people are to participate in the management of the company, the inheritance agreement may also contain a specific document to this effect, the so-called *family business protocol* (art. 431-7.1, 431-25.2 CC Cat).[85]

It remains to be seen whether this new regulation will lead to an increase in the number of inheritance agreements that are entered into. It seems that in 2009, 2,956 marriage settlements were executed, of which only 90 were inheritance agreements.[86] There may be different reasons for this low popularity,[87] but maybe some are related to the fact that inheritance agreements still cannot be entered into by people who are not members of the same family. If the idea behind the reform was to abandon the traditional notion where inheritance agreements were designed to maintain the estate within the family, since this is considered anachronistic (maybe none of the children is capable of carrying on with the family business or has no interest in it whatsoever), it does not seem adequate to still impose a restriction as to who may enter into such an agreement, as provided in art. 431-2 CC Cat, which still circumscribes this possibility to family, albeit in a much broader sense than in the previous regulation. As already mentioned, it is possible for two of the people included in art. 431-2 CC Cat to enter into an inheritance agreement for the benefit of somebody else, but it is difficult to understand why someone who is neither appointing an heir, nor being appointed, would wish to participate in such a scheme. This party's presence is only required so that the agreement is irrevocable, but we must admit this is a very weak design. It is obvious that in many cases the decedent will feel closer to a third party than to some of the relatives with whom he or she may enter into an inheritance agreement (especially if we bear in mind that in-laws are included in the list provided by art. 431-2).[88]

---

[85] González Bou (2005) 757; Egea Fernández (2010) 15-16, 24; Cerdà Albero (2009) 181 ff.

[86] Data on the total number of marriage settlements and other contracts directly linked to a marriage in *Anuario DGRN* (2009/III); data on the number of inheritance agreements, whether covering the entire estate or only certain assets in Lamarca Marquès (2010) 1171, fn. 6.

[87] See Navas Navarro in this book (section 3).

[88] Egea Fernández (2009) 22; Puig Ferriol (2009) 447-448; Garrido Melero (2008) 284; Trigo García (2009) 508-511.

5 Changes within Tradition: The Incomplete Reform of the Forced Share

Whilst under the Spanish CC the forced share is, as a general rule, a *pars bonorum* (i.e. it needs to be paid in kind) and it amounts to two-thirds of the augmented estate when the forced heirs are descendants, in Catalonia it is a *pars valoris* (i.e. it can be paid in money even if there is none in the estate) and it only amounts to a quarter of the augmented estate. Therefore, the restraint on freedom of testation is much less severe. But for both systems there is still more support for maintaining the forced share, albeit modified (in different directions: increasing the grounds for deprivation and unworthiness, limiting the list of beneficiaries or the amount, facilitating payment and the deferment thereof, reducing the donations *inter vivos* that are included in the augmented estate), than for its complete repeal.[89] This trend of modifying (sometimes substantially) the forced share in order to weaken it has been followed lately in a number of European systems, including Spain.[90]

It is arguable whether the forced share is constitutionally protected in Spain.[91] The German Constitutional Court considers it is (judgment of 19 July 2005)[92] and, undoubtedly, many of the opinions given for Germany could be extrapolated to Spain, since art. 33 and 39 of the Spanish Constitution are substantially equivalent to their German counterparts. However, the constitutional goal of family protection does not seem to suffer when those not benefited in an inheritance do not need a share of the estate and it does not demand that the beneficiaries are the children to the detriment of the surviving spouse or

---

[89] On the debate in Spain, Delgado Echeverría (2006) 122-130; Torres García (2006) 214-224; Cámara Lapuente (2007) 31-35 and also in this book (sections 3.1 and 3.2); Vaquer Aloy (2007) 12 f; Arroyo Amayuelas (2007) 270-272; Parra Lucán (2009) 495 ff.

[90] For a general comparative law perspective, Kroppenberg (2009) 1156, 1158; Vaquer Aloy (2007) 3-7; Parra Lucán (2009) 477-495; Miquel González (2009) 495-497; Foqué-Verbeke (2009) 211-217. See Pintens, in this book (section 3.1.2). The change of perspective in Louisiana is also interesting to note: Rougeau (2008) esp. 17 ff. For detail on the new forced share system in France, Ferrand (2009) 192-198. For the German situation prior to the reform that came into force in January 2009, Pintens-Seyns (2009) 174 ff.; on the new law, Arroyo Amayuelas (2009) 1 ff. and Röthel, in this book (section 3). Concerning the regulation in force in Belgium and reform proposals, Casman (2009) 155-156, 160 ff. For Scotland, Clive, in this book (section 2.2); for The Netherlands, Milo, in this book (section 4.3); for Scandinavia, Hambro, in this book (section 2). No reforms have succeeded in Italy (see Fusaro, section 3.1, and Vaquer Aloy, section 2, in this book) nor in Hungary (see Csehi section 3.3.8 in this book).

[91] Arguing that it is, Bustos Lago (2009) 414-415; Ollé Favaró (2009) 466 and Vaquer Aloy, section 2, respectively. Against, Miquel González (2009) 498-499; Valladares Rascón (2004) 4901; Del Pozo Carrascosa – Vaquer Aloy – Bosch Capdevila (2009) 384; Parra Lucán (2009) 501.

[92] At least the children's forced share. The judgment does not decide on the forced share of other descendants (§ 2303.2, I BGB), parents or surviving spouse (§ 2303.3, I BGB) or cohabitant (§ 10.6 LPartG). See Otte (2005) 1007-1010; Gaier (2007) 161-168; Karpen (2007) 173-184; Pintens-Seymar (2009) 169-174; Pintens, in this book (section 3.1.2).

cohabitant. Moreover, the law of succession is not the only mechanism to protect family members. The arguments in favour of eliminating the forced share, which operates as a mandatory limit on testamentary freedom, are solid. Nowadays, the relevant family (the nuclear family) is no longer a productive unit; the children do not work for the family and, usually, they do not look after their elderly parents (and if one of the children does, it does not seen fair to equalize his or her position with that of his or her siblings). In addition, the family assets to be transmitted have not usually been acquired thanks to the joint efforts of all the family members – which traditionally justified the children's participation upon the death of the head of the family; generally, the estate has been generated by the decedent's work, and his or her spouse or partner will have contributed towards it. A person's assets, leaving the family home aside, are usually fungible and they can be transmitted during that person's lifetime, which is often the case when the decedent has invested in his or her children's education or career. It is not justifiable to impose principles of family solidarity upon the testator when the beneficiaries of the forced share do not require it for their maintenance, and this is a frequent occurrence, due to the increase in life expectancy, which leads to the decedent's children being at their best financial moment at the time of the testator's death.[93] An alternative to eliminating the forced share would be to skip a generation and offer it to the grandchildren, or to limit it to minor and incapacitated issue.[94] But probably these solutions would encounter the same opposition as the proposal to allow the testator to benefit only one of his or her children – which however is accepted in some regions – or, even more *shockingly,* to leave the entire estate to his or her new girlfriend. It is obvious that this is a cultural and, above all, emotional problem.[95]

Probably this explains why the Catalan legislature has not considered it to be the right moment to eliminate the forced share. The beneficiaries are the decedent's children (and their descendants by right of representation) and, if there are no descendants, the decedent's parents (but not further removed ascendants). Nevertheless, the new regulation follows the trend that appeared in the 1990s towards weakening the forced share. Modifications are implemented in different areas: the donations that are added to the estate to calculate the forced share are now only those made during the last 10 years of the decedent's life (art. 451-5 b CC Cat), except for certain donations made to the forced heirs that count towards their entitlement (art. 451-8 CC Cat) regardless of the date when they were made; the generalization of the *cautela socini* (art. 451-9 CC Cat), i.e. the possibility to give a forced heir more than he or she is entitled to, but with some encumbrance, so that the forced heir may choose to accept this gift or disclaim it and demand payment of the strict forced share; the controversial widening of the grounds for disinheritance, as already explained (art. 451-17.2

---

[93] Data in Vaquer Aloy (2007) 8-11.

[94] Vaquer Aloy (2007) 14 ff.

[95] Reher (1996) 345; Miquel González (2009) 499; Bouckaert (2009) 94, emphasizing the importance of testamentary freedom from the point of view of economic efficiency (95-100).

e CC Cat), and the reduction of the time during which the forced share can
be claimed from 15 to 10 years (art. 451-27 CC Cat). But the legislature did not
take the opportunity to eliminate the parent's forced share, as has been done
in France (art. 914 and 916 French CC),[96] and benefit the surviving spouse or
cohabitant.

On the other hand, the fact that not all donations made to the forced
heirs count towards their forced share does not seem to be the best solution.
As already mentioned, the forced share in Catalonia is only a quarter of the
augmented estate, which explains why, as a general rule, donations made to the
beneficiaries are not counted towards their share, unless otherwise stated at
the time when the donation was made (art. 451-8,1 CC Cat). Therefore, technically the rule is coherent, but it must be noted that there is a sociological reason
behind the proposal put forward by German academics (although in Germany
the forced share is half the intestate entitlement [§ 2303 BGB], which can
amount to half the estate) to reverse the rule: this would be the effect that most
parents would consider natural when donating assets to their children.[97] Catalan
case-law shows that many testators thought that the default rule was that donations to their children counted towards their forced share, which explains why
so many judgments deal with testamentary clauses providing that the will leaves
nothing to a forced heir because he or she has already received during the testator's lifetime. Some authors believe that these are cases where the testator really
wishes to deprive the forced heir of his or her share without any valid reason to
do so.[98] But, since testators are not usually versed in law and not all donations
are executed by notaries, it is also possible to presume the contrary, i.e. that the
testator thinks that the forced share has already been paid during his or her
lifetime and does not wish to benefit the donee any further.

However, the Catalan legislature has preserved the rule that donations do
not count towards the forced heir's share, except for those made to promote the
children's personal and economic independence (art. 451-8.2 a, b CC Cat).[99]
Some consider this rule to be a sign of social paternalism and intervention-
ism in the economic relation between parents and their children. But it must
be noted that the decedent can always exclude this legal effect at the time of
making the donation or when executing his or her will.[100] Notwithstanding, the
fact remains that the rule can be perceived as arbitrary and need not necessarily
respond to the testator's designs. For instance, if a parent gives one of the children his or her first home, the value thereof will be taken into account to reduce
this child's forced share; by contrast, the donation made to his or her brother of
a holiday home (probably to compensate for the fact that the parents were unable

---

[96] Ferrand (2009) 195-196.

[97] Arroyo Amayuelas (2009) 18-19.

[98] Lamarca Marquès (2009a) 286.

[99] This is a modernization of the old *donationes ob causam*, on which Puig Ferriol – Roca Trías (1980) 344-
348, esp. 347-348.

[100] Ferrer Riba (2009) 24-25.

to contribute when this other child acquired his or her first independent home), will not reduce the forced share. Again, for a decedent unversed in law, this differentiated treatment will come as a surprise and be perceived to be absurd.

On the other hand, the donor may have stated, at the time of the donation, that the value thereof is to be discounted from the donee's forced share. The CC Cat thus clarifies the previous provision in art. 359 CS, following the judicial construction whereby the testator cannot impose the reduction at the time of executing the will.[101] The courts justify this restraint on testamentary freedom because it is thought that the donee is entitled to know whether the donation is going to count towards the forced share in order to decide whether to accept it or not,[102] but it hinders the testator's ability to adapt to changing circumstances, when maybe the forced heir's conduct should allow the testator to change his or her mind. It is very arguable that the donee's reliance deserves more protection than the testator's freedom. The fact that "the donee cannot have his or her unwaivable and forced right affected"[103] does not justify the legislature's choice, since the fact that the donation counts or not towards the forced share is not detrimental to the right to receive it (art. 451-10 CC Cat). The right to the forced share remains intact, whether it has been received (totally or partially) during the decedent's lifetime or not. If the donation does not cover the forced share, the difference can be claimed from the heir (art. 451-10.1 and 2 CC Cat); if the donation exceeds the forced share, the difference will be pure lucrative enrichment. Even if it then turns out that, for this part that exceeds the forced share, the donation is to be reduced to cover the share of other forced heirs (art. 451-22.3 CC Cat), the donee's right to the forced share still remains untouched, which is what the legislature is supposed to be protecting. It would have been much better to either generalize the default rule under art. 451-8.2 CC Cat (regarding donations that *are* taken into account towards the forced share) or, at least, to allow the testator to counteract the legal effect of the contrary general rule at any time.

6 Conclusions

In general terms, the recent reform of the Catalan law of succession is an important step towards the modernization of this highly technical area of the law that brings with it huge practical implications. The legislature has endeavoured to adapt the existing provisions to sociological changes and in many instances has attained its goals, which are in line with those guiding other

---

[101] STSJC 12 March 1998 (RJ 10050); SsAP Lleida 29 April 2005 (JUR 171481) and 6 March 2009 (JUR 385996); SAP Barcelona 26 October 2006 (JUR 2007/144825); SAP Tarragona 3 October 2007 (JUR 2008/41733); SAP Barcelona 15 July 2009 (RJ 407944). The opposite opinion in SAP Barcelona 17 January 2000 (AC 1039).

[102] STSJC 4 April 2005 (RJ 2007/1812); ATSJC 28 November 2005 (RJ 2006/552).

[103] STSJC 4 April 2005 (RJ 2007/1812).

European reforms that have been enacted during the last decade or that are still being drafted.

Nevertheless, as well as presenting a few technical flaws, the overall impression is that innovations could have been more radical. Maintaining the old principles, such as the *nemo pro parte* rule, generates important problems, as explained, which require forcing the construction of the testator's will to limits that often lead to clearly disregarding his or her wishes; this is, we think, beyond any doubt. Therefore, the question is whether there is any solid reason why partial intestacy is forbidden. The only justification that springs to mind is the preservation of a differentiating legal tradition. It goes without saying that this cannot be sufficient.

On the other hand, the legislature has eagerly embraced the equalization of cohabitants and spouses, but has been reticent in other areas. If in most testaments the surviving spouse or cohabitant is the sole heir, why not transfer this practice to the regulation on intestacy, thus granting the surviving partner a preferent position over the decedent's issue? Another example of these half-hearted reforms is that inheritance agreements, which should contribute towards efficient succession within the family business, can only be entered into by family members; the list of these is longer than in the old law, but it is still not possible to decide irrevocably on one's succession by means of a contract with a business partner, for instance.

Finally, the debate is still open regarding the elimination of the forced share. The legislature decided that it was not the right moment to repeal the rules on the forced share altogether, so the alternative was to weaken the forced heir's rights. This has been carried out in different ways, sometimes through provisions that are considered too vague, thus leading directly to more judicial conflict. But, more importantly, of all the reasons for and against the forced share, there is one that is often overlooked: it generates complexity in an area of the law where technical problems are frequent enough. Probably this consideration should be present in the legislature's mind whenever another reform process is undertaken.

CHAPTER 4

Testamentary Freedom and Its Limits

Esteve Bosch Capdevila

1 Introduction

1.1 The Testator's Will as the Supreme Law of Succession

The general principle that the will of the testator is the supreme law of succession manifests itself in several ways in the Catalan Civil Code (CC Cat): First, the CC Cat specifies the prevalence of voluntary succession. This principle means that the rules of intestacy will only apply if there is no testament or inheritance pact (art. 411-3.2 CC Cat). Second, the testator's will prevails when interpreting the provisions of the testament (art. 421-6.1 CC Cat). And, finally, there is the principle of freedom of testation. Art. 421-1 CC Cat, which itself is entitled "testamentary freedom", provides that:

> "testate succession is governed by the volition of the decedent as is manifested in the decedent's testament in accordance with the law".

In this study, I will be looking at this latter area of testamentary freedom and, in particular, at its limits.

1.2 Protecting Testamentary Freedom

First of all, it should be said that law protects testamentary freedom in general and, more specifically, it protects the testator's freedom from attacks by thirds parties.

The CC Cat declares void any will, or provision in a will, that has been made under the threat of "violence or grave intimidation" or that has been executed due to "fraud" (as is the case in contract law and other manifestations of a person's freedom).

The CC Cat also declares void any provisions in favour of ineligible persons. The mere suspicion that a person (for example, the notary who has authorized the will) could have influenced the testator, causes this person to be declared ineligible as an heir to that specific testator, regardless of any assertions to the contrary made by the testator (this is in contrast to what happens, for example, with indignity or unworthiness, in which case the testator may forgive the beneficiary's behaviour).

1.3 The Types of Limits to Testamentary Freedom

The law, therefore, protects testamentary freedom. This, however, does not mean that testamentary freedom is absolute; the testator cannot bequeath or devise everything in the manner that he or she sees fit and to the persons he or she chooses. Certain limits apply.

When referring to the limits to testamentary freedom, surely the first limit must be the *legitima portio* (forced share). Regarding this issue, the Duran i Bas

Memoria (Report)[1] reflected in depth on whether it was appropriate or not to maintain the so-called principle of testamentary freedom and concluded that this freedom depended on the *legitima portio* continuing to be small (that is, a quarter of the *relictum* plus the *donatum*); if, as some jurists were demanding at the time, the forced share is increased, the principle of testamentary freedom is called into question.

In any case, whether the forced share is larger or smaller, it is clear that it places a limit on testamentary freedom, possibly the most important limit given that the testator cannot dispose freely of a part of the estate to whoever he or she wishes. However, the forced share is not the only limit to testamentary freedom, indeed limits can come from various sources. The most important limit is the law. The law awards certain rights to a series of people, these being the beneficiaries of the forced share, as we have seen, but also the surviving spouse, by means of the so called *"widow's quarter"*, i.e. a share of up to a quarter of the estate in case of need, which is also granted to the cohabitant. These rights mean that the testator cannot leave the entire estate to whomever he or she chooses. Other legal limits to testamentary freedom are the *"Falcidian quarter"* (granted so that the heir receives a portion unburdened by legacies) and the *"Trebellian quarter"* (granted to the fiduciary heir in a fideicommissum, so that he or she can detract a share form it), although they are not mandatory for the testator. The law also specifies that testamentary provisions are subject to certain formalities, so that a will drafted in any other manner is not valid. Furthermore, the law establishes certain other limits regarding the specific content of the will. Due to the principles governing Catalan inheritance law, and several other reasons, not all provisions are considered acceptable.

The second limit does not have a legal origin, rather it is voluntary: it is the result of the fact that the decedent entered into a succession agreement. Testamentary freedom is conditioned by the terms thereof, unless there is cause for the revocation of the agreement (arts. 431-14 ff. CC Cat).

The third limit could also be voluntary, but rather than deriving from an agreement with a third party, it is the result of the testator's unilateral wishes or of those of a third party, for example, when the testator states that he or she will not make a new will, or when a third party manages to get the testator to make a certain provision. However, the general rule is that these limits are not accepted by the law.

In this article I will discuss some of these limits (both those that are accepted and those that are not). Although those limits derived from legal rights and the succession agreements are surely the most important, I will not be discussing them in this article because they have already been dealt with in other studies included in this publication.

---

[1]   Duran i Bas (1883).

2   Limits Derived from the Testator's Wishes

This first limit to testamentary freedom can originate with the testator himself, who in his or her will may attempt to preclude or condition the creation of a new will. It is necessary to distinguish between two types of limit that fall within this category. The testator may:

a) Waive the right to subsequently modify or revoke the will so that this is the one that will definitively and irrevocably govern his or her succession

b) Specify that certain signs, formulae or words, that is, the so-called clauses *ad cautelam*, should be used in order to revoke the will.

There are numerous Civil Codes that expressly prohibit or state the ineffectiveness of these limits regarding the right to revoke a will, among them art. 737 Spanish CC (to which we will refer later), art. 1001 Chilean CC of 1855, art. 2311 Portuguese CC and art. 679 Italian CC. The CC Cat is not so explicit. It simply states in art. 422-8.1 that "testamentary provisions are essentially revocable". We will now look at the scope of this regulation.

2.1   Provisions in a Will Aiming to Prevent Future Testamentary Modification or Revocation

Although Catalan law, unlike other systems, has no explicit provision regarding this matter, I understand that there are no doubts regarding the ineffectiveness of provisions in a will that seek to render it, or a part thereof, irrevocable or unmodifiable. The "essentially revocable" nature of the will would be contradicted if such provisions were considered effective.

Surely the Catalan legislator could have added a provision to art. 422-8.1 CC Cat such as that included, for example, in art. 679 Italian CC which says that the right to revoke or modify will provisions cannot be renounced in any way: any clause or condition to the contrary will have no effects. It should be said that this rule was explicitly laid down in one of the current regulation's precedents, specifically in art. 474 of the 1955 *Projecte de Compilació* (Draft Compilation), which said "any clauses will be regarded as completely invalid if these clauses are intended by the testator to order the ineffectiveness of future wills [...]."

2.2   *Ad Cautelam* Clauses: Do They Protect or Limit Testamentary Freedom?

More controversial is the case of the so-called *ad cautelam* clauses, which do not prevent the revocation of a will, but rather make this revocation conditional on the testator using certain words or signs established in a previous will. Although the general rule, in comparative law, is to prohibit such clauses, it has not always been this way in Catalonia.

2.2.1　The Admission of *Ad Cautelam* Clauses in the Catalan Legal Tradition and in the Precedents of Book IV of the CC Cat

The effectiveness of *ad cautelam* clauses was admitted in the Catalan legal tradition, thus accepting that the revocation of a will could require the use of certain words specified in the previous will. This was mentioned in the Duran i Bas *Memoria* in 1883, when the learned jurist said that the use of what he called the *ad cautelam* clause was very frequent in Catalonia.

Ad cautelam clauses for the revocation of future provisions were also admitted in the different projects for an appendix to the Spanish CC covering Catalan law specialities, which would never be enacted (art. 258 of the 1930 appendix project) and Draft Compilations (art. 474 of the already mentioned 1955 Project). The latter provided that:

> "the so-called repealing or *ad cautelam* clause will be effective in a open will [i.e. drafted by a notary] when the testator uses this clause to specify that the will can only be subsequently revoked by another will if in this new will the testator uses certain words or phrases specified in the original will. The initial will can be revoked if the subsequent will makes express mention of this clause, either by repeating the same words or phrases contained in this clause or by specifically referring to the initial will that contains it and the approximate date thereof. If the person is unable to do this, the subsequent will shall be considered invalid. If the previously mentioned repealing *ad cautelam* clauses are not contained in an open will, these shall be regarded as completely invalid [...]",

Thus, the main features of article 474 of the 1955 Project were that:
  a) It required the *ad cautelan* clause to appear in an open will for the clause to be effective;
  b) It also allowed the revocation to be effective if the testator merely referred to the previous will containing the specific words or phrases and the approximate date of this will, without having to repeat those words or phrases exactly. This was surely done to facilitate the revocation of the will if there was the wish to do so and in the event that the testator should have forgotten the specific words or phrases because of his or her advanced age.

However, the *Comisión de Justicia de las Cortes Españolas* (Justice Commission of the Spanish Courts) eliminated the article dedicated to *ad cautelam* clauses, with the result that the definitive text of the 1960 Compilation only referred to them in its third transitory provision, which recognized the effectiveness of *ad cautelam* clauses only in open wills that had been executed before the 1960 Compilation came into effect. Therefore, the Compilation implicitly negated the validity of *ad cautelam* clauses in wills executed after the Compilation came into effect. Nevertheless, all cases were subject to the supplementary provision of art.

737 Spanish CC, which expressly specifies the ineffectiveness of testamentary provisions that aim to render the will irrevocable and of those clauses where the testator uses an *ad cautelam* formula to limit the right to revoke the will.

2.2.2 The Silence of Book IV of the CC Cat Regarding the *Ad Cautelam* Clauses

As with the Catalan 1991 CS, Book IV CC Cat contains no specific provision on *ad cautelan* clauses, thus it does not allow them (as did the 1955 Draft) nor forbid them (as does the Spanish CC). This does not mean that *ad cautelam* clauses have disappeared from current law, but rather that their use is accepted for the so-called *testamentary briefs*, i.e. informal documents left by the deceased to complement a will and which can contain, among other provisions, legacies the value of which does not exceed 10% of the estate. Art. 421-21.1 CC Cat states that, for testamentary briefs to be valid, one of the requisites is compliance, if appropriate, with the "formal requisites specified by the testator in his or her will".

Currently there is a legislative gap regarding the use of *ad cautelam* clauses, which has to be resolved using analogy and resorting to the Catalan legal tradition (the Spanish CC cannot be applied as supplementary law for succession matters). It is clear that there are arguments both in favour and against the validity of these clauses.

In favour of *ad cautelam* clauses, it can be argued that:
a) They must be considered valid if they are not expressly prohibited by the law;
b) They were admitted in the Catalan legal tradition, whereas their prohibition was imposed by the Spanish legislation;
c) They do not infringe the general rule regarding the revocability of testamentary provisions, since they remain revocable even if the testator has used an *ad cautelam* clause;
d) They do not restrict testamentary freedom, but rather are used precisely to reinforce this freedom, as they may protect the testator against leaving a will made under duress or in a frail state of mind. This is the interpretation made by some notaries;
e) They are admitted, as we have seen, in the case of testamentary briefs.

Against *ad cautelam* clauses, it can be argued that:
a) If the legislator had wished to recognize their validity, the CC Cat would have expressly so provided, especially given that such recognition would have meant changing the criterion held in the Compilation.
b) The fact that *ad cautelam* clauses are admitted in testamentary briefs may be because the testator can always enact a codicil if he or she forgets or wants to obviate one of these clauses, with the result that there are no insurmountable consequences arising from the testator's lack of respect for the clause.

The crucial question, in my opinion, is whether *ad cautelam* clauses restrict or reinforce testamentary freedom.

As we have seen, the validity of these clauses has been upheld on the grounds that they reinforce the testator's wishes in the face of possible external pressures. However, we must not forget that any will executed without testamentary freedom has no legal validity. Also, the testator can immediately revoke any such will by executing a new one.

Furthermore, the dangers of using *ad cautelam* clauses outweigh the benefits. Older people in particular may find that *ad cautelam* clauses constitute a mechanism that prevents them from making a new will because they have forgotten about the existence of the clause in question or because they cannot remember the words or phrases that they are supposed to use. This must surely be more likely to occur than a situation in which a will is executed as a result of violence or intimidation.

For this reason, I believe that despite the silence of Book IV, *ad cautelam* clauses cannot be admitted and that their use cannot be justified within the boundaries of testamentary freedom. Nevertheless, a regulation that does not require a literal transcription of the clause in question (such as the aforementioned provision in the 1955 Draft Compilation) is a more or less neutral solution, which, on reflection, I would recommend.

3 The Limits Imposed by a Third Party: The Problems Caused by *Captatorias Institutiones*

In a previous section of this study we have seen how the law protects testamentary freedom from third parties applying violence, intimidation or deceit. However, a third party may influence the testator's wishes through apparently legal actions. An example of this would be when the third party making a gratuitous transfer, either *inter vivos* or *mortis causa*, imposes the condition that the testator must subsequently include a certain provision in his or her will. For example, "I will give you the house, but if you die without heirs, you must leave it to my grandchildren"; or "I will make you my heir, but you must include a provision in your will in favour of my grandchildren".

The CC Cat takes into account these *captatorias institutiones* in its provisions governing the conditions imposed on heirs. It makes no reference to the ineffectiveness of a *mortis causa* provision made under the influence of the *captatoria conditio*, but rather only refers to the invalidity of the provision containing such condition. Therefore, according to article 423-19 CC Cat, the *captatoria conditio* imposed on an heir renders the appointment of the heir null and void.

The CC Cat refers to, but does not define, *captatoria conditiones*. According to Borrell i Soler, these conditions are made "on the condition that the beneficiary or a third party leaves a bequest or a devise to the testator or to a person designated by the testator".[2]

There are various issues regarding this matter that need to be discussed. First of all, the conditions we are dealing with are considered unlawful conditions, but they do have their own special regulations. The general rule in Catalan succession law is that unlawful conditions are regarded as not having been formulated; they can only invalidate the appointment of the heir "if the fulfilment of an unlawful condition was the determining reason for the appointment of an heir" (art. 423-17 CC Cat). Instead, as we have seen, a *captatoria conditio* always has this effect.

On the other hand, is a provision also null and void if a *captatoria conditio* is imposed in an *inter vivos* donation, for example, when a donation is made on the condition that the donee includes a certain provision in his or her will? There is a legislative gap concerning the conditions imposed on gifts that I believe should be covered by the rules governing testamentary provisions. If this were the case, the donation could be considered null and void.

A third question is whether art. 423-19 CC Cat is solely intended to protect a person's testamentary freedom, or whether it is intended to also protect this person's privilege to dispose *inter vivos*. The answer depends on what kind of transfer we are thinking of.

The beneficiary of the gift subject to a *captatoria conditio* cannot be required to make a donation, since the latter can only be considered as such if there is *animus donandi*. However, what the testator can do is appoint a person as heir and then encumber this heir with the condition whereby the heir must give something that already belongs to him or her to a third party (art. 427-24.1 CC Cat). This may seem paradoxical: the law allows the testator to impose a condition on us whereby we must give, for instance, our house to a given person; but it does not allow the testator to impose a condition whereby when we die, we leave our house to this person. This shows that art. 423-19 CC Cat is possibly one of the main exponents of the principle of testamentary freedom in the CC Cat. The testator can encumber the heirs or legatees with bequests, limit their privilege to dispose by means of a prohibition (art. 428-6 CC Cat) or establish a fideicommissum. However, what the testator cannot do is place conditions on those persons' freedom of disposition *mortis causa*, whether these conditions are positive (by imposing a disposition *mortis causa* in favour of specific individuals, art. 423-19 CC Cat), or negative (by prohibiting a disposition *mortis causa* in favour of specific individuals, art. 428-6.3 CC Cat, which restricts the prohibitions on disposing established in the will to *inter vivos* acts).

It should be pointed out that the imposition of a fideicommissum (arts. 426-1 ff. CC Cat) does not technically constitute a limit on testamentary freedom. A fideicommissum restricts freedom of disposition *inter vivos* of the assets affected by it, but not the freedom of disposition *mortis causa*, given that these assets do not belong to the first heir's estate.

---

[2]   Borrell i Soler (1944) 82.

Finally, it should be noted that the CC Cat specifies the invalidity of *captatoria conditiones*, but it does not say whether a *mortis causa* disposition that is a consequence of the *captatoria conditio* is effective or ineffective. Some of the Catalan academics insist on the invalidity of this disposition so as not to benefit the person who has limited the testator's freedom. This position would only be defensible if one accepts the validity of the *captatoria dispositio*. However, if this provision is declared invalid, as it is in the CC Cat, and is therefore ineffective, it is clear that it cannot realize its aim of limiting the beneficiary's testamentary freedom, and that therefore the testator's provision has been made freely and is valid, unless the testator is unaware of the ineffectiveness of the *captatoria dispositio*.

It is possible that the beneficiary of the *captatoria dispositio* is unaware of the invalidity of the provision made in his or her favour and that, in his or her own will, he or she fulfils the condition in accordance with the instructions received. In this case, the testator's provision is certainly null and void. It can be claimed that the beneficiary has made a mistake: he or she believed that, in order to receive the gift, a certain provision had to be made in his or her own will, but it turns out that he or she will not receive that gift, because the law states that the *captatoria dispositio* is null and void (art. 423-19 CC Cat). It is clear that the beneficiary's motives are mistaken and this will invalidate the provision that he or she has made in his or her will "because the testator would not have made this provision if he or she had been aware of the mistake" (art. 422-2.1 CC Cat).

4 The Legal Limits to the Content of Testamentary Provisions

I will now discuss the legal limits referring to the content of testamentary provisions.

4.1 Limits that Affect the Conditions that a Testator Can Impose

There are two types of limit to the conditions that a testator can impose: Those limits deriving from the principle *semel heres semper heres*, which precludes the heir to be subject to any condition subsequent or the appointment to be postponed or finalized at a certain time; and the limit deriving from the fact that conditions cannot be unlawful.

4.1.1 Limits Deriving from the Principle *Semel Heres Semper Heres*

The *semel heres semper heres* principle, which applies in the Catalan law of succession, means that no condition subsequent is to be imposed on the heir, and that his or her appointment cannot be delayed or finalized at a certain time. The litteral translation would be: "Once an heir, always an heir". Therefore, any condition or time limit that contravenes this rule is regarded as not having been formulated (art. 423-12.1 CC Cat)

However, the importance of this principle as a possible restriction on the testamentary freedom should be qualified as follows.

a) This principle applies only to the appointment of heirs, but not to legacies.

b) If the reason for the condition is to encourage the heir to behave in a certain way (for example, the heir must carry out a certain act), the testator can establish this as a condition precedent, or, if the testator wants the heir to become heir with immediate effect, he or she can impose a "mode" (or charge) on the heir. In this latter case, if the heir does not perform, the *haeredis institutio* (appointment of an heir) is not void; art. 428-4 CC Cat provides a series of different guarantees to ensure that the testator's wishes are fulfilled.

c) The restriction imposed by the principle, regarding the condition subsequent and the establishment of a deadline to the appointment of an heir is questioned, because the testator can impose a fideicommissum, whereby the first heir (fiduciary heir) acquires the estate but has to transfer it to the fideicommissary once the term has expired or the condition has been fulfilled (art. 426-1.1 CC Cat). The CC Cat admits universal fideicommissa whereby there are two heirs: the fiduciary heir, who will be considered the heir until the condition is fulfilled (hence the condition subsequent) or until the end of the period (hence, the "subsequent period"), and the fideicommissary heir (the beneficiary), who becomes the heir thereafter once the condition is fulfilled (hence, the condition precedent) or once the period has ended (hence, the suspensive period). Therefore, the correct interpretation of the principle *semel heres* is that the heir cannot cease to hold the status of heir unless the testator has named a subsequent heir. In such a case it is understood that a fideicommissum has been established (and this, according to art. 426-13.1 CC Cat, need not be expressly stated).

If there is no subsequent heir, it would seem that article 423-12.1 CC Cat must be applied, and that therefore it will be understood that the condition or the time limit have not been formulated. In this context, it is surely a step too far to interpret that there is a tacit recognition of the intestate heirs as the fideicommissary substitutes (a solution which would not be contrary to the *nemo pro parte* rule)[3] if we apply a strict interpretation of article 423-12.1 CC Cat.

Accordingly, the conclusion that can be drawn from this is that if the testator no longer wants a certain person to be his or her heir, then a subsequent heir must be designated.

---

[3]   See below 4.2.1.

4.1.2   Limits Derived from Certain Conditions Being Unlawful

Art. 423-17 CC Cat states that:

"Unlawful conditions will be deemed as not being set; however, if the fulfilment of an unlawful condition was the determining reason for the appointment of an heir, such appointment shall be deemed null and void."

Therefore, when there is a conflict between the testator's wishes (the fulfilment of the condition) and the law (which prohibits unlawful conditions), the law takes precedence. Because it is unlawful, the condition is regarded as not having been included in the will, except in cases where it can be shown that the heir would not have been chosen unless the condition were to be fulfilled. As we can see, this is a different solution from that provided in the law of obligations, where the imposition of an unlawful condition invalidates the obligation (art. 1116 Spanish CC).

The most important problem is determining the precise meaning of the term "unlawful condition". Art. 423-17 CC Cat refers to unlawful conditions without specifying the scope of this concept. Nor do the precedents of the CC Cat clarify the issue; in the 1955 Draft Compilation, unlawful conditions were mentioned in art. 266, with no further elaboration.

Let us try to define the concept of the unlawful condition. Unlawful conditions can be used for unlawful acts and for other reasons, so it is necessary to distinguish between the different kinds of unlawful condition.

The concept of unlawful condition includes those conditions that are used to carry out unlawful acts, for example, murder. The term "unlawful acts" does not only refer to crimes, but also to direct and indirect infractions of the law. Thus, for example, if a condition states that someone has to travel by car from Barcelona to Madrid in less than two hours, this condition must be considered unlawful because to fulfil it would require that person to seriously exceed the speed limit. Less clear is the case where, rather than crimes, the condition requires someone to carry out acts that contravene "appropriate behaviour" or "morality" (e.g. "I will leave my house to you on the condition that you seduce your three sisters"). The imprecise nature of these concepts means that we cannot include them within the concept of unlawful conditions as specified by the CC Cat. A condition can also be unlawful not because its fulfilment requires carrying out unlawful acts, but because the law states that it should not be admitted as a condition in a will. For example, the law will not admit a condition that prevents a given person from challenging a will, even though the act in question (that of not challenging the will) does not constitute an unlawful act (art. 423-18 CC Cat). The same thing occurs regarding the *captatoria conditiones* to which we have already referred. The most doubtful case is when an unlawful condition involves a certain level of coercion in the personal sphere, without this being expressly condemned by the law. A large number of academics regard as unlawful those conditions which imply a certain unjustified coercion in the personal sphere, in that they constitute an attack to the constitutionally recognized individual rights and liberties of the person. If the Spanish Constitution recognizes as a fundamental right, among others, the right to ideological and religious freedom (art. 16), or the right to freely choose a place of residence (art. 19), and if art. 32.1 establishes that men and women have the right to enter into marriage with full legal equality, then it may be considered that the notion of public order has been contravened if a condition requires an individual to join a certain political party, or follow a particular religion, or to live or not to live in a particular city, or to marry or not marry. Nevertheless, for various reasons I believe that as a general rule these conditions must be regarded as valid. First, it is not at all clear that respect for individual rights and liberties should be not only vertical (from the State towards the citizen), but also horizontal (in relations between citizens), particularly in this case, where the individuals are regarded as equals (we are not dealing with the relationship between an employer and an employee, for example). Second, there will often be a legitimate or respectable motive leading the testator to set the condition; and in any case, even if this were not so, I believe that whether or not there is a legitimate motive is not a matter for investigation. For example, if the testator imposes a condition that requires the legatee to cease being a member of a particular political party, such a condition may be founded on the belief that this is the best thing for the legatee, without there being any intention to harm him or her or restrict his or her freedom. Third, the beneficiary is not obliged to do anything. In fact, he or she can always disclaim the gift. On the other hand, we must remember that prohibitions must be interpreted restrictively. And finally, the CC Cat also (implicitly) admits a certain condition that could be classified as coercing individual freedom: the requirement to marry. Some authors have said that these kinds of condition should not be admitted because they involve the coercion of the heir's free will. But in my opinion, the condition to not enter into marriage is just as coercive as the condition to do so, this latter condition being implicitly admitted in the CC Cat (art. 423-15.1), which therefore means that it is not considered unlawful. Therefore, we can conclude that the law not only fails to prohibit these conditions, but also takes them into account. And if the "coercion" to enter into marriage is admitted, then this must mean that coercion in other personal spheres is also admissible.

4.2   Limits Affecting Specific Clauses

In addition to the situations that have already been mentioned, the law also places the following additional specific limits on testamentary freedom.

4.2.1 The Incompatibility between Testate and Intestate Heirs and Testamentary Freedom

In Catalan law, the *nemo pro parte* principle applies, which means that we cannot have, for the same decedent, a testamentary heir and an intestate heir.

Let us imagine, then, that the testator chooses a certain person as heir, but giving this person only part of the estate or a specific asset, with the express condition that the heir cannot receive more than said part or asset. If there is no other designated heir, the fulfilment of the testator's wishes would violate the *nemo pro parte* principle, because these wishes would mean that we would have partial intestacy.

The following solution could be used to try and respect both the wishes of the testator and the principles of succession: If a prohibition of accretion has been imposed on the only heir (the *heres ex re certa* of our example), this heir (*ex re certa*) could be regarded not as an heir, but rather as a legatee. The result of this would be that if a process of intestate succession were initiated regarding the rest of the inheritance, this would not go against the *nemo pro parte* principle, because there would not be a testamentary heir alongside the intestate heirs, but rather a legatee. This solution might seem to contradict article 423-3 CC Cat (which provides that an heir to a specific asset must be considered a legatee for that asset, and an heir for the remainder), but this is a default rule applicable only when it is not possible to determine what the testator really wanted. However, if the testator's wishes are clear, then they must be respected in accordance with article 423-2 CC Cat.

If the prohibition of accretion has been imposed on the heir of only part of the estate and there is no other heir, the legal tradition has applied several possible solutions. The solution that would most readily coincide with the testator's wishes, whilst also respecting the *nemo pro parte* principle, would be a tacit recognition of the intestate heirs eligibility to receive the rest of the inheritance (by which means all the heirs become testamentary heirs).

4.2.2 The Limits Imposed on Fideicommissum

Another restriction to testamentary freedom comes in the form of the limits imposed on fideicommissum. When several fideicommissary heirs are appointed successively, the law prevents the fideicommissum from being indefinitely or excessively prolonged by imposing a series of limits on it. These limits mean that if a testator has appointed more fideicommissary heirs than the number permitted by law, then these appointments are regarded as not having been formulated.

If the persons appointed as fideicommissary heirs are not born at the time of the testator's death, then only one fideicommissary appointment can be effective (art. 426-10.2 CC Cat). The testator can appoint several successive fideicommissary heirs, but when one of them acquires the fideicommissum, the other appointments are not effective. For family fideicommissum (whereby the fideicommissary heirs are the testator's descendants, siblings or nephews or nieces), then any number of appointments is permitted as long as it does not surpass the second generation (art. 426-10.3 CC Cat); if, in accordance with art. 426-10.3 CC Cat, the first generation is considered to refer to the testator's children or nephews or nieces, this means that all the testator's siblings, children and grandchildren, nephews and nieces and grandnephews and grandnieces can be appointed as fideicommissary heirs.

Another limit on the testator's freedom, which also relates to the entailment of assets, can be found in art. 428-6.2 CC Cat, under which limitations to the privilege to dispose cannot exceed the lifetime of a specific physical person or, otherwise, a period of 30 years.

4.3   The Lineage Principle

The lineage principle also constitutes a restriction on testamentary freedom because it means that a set of assets that the decedent acquired during his or her lifetime from certain relatives without consideration must, under certain circumstances, go to the relatives in direct line of succession of the relatives from whom these assets were acquired. However, the application of the lineage principle is very limited in Catalonia, where it only surfaces in the context of hereditary substitutions, for children who die before attaining testamentary capacity and only regarding assets that the prepubescent has acquired from the parent who has not appointed a substitute heir.

Let us suppose that the testator wants to appoint his prepubescent son as his or her successor. Art. 425-7 CC Cat, which incidentally carries the title of "Lineage Principle", provides that a parent may only appoint one or more siblings of the prepubescent who are common children or, failing this, relatives from the other line up to the fourth degree as substitutes for the assets of the prepubescent that stem from the inheritance of the other parent, if this other parent has not done so.

4.4   Discriminatory Clauses

Finally, let us suppose that the testator establishes apparently discriminatory clauses in his or her will. For example, let us suppose that I appoint my male children as my heirs; or I exclude from the succession any people related to me through adoption. Are these provisions valid? In my opinion, the testator can choose whoever he or she wants to be his or her heirs; that is, once the *legitima portio* has been respected, the testator has the right to freely choose his or her successor or successors.

It is the law, rather than the testator, that cannot discriminate. Exercising the right to choose a successor, however it may be done, cannot give rise to discrimination. Let us imagine that the testator has three children, two of which (A and B) are his or her direct natural children, and a third (C) who is the testator's son through adoption. If the testator says "I appoint A and B as my heirs", would anyone doubt the validity of such a provision? And does it not amount to the same thing if the testator says "I appoint my direct natural children"?

However, our opinion is not the same as that of the European Court of Human Rights, which in ECHR ruling 13 July 2004 declared that a judgment by the Andorran Supreme Court violated article 14 of the European Convention on Human Rights because it excluded adopted children from the succession by virtue of the phrase "child of a legitimate and canonic marriage".[4] And STC 9/2010, 27 April, invoked this ECHR ruling 13 July 2004 when it stated that the expressions "legitimate children" used in a will made in 1927 could be interpreted as also including adoptive children.

---

[4]   Arroyo Amayuelas – Bondia Garcia (2004) 7 ff.; Marsal Guillamet (2005) 477 ff.

Freedom of Testation, Compulsory Share and Disinheritance Based on Lack of Family Relationship

Antoni Vaquer Aloy

1 Preliminary Remarks

Can a law of succession be modern? The question seems to entail a contradiction. The law of succession has a conservative character,[1] it regulates the transmission of a decedent's estate to his or her successors.[2] Despite the many legal reforms in most modern legal systems, the institutions in the different national laws are often those that figured in Roman law. Of course, one could object that the contract of sale was also regulated in Roman law. Nonetheless contract law has evolved and new contracts have been developed to meet the requirements of economic activity. Similar innovations have not deeply affected the law of succession. Some modest changes address freedom of testation and the protection of spouse and descendants needing care. Fontanellas has clearly pointed out three trends in the law of succession: strengthening the spouse's position, maintaining the compulsory share of descendants but aiming at reducing its amount, and the suppression of the compulsory share of ascendants and other relatives.[3] Also appearing in Catalan law, these trends show the change of paradigm in intergenerational wealth transmission.[4] But the fundamentals

---

*   This essay is part of the activities of the consolidated research group 2009SGR689, funded by the Government of Catalonia. The author is indebted to Prof. Shael Herman for his lucid comments on an early draft of this essay and language checking.

1   Parra Lucán (2009) 537 explains that the law of succession is burdened with tradition. A token of this conservative character is visible when some institutions are identified as distinctive cultural elements of Catalan identity applied to inheritance law. Some institutions of the Catalan Civil Code not only still have an unquestionable Roman taste, such as *quarta trebellianica* (art. 426-31 ff.) or *quarta falcidia* (art. 427-44), but in addition –and because of that– are considered as hallmarks of Catalan law. It is enough to quote two interventions at the Parliament of Catalonia during the discussion of the bill on Book IV on the law of succession of the Catalan Civil Code (CC Cat). Ms Núria de Gispert (CiU, opposition and former Catalan Minister for Justice) said: "let me identify briefly those modifications in relation to the original bill that are substantive for the law of succession (...) the recovery of the *quarta trebel·lianica* and *falcidia*. If someone considers that they had an old-fashioned denomination, not modern enough, he or she must know that they stem from Roman law and that they are still useful in the XXI century. We have a historical law and we know how to adapt it to the current necessities of the Catalan society". In his turn, Mr Miquel Àngel Estradé (ERC, party supporting the government) added: "It is very important that we have recovered *quarta falcidia* and *quarta trebellianica*, it is good to recall the origins, to keep the historical denomination". *Diari de Sessions del Parlament de Catalunya*, sèrie P, No. 54, June 18, 2008, p. 8 and 11, respectively.

2   Hirsch (2009) 9, stresses that giving people the right to make a will encourages them to produce and to save more wealth. The author quotes Kopcuk – Lupton (2007) 207, on the basis that in 2005 the cohort of those aged 50 years or more had amassed a level of wealth never held before by a single generation, giving empirical evidence that freedom of disposal upon death makes households increase their rate of savings.

3   Fontanellas (2010) 287. See also Vaquer (2009) 552 ff.; Foqué-Verbeke (2009) 219-221.

4   The thesis of J.H. Langbein (1988) 722 ff., arguing that at least as far as the middle-class population is concerned, the importance of lifetime transfers has increased while the importance of wealth transfers

of the Catalan law of succession remain untouched, as proven by the fact that the old principles of Roman law are still invoked in the Preamble of the Civil Code.[5] Not surprisingly therefore, a thorough discussion of the enduring system of compulsory share has been absent during the preparation of the new law of succession.

2 Reforms of the Compulsory Share in European Laws of Succession: No Abrogation, Only Reduction

A few years ago, a South African lawyer labelled the compulsory share a "relic" and called upon modern systems of law to abolish it.[6] For the time being, European legislatures dare not do so.[7] Only in Italy we find an open attempt to suppress the compulsory share. A bill, the *Disegno di legge* No. 576,[8] sought the abrogation of the "archaic institution of the compulsory succession". The bill invoked freedom of testation as a constitutionally granted right. A crucial argument for suppression was the fact that although the *ratio legis* of any compulsory share resides in intergenerational solidarity, the share was not dependent on a descendant's need. Moreover, it was affirmed that parents during their lifetimes invest in their children's education and welfare huge amounts of money. The bill even considered that the Italian compulsory share system was unconstitutional. However, doctrine has judged the bill too radical; it has also pointed out that a stress on freedom of testation would require a stricter regulation of vitiated consent to prevent undue influence upon the testator's intention; lastly, it has also been said that the defence of freedom of testa-

---

on death has decreased, is well known. Lifetime transfers include the investment in education of descendants. Along these lines, art. 451-8.2 a CC Cat provides that donations to children to buy their first dwelling or begin the exercise of a profession or a business are to be taken as an advancement of the compulsory share, thus reducing it. Lamarca Marquès (2009) 278-279, has expressed his criticism to this regulation.

[5] The Preamble reads: "In substantive terms, the fourth book preserves the inheritance principles of Catalan law as they were provided for in the Code of Succession" (English edition by the Government of Catalonia, 2010). The Succession Code passed in 1991 said in its Preamble: "the great principles inherent to Roman Law, which are so deeply rooted in Catalan Inheritance Law, are not modified" (English edition by the Government of Catalonia, 2000).

[6] Sonnekus (2005) 84: "the continental systems that still retain a form of legitimate portion or reserve will most probably be compelled, by virtue of the movement towards a unification of European law, to abandon this relic".

[7] See, in addition to the references to other legal systems contained in this essay, Parra Lucán (2009) 488 ff., showing that the compulsory share has not been completely abolished in any country where it was in force.

[8] Available at http://www.senato.it/leg/16/BGT/Schede/Ddliter/testi/31203_testi.htm.

tion does not require a complete derogation of the compulsory share.[9] Finally, the bill was not taken up for consideration by the Italian legislative.

In force since January 1, 2010, the German *Gesetz zur Änderung des Erb- und Verjährungsrecht* has amended the regulation of the compulsory share. A modest legal reform,[10] the law has not questioned the foundations and the essential principles of the regulation. The German lawmaker faced a social reality in which the families take care of their older members without remuneration. According to the new law, descendants who have cared for a decedent may obtain from the other intestate successors collation of the expenses incurred in caregiving even if the expenses have not caused a reduction of their income.[11] Despite the modesty of the legal modification, the law has taken into account that an elderly testator's welfare may depend on only one or only some of his or her descendants.

Concerning the compulsory share, the last major reforms of the European national laws of succession lead to the conclusion that there is a tendency to characterise compulsory share as a mere obligation instead of a right to the assets themselves, so that it does not have to be paid in kind (*pars valoris bonorum* instead of *pars bonorum*, avoiding the forced heirship). This approach means to limit the relatives entitled to the compulsory share, and to look for indirect ways to lower its amount, for example, by reducing the donations that are added to the estate in order to form the basis over which the compulsory share is calculated.[12] Hence, the compulsory share survives, but in an attenuated form.

3   A Weaker Compulsory Share in Catalonia

During the debate preceding the enactment of the Book on successions of the Catalan Civil Code, the subsistence of the compulsory share has not raised any controversy. This mildness contrasts with the reform of the Compilation of 1984 and the preparation of the Succession Code of 1991, when some voices claimed a radical amendment.[13] Now, the Catalan legislature seems to prefer the agony of regulating the compulsory share by way of successive

---

9   Dossetti (2009) 35 ff. More sympathetic with the bill was Bonilini (2009) 732 ff. With strong criticism, Amenta (2009) 605-633.

10 It has to be borne in mind that the decision of the Constitutional court handed down on April 19, 2005 (*NJW*, 2005, 1561), considered the right to the compulsory share constitutionally secured and unconstitutional the disinheritance based on lack of family relationship with the decedent. See Pintens/Seyns (2009) 169-174.

11 See Arroyo Amayuelas (2010) 13 f.

12 Vaquer (2009) 564 ff.

13 Fundamental, Puig Salellas (1985) 211 ff. For the debate in Spain concerning compulsory share in the *Código civil*, see Cámara Lapuente (2007) 31 ff.

small reforms aimed at diminishing its amount.[14] This becomes apparent from the following amendments:[15]

a) The reduction of the donations that are added to the estate in order to form the basis over which the compulsory share is calculated, since only the donations made in the last ten years before the testator's death must be added to the *relictum* (art. 441-5 b). This rule brings Catalan law quite close to Dutch law.[16]

b) The establishment of a tacit *cautio Socini* (art. 451-9.2).[17]

c) The abolition of the ascendants' compulsory share provided that the deceased leaves descendants even if the latter are not entitled to the compulsory share (art. 451-4.1).[18]

d) To dispel any doubt, art. 451-3.2 shows that when the beneficiaries are entitled to the compulsory share by representation, the subject matter of their right is precisely the compulsory share, and not the concrete assets that the decedent may have set aside to pay the compulsory share.

e) The propaedeutic statement according to which the so called simple bequest in payment of the compulsory share *(llegat simple de llegítima)* in favour of one appointed as an heir does not entail any other attribution than the appointment as an heir (art. 451-7.4).[19]

This list contains minor changes, but altogether should reduce the amount of money granted to the beneficiaries of the compulsory share.

---

[14] According to the Preamble of the Catalan Civil Code, "The fourth book maintains the legitime as a legal inheritance attribution and a limit to the freedom of testation, though it enhances the secular tendency to weaken it and make it more difficult to claim" (English edition by the Government of Catalonia, 2010).

[15] See also Arroyo Amayuelas (2007) 274 ff.

[16] See art. 4:67 NBW, that establishes that only donations performed within five years before the decedent's death must be added to the *relictum*. See Mies de Bie (2008) 1073 f., No. 90.

[17] The testator can attribute encumbered assets in payment of the compulsory portion provided that their value exceeds that of the compulsory share. This is valid even if the testator does not give the beneficiary the express option to claim payment in money free of any encumbrance instead of the encumbered assets, since this alternative is granted by law.

[18] According to one of the members of the legislative commission, Lamarca Marquès (2009) 272, maybe this innovation may be explained "as a compromise with part of the doctrine that claimed abolition of the compulsory share" (among those scholars, myself; see Vaquer, 2007) (originally in Catalan, author's translation).

[19] For example, the testator appoints as his sole heir his daughter Miriam and devises the compulsory share to whoever should be entitled to it. Miriam is heir and obtains all the assets, but she cannot claim, in addition, her compulsory share.

4 The New Gorund for Disinheritance in Art. 451-7.2 e of the Catalan Civil Code

4.1 Subsistence of the Compulsory Share, with Widening Grounds for Disinheritance

Let us consider the innovation in Book IV of the Catalan Civil Code to clarify the subsistence of compulsory share in relation to the evolution that some legal systems have experienced. The Catalan Civil Code incorporates a new ground for disinheritance[20] in art. 451-17.2 e: "the evident and continued lack of family relationship between the deceased and the beneficiary of the compulsory share provided that it is solely imputable to the beneficiary". Lamarca has justified the subsistence of the compulsory share in the civil law of Catalonia: "if we start from the existence of the family ties originated by filiation, with the formation of a *family community* in most of the cases, a legal participation in the parents' estate, in the lower extension that Catalan law allows, seems reasonable to me, with solid material foundations". Still more: "I do not think that the proposed alternatives, whether in form of abolition or modification, could lead to a significant improvement in terms of *social welfare* in comparison with the law in force". And he adds: "confrontations because of *opportunist behaviours aimed at gaining the parents' favourable disposition,* that a system of absolute freedom of testation would encourage, to the detriment of the other siblings, is mitigated by the existence of a quarter of the estate reserved to all of them".[21]

4.2 Behaviour-Based Succession Systems

Some scholars and even some legal systems suggest linking legal succession rights with the attitude of the beneficiaries toward the *de cujus,* an opinion that partially shares the same aim as the new Catalan ground for disinheritance. Linking succession rights and caregiving would be more feasible than trying to avoid opportunism. In the end, the lawyer's point of view is important, i.e. whether he or she focuses on the decedent or on the descendants, thus lending more weight to freedom of testation or to intergenerational solidarity within the family. The *ratio legis* of this behaviour-based approach to succession rights is, precisely, to avoid opportunist attitudes of the descendants and to grant the decedent the best possible conditions during his or her lifetime.[22]

---

[20] Pintens (2001) 643 had already pointed out that one of the trends in the European laws of succession was the widening of the legal grounds for disinheritance. For Louisiana, see the debate in Nathan Jr (2000) 1043, who concludes that "the bases for disinherison are more expansive than before".

[21] Lamarca Marquès (2009) 265-266 (originally in Catalan, author's translation and emphasis).

[22] From a law and economics approach, Bouckaert (2009) 95 ff. has found an argument in favour of freedom of bequest in the informal exchange with potential heirs. In the author's opinion: "Because the devisor controls, up to the moment of his death, full control on the assignment of his inheritance, he/ she can use this position to attract services from potential heirs. Freedom of bequest stimulates in this

In the United States, the compulsory share is still a hot topic. The starting point is the inexistence of the compulsory share in favour of the descendants.[23] The only exception is Louisiana: although the general Hispano-French compulsory share has been abolished, descendants who are under 24 years of age or suffering mental incapacity or physical infirmity are entitled to a share of the estate.[24] Different proposals have been made, some advocating the introduction of a system of family provision like the English or New Zealander,[25] but some still supporting the current legal regime without compulsory share, with arguments that deserve attention.[26]

J.C. Tate,[27] on the basis of population statistics, in particular the data warning about the increasing number of elderly people, has suggested linking a broad freedom of testation for American testators[28] with parents benefitting, *mortis causa*, only children who have taken care of them. This would mean a sort of reward, since not all children wish or can take care of their parents. Descendants do not find any incentive to take care of their ascendants where the compulsory share is equal for all irrespective of their attitude toward the decedent, in particular where the reserved portion takes the lion's share of the estate. On the contrary, and especially when an economic crisis erodes the foundations of the welfare state and endangers the public pensions system, rewarding the child or the children concerned about their elder parents entails an efficient use of personal wealth.

In the context of behaviour-based succession rights, section 259 of the California Probate Code is notable. According to paragraph a):

way voluntary help for high-aged people which can relieve the welfare state from a part of its financial burden".

[23] This does not mean that freedom of testation is absolute. The spouse is entitled to an elective share of the estate in all states but Georgia. See Turnipseed (2006) 737; Dukeminier – Sitkoff – Lindgren (2009) 469 ff.

[24] Art. 1493. A Louisiana Civil Code: "Forced heirs are descendants of the first degree who, at the time of the death of the decedent, are twenty-three years of age or younger or descendants of the first degree of any age who, because of mental incapacity or physical infirmity, are permanently incapable of taking care of their persons or administering their estates at the time of the death of the decedent". On the evolution of compulsory share in Louisiana and the legislative history of current art. 1493 Louisiana Civil Code see, critically, Rougeau (2008), available at http://papers.ssrn.com/sol3/papers.cfm?abstract_id=1396678; Lorio (2002) 7 ff.

[25] Chester (1998) 1; Knaplund (2006) 1.

[26] Even if descendants are not entitled to a compulsory share in the United States, testators should "think twice or, better, three times, before exercising the power" to disinherit children, unless the parent does so in favour of a surviving spouse. This warning is made by Dukeminier- Sitkoff- Lindgreen (2009) 520.

[27] Tate (2008) 131.

[28] Of course, a lawyer could argue that a compulsory share, in a context where people often remarry, avoids rivalries among kids of different marriages. But denying a fixed share might also attain the same goal.

Any person shall be deemed to have predeceased a decedent to the extent provided in subdivision (c) where all of the following apply:

1) It has been proven by clear and convincing evidence that the person is liable for physical abuse, neglect, or fiduciary abuse of the decedent, who was an elder or dependent adult.
2) The person is found to have acted in bad faith.
3) The person has been found to have been reckless, oppressive, fraudulent, or malicious in the commission of any of these acts upon the decedent.
4) *The decedent, at the time those acts occurred and thereafter until the time of his or her death, has been found to have been substantially unable to manage his or her financial resources or to resist fraud or undue influence.*

Similarly, Oregon Statutes section 112.465 lays down that:

1) Property that would have passed by reason of the death of a decedent to a person who was a slayer or an abuser of the decedent, whether by intestate succession, by will or by trust, passes and vests as if the slayer or abuser had predeceased the decedent.

The provision includes both physical abuse as described in section 124.105 and financial abuse defined in section 124.110.[29]

Some commentators have argued that behaviour-based systems of succession rights strengthen family ties and avoid abuses to elder people. In this sense, section 259 California Probate Code would be a first step, even if insufficient, since it does not entail a ground for disinheritance, but it simply prevents abusers from obtaining any attribution or compensation resulting from the facts listed in the said section 259 (paragraph a).[30]

China has carried to an extreme a behaviour-based system of succession rights. According to Law of Succession of the People's Republic of China art. 13.4:

At the time of distributing the estate, successors who had the ability and were in a position to maintain the decedent but failed to fulfil their duties shall be given no share or a smaller share of the estate.[31]

Conversely,

At the time of distributing the estate, successors who have made the predominant contributions in maintaining the decedent or have lived with the decedent may be given a larger share (art. 13.3).

---

[29] Available at http://www.leg.state.or.us/ors/.

[30] Korpus (2000-2001) 537.

[31] Available at http://www.novexcn.com/law_of_succession_1994.html.

Moreover, there is a specific ground for disinheritance consisting of committing serious acts of abandonment or mistreatment of the decedent.[32] Lastly, the court may even in its discretion grant a portion of the estate to a decedent's caregiver who meets the requirement set out in art. 14:

> An appropriate share of the estate may be given to a person, other than a successor, who depended on the support of the decedent and who neither can work nor has a source of income, or to a person, other than a successor, who was largely responsible for supporting the decedent.

This set of rules gives Chinese courts great discretion to distribute the estate in accordance with the behaviour of the successors with respect to the decedent;[33] but, at the same time, the testator's intention – hence, freedom of testation – is pushed into the background, since the court distributes the estate without taking it into account.

Other legal systems contain grounds for disinheritance along the lines of the new art. 451-17.2 e CC Cat. In the Czech Republic a successor may be disinherited because of his or her failure to care for the decedent who needs assistance because of illness, age or another serious circumstance, and also if he or she has not shown the interest he or she should have shown as a descendant for a long time.[34] The new Croatian law of succession lists among the grounds for disinheritance the serious infringement of a legal or moral family obligation toward the deceased, for instance not giving him or her care when needed.[35] The Brazilian Civil Code of 2002 establishes as a ground for disinheritance the neglect of ascendants mentally alienated or seriously ill (art. 1962. IV, whilst art. 1962. V lays down the same rule in relation to descendants). The Peruvian Civil Code of 1984 permits disinheritance of descendants that have neglected ascendants who were seriously ill or incapable of taking care of themselves.

4.3 Compulsory Share, Disinheritance and Descendants' Behaviour in Catalan Law

The Chinese approach is incompatible with the Catalan legal system, since courts cannot make a will for a testator. This system may be suitable for China because of its morals and its political and judicial system.[36] Wills

---

[32] Art. 7.3: "A successor shall be disinherited upon his commission of any one of the following acts: (3) a serious act of abandoning or maltreating the decedent".

[33] See, for a range of judicial decisions, Foster (1998) 77 and Foster (1999) 1199. For example, the daughter given up for adoption –and therefore lacking any legal succession right– that many years later found her biological mother and took care of her was rewarded with 8000 Yuans (aprox. 900 Euros) from the estate.

[34] Rombach (2008) 1501 f., No. 72; Hrušáková (2002) 196, No. 530.

[35] Süß (2008) 943, No. 32; Gliha (2005) 252, No. 442.

[36] Nowadays all new judges in China must be university graduates, but still half of the active judges have no university studies, although this rate is in turn half of what it was in 1990, according to Liebman

are strictly personal in Catalan civil law.[37] Several reasons make the Chinese
solutions unworkable in Catalonia: a) the solemnities required for a valid will, b)
freedom of testation as a concretion of the constitutional guarantee of property
enshrined in art. 33 Spanish Constitution, c) the role of judges simply applying
legal rules, neither creating them nor acting as equity arbitrators. However, Chinese law reflects a tendency, also present in the United States, where the social
and economic model is completely different, aimed at using the law of succession instrumentally both to decide the *mortis causa* destination of the decedent's
assets, and to achieve through the *mortis causa* destination welfare and equity
goals.

Catalan law is not immune from the noted tendency to behaviour-based
regulation of succession. The ground for disinheritance enshrined in art. 451-7.2
e CC Cat comes again into the picture. Testators may disinherit their descendants provided that there is an evident and continued lack of family relationship
solely imputable to the beneficiaries of the compulsory share. Additionally, the
grounds for unworthiness must also be kept in mind, since according to art.
451-7.2 a CC Cat, they also constitute grounds for disinheritance.[38] Therefore,
the decedent may invoke any of the grounds for unworthiness listed in art. 412-3
CC Cat in order to disinherit one or more of his or her descendants provided that
the decedent fulfils the requirements established by art. 451-8,[39] i.e. mentioning
the ground for disinheritance in the will, the codicil or the succession contract,
and naming the disinherited successor. But unworthiness also deprives successors of their succession rights and, consequently, the unworthy beneficiary may
be prevented from receiving a compulsory share even if the testator has not
formally disinherited him or her.

The new ground for disinheritance of art. 451-17.2 e CC Cat takes into
account the personal aspect resulting from kinship, since only the closest
members of the decedent's family can be beneficiaries of the compulsory share
(descendants; only if descendants are lacking, the decedent's parents, art. 451-3
and -4 CC Cat). It can be said that the law faces up to the "social or moral side"
of family relationships.[40] Nevertheless, the ground for disinheritance is not
based on any lack of relationship. It is qualified by two adjectives, "evident" and
"continued". "Continued" means long-lasting, but also that the absence of relationship must remain at the time of the decedent's death; "evident" entails serious, external acts.[41] Moreover, the ground for disinheritance must be exclusively

---

(2010) available at http://www.pbs.org/wnet/wideangle/lessons/the-peoples-court/legitimacy-through-
law-in-china/4332/.

[37] Pozo Carrascosa – Vaquer Aloy – Bosch Capdevila (2009) 61 f.

[38] On the duality grounds for unworthiness/grounds for disinheritance from a comparative point of view,
Zimmermann (2010) 503 ff.

[39] Ribot Igualada (2009) 1395 f.

[40] Ribot Igualada (2009) 1400.

[41] This fragment of the decision handed down by the Court of Appeal of Barcelona on October 21, 2009
is revealing (available at http://www.poderjudicial.es ROJ: SAP B 10746/2009): "The appellants argue

imputable to the successor. If this was to be interpreted strictly, art. 451-17.2 e CC Cat would be inapplicable in many cases, since often it would be impossible to prove that the disagreements between relatives can be blamed on only one person rather than the testator as well. In my opinion, the rationale of the legal rule must permit disinheritance when a beneficiary's behaviour becomes the efficient cause in view of all the surrounding circumstances suggesting lack of family relationship; otherwise the application costs of the legal rule already predicted by the Preamble of the Civil Code of Catalonia would be excessive. Without intending to be too casuistic, let us consider a son who intermittently contacts his father but does not allow him any contact with his grandchildren; of course, it is possible to imagine justifications for that attitude (perhaps the father was convicted of child abuse), but it is not admissible to construe the term "family relationship" as exclusively the relation between parent and child disregarding the extended family. Certainly, the Catalan legislature has resorted to a vague notion when describing this new ground for disinheritance. Yet, as Rhodes has pointed out, the legislature acknowledges a beneficiary's misbehaviour may be difficult to apprehend and grants discretion to courts in order that in each case they try to find the balance between the decedent's intention, the disinherited beneficiary's attitude and the underlying policy principle.[42]

It is worth referring to some statistics. There are almost 3 million people living alone in Spain, of which 450,000 are 80 years or older. In particular, more than 25% of people aged more than 90 live alone, this is to say, 60,000 elderly people. If we take the age range between 85 and 89, the number of elderly people living alone raises to 140,000, to 250,000 if the range is between 80 and 84.[43] On the other hand, and according to Fundación Rais, almost

---

the difficulty of proving facts that remain within the family. This is true, but this is at least partially a consequence of the proportionality of disinheritance and the seriousness of insults and mistreatment. Since when the alleged mistreatment or insult does not transcend the direct inner family core, usually it is because these are ordinary controversies that render disinheritance disproportionate. It has to be borne in mind that the Spanish Civil Code, former art. 370.3 Catalan Succession Code and current art. 451-17.2 e require a serious mistreatment or insult so that the Court understands that there is ground for disinheritance" (author's translation). This does not mean, however, that the courts cannot be flexible when assessing evidence, precisely because the facts arise within the family. It is worth quoting the decision of the Court of Appeal of Barcelona handed down on May 4, 2006 (available at http://www.poderjudicial.es ROJ: SAP B 5473/2006): "One thing is that the grounds for disinheritance –because they entail a civil penalty– must be restrictively construed, and a different one that the assessment of evidence of the existence of the ground for disinheritance is equally strict. On the contrary, flexibility must prevail, since the facts in which disinheritance is based occur in a domestic environment, the realm of privacy, so that only the members of the family or persons knowing for friendship or professional reasons the family secrets could explain them" (author's translation). By the way, some Spanish scholars advocate for a more flexible construction of the grounds for disinheritance: see in particular Lasarte Álvarez (2007) 363 ff., and Rebolledo Varela (2010) 410 ff.

[42] Rhodes (2007) 989.

[43] Source: http://www.ine.es/prensa/np275.pdf. See also the INE report "Men and Women in Spain 2009" available athttp://www.ine.es/prodyser/pubweb/myh/myh09.pdf, p. 18.

300,000 old people suffer some kind of abuse or assault; this means a 5 per cent, being in most cases maltreated by their own descendants.[44] If we use Catalan statistics, in 2001 more than 20.4% elder people residing in family dwellings lived alone, in particular women, which represented 15.9%, i.e. 220,000 elderly people living alone.[45] In the coming decades, all EU countries will experience steep increases in the share of elderly persons in the total population.[46] Of course, I neither pretend to say that most elder people suffer from physical or economic abuse or maltreatments committed by their descendants, not that most descendants leave their parents unattended. Nevertheless, abuses do exist and they may increase because of the economic crisis. In fact, the Catalan legislature has realized that a number of vulnerable old people are attended by professional caregivers without family ties. Consequently, it has established a caution according to which whenever an elder person wants to favour in his or her will a professional caregiver, he or she must make a notarial will or a succession contract, so that a notary must intervene and assess in addition to his or her capacity the true intention of the testator.[47] The Catalan legislature is thus aware that many elder people live without relatives taking care of them. Yet, it has adopted the perspective of the caregiver that may wish to take advantage of the situation of vulnerability. It is thus also necessary to recall the complementary perspective, this is to say, the testator who foresees his or her death and wants to favour or to exclude his or her descendants depending on the relationship they have developed.

On the other hand, there are not many judgments deciding disinheritance cases. This allows us to conclude that only a few testators wish to disinherit their descendants. If one looks up the databases of the Spanish judicial power (CENDOJ), there are 79 decisions since 1997 in which the term disinheritance appears, and disinheritance is not a crucial question in all of them. 48 other judgments deal with cases of omitted successors (pretermission). Even if this statistic is not too reliable, I think it can be stated that the vast majority of testators are not disinheriting their descendants. That is the reason why this new ground for disinheritance enshrined in art. 451-17.2 e CC Cat cannot be disapproved. Nothing leads one to think that there are thousands of testators eager to disinherit their descendants on the basis of this new legal provision; on the contrary, it will be useful to solve some imbalance in the grounds for disinheritance as regulated in the former Succession Code.

This new ground for disinheritance may avoid forcing the other grounds when the intention to disinherit does not fit exactly with the wording of the grounds and nevertheless the court considers that there are good reasons to deprive the beneficiary of the compulsory share. The decision of the Court of

---

[44] http://www.fundacionrais.org/Elemento.aspx?id_elemento=767.

[45] Source: Catalonia Ageing Yearbook 2004, p. 24, available at http://www.envelliment.org/documents/
      docs/Anuari2004cat.pdf.

[46] See http://ec.europa.eu/economy_finance/structural_reforms/ageing/index_en.htm.

[47] Pozo Carrascosa – Vaquer Aloy – Bosch Capdevila (2009) 447 f.; Gómez Pomar (2009) 123 f.

Appeal of Barcelona handed down on May 5, 2006,[48] provides us with a good example of how the courts operated even before the reform was in place. The testator alleged the third ground for disinheritance as set out in art. 357 Succession Code, i.e. physical maltreatment or serious slanderous allegations against the testator. According to the testator, his daughter had often stolen money from her parents, she had offended him using insults such as "cabrón" or "maricón", she had thrown him out of their home, latterly she had ignored him and when she talked to him it was only to insult him and tell him that she did not love him any more and she considered they were not a family. There was evidence that the daughter impeded any contact with his grandson. The Court of Appeal reversed the decision of the district judge who considered that art. 357 c Succession Code could not be applied where there was neither physical maltreatment nor slander.[49] For the Court of Appeal, the daughter's behaviour had affected her father's dignity. The following fragment of the judgment deserves attention:

> "Evidently the legislature cannot coactively impose the affective ties that parental relationship usually entails, but it strives to foster them (parental authority implies care of children of minor age by means of living together, maintenance, education; once the children are of full age, the law imposes a reciprocal duty of alimony) and it establishes the duty of mutual respect between closest relatives. (...) This respect is violated when there is an offence consisting not only in proclaiming the irrelevance of the parents for the children but also making clear the personal rejection with expression like 'I don't love you', 'you are not my family'. Such expressions, even if they are not sincere, are completely unnecessary and hurt parents' dignity".[50]

This judgment is interesting because, although it applies the ground for disinheritance consisting in maltreatment and slander, it redirects the issue towards affective ties in the parental relationship, and bases the disinheritance on its absence due to the daughter's behaviour. Other judgments can complete this approach to behaviour-based disinheritance. The Court of Appeal of Barcelona in its decision of September 19, 2008,[51] again on the basis of art. 370 c Succession Code, upheld the ground for disinheritance because the plaintiff did not succeed to prove that the reason why he lacked any relationship with his father was his sister's attitude. Once more under the coverage of maltreatment the lack of family relationship comes to the scene as the true ground for disinheritance. Lastly, the decision of the Court of Appeal of Barcelona handed down on June 9, 2009,[52] needs to be mentioned. The issue was the refusal to pay alimony to

---

[48] Westlaw Aranzadi databases JUR 2006/272116.

[49] New art. 451-17.2 c CC Cat only considers the serious maltreatment to the testator, his or her spouse or cohabitee and closest relatives.

[50] Author's translation.

[51] Available at http://www.poderjudicial.es, ROJ: SAP B 8510/2008.

[52] Available at http://www.poderjudicial.es, ROJ: SAP B 7322/2009.

the claiming mother on the basis of the application of the grounds for disinheritance according to art. 271.1 d of the recently repealed Family Code. The
Court accepts that the mother's behaviour went far beyond what was necessary
to keep under control a family of a young widow mother with seven children.
The Court considers that the disproportionate punishments to the children for
irrelevant facts, that even made the children abandon the family domicile before
coming of age, along with some physical maltreatment episodes, the necessity
for some of the children to get psychological treatment, the mother's refusal to
maintain family relationships with some of the children and their own families,
amounted to a ground for disinheritance. The most important aspect is the
lack of family relationship with the descendants, not the concrete mistreatment
inflicted.

5 Concluding Remarks

Ribot Igualada has stated that the new ground for disinheritance enshrined in art. 451-17.2 e CC Cat is one of the last attempts to save the
compulsory share. He also considers that this regulation shows the fear to abolish the compulsory share in Catalonia by escaping to a general clause in order to
clear the legislature's conscience in the face of certain groups of cases.[53] I prefer
to stress the reinforcement of the role of freedom of testation,[54] giving testators the opportunity to disinherit the descendants that have not kept a family
relationship and to favour the spouse or those descendants who have taken care
of him or her. Otherwise it is not possible to hold that the compulsory share sets
a balance between freedom of testation, succession and family protection;[55] or
that the compulsory share contributes to the social necessity of strengthening
the family.[56] For then only testators would be burdened with duties, compelled
to favour their descendants *mortis causa*, whilst the descendants would feel
legally –maybe not ethically– free to take care of their parent or not. Only if they
committed criminally relevant facts against the testator he or she could deprive
them from any legal succession right, although it is more usual –luckily!– that
the descendants simply disregard the testator. It is by no means clear that the
new Catalan ground for disinheritance leads to an increase of disinherited
descendants.[57] Probably it will only imply an adjustment of the invoked grounds
for disinheritance, since it will not be necessary any more to force the wording of
former art. 370 c Succession Code. In my opinion, this new ground for disinher-

---

[53] Ribot Igualada (2009) 1402.

[54] Obviously, the testator is completely free to favour despite his or her behaviour the descendant. According to Zimmermann (2010) 505, the grounds for disinheritance imply that freedom of testation prevails
over intergenerational solidarity.

[55] Badura (2007) 151 ff.

[56] Zacher (2007) 135 ff.

[57] Such prediction has been made by Lamarca Marquès (2009) 293.

itance, even if it does not constitute a token of modernisation, evidences a spontaneous convergence with sensibilities already reflected in other legal systems based on different succession principles, though equally concerned about the welfare and the freedom of testators.

Freedom of Testation Versus Freedom to Enter Into Succession Agreements and Transaction Costs

Susana Navas Navarro

1 Introduction

As we are aware, one of the more noteworthy amendments implemented by the Catalan legislator is that concerning succession agreements (Preamble IV of Law 10/2008, of 10 July, *of the fourth book of the Civil Code of Catalonia, regarding successions,*[1] hereinafter Book IV CC Cat). Said amendment sought, as one of its objectives, to ensure that these agreements recover their value as a legal instrument used in estate planning, particularly in cases where a generational change takes place within a family business.[2] In this respect, the legislator states, while highlighting the obsolescence of marriage settlements:

> "Indeed, these agreements were the driving force behind inter-generational transfer of typically agricultural family assets by means of the establishment of a unique heir agreed on in marriage settlements. Despite the historical significance of inheritance pacts, their regulation, which has been immersed in social and economic circumstances and a concept of family relations that belong to another era, was more useful when it came to interpreting old marriage settlements rather than as an instrument for inheritance planning".[3]

In view of this, the legislator has chosen to separate succession agreements from marriage and from the requirement to execute them *ad solemnitatem* within a marriage settlement (art. 431-7 CC Cat) and to extend the subjective scope so that succession agreements may be entered into not only by spouses or future spouses or their ascendants or descendants, but also by partners in stable relationships and between collateral relatives related through blood and through marriage (art. 431-2 CC Cat).[4] These agreements therefore facilitate handing

---

*   This study falls within the scope of the research project entitled "Grup de dret civil català" (2009 SGR 221). I would like to extend my gratitude to Santiago Espiau Espiau, Professor of Civil Law at the University of Barcelona, and Antoni Vaquer Aloy, Professor of Civil Law at the University of Lleida, for their observations further to reading the present paper. Any errors are attributable only to its author.

[1]   "The system on succession agreements is unquestionably the foremost new aspect in the fourth book with respect to the previous Code of Succession" (Preamble IV Law 10/2008; DOGC No. 5175, 17 July 2008, English edition by the Government of Catalonia, 2010).

[2]   There is no regulatory concept of family business, on account of the diverse nature of the phenomenon; authors are not even able to reach an agreement on the definition of the term "business"; see Palazón (2003) 27 ff. This is acknowledged in the report entitled *Informe de la Ponencia de Estudio para la problemática de la empresa familiar,* drafted at the Senate Treasury Committee on 12 November 2001 (BOCG – Senado, VII Legislature, series I, No. 312, dated 23 November 2001, 25). In an attempt to clarify, Cerdà (2004) 91-92 states that the family business is that under the management of a family, that would hold the majority of the voting rights, the power to appoint or dismiss most members of the governing body and the option to dispose, by virtue of agreements, of the voting rights. See, Casillas –Díaz – Vázquez (2005) 6-7; Steier – Chrisman – Chua (2004) 296.

[3]   Preamble IV, Book IV CC Cat (English edition by the Government of Catalonia, 2010).

[4]   For references to other amendments introduced by the Catalan legislator in relation to succession agreements, see Brancós (2009) 953-982; Egea (2009) 9-58; Pratdesaba (2008) 151-181.

over the family business.[5] This is one of the issues that will be addressed from an economic perspective in this paper (*infra* section 3).

Another innovation introduced by the 2008 legislator as regards succession agreements is the possibility of executing succession agreements the subject matter of which are only certain assets (and not the whole estate). These are governed by arts. 431-29 and 431-30 CC Cat.[6]

Before addressing the issues that are central to our analysis, the alternative outlined in the title of this paper "Freedom of testation versus freedom to enter into succession agreements" is also worthy of mention, since it presents a two-pronged approach. Indeed, the first approach is that of the legislator who, when regulating the transfer *mortis causa* of an individual's assets, may choose, based on the provision set forth under art. 33.1 of the Spanish Constitution, to protect private property and, therefore, inheritance rights, much in the same way as the Catalan legislator has already done, by providing the deceased with three options: to dispose of the estate as he or she sees fit, unilaterally, by appointing one or several heirs in a will (testate succession, arts. 421-1 to 429-15 CC Cat); to agree with one or several other person(s) who will be appointed future heir(s) (succession agreement or contractual succession, arts. 431-1 to 431-30 CC Cat); or to establish no disposition of any kind, in which case, the law itself will propose a list of heirs (intestate succession, arts. 441-1 to 444-1 CC Cat). When faced with the choice which a person may make between a will or a succession agreement, the legislator must specify the relation between both sources of inheritance rights (art. 411-3 CC Cat, which inaccurately refers to "*the foundations for eligibility*"), stating, where applicable, preference for one over the other or, where applicable, rendering them partially or fully incompatible (art. 411-3 CC Cat). This issue will be covered in the next section (2).

The second approach, and perhaps the most interesting, is that of the *deceased*; of the person for whom succession is sought, and who, under Catalan law, is faced with the above mentioned options provided by the legislator: 1) to make no provision for the transfer of his or her assets for after his or her demise; 2) to make certain provisions, appointing one or several universal heirs by means of a will or succession agreement (art. 411-3.1 CC Cat). The deceased's decision in this respect, in addition to personal, internal and psychological and even strategic reasons, is also determined by economic factors and this, in our view, is of particular significance in the case of succession within a family business.[7]

---

[5]   At the Ninth *Congreso notarial español* held in Barcelona from 12 to 14 May 2005, a proposal was put forward to extend the freedom to organise succession *mortis causa* using succession agreements, joint wills and trusts as legal instruments for planning succession within the family business. See Cámara (2007) 6. This topic is also mentioned by Albiez (2006) 216-256.

[6]   On this topic, see Navas (2009) 1-35.

[7]   Bernheim – Shleifer – Summers (1985) 1045-1076; Shavell (1991) 401-421.

2   The Legislator's Choice: An Inheritance Agreement Prevails Over and Is Sometimes Incompatible With a Will

In art. 411-3.3 CC Cat ("universal testate succession can only take place if there is no inheritance pact"), the legislator has chosen to grant the succession agreement in which the heir is instituted priority over a will; the precedent of this provision can be found in the now repealed art. 3.3 of the Catalan Succession Code 1991 (hereinafter CS), the wording of which was very similar. Most Catalan academic writing maintains that art. 3.3 CS points to incompatibility between succession by means of a succession agreement (the inheritance pact) and testate succession; specifically, between the inheritance rights derived from the will and the inheritance rights derived from the inheritance pact.[8] Recent academic opinion, however, has understood that the rule of art. 3.3 CS actually established precedence, and not incompatibility, between both hereditary entitlements. Such precedence also constituted material and legal incompatibility cases where the deceased disposed of the entire estate by means of an inheritance pact. However, in the literal rendering of the CS, the material compatibility between the inheritance pact and the will did not constitute legal incompatibility when, in the inheritance pact, the deceased only disposed of a portion of the estate.[9]

Book IV of the CC Cat has chosen to convert material compatibility into legal incompatibility. In fact, art. 431-23 CC Cat, in regulating the revocatory effect of the inheritance pact, establishes in its first paragraph that:

> "A valid inheritance pact revokes the will, codicil, testamentary brief and bestowal *mortis causa* made prior to its execution, even if the former is compatible with the latter".[10]

This material compatibility will appear where the deceased had disposed of only a portion of the estate in the will, and in the subsequent inheritance pact he or she disposed of the remainder. According to the literal sense of the precept, it would seem that the will and the succession agreement cease to be compatible in the eye of the law, so that the (partial) inheritance pact revokes the will, which means that a portion of the estate — that provided for in the will — is considered not to have been disposed of by the deceased. Hence, by applying the rule of legal incompatibility to what is materially compatible, a portion of the estate

---

8   Marsal (2003) 587; Puig Ferriol – Roca Trias (2009) 47; Puig Salelles (1994) 22.

9   Bosch (2004) 115-118. This interpretation seems to be at odds with the wording of art. 431-23 CC Cat. See Del Pozo – Vaquer – Bosch (2009) 51.

10 English edition by the Government of Catalonia, 2010, which is used throughout the text when transcribing provisions contained in Book IV. In this translation "bestowal" refers to *donatio mortis causa* and the expression "testamentary brief" is used to refer to informal documents left by the deceased to complement a will and which can contain, among other provisions, legacies the value of which does not exceed 10% of the estate (art. 421-21 CC Cat).

goes from having a destination predetermined by the deceased, to having none at all. As a result, the deceased must subsequently (and once again) dispose of this portion under codicil, testamentary brief or another succession agreement or *donatio mortis causa* (arg. ex art. 431-22.1 CC Cat) so that this portion, now vacant, is suitably apportioned and not incorporated into the inheritance pact (art. 431-28.2 CC Cat). This understanding of art. 431-23.1 CC Cat is clearly at odds with the deceased's wishes, its only ground being the legal incompatibility between inheritance titles. This interpretation derives from the fact that the Catalan legislator has introduced, in art. 431-23.1, a final clause which was not included in art. 70.1 CS. In fact, art. 70.1 CS only established, in its first section, that a valid inheritance pact revokes the will, codicil, testamentary brief and *donatio mortis causa* made prior to its execution. This provision could be construed as to refer to the general rule only, that is, to the case in which the will had disposed of the entire estate and likewise had been done in the inheritance pact, so that the latter revoked the former. When only a portion of the estate has been disposed of, on the other hand, there was no obstacle to reasoning that material compatibility would result in legal compatibility.[11]

Art. 431-23.1 CC Cat is not well reconciled with its second paragraph, where it assumes that the inheritance pact covers the *entire* estate, on stating that:

> "Dispositions mortis causa subsequent to the inheritance pact shall only be effective if the inheritance pact is preventive or inasmuch as the reservation for disposition will allow".

The main aim of the so-called preventive inheritance pacts is to avoid intestacy; therefore, a subsequent will prevails over the succession agreement. This proves that the Catalan legislator decides based on the fact that the preventive inheritance pact is universal, or rather, that it comprises all estate assets and not only a portion thereof. This general approach, as far as we understand, is also that referred to in the first paragraph of the precept under study.

Hence, art. 431-23.1 CC Cat can be interpreted as meaning that the inheritance pact executed subsequently — and which revokes a will executed before — must be an inheritance pact for the entire estate; in the revoked will, only a portion of the estate had been disposed of; therefore, in principle, it was materially compatible, but it ceases to be so further to execution of the inheritance pact which comprises all estate assets. If, on the other hand, the inheritance pact were to comprise only that portion of the estate that was not disposed of under the will, we think that material and legal compatibility ought to be upheld, since this coincides with the deceased's wishes with respect to the apportionment *mortis causa* of his or her assets. This interpretation is also supported by the legal argument that in art. 431-23.1 CC Cat the will appears named together

---

[11] Bosch (2004) 117-118. Academic opinion accepted that the deceased could confirm the validity of a will, in whole or in part, in a subsequent inheritance pact, and even that such confirmation could be inferred from the pact, even if it did not state it in express terms [López Burniol (1994) 346].

with the codicil, the testamentary brief and the *donatio mortis causa*, in which
only certain assets or a portion of the estate may be disposed of, but not the
entire estate (arts. 421-20, 421-21 and 432-2.1 CC Cat). The legislator is therefore making decisions which are effectively based on a *de facto* assumption, in
referring to the (material) compatibility, that in the provisions governing the
succession executed prior to the inheritance pact, only a portion of the estate has
been disposed of and, therefore, may be deemed compatible, and the subsequent
inheritance pact, which must necessarily dispose of the entire estate (universal
inheritance pact), has the revocatory effect as provided under the regulation.

If, however, the deceased executes an inheritance pact and several assets are
set aside for subsequent disposition, the disposition of such assets may only be
performed by means of codicil, testamentary brief, succession agreement or
donatio mortis causa, but not by means of a will (art. 431-23.2 in relation to art.
431-22.1 CC Cat). If not disposed of, the vacant portion is incorporated into the
inheritance pact (art. 431-28.2 CC Cat). Hence, it would seem that material and
legal compatibility between the contractual heir and the testamentary heir is
reduced in Book IV, since it will only operate if the will disposing of a portion of
the assets is executed prior to the inheritance pact, but it will not if the execution of the will takes place subsequently to that of the inheritance pact. We think
this unnecessarily limits the legal channels through which the deceased's final
wishes may be expressed. The fact that art. 431-22.1 CC Cat has acknowledged
that, in an inheritance pact, the deceased may set aside an *aliquot share* of the
estate to dispose of freely (a provision not established under the old art. 82.1 CS
on which the new article is based), shows that it cannot be held that art. 431-23.1
refers to a complete universal inheritance pact (the estate in its entirety) and
the deceased seeks solely to subtract a certain singular asset or assets from the
estate in its entirety.[12]

We must also highlight that this restriction, today, is justified only by the
strict observance of succession principles existing under Catalan law.[13]

What is certain is that, whether or not legal incompatibility exists, in practice, this is of little or no relevance, due to the dearth of succession agreements
(particularly inheritance pacts) entered into and, conversely, the significant
increase in wills. One must bear in mind that under the CS, inheritance pacts
could only be agreed upon within marriage settlements (art. 67.1 CS), and that,
as statistics show, the execution of the latter has also decreased considerably.[14] In
fact, according to the *Anuario de la Dirección General de los Registros y del Notariado*, 110,575 wills were executed in Catalonia in 2007 compared to the 3,024

---

[12] This was the interpretation given by Bosch under the CS (2004, 117-118). On the contrary, see: López
Burniol (1994) 372.

[13] For critiques on the observance of said principles in Book IV of the CC Cat, see Salvador/López Burniol
(2009) 71.

[14] One of the reasons to promote a revival of marriage settlements has been precisely so that they can be
used to agree on heirs to continue the family business started by their ascendants, see López Burniol
(1999) 46 ff. This concept is covered by Gortázar (2005) 123-130.

instruments drafted referring to marriage, cohabitation and separation. Further data is provided under the title "Herencias" [Inheritances], of which there were 64,480 in total, even though the grounds for inheritance rights are not known.[15] In short, if from those 3,204 public documents we subtract those relating to long-term cohabitation, those governing *de facto* separations, those restricted to the establishment or dissolution of matrimonial property regimes and those containing agreements in case of a future separation, it can be seen that inheritance pacts are disappearing through lack of use.[16] Within the European Union, in relation to the total number of deferred inheritances, the country in which most wills are executed is Spain (50%), compared to Italy (45%), Belgium (10-15%), France (10%), Germany (20%) and England (33%).[17]

This highlights, initially, the lack of interest in (or even, perhaps, lack of awareness of) succession agreements when planning, during one's lifetime, the transfer of assets by means of succession.[18] From an economic perspective, however, such behaviour may be considered to be perfectly rational.[19]

3 The Deceased's Choice: Succession Within the Family Business

3.1 Preliminary Remarks

As pointed out at the beginning of this paper, we will primarily focus on succession within family businesses, given that this is one of the factors that prompted the Catalan legislator to incorporate largely new rules for succession agreements. Indeed, it is a fact that there is an industrial sector essentially comprising family businesses struggling to reach the third generation. In Spain, according to information issued by the Family Enterprise Institute, it is estimated that there are some three million family businesses, which make up 85% of the total number of established firms. This means that they provide employment to 75% of the workforce (13.9 million workers). They are also responsible for 59% of Spanish exports. Their total revenue is equal to 70% of Spanish GDP. 50% of Spanish firms listed on the Stock Exchange are family businesses, a figure which shows us that family businesses do not only comprise small and medium enterprises — there are also large companies run by families. In Catalonia, two-thirds of small and medium enterprises are family businesses, representing 65.6% of the total number of existing companies.[20] If we now look at generational change, we see that only 65% of companies are

---

[15]   *Anuario DGRN* (2008/IV).

[16]   López Burniol already drew the same conclusions in 1990 (1994) 330.

[17]   This information has been contributed by Cámara (2007) 6-7.

[18]   Jou (2005) 367 ff.; Giménez (2005) 745-749.

[19]   See section 3.3 of this paper.

[20]   Guinjoan- Murillo – Pons (2004) 21-22.

passed on to the first generation of successors; 26% make it to the second; 9%
to the third, and just 1% make it through to the fourth generation or beyond.[21]
On a macro-economic scale, there are 17 million family businesses within the
European Union, which employ 100 million people and represent 60% of the
EU's business sector, and out of the top 100 European companies, 25% are
family businesses.[22] Another interesting statistic comes from the United States,
where 80% of all companies are family businesses, which means that they
provide employment to over 50% of the population.[23] The social reality, however,
shows that business owners – particularly first generation – are often reluctant
to plan succession in a timely and ordered fashion; therefore it is rare, during
their lifetime, to see the business itself or the assets owned by it being passed
on.[24] We will therefore focus on the transfer *mortis causa* of the family business
and, to this end, we will draw from information provided in the report entitled
Radiografía de la empresa familiar española. Fortalezas y riesgos, directed by Professor Gimeno Sandig, in which it was concluded that 78% of family businesses
have not planned their succession and that only 51% of subsequent generations
are familiar with the succession guidelines, which means half of the successions
in family businesses are planned without the due participation of the generation
that is to inherit ownership of the business.[25] When planning this succession,
the instrument used, as shown by the statistics outlined above, is the will, and
not the succession agreement.[26] It is often the case that, within certain companies, by means of shareholders' agreements, family members establish clauses

---

[21] A similar scenario was observed in Germany, see Bös – Kayser (1996). I would like to thank the *Institut
für Mittelstandsforschung Bonn* for having kindly provided me with this study.

[22] The realization that family businesses were disappearing, without being passed from generation to
generation, was proven by the publication of the Commission Recommendation of 7 December 1994 on
the transfer of small and medium-sized enterprises (OJ C 204, dated 23 July 1994), further to the meet-
ing held in the French city of Lille, which addressed the need to seek solutions, amongst others, based
on succession rights which favour generational handovers within family businesses, and to which end,
the importance of succession agreements was raised (The European Forum on the Transfer of Business
on 3 and 4 February 1997 in Lille). The situation is one of the reasons that led to the amendment of art.
1056.2 Spanish CC through Ley 7/2003, 1 April, *de la sociedad limitada nueva empresa* (BOE No. 79, 2
April 2003). A general reference to this Law is covered in Reyes (2003) 771 ff. The Communication from
the Commission to the Council, the European Parliament, the European Economic and Social Committee and the Committee of the Regions [COM(2006) 117 final, p. 20] examines the problems inherent to
the handover of family businesses.

[23] http://www.iefamiliar.com/empresafam/datos.asp.

[24] Casillas – Díaz – Vázquez (2005) 234 ff.; Fuentes (2007) 93 ff, 271 ff.; García – López (2004) 47-48.

[25] Gimeno (www.fbkonline.com/es/eventos/evento_01.html). Timely planning of succession within the
family business is a guarantee of its survival, in spite of the generational handover. See Sherma – Chrisman – Chua (2003) 1-16.

[26] See section 2 of this paper. In Germany, where the inheritance contract (*Erbvertrag*) has a long tradition,
it has even been proposed that it be eliminated, given the low number of contracts entered into and the
comparatively greater number of wills executed. See Mayer (2000) 26-30.

clearly indicating how succession is to take place (the transfer *mortis causa* of shares to a specific person, for instance).[27] A "family protocol" is a legal instrument which serves as a backup to said agreements,[28] the publication of which is regulated under Real Decreto 171/2007, de 9 de febrero, *por el que se regula la publicidad de los protocolos familiares.*[29] Family protocols often contain succession agreements, the validity of which is uncertain. Currently, approximately 25% of family businesses have established a family protocol,[30] even though evidence would suggest there is a certain level of disenchantment with the document in question.[31]

The question that immediately presents itself is this: To what can we attribute — or what is the economic reason for — the preference for wills over succession agreements? Before we can address this question correctly, from an economic perspective, it is worth noting that, in our view, the modern family business is not equivalent to the old "homestead", a family estate that was typically agricultural in nature, which in Catalonia was inherited through the appointment of a sole heir, during the deceased's lifetime, by means of an inheritance pact.

---

[27] As highlighted in the aforementioned European Forum on the Transfer of Business on 3 and 4 February 1997 in Lille. For academic opinion, see Egea (2007) 23. This type of shareholders' agreement is referred to, in academic opinion, as an "organisational agreement". See Paz-Ares (2003) 2-3. The problem inherent to this type of agreement is its enforceability, that is, whether its performance can be imposed or not. It is held, in this case, that the behaviour of the debtor would amount to a *volere*, that is, making a statement, which the court cannot make in the debtor's place (art. 708 LEC). Rodríguez (2007) 1148 ff., believes that these types of agreement – those which make provision for the inheritance of a specific asset – are viewed merely as "guidelines". It would be a case, based on analysis of the Law of Succession, of a "mere recommendation" which, if entailing "non-disposal", is not legally enforceable (art. 428-6.6 CC Cat). Another possible agreement would involve stipulating the non-revocation of a will having been executed prior thereto. The will is, however, essentially revocable (art. 422-8.1 CC Cat, art. 737 Spanish CC) and may not be rendered irrevocable further to agreement by the parties, since this is the general rule under all legal regulations which apply to us. See Vaquer (2009) 559 fn. 16.

[28] We must bear in mind that succession agreements may be established by means of a notarised family protocol (art. 431-7 CC Cat), which in turn constitutes a shareholders' agreement or pact that allows, from a business perspective, the succession agreement to be considered as a shareholders' agreement governed by its own rules. See Grima (2004) 117 ff.

[29] BOE No. 65, 16 March 2007. Real Decreto 171/2007 defines the "family protocol" under art. 2.1 as "a series of agreements signed by and between the members themselves or third parties as a means to upholding those family ties which impact on an unlisted company and in which there is a common interest to govern the relationships between family, property and company affecting the entity". On publication, see Fernández del Pozo (2008); Rodríguez (2007) 1148 ff.

[30] http://www.iefamiliar.com/asocterr/datos.asp.

[31] Cerdà (2009) 182.

3.2   The Family Estate: From "Homestead" to "Business"?

Vicens Vives states that, historically speaking, a fundamental
element of Catalan society was the homestead and not the person. The homestead (the *mas*) and the family that belonged to it comprised the social substruc-
ture of Catalonia both before and after the 14th century.[32] The prosperity and
stabilisation of Catalan agriculture contributed in turn to social stability. What
was important was the ownership of the family estate, which was transferred to
a sole heir, the first-born son, who would bring his spouse or future spouse and
offspring to the homestead and would continue to observe his duty of maintaining the unity and production of the agricultural family estate.[33] As we know,
the standard procedure for transfer *mortis causa* of this estate was by means
of a marriage settlement executed by the son upon his marriage,[34] and under
which his appointment as heir was agreed by his ascendants — this sometimes
entailed even a third generation who were the future offspring of the contracting parties. This inheritance pact also incorporated, in the same document,
amongst other provisions and depending on the area, the dowry, the mortgage
guaranteeing its reimbursement or a usufruct in favour of the future widow,
and even other provisions that could be stipulated by other family members.
Marriage settlements therefore represent a transaction among conflicting legal
positions and interests around the marriage that is going to be entered into. The
main problems arose in relation to the bride's dowry (amount, payment terms,
circumstances under which it may be reimbursed, etc.), but the bride's family
was also concerned with the status of the assets that comprised the "homestead"
that she would become part of, that is, any debt or credit levied thereupon, as
well as other dowries or forced shares yet to be paid out of it. Barrera states that
"all of this necessarily arises in prior negotiations and is perhaps reflected in
the drafting of the actual settlements".[35] These negotiations, when analysed
from a more current perspective, enable us to deduce that a few, certainly high,
"transaction costs" (information costs and negotiation costs) were involved. In
spite of these costs, however, the usefulness in terms of social wellbeing derived
from this type of succession agreement resulted in an efficient cost-benefit ratio.
Indeed, marriage settlements and, therein, inheritance pacts in favour of a
sole heir – the first-born son – served as a regulatory instrument governing the
economic life of Catalan families at that time, which brought peace and social
stability.[36]

The previous social conception of the land gradually disappeared and the
prevalence of a bourgeois concept of private property[37] under a market economy

---

[32] Vicens Vives (1980) 28.

[33] Barrera (1990) 50.

[34] Unless this had already been done in the marriage settlements previously executed by the parents.

[35] Barrera (1990) 92 ff.

[36] López Burniol (1994) 328; De Hinojosa (2003) 128 ff.; Vallet de Goytisolo (2007) 98-101.

[37] Peset (1990) 172 ff.; Tedde de Lorca (1994) 42-43.

system viewed land as a good that could be bought and sold, and from which an individual utility could (and still can) be extracted and entered in the books.[38] As Vicens Vives reminds us:

> "the deep-rooted concept of the social service of the land disappeared amidst the numerous legislative barriers and judicial sentences, geared towards the defence of the individualistic personalisation of society".[39]

This change in concepts, together with the evolution from extended family to nuclear family in which the interests of the individual were legally protected,[40] brought about the decline of marriage settlements and their gradual abandonment.[41] The inheritance pact entailed an immobilisation of land, which remained outside of commercial use and which was at odds with bourgeois legal logic.[42] Hence, when socio-economic circumstances change and capital is devalued, the execution of marriage settlements begins to decrease and the inheritance pact along with them. We must also take into account that the division of estates, at a specific historical-social point in which there is no market system, means that there are no mechanisms to absorb this offer, thus rendering the fragmentation of land economically inefficient.[43]

This new individualistic conception of property rights, as we see it, means that the current family business cannot be viewed as the modern (or postmodern) successor to the old "homestead" of Catalan historical society. Furthermore, the rise of the individual rights of the person and the change in the conception and composition of the nuclear family do away with the concept of a family tied to an estate.[44] This change in the legal and social mentality entails a further change with respect to those transaction costs worthy of consideration which, at a certain point in history, were met, since they were compensated by the social benefit. With the bourgeois concept of property and the emergence of the market economy system, estate division no longer poses a problem, since the market incorporates mechanisms which allow said offer to be absorbed. Hence, the importance of transaction costs certainly becomes evident at this moment, and thus the need to contemplate, from an economic perspective, the behaviour of the individual who chooses to incorporate his or her succession into a will

---

[38] Beckert (2008) 17.

[39] Vicens Vives (1980) 40.

[40] Barrera (1990) 377; Flaquer (1999) 66; Flaquer (1998) 97 ff.

[41] Barrera (1990) 142-145.

[42] Barrera (1990) 368 ff. For an economic explanation, refer to Baker – Micelli, (2005) 82 ff.

[43] Lueck – Miceli (2007) 223.

[44] Magariños (2005) 21, points out the reluctance to include the family name in the family business, in order to protect it against being damaged by economic vicissitudes, as well as the interest of preserving anonymity through the legal personality of a capitalist company.

as opposed to a succession agreement. From this perspective, such behaviour would be rational.[45]

Currently, transaction costs are not compensated by utility and social wellbeing (social stability and peace), which were the cornerstone of the previous socio-economic system; that is not to say that no social benefit may be generated indirectly. Therefore, the question nowadays is whether or not those transaction costs are compensated by the individual benefit for those who have to meet them, so that if there are alternative legal instruments which produce the desired benefit at a lower cost, the individual will "rationally" opt for those. Organising succession *mortis causa* through a succession agreement, instead of a will, entails greater costs, which the rational and self-interested *homo economicus*[46] tends to avoid and which, therefore, explains the preference for wills over succession agreements. For a legal regulation to be efficient, it must be managed in such a way so as to reduce transaction costs as much as possible and provide, in return, wellbeing or utility to the parties, to individuals. Conversely, if a regulation is inefficient, this would lead to it being difficult to apply in practice.

3.3   Economic Costs Derived from Entering into Succession Agreements

It is known that one of the difficulties faced by family businesses is the succession of its founder or founders. Said succession entails both the succession in the business management and in the ownership of the company. The reality is that business owners, particularly those of the first generation, are often reluctant[47] to proceed with the generational handover and that this delay is in itself one of the factors contributing to the failure of the next generation to take over and therefore the reason why the company ends up disappearing.[48] These hindrances are not only of an organisational nature, such as the delay in the training of a future successor in the case of one having been chosen, his or her decision to be incorporated definitively in a managerial capacity within the company,[49] the undertaking of various and diverse duties,

---

[45] Posner (1998) 11: "Behaviour is rational when it is adapted to the model of rational choice, whatever the mental state of whoever is choosing". An attempt to introduce other factors into the behaviour of *homo economicus* which, it is thought, ought to have been taken into account by law analysis experts, can be found in Jolls – Sunstein – Thaler (2000) 13-59.

[46] Schäfer – Ott (1991) 61 ff.; Paz-Ares (1981) 627-628.

[47] This is partly attributable to certain characteristics in the personality of the founder, classified by the business scholars as "monarch" or "general", which hinder the handover. When, however, there are "governors", said handover is carried out in a much less conflictive way. In the first case, the successor is seen as a "competitor"; in the latter case, the identities have already been separated so that one is that of the company, and the other that of the founder, which prevents the successor to be perceived as a "competitor". See Moore – Fialko (1999) 164; Staurou – Kleonthous – Anastasiou (2005) 188.

[48] Bjuggren – Sund (2001) 11 ff.

[49] Barbeito – Guillén – Martínez – Domínguez (2004) 32 ff.; Brockhaus (2004) 167; Lubatkin – Schulze – Ling – Dino (2005) 313-330.

the payment of an independent salary for the work performed,[50] or psychological factors such as the relationship between the founder and the successor; the delay is also noticeable when transferring the ownership of the company (or its shares or holdings) to future successors.[51]

3.3.1   Transaction Costs and the Choice of the Successor

There is an information cost which corresponds to the resources that the deceased must invest in as a means to finding out more about the person (or persons) to whom he may bequeath a particular asset or assets, or the entire estate (in our case, the family business), that is, the extent to which the successor's character encompasses the characteristics valued by the deceased and which would make the deceased want to institute him or her as successor.[52] Savings are made on these costs when legislation stipulates that the heir must be the first-born child. The right of primogeniture entails lower costs, as was the case with succession in the "homestead".[53] Such right having disappeared, the deceased must endeavour to determine which of the possible successors is the most suitable to acquire all or a portion of his or her estate.[54]

At this point, we must take into account the type of family business we are dealing with,[55] since information and evaluation costs in relation to the appointment of the successor will vary. In fact, in a family business with a straightforward structure, such as an establishment open to the public, the appointment costs of the successor are unlikely to be very high, since the person or persons

---

[50]   One of the inherent risks within a family business is the overlapping of family relationships with business relationships, which may have both advantages and disadvantages; among the latter, we may highlight the lack of a salary allocation for the performance of a specific labour or professional activity. See Harvey (1999) 61-72.

[51]   Even though under some legal systems the regulation of forced shares may be disadvantageous for the transfer *mortis causa* of the family business, we do not think that this is the case under Catalan law due, firstly, to the *legítima corta* forced share system and, secondly, due to the possibility of paying the forced share in cash, even if there is none in the estate, which is a result of conceiving the forced share as *pars valoris* (art. 451-11 CC Cat). With respect to the relationship between the forced share system and the handover of the family business, see López Burniol (1999) 48; Parra Lucán (2009) 481-554.

[52]   From a contractual perspective, in relation to information costs, see Alfaro (1996) 131 ff., 141; Le Breton-Miller – Miller – Steier (2004) 305-328, 308-309.

[53]   See section 3.2 of this paper.

[54]   From the perspective of company law, see Fuentes (2007) 289 ff. In practice, the founder of a family business often transfers ownership to the "chosen" son or daughter, irrespective of his or her skills or contribution to the success of the company. See Staurou – Kleonthous – Anastasiou (2005) 191. In many cases, the fact that a sole successor is chosen in order to avoid the disappearance of the family business leads to a preference of male over female, which represents a major obstacle to the appointment of women to management positions within these enterprises. See Parra Lucán (2009) 538.

[55]   Miller – Steier – Le Breton-Miller (2003) 513-531.

appointed as successors are often part of the deceased's close family circle.[56]
Hence, the deceased already has a certain amount of information which serves
as a sufficient basis on which to make his or her decision, since the successor is
often linked to the company, works within it, occupies an important position[57]
or, depending on the legal form adopted by the company, may even already hold
a certain amount of shares.[58] Moreover, during the deceased's lifetime, even at
the end of his or her professional life, the person or persons who will take over
the family business upon his or her death can be trained.[59] The deceased may
already have a certain amount of information which serves as a sufficient basis
on which to make a decision without incurring excessive information costs. The
current owner is also familiar with the status of the company, the guidelines
on future objectives, the future planning and the strategies for avoiding conflict
once the successor has been chosen.[60] This information is held by the deceased-
founder and not always by the successor(s).[61]

However, in a family business with a more complex structure (medium or
large company), comprising various family lines, the discussion and subsequent selection of the successor (or successors) will be preceded by an inevita-
ble negotiation phase, since there will normally be various "candidates"[62] and
future strategies must be agreed by the existing family organisations,[63] such as
the Family Assembly, Council or Advisory Board, to cite those most frequently
encountered.[64] Possible future effects of said choice must also be foreseen.[65] In
such cases, the resources invested in gathering information and negotiating
the choice of the successor or successors (transaction costs) may be considerable, even though the reputation of the "chosen" person yields complementary
information about his or her behaviour and professional conduct.[66] The fact that
a family protocol, as mentioned previously, may exist must also be taken into

---

[56] It must not be forgotten that only certain persons can enter into succession agreements among each
other (art. 431-2 CC Cat).

[57] Amat (2004) 127 ff.; Fuentes (2007) 257 ff.

[58] The legal basis of the family business may certainly be heterogeneous: from sole proprietorship to
corporation. See Cerdà (2004) 99 ff; Grima (2004) 145 ff.

[59] Gallo (2004) 115 ff.

[60] Barbeito – Guillén – Martínez – Domínguez (2004) 29.

[61] It should be borne in mind that, according to the study carried out by Professor Gimeno Sandig, 51% of
subsequent generations do not participate in the succession of the family business into which they have
most likely already been incorporated. See section 3.1 of this paper.

[62] Brockhaus (2004) 167 ff. highlights the difficulties inherent to choosing a successor and the related
negotiations when various family lines are involved.

[63] This approach would allow for the growth in the use of a Catalan provision that is rarely applied in practice. I refer to the appointment of an heir by the deceased's spouse or cohabitant (arts. 424-1 to 424-4 CC
Cat) or two closest relatives (arts. 424-5 to 424-10 CC Cat).

[64] Le Breton-Miller – Miller – Steier (2004) 316; Rodríguez (2007) 1144.

[65] Le Breton-Miller – Miller – Steier (2004) 315-316.

[66] Brockhaus (2004) 168.

account, since the strategy to be followed during succession *mortis causa* has been duly negotiated and established therein. One must not forget, however, that only 25% of family businesses have a protocol in place,[67] thus, if there are no other "shareholders' agreements" governing these aspects and, in particular, the transfer *mortis causa* of the company, the entire issue in all its complexity will be raised at a later date, which may result in very high transaction costs.[68] In short, the institution of a successor in the family business is not an occasional or isolated act; rather it must be analysed according to its context, whereby a series of preliminary negotiations are held and other family members may take part. Therefore, it makes sense for the legislator to have acknowledged that, in a notarised family protocol,[69] under which the company's objectives and strategies have been agreed,[70] the institution of an heir may likewise be agreed (art. 431-8 CC Cat).

3.3.2 Economic Costs Derived from the Deceased's Change of Mind

In practice, the transfer of ownership of the family business, by means of donations (arts. 531-7 ff. CC Cat) or even of succession agreements incorporating an *inter vivos* donation of certain assets (arts. 431-19.1 and 431-29.3 CC Cat), is not often undertaken during the lifetime of the current owner. It is more common to encounter a strategic[71] announcement or promise to a person who will be named as (universal or particular) successor to ownership of the family business in which he or she most likely already works. The objective is therefore to influence the behaviour of the future successor so that he or she becomes more involved and identifies more with the corporate culture of the family business. The extent of influence on the behaviour of the future successor may still be greater than that provided by a mere promise, depending on whether or not such a promise is enforceable.[72] The extent of influence is greater if the "successor" is appointed as such in the will. However, the successor's behaviour is more heavily influenced if he or she is instituted in the succession agreement,[73] whether as heir (inheritance pact) or as "particular" succes-

---

[67] See section 2.1 of this paper.

[68] Alfaro (1996) 145 ff.

[69] Tena (1992) 10 ff.

[70] In relation to these agreements, academic opinion often distinguishes between "relationship agreements", "function agreements" and "organisation agreements". See Paz-Ares (2003) 3-4.

[71] On donations, see: Bernheim – Shleifer – Summers (1985) 1045-1076; Perozek (1998) 423-445; Shavell (1991) 401-421.

[72] Kull (1992) 39-65. Recoverable extra-contractual damage may, in any event, be sustained as provided under art. 1911 of the Spanish CC. See Pintens (2001) 628-648, 644. The "trust cost" may have been incurred in such case whereby an opportunity has been allowed to pass by. See Eisenberg (1979) 18 ff.

[73] In favour of the introduction of succession agreements within the scope of the Spanish CC, see, for all, Sánchez Aristi (2006) 477-543.

sor (i.e. the beneficiary in a succession agreement that does not comprise the entire estate). In the latter case, the extent of influence is greater if the subject in question is party to the agreement (art. 431-2 CC Cat) than if he or she is only a third party beneficiary (art. 431-3 CC Cat) since, in the former case, the successor's consent is required in order to be able to terminate the agreement by means of mutual rescission (art. 431-12 CC Cat); whereas in the second case, consent is not required, since no right to succession is acquired until the demise of the deceased, because there has been no acceptance (art. 431-3.1 CC Cat). In both cases irrevocability applies (arts. 431-18 and 431-30.5 CC Cat), as a general rule inherent to the succession agreement, insofar as it constitutes a contractual framework, as opposed to wills, which are essentially revocable (art. 422-8.1 CC Cat).

It would therefore seem, from the deceased's perspective, on first approach, that the succession agreement is a legal instrument for succession planning which may motivate the successor more because of the fact that it is carried out during the deceased's lifetime. However, is the succession agreement which is, generally speaking, irrevocable, an economically efficient succession planning instrument? This is where doubts begin to arise. Firstly, from the successor's perspective, "already" knowing that he or she is the owner of the family business may well produce the opposite effect, that is, that the successor has no incentive to behave in the desired way and changes his or her attitude towards the family business[74] –albeit not in such a way for this change in attitude or behaviour to constitute grounds for the institution to be revoked (art. 431-13 in relation to art. 412-3 CC Cat); the successor may change his or her goals and personal objectives, or be influenced by third parties, which would result in a loss of interest in the company, thereby eventually giving rise to the opposite effect of what is sought. Other changes may also occur, such as the impact on the choice of company employees, potential clients, the company's reputation or share values altering, a specific legislative change that affects the family business in a certain way; or the onset of a serious illness that leads to a change in fundamental strategies. It may also be the case that the deceased is overcome with "fear" of being left without sufficient assets on account of the uncertainty inherent in the final phase of human life,[75] realises his or her misjudgement or underestimation of reality, and over-optimism and excessive confidence in both him or herself and in the choice are subsequently dispelled, forcing careful reassessment of the situation. Any number of other circumstances may lead to the deceased (business owner) changing his or her wishes. If no provision has been made for this under the succession agreement (art. 431-14.1 a CC Cat states that grounds for revocation of the succession agreement must be expressly agreed), it may be difficult to successfully plead an unforeseeable change in circumstances (art. 431-14.1 d CC Cat), given the restrictive interpretation sustained by the Supreme

---

74 This is one of the reasons that justify the individual avoiding the donation of assets during his or her lifetime and postponing it until his or her death. See Shavell (2004) 60.

75 Davies (1981) 561-577.

Court.[76] As a result, and as a means to avoiding irrevocability, the potential risks inherent to the succession agreement itself must be foreseen. Such foresight will need to have already been achieved upon entering into the succession agreement and requires that certain clauses be established in the succession agreement, such as those governing the specific grounds for revocation agreed by the parties (art. 431-14.1 a CC Cat), burdens or purposes (art. 431-6 CC Cat),[77] trusts (art. 431-5.1 CC Cat) or reversals (art. 431-5.1 CC Cat), amongst others, which facilitate the process in case of the deceased changing his or her wishes,[78] in other words, which entail a lower economic cost in such cases. Information costs and, therefore, transaction costs[79] will already have been incurred.

It is, however, impossible to foresee all risks, and even the foreseen ones may never occur, whereas others occur unforeseen. It is therefore economically inefficient to seek to foresee all possible future events that facilitate the process of revoking the succession agreement ("expressly agreed causes"), since very high information costs would be incurred on account of the fact that it requires investment in many resources in order to gather information on all possible future events.[80] If, therefore, not all risks are foreseeable and an unforeseen event occurs that brings about a change in the deceased's wishes, the legal channel open to the deceased is to eliminate the appointment of the successor by means of mutual rescission (art. 431-12.1 CC Cat), which requires the agreement of all parties to the succession agreement that are affected by the amendment or termination (art. 431-12.2 CC Cat). This would therefore require that the parties are, firstly, informed thereof beforehand, and secondly, that they agree to terminate or amend the succession agreement, which would incur new economic costs derived from investing resources in gathering information on the events having occurred, on the amendment or termination of the agreement and how they may be affected by this.

Hence, it would seem that, generally speaking, succession agreements are not sufficiently "efficient" legal instruments so as to encourage people to enter into them. In practice, this will most likely mean that succession agreements are

---

[76] Egea (2009) 1127-1128. Under Aragonese law, however, the unforeseen inefficiency of the agreement due to a change in circumstances is taken into account. See Bayod (2005) 1-10.

[77] For critique on the outlook provided under art. 431-6 CC Cat with respect to "burdens, conditions and *purposes*", see García Rubio – Herrero Oviedo (2008) 465 ff.

[78] Rodríguez Aparicio (2004) 306, mentions the need to periodically review the business owner's will so as to reflect the economic circumstances of the family business.

[79] We must base this on the fact that, even though the succession agreement is a unilateral agreement [see Egea (2009) 17; Navas (2009) 5-7], it falls into the category of contracts and, on this basis, the same conceptual tools used to analyse any other contract from the perspective of the economic analysis of law (opportunity costs, transaction costs) may be used, applying the appropriate adaptations, since it does not concern the exchange of goods and/or services, which is the paradigm of the economic analysis of contractual law.

[80] Posner (1998) 93.

not executed. We may also conclude that succession agreements are not "efficient" enough so as to influence the successor's behaviour.

3.4   Possible "Efficient" Instruments for Succession Within the Family Business

The above statement requires clarification, since there is a type
of succession agreement that may indeed be sufficiently efficient as a means to
organising succession in the family business: In other words, the cost derived
from entering into it is lower than the benefit/utility that may be generated,
although it does have its drawbacks. We are referring to the *preventive succession
agreement* in which the heir is instituted or preventive succession agreements
referring only to certain assets (art. 431-21 CC Cat). These agreements are unilaterally revocable through execution of another succession agreement or even of a
notarised nuncupative will, since their essential purpose is to avoid intestacy.[81]
Hence, certain risks having occurred, such as those outlined previously, which
may change the deceased's wishes, all that remains to be done is to execute a
new will or agreement (arts. 422-8.1 and 431-23 CC Cat). However, as pointed
out under art. 431-21.3 CC Cat, it must be clearly expressed that the succession
agreement is of such a nature and, therefore, revocable. We believe that this
precept accepts either an express provision by the parties stating the preventive
nature of the agreement, or that this may be clearly and categorically deduced
on establishing the right of revocation. In contrast to some academic opinion,[82]
we do not think it is possible for there to be a succession agreement that is not
preventive but which, nonetheless, provides therein, the option of *ad libitum* revocation by any or just one of the parties, as this would leave the validity and fulfilment at the discretion of one of the parties (art. 1256 Spanish CC); moreover,
it would distort the meaning and purpose of the succession agreement.[83] If no
such preventive provision has been made, the agreement may not be revoked
and it will be classified as an "ordinary" succession agreement; that is, subject to
the general grounds for revocation provided by law (art. 431-14 CC Cat).

The cost of preventive provision, in one form or another, does not exist in
the will. Moreover, the other executors must be notified of the revocation of the
preventive succession agreement, bar exemptions, which is not required when
revoking a will (art. 431-21.2 CC Cat). To this we must also add the economic cost
inherent to a certain type of succession agreement, called reciprocal or mutual;
we are referring to the cost derived from the need to obtain the consent of the
other party to the agreement in order to be able to dispose of the assets even
inter vivos. This will inevitably incur transaction costs (art. 431-25.3 CC Cat),[84]
which are also not incurred under a will. On the other hand, succession agree-

---

[81] Egea (2009) 1152-1153.

[82] Egea (2009) 1125, 1157.

[83] Del Pozo – Vaquer – Bosch (2009) 318.

[84] Egea (2009) 1153.

ments, although preventive, whether they institute an heir or refer to certain assets only, will always be subject to formal requirements (art. 431-7 CC Cat).

One possible alternative, in terms of efficiency, depending on the legal regulation laid down, is the *joint* will. Joint wills are not accepted under Catalan law or the Spanish CC, even though most academic opinion favours the repeal of the prohibition of the joint will in the latter[85] and the inclusion of a provision to this effect in the CC Cat,[86] as has been done under Aragonese law without any problems (arts. 91 and 102-107 Law 1/1999, 24 February, on succession *mortis causa*, hereinafter LASMC).[87] This type of will is essentially revocable; it is not even necessary to make such a provision when drafting the will, as must be done, conversely, for the preventive provision in a succession agreement (art. 431-23.3 CC Cat), but still the joint will allows for a certain degree of agreement between family members or relatives when deciding on who will be the successor to the family business. It may even be a holographic will (art. 96 LASCM), for which there would be no drafting costs; instead, this kind of cost is incurred when executing preventive succession agreements. A drawback lies in the unilateral revocability of the joint will in cases where said will is reciprocal. But this would depend, however, on the publicity or notice regime established for said revocation; i.e., it may require a notarised document or acknowledgement of having received notice by the other executor of the will so that the revocation does not become effective without his or her knowledge,[88] although the validity of the revocation need not depend on said knowledge, where a notification issued by a notary to the other executor of the will is sufficient (art. 106.4 LASCM). Depending on the legal regime governing these issues, the costs attributable thereto may be lower than those derived from the revocation of preventive succession agreements.

The economic costs we have just referred to do not accrue if one decides to make an ordinary will. The information phase (transaction costs) and choice of the successor always exist, whether one makes a will or enters into an agreement, but subsequent costs may be circumvented, such as those deriving from a change in the deceased's wishes. Thus the will is regulated more efficiently than the succession agreement. Wills, as we know, are essentially revocable (art. 422-8.1 CC Cat), regardless of the reason for doing so – even a will that merely revokes the previous one is valid (arts. 422-8 and 422-9 CC Cat) – and this facilitates the adaptation of the future succession to unforeseen changes that may arise within the family business, the deceased or the successor's character. No notification of the revocation is required, and the executor may dispose of his or her assets *inter vivos* in any way he or she sees fit. It may also be executed in holographic form (art. 421-17 CC Cat), thereby saving on notarial costs. It entails, in short, a greater economic cost saving in relation to the other two instruments

---

[85] Castiella (1993) 35-53; García Vicente (2006) 289-299; Magariños (2005) 20.

[86] For all, see Salvador Coderch – López Burniol (2009) 70.

[87] BOA No. 26, 4 March 1999. For academic opinion, see Tobajas (2000) 693 ff.

[88] García Vicente (2006) 295.

that we have covered: the preventive succession agreement and the joint will.
Therefore, the will is the most efficient instrument for estate planning, since it
provides greater utility at a lower cost, which shows that its legal regulation is
efficient as well.[89]

It must be noted that both the will (joint or ordinary) and the preventive
succession agreement, because of being revocable, serve the objective of motivat-
ing the successor in his or her involvement in the family business; acting otherwise could lead to the loss of all rights over the estate or over part of it.

4   Final Conclusions

Based on the foregoing, the future points to the scant practical application that succession agreements are likely to have. Only those agreements in which costs are kept to a minimum, as may be the case with preventive
succession agreements, will have a certain amount of relevance, although not
to the same extent as wills have and are expected to have. Therefore, in spite of
amendments introduced by the Catalan legislator, the legal regulation of succession agreements is not efficient enough to govern succession within the family
business.

We must also conclude that, in spite of the precedence – and even incompatibility – of succession agreements over testamentary succession, in practice, the
regulation set forth under art. 431-23 CC Cat shall have little, if any, practical
relevance. It should also be kept in mind that, pursuant to art. 431-23.2 CC Cat,
the exception to this rule is the preventive inheritance pact. The legal regulation
which generates lower costs and which, as a result, is the most economically
efficient is the regulation of the will,[90] which correlates both with the statistics
provided[91] and with the "rational" behaviour of the average citizen as defined by
economists.

From a different perspective, we must note that succession agreements do
not constitute an insurmountable obstacle to the unification of the law of succession in Europe, particularly if we take into account their scant practical application. As we know, there is a fundamental distinction whereby countries with a
Roman-Germanic tradition accept the inheritance contract (*Erbvertrag*), unlike
their Roman-French counterparts,[92] although alternative concepts have been
sought in the latter, such as, in France, irrevocable donations or the contrac-

---

[89] In terms of flexibility of the will versus the succession agreement, see Salvador Coderch – López Burniol
      (2009) 70.

[90] And this, bearing in mind that one of the characteristics of the most recent legislative amendments in
      relation to the will is the softening of testamentary formal requirements, resulting in enhanced "effi-
      ciency" over other inheritance schemes.

[91] See section 3 of this paper.

[92] Cámara (2003) 1229; De Waal (2007) 16-17; Grimaldi (2001) 356.

tual institution of the heir under marriage settlements.[93] English law refers to "contract to leave a gift" or "contract not to revoke a will" as legal concepts that may have similar legal effects to the succession agreement.[94] In other words, the different approach towards succession agreements should not hinder the unification of the law of succession based on freedom of testation, which is acknowledged by all legal regulations governing our area of influence.[95]

---

[93] Loi n° 2006-728 du 23 juin 2006, portant réforme des successions et des libéralités (JO dated 24 June 2006). For academic opinion, see Delfosse – Peniguel (2006) 260 ff.; Pereña (2005) 2485-2500.

[94] See, in this same book, the contribution by R. Kerridge; Anderson (2006) 1262-1263; Hiram (2006); Pintens (2001) 644; Parry – Kerridge (2009) 95-96, 6.01.

[95] Van Erp (2007); De Waal (2007) 16-17; Vaquer (2009) 556 ff.; Verbeke – Leleu (1994) 335-350.

PART III

National Perspectives on the Law of Succession in the 21st Century

CHAPTER 7

Freedom of Testation in England and Wales

Roger Kerridge

1 Introduction

Although the United Kingdom has one single tax régime, England (including Wales), Scotland and Northern Ireland each has its own set of laws relating to succession. This chapter is concerned with England (including Wales) which will, to avoid the need for repetition, henceforth be referred to simply as 'England'. 'English law' in this chapter means the law applicable in England and Wales.

It is generally said, and generally accepted, that English law applies the principle of freedom of testation, so that, when someone dies he is free to do whatever he likes with his property. In fact, few things in the world of the law are as simple as at first they appear, and different legal systems are, in the rules they apply, seldom as distinct from one another as at first they look. The idea that English law provides, or has ever provided, for complete freedom of testation is one which is, at best, open to question. The general rule of freedom of testation, in so far as it has existed, has always been subject to qualifications, or restrictions, of one sort or another, though they have varied in form and extent over the years.

2 History

Until the early years of the twentieth century, English law applied radically different rules to succession to real property and succession to personal property. 'Real' property (or 'realty') was property which could be recovered specifically by real action, and the main form of real property was freehold land. 'Personal' property (or 'personalty') included not only moveables, but also land held by lease. From the early Middle Ages, it became established, for reasons which are not now entirely clear, that jurisdiction over succession to personalty belonged to the ecclesiastical courts, while jurisdiction over realty lay with the common law courts. England seems to have been one of the few jurisdictions, or possibly the sole jurisdiction, in Western Europe, where the ecclesiastical courts obtained this control over succession. And it seems to have been the Church which encouraged the faithful to make wills which dealt with their personalty.[1] Total freedom to dispose of personalty on death was established throughout the greater part of England during the Middle Ages. Having said that, it was not extended to the Province of York[2] until 1692, to Wales until 1696, and to London until 1724. So it was only from 1724 onwards that there

---

[1]   A will of personalty was, in former times, more usually referred to as a 'testament'. A 'testament' disposed of personalty while a 'will' disposed of, or attempted to dispose of, realty. Having said this, the terminology has never been strict and the umbrella term nowadays is 'will'. The term 'testament' is used today in the phrase which appears at the start of most formally drafted wills, 'Last Will and Testament'.

[2]   I.e. the Archdiocese of York – most of northern England.

was freedom of testation over personalty throughout the whole of England and
Wales. And it is worth noting that until the enactment of 'An Act for the Prevention of Frauds and Perjuries' commonly called the Statute of Frauds,[3] in 1677,
testaments of personalty required no formalities. They could be oral and were
often, if not usually, spoken shortly before death in the presence of some reliable
person. And who more reliable than the local priest? He could then confirm the
deceased's wishes which would often have included a gift to the Church. The
double control, whereby the clergy evidenced the making of testaments and the
ecclesiastical courts then sat in judgment on the validity of dispositions, helps
to explain much concerning the power and wealth of the Church in England
from the Early Middle Ages onwards. Freedom of testation, freedom *not* to leave
property to one's family, would have suited both the Church and all those in holy
orders.

But there was no freedom of testation over realty in England in the Middle
Ages. In fact, there appears to have been some doubt as to the position until
the thirteenth century, but it became established by then that on someone's
death, his realty could not be devised[4] but that it had to pass to the heir – usually
the eldest son.[5] Realty (freehold land) could not be devised by will *but* those
who did not want all their realty to pass to their heirs sought ways of overcom-
ing the problem. This is what lead to the creation and development of the use,
the precursor of the trust. The use, which was upheld by Chancery, enabled
landowners both to avoid feudal incidents (a form of tax) and to control what
happened to their property, including their realty, after their deaths. So, landowners could not devise their freeholds on death, but could achieve the same
result in a slightly roundabout way by creating uses while they were alive. A
principal attraction of uses to landowners was that they assisted in the avoidance of feudal incidents. But while this made them attractive to landowners, it
meant that the Crown was bent on their destruction. In 1535, Parliament passed
the Statute of Uses,[6] the effect of which was to place severe limitations upon the
effectiveness of uses, and, in particular, to restore to the Crown the revenue lost
by the avoidance of feudal incidents. The 1535 Act was *not* a popular measure. It
was, as Maitland put it, 'forced upon an extremely unwilling Parliament by an
extremely strong-willed king'.[7] King Henry's problem was that there was a limit
to how much support he could risk forfeiting. He was engaged in a potentially

---

[3]   29 Car. II c.3.

[4]   A 'devise' is a gift of realty by will, and the corresponding verb is 'to devise'. The recipient of a devise is
'a devisee'.

[5]   The 'heir' in English law is quite different from the 'heir' in Roman law. The heir in English law was
not a universal successor, but the person who took the realty. Among persons of the same degree, males
took before females and, among males, elder took before younger. So, if a deceased left children, his
eldest son was his heir.

[6]   27 Hen. VIII c.10.

[7]   Maitland (1936) 35. The king was, of course, Henry VIII. He could be very persuasive. He executed not
only two of his six wives, but also a number of his ministers.

damaging dispute with the Church of Rome. He was in the process of suppressing the monasteries, whose wealth he coveted, and he needed the support of the
landowning classes, the people whom Parliament represented. That is why, in
1540, Henry permitted Parliament to enact the Statute of Wills,[8] an Act which
entitled freeholders to devise their freehold lands[9] on death. This was the pay-
back for passing the Statute of Uses and was a victory for the landowning class.
Freehold land was, thenceforth freely devisable.

The 1540 Act appeared to usher in a period of almost total freedom of testation in England[10] but to look simply at the rules made by the judges and the
rules enacted by Parliament is not to see the whole picture. It is not easy for any
society to survive with a system which permits total, or almost total, freedom
of testation. True freedom of testation means, by definition, the freedom to act
in a way which is arbitrary, and which many people would regard as unfair. To
permit this to all owners of property over a long period is something which
no advanced legal system is likely to contemplate. And in what at first sight
appears as a curious reversal of rôles, it was the trust (as the use came to be
renamed after 1535) which acted as a fetter on freedom of testation. The Statute
of Uses of 1535 had been designed to prevent the avoidance by landowners of
feudal incidents. Feudal dues were, in effect, abolished by Parliament during
the run-up to the English Civil War and the Interregnum in the middle years
of the seventeenth century. And, when the monarchy was restored in 1660, the
Crown was obliged, as part of the overall settlement, to confirm, by the Tenures
Abolition Act of 1660[11] that all burdens from feudal dues were to cease to apply.
This meant that the 1535 Act no longer served its original purpose, and no one
had an interest in opposing the resurrection of the use, although it was slightly
disguised by being renamed the trust. As Professor Simpson put it: 'The history
of the steps by which trusts came to be recognized forms an intriguing but
somewhat obscure chapter of legal history'.[12] But trusts *were* recognised by the
latter part of the seventeenth century and they acted as a significant restraint on
freedom of testation.[13]

---

[8]   32 Hen. VIII c. 1.

[9]   There was still one relatively minor limitation under the Statute of Wills, it related to those who held by
      military tenure. This limitation disappeared in 1660.

[10] There were still limits on the freedom to bequeath personalty in the Province of York, in Wales and in
      London, and these lasted until 1724 – see above.

[11] Car. II, c. 24. This extraordinarily ill-drawn statute confirmed legislation which had been passed in the
      run up to the Civil War and during the Interregnum.

[12] Simpson (1986) 200.

[13] Maitland's description of what happened to the Statute of Uses was more colourful than Simpson's.
      He referred to it as '...that marvellous monument of legislative futility, the Statute of Uses, the statute
      through which not merely coaches and four, but whole judicial processions with javelin-men and trum-
      peters have passed and re-passed in triumph.' See, Fisher (1911) para 273.

3 Trusts as a Restraint on Freedom of Testation

What was developed in England, at the end of the seventeenth century, and perfected during the eighteenth century, was the strict settlement. Uses had been brought back to life and renamed trusts, but there were good policy reasons which dictated that nobody should be permitted to create trusts which restricted the power of alienation for excessively long periods. The judges developed a series of rules which were designed to prevent the creation of perpetual trusts, and the two principal rules were the so-called Modern Rule Against Perpetuities, fashioned by Lord Chancellor Nottingham in *The Duke of Norfolk's case* in 1681[14] and the Rule in *Whitby v Mitchell*[15] otherwise known as the Rule Against Double Possibilities. The former Rule was the more significant, and was to the effect that a future interest would be void unless it was certain to vest within a maximum period of a life in being plus 21 years. There is insufficient space here to go into the details of 'vesting', but the effect of the Rule was that property could only be tied up for one generation at a time. The trick, if it is appropriate to call it that, with a strict settlement, was to re-settle the property once every generation. If a life tenant died leaving a successor who had a freehold, or an entail,[16] such a successor would be free to do what he liked. But the system operated in such a way as normally to prevent anyone from getting into this position. When an eldest son reached majority, or possibly when he married, he would be summoned by his father and persuaded to agree that he should give up the freehold or entailed interest which he would obtain on his father's death, and should accept instead a life interest. In exchange for this, he would be provided with an immediate income (something he would need), and so the family property would be tied up for another generation, with modest provision for the younger sons and the daughters.

This form of strict settlement, the brainchild of the conveyancer Sir Orlando Bridgman at the end of the seventeenth century, lasted right through the eighteenth and nineteenth centuries and only fell from favour early in the twentieth century when Estate Duty, a tax on death, caused it to lose ground to other more tax-effective arrangements.

But the point that is being made here is that, during the eighteenth and nineteenth centuries, there was no true freedom of testation for most substantial landowners in England and Wales. Most large landed estates would have been preserved intact and would have passed from father to eldest son. Yes, a man was free to make a will devising and bequeathing all his property to whomsoever he wished *but* the greater part, in many cases almost the entirety, of the landed estate a man appeared to own would in fact be held in a settlement of which he was merely the tenant for life, and so he would have no power on his death to control what happened to it.

---

[14] Ch. Cas 1, 2 Swanston 454.

[15] (1890) 44 Ch.D 85.

[16] Entailed land passed only to the descendants of the original grantee, and not to his heirs general, i.e. not to collaterals. But a tenant in tail could, while living, bar the entail and turn it into a freehold.

The point is graphically illustrated by the nineteenth century reported cases where wills are being challenged on the grounds of lack of capacity, undue influence, lack of knowledge and approval, or lack of due execution. Before 1858, any such challenge would be made in one of the ecclesiastical courts if the property involved were personalty, whereas it would be made in a common law court if the property were realty. The reported cases are almost all in the ecclesiastical courts – usually the Prerogative Court, the court of the Province of Canterbury, which sat in London at Doctors' Commons.[17] There appears to have been only one reported case during this period[18] which involved realty and that was *Boyse v Rossbrough*.[19] There were a large number of cases involving personalty. It is easy nowadays for somebody reading these cases to fail to note that they did not involve realty. Take, for example, the very well-known case of *Barry v Butlin*[20] where a father had disinherited his son in favour of the father's solicitor, his doctor and his butler. The son challenged the will and his challenge failed. That was the standard result in this type of case, especially where one of the beneficiaries under the disputed will was a lawyer, the legal profession was good at looking after itself. But what is not so obvious on a quick reading is that the will covered *only* the testator's personalty. The realty was held in a strict settlement and the son took it anyway. Whatever happened, the father was not able to devise the land to anyone, it passed to his son, whether or not he wanted it to. The value of the personalty in dispute in this case was somewhere between £13,000 and £14,000; while the realty provided an annual income of between £3,000 and £4,000; meaning that it would have had a capital value in excess of £100,000. In other words, somewhere between 80% and 90% of the old man's apparent property was held in settlement and this would have been quite standard in those days. So called 'freedom of testation' was hugely circumscribed by the existence of settlements.

Strict settlements were largely for the benefit of eldest sons. What may well be the best-known of all early nineteenth century novels is Jane Austen's *Pride and Prejudice* at the centre of which is the so-called 'entail' which prevents Mr Bennett from providing properly for his daughters on his death. In fact, the arrangement in question would probably have been not an 'entail' but a strict settlement, but the terminology would not have bothered most of the book's readers. The point is that the property was *not* freely devisable by will.[21] And, quite apart from the strict settlements which favoured eldest sons, there were

---

[17] The doctors were not medical doctors, they were the ecclesiastical lawyers, the advocates who practised in the ecclesiastical courts – the doctors of law or of civil law of the universities of Cambridge and Oxford.

[18] The period begins only at the start of the nineteenth century because cases in the ecclesiastical courts were not reported until about 1800.

[19] (1856/7) 6 HL Cas 2.

[20] (1837/8) 1 Curt 614, 2 Moo PC 480.

[21] There is a complication in relation to the strict settlement in *Pride and Prejudice*, and it relates to the impact of the Modern Rule Against Perpetuities and as to who could have wanted to create a settlement

marriage settlements designed to protect women's property from their husbands and to ensure that it was passed on to their children and not squandered. Again, this meant that the property in question would not have passed by will – it was outside the sphere of so-called freedom of testation.

And quite apart from settlements and trusts, there were, in the eighteenth and nineteenth centuries, two other restrictions on freedom of testation. The Mortmain Act and the literal approach to the construction of wills.

4   The Mortmain Act

In 1736 Parliament passed *An Act to Restrain the Disposition of Lands Whereby the Same Become Unalienable*, a statute more commonly referred to as the Mortmain Act.[22] The Act provided that from and after 24th June, the Midsummer Quarter Day, 1736, no land was to be devised to charity[23] by will. A gift of land to charity would be valid only if made more than a year before the donor's death. Although the Act began by appearing to cover gifts of land to all charities, it went on, in section 4, to state that it did *not* extend to the two universities,[24] to any of their constituent colleges or to the three best-known, and richest, schools in England – Eton, Winchester and Westminster. The Act was, in fact, directed against the one major charity which it did not name, the richest of all the charities, the Church. What lay behind the Act, apart from a general mood of anti-clericalism, was the suggestion that greedy clergymen were hovering around the death-beds of the rich and were persuading them to execute wills to the dis-benefit of their families and to the great advantage of an organisation which, in the eyes of those who sat in Parliament, needed no further financial support. The significance of 'land' in the scheme of things is that land was, in the days before the Industrial Revolution, the principal form of wealth. The object of the 1736 Act was to prevent people from making significant dispositions to the Church on death.

It is worth thinking about how the system of strict settlements and the Mortmain Act complemented one another. Marriage settlements and strict settlements would have applied particularly to those who were married and to those who had children. The Mortmain Act would have applied to those who had fewer close family ties and who might have been tempted, in their concerns about the after-life, to leave property to an outside organisation (the Church) rather than to retain it within the wider family.

The Mortmain Act 1736 was eventually repealed in 1891, but had been in place for 155 years and its effect during that time, though nowadays often overlooked, must have been significant.

---

whereby Mr Bennett had a life interest, followed by a remainder to a seemingly distant cousin with a different surname – but there is no space to discuss this here.

[22]   9 Geo. II c. 36.

[23]   I.e. devised to trustees to hold for charity.

[24]   There *were* only two universities in England before the nineteenth century.

5 The 'Construction' (or Interpretation) of Wills

Then there was, until very recently, another disguised restraint on true freedom of testation and this concerned the *interpretation*, or as it is more traditionally called, the *construction* of wills. There are two basic approaches to the interpretation wills. On the one hand, there is the *literal* (or *grammatical*) approach which concentrates on the 'ordinary' meaning of the words in the will; on the other hand, there is the *intentional* (or *inferential*, or *liberal*, or *purposive*) approach, which focuses on the testator's intention. The conflict between the two approaches is the Roman law conflict between the Proculians and the Sabinians,[25] what F.V. Hawkins, in a paper published by the Juridical Society in 1863[26] called 'the fundamental antithesis' between expression and intention, between the letter and the spirit, and it occurs whenever legal texts fall to be construed.

There was in England, during the eighteenth and nineteenth centuries, a running battle between the proponents of the two approaches. The leading literalists were Sir James Parke, who later became Lord Wensleydale, and Sir James Wigram, who wrote a textbook on *The Interpretation of Wills* which ran to five editions.[27] In the rival camp were Sir Edward Sugden, who became Lord St Leonards, and Hawkins himself, whose textbook has also run to five editions. During the latter part of the twentieth century, the intentional approach has slowly but surely gained ground, *but* in the two earlier centuries the literal approach tended to prevail. It was the approach favoured by Chancery lawyers,[28] and it was Chancery lawyers who interpreted wills.[29] But the significance of this, in the present context, is that, whenever the literal and the intentional approaches produce different results (and they do produce different results in almost all disputes concerning the interpretation of wills) the literal approach gives a result *not*

---

[25] The Proculians and Sabinians were two schools of Roman jurists during the imperial period. They held differing views on many topics, including construction.

[26] Hawkins's paper was read before the Juridical Society in 1860 and published in Volume II of the Society's Papers, in London, in 1863. It was then republished as Appendix C to Prof. Thayer's *Preliminary Treatise on Evidence at the Common Law*, Boston, 1898.

[27] The first edition was published in 1831 and the 5th (which was by C.P. Sanger), in 1914. All editions were published in London and all from the 2nd, in 1834, were respectfully dedicated to Sir James Parke.

[28] There have, altogether, been three sets of lawyers who have practiced before the English courts, the common lawyers, the chancery lawyers and the ecclesiastical lawyers. The distinction between the common lawyers and the chancery lawyer was less marked than the pre-1858 distinction between both of them, on the one hand, and the ecclesiastical lawyers, on the other: but it was, and is, a clear distinction. Chancery lawyers deal with technically complex areas of the law, such as trusts and tax, common lawyers deal with contract, tort and crime. But there are, of course, areas of overlap, especially in the field of commercial law.

[29] The *interpretation* of wills has always belonged to Chancery, *not* to the court which has granted probate. In 1971, contentious probate was, itself, moved to Chancery, but common form probate, where there is no dispute, is still dealt with in the Family Division, which is the successor to the Court of Probate and so to the ecclesiastical courts.

intended by the testator.[30] And this, in the present context, amounts to an indirect infringement of the principle of freedom of testation. If a testator does not use the 'correct' words (the 'usual' words) to express his intention, his intention will be thwarted. This becomes clear if one looks at Wigram's book. The 'correct meaning' or 'usual meaning' (or, as Wigram would have put it, 'the strict and primary acceptation') of the word 'child' was, in the eighteenth and nineteenth centuries, held to be 'legitimate child'. So, a gift to 'the children of X' was read as meaning a gift to 'the legitimate children of X' and if, for example, at the date of the bequest, X had only illegitimate children, the gift would be interpreted to exclude them and include only future legitimate children.[31] This form of 'interpretation' allowed the court to decide that the effect of the wording in a will was to pass the testator's property to someone whom the court knew that the testator did not intend to benefit, but who, the court believed, was somehow more deserving of the testator's bounty. There appear to have been two half-disguised justifications for the literal approach to the construction of wills, as it was applied during the eighteenth and nineteenth centuries. The less creditable one was that it provided extra work for the lawyers, who could spend time arguing over the 'correct' meaning of words and in working out what exceptions there might be to the basic rule which applied the 'correct' meaning in cases where it was quite obvious that the testator, or his draftsman, had intended some other meaning. The more creditable one was that it could be used as a form of public policy back-up, whereby, for example, illegitimate children could be excluded from benefit, and so indirect support could be given to the institution of marriage.

The literal approach to the interpretation of wills began to lose ground during the middle part of the twentieth century. It was a slow process, starting with the House of Lords case of *Perrin v Morgan*[32] and ending, or hopefully ending, with the enactment of section 21 of the Administration of Justice Act 1982. This section says, in effect, that the meaning of the words in a will should be the meaning intended by the person who used them, *not* some 'correct' or 'ordinary' meaning intended by someone else.[33]

---

[30] See (2000) 116 LQR 287 – 317.

[31] A clear early example of the disinheritance of an illegitimate daughter, when it was perfectly clear that the father intended her to take, is *Cartwright v Vawdry* (1800) 5 Ves Jun 530.

[32] [1943] AC 399.

[33] Even after the enactment of section 21, there are cases where old-fashioned lawyers find 'clear' meanings in words and phrases which are not clear, and they still sometimes end up by interpreting wills in ways almost certainly not intended by those who wrote them. A recent example of this tendency is *Re Owen* [2002] WTLR 619.

6   The *Pla and Puncernau* Case Viewed from England

A discussion of the literal approach to interpretation in England, and how it could act as a disguised *half-limitation* on freedom of testation, leads on to a review of the European Court of Human Rights case of *Pla and Puncernau v Andorra*,[34] because it is a good example of literal interpretation leading to a result not intended by the testatrix.

First of all, what happens if, in England, there is a will which leaves property to 'the children of X' and X has children, some or all of whom are adopted? Do such children take? The answer, in England, would depend in part on the date when the will was executed. Legal adoption did not exist in England until 1926 and, until 1950, adoption normally conferred on an adopted child no right or interest in property as a child of his or her adopter. Between 1950 and 1976 there were a number of detailed rules, but it was not normally possible for an adopted child to take as a child of his adopter *unless* the will under which he claimed had been executed on or after 1 January 1950. If someone dies on or after 1 January 1976, a reference in his will to a 'child' will normally include an adopted child *but* this principle applies 'subject to any contrary indication'.[35] The English rules are based on the premise that the word 'child' does not, in this context, have a clear meaning, it is essentially ambiguous, and it may, or may not, include an adopted child. Whether the word is interpreted to include an adopted child will depend on the date of death and may, subject to the date of death, also depend on the date when the will was executed. The words 'subject to any contrary indication' mean that it is possible to call evidence (including evidence extrinsic to the will) to show how the testator used language and to show who he or she thought were 'children' in the context of the gift. This appears to the present writer to be perfectly reasonable. The word 'child' in the context of adoption is classically unclear. Whether someone who referred, or refers, to 'the children of X' did or did not, or does or does not, intend to include X's adopted children must depend both on date and context. If this is right, the approach taken by the European Court of Human Rights in the *Pla and Puncernau v Andorra* case, which is based on an odd mixture of an old-fashioned approach to interpretation, combined with a modern approach to anti-discrimination, is quite clearly wrong.

In *Pla and Puncernau* an Andorran woman, Carolina Pujol Oller, made a will in Andorra in 1939 and in this will she settled her estate on her son, Francesc-Xavier, for life. On his death it was to pass (by way of an arrangement which appears to be equivalent to a non-fiduciary special power under an English settlement) to one of Francesc-Xavier's sons or grandsons, provided such son or grandson was the issue of 'a lawful and canonical marriage', i.e. provided such son or grandson was legitimate. In due course, Francesc-Xavier married, and, in 1969, he and his wife adopted, in Spain, a child called Antoni. In 1995,

---

[34]   No. 69498/01, ECHR 2004-VIII.

[35]   See now the Adoption and Children Act 2002, ss. 67 and 69(1).

Francesc-Xavier made a will in which he purported to appoint the property from his mother's estate to Antoni. The question in the case was; was Antoni a 'son' of Francesc-Xavier within the meaning of the relevant clause in Carolina Pujol Oller's 1939 will trust? The Court of Appeal in Andorra adopted what appears to a twenty-first century English succession lawyer to have been a straightforwardly correct approach. The Court put itself in the position of Mrs Pujol Oller, the person who executed the will, at the time it was written, and attempted to work out what it thought she, Mrs Pujol Oller, would have meant by the word 'son'.[36] It thought that she would not have intended to include an adopted son, and so an adopted son did not take. No one will ever know if the court's conclusion as to the testatrix's intended meaning was correct, but it is submitted that the court asked itself the right question and attempted to answer it in the right way. There appears to the present writer to be no ground whatsoever for criticising this approach. By contrast, the Human Rights Court in Strasbourg based its judgment on the 'general legal principle that where a statement is unambiguous there is no need to examine the intention of the person who made it' and then followed this by repeating it in Latin: *'quum in verbis nulla ambiguitas est, non debet admitti voluntatis queastio'*. It is interesting that lawyers in different legal systems often use the same tricks. Trying to give an ill-founded assertion extra authority by repeating it in Latin is a traditional technique of English judges, though it has to be said, on their behalf, that when they adopt this method, they usually get the Latin spelling right. The final word should be *quaestio*, not *queastio*. The general point about any 'general legal principle' which relates to 'unambiguous statements' in wills is that it has to be regarded with the greatest possible circumspection. Who says that the 'statement is unambiguous'? The words 'child' or 'son' in wills are notoriously ambiguous. They will mean different things to different people in different places and at different times. English judges in the eighteenth and nineteenth centuries would assume that these words implied legitimacy, *and* that they excluded adoption. This will no longer be the case, *but* neither word has a clear, fixed meaning. And what is particularly hard to justify in the *Pla and Puncernau* case is that a group of judges in Strasbourg were discussing, in French, a language which was not, for most of them, their mother tongue, the interpretation of a will written more than sixty years earlier in Catalan, a language with which most of them would have been unfamiliar. This way of going about things was, quite simply, wrong.

And as for the question of 'discrimination', which is supposed to lie at the heart of the Strasbourg court's judgment, freedom of testation is all about 'discrimination', except that that is not, in the context of succession, what it is called. Again, it is a question of the use of words.[37]

---

[36] In Part V of the judgment of the Andorran Court of Appeal, there is a (correct) reference to 'the scope of the expression…analysed in the light of the social, family and legal conditions in which [the testatrix] lived.'

[37] A long time ago, the present writer worked as a member of the Secretariat of the European Commission of Human Rights in Strasbourg, before it was amalgamated with the European Court of Human Rights.

Freedom of testation means that someone is permitted, when he dies, to leave his property to whomsoever he wishes. It is, of course, possible to have a system which does not permit freedom of testation, but which says that when someone dies he must devise and bequeath his property to X, Y and Z. Or, it is possible to have limited freedom of testation. But, to the extent that someone is given freedom, he is entitled to choose and he is entitled to make choices which others might find odd, or unattractive. As Sir James Hannen, the judge of the Court of Probate, put it when directing a special jury in the case of *Boughton v Knight*:[38]

> '....the law does not say that a man is incapacitated from making a will if he proposes to make a disposition of his property moved by capricious, frivolous, mean, or even bad motives. We do not sit here to correct injustice in that respect... In fact, this question of justice and fairness in the making of wills in a vast majority of cases depends upon such nice and fine distinctions, that we cannot form, or even fancy that we can form, a just estimate of them. Accordingly, by the law of England everyone is left free to choose the person upon whom he will bestow his property after death entirely unfettered in the selection he may think proper to make. He may disinherit, either wholly or partially, his children, and leave his property to strangers to gratify his spite, or to charities to gratify his pride, and we must give effect to his will, however much we may condemn the course he has pursued.'[39]

Freedom of testation means freedom to discriminate, the greater the freedom, the greater the possible discrimination. If someone is free to devise and bequeath his property to whomsoever he likes, he can choose to benefit the males rather than the females, or vice versa, the legitimates rather than the illegitimates, or vice versa, and so on. And a particularly odd aspect of the *Pla and Puncernau* case is that the judges did not find fault with the preference in the 1939 will trust for someone who was both male and legitimate. Was this not discrimination? Of course it was! But non-discriminatory freedom of testation is a contradiction in terms. Under a system of freedom of testation, Mrs Pujol Oller was entitled to benefit her son in preference to her daughters, which she had done in 1939, and she was entitled to express a preference for grandsons and great-grandsons, over granddaughters and great-granddaughters, as well as a preference for legitimates over illegitimates. So, of course, she was, if she chose, entitled to express a preference for the blood-line over an adoptive line. Preventing her from doing this by pretending that her words were clear, when they were classically ambiguous, was ridiculous.

In the years that have gone by since then, he has sometimes wondered why he left the well-paid and easy existence of an international civil servant to become an ill-rewarded academic. Having read the judgment in *Pla and Puncernau*, he remembers.

[38] (1872-75) LR 3 P&D 64.

[39] At p.66, the case concerned incapacity.

7 Contracts to Leave Property by Will, Proprietary Estoppel and Mutual Wills

English law differs from Roman law in that there appears never to have been a rule of English law to the effect that a contract or agreement to leave property by will is unenforceable. There seems to be no suggestion in English law that there might be a public policy objection to an arrangement of this sort. There have always been problems in this area, but they relate to matters of detail, detail as to what has been agreed, not to principle.

There are three ways in which agreements or assurances to leave property by will may be enforced in England: as contracts, through the doctrine of proprietary estoppel, or as mutual wills. The English courts do not appear to regard any of these as an infringement of the principle of freedom of testation.[40]

7.1 Validity of a Contract to Leave Property by Will

A contract by which T promises P to leave to P by will specific property[41] or the whole or a specified share of his residuary estate, is valid. Under general principles of English contract law, such a promise must either be supported by valuable consideration[42] or be made by deed; there must be an intention to create legal relations, and the terms of the contract must not be uncertain. Moreover, if the contract relates to land and was made after September 26th, 1989 it is void if it is not in writing.[43] Similarly, a contract by which T promises P not to revoke or alter T's existing will, or a particular gift in it, is valid.[44] If T commits a breach of his contract with P, after T's death P is entitled to recover damages from T's estate for loss of the promised benefit.[45]

7.2 Proprietary Estoppel

As an alternative to making a claim in contract, someone who has relied upon an assurance given by the deceased to the effect that the deceased will dispose of some or all of his property in a particular way on his death may be able to bring a claim based on the equitable doctrine of proprietary estoppel.

---

[40] Or, it could be that English lawyers, when faced with a potential conflict between freedom of testation and freedom of contract, favour freedom of contract.

[41] *Parker v Clark* [1960] 1 W.L.R. 286 (contract to leave house and contents to P, Q and R jointly); *Hammersley v De Biel* (1845) 12 Cl. & F. 45 (cash legacy).

[42] 'Consideration' is a standard requirement of a contract in English law, it implies a bargain, as opposed ot a gift.

[43] Law Reform (Miscellaneous Provisions) Act 1989, s.2(1). If it was made before September 27th, 1989 it is not enforceable unless there is a signed memorandum satisfying section 40 of the Law of Property Act 1925, or the equitable doctrine of part performance applies.

[44] *Robinson v Ommanney* (1882) 21 Ch.D. 780; (1883) 23 Ch.D. 285.

[45] *Hammersley v De Biel*, above; *Schaefer v Schuhmann* [1972] A.C. 572, 585 *et seq.*

The earlier cases where successful claims were based on the doctrine of proprietary estoppel concerned assurances about existing rights, and they covered clearly identified property, not all or part of someone's property on his future death. But in *Re Basham*[46] Edward Nugee QC[47] extended the doctrine of proprietary estoppel to cover promises which related to what would happen to the promisor's property when he died. He formulated the doctrine in the following way:

> '... where one person, A, has acted to his detriment on the faith of a belief, which was known to and encouraged by another person, B, that he either has or is going to be given a right in or over B's property, B cannot insist on his strict legal rights if to do so would be inconsistent with A's belief.'[48]

The Court of Appeal have since approved the extension of the doctrine of proprietary estoppel to cover promises to leave property on death in five cases.[49] Not everyone has been enthusiastic about the extension of the doctrine of proprietary estoppel into the law of succession.[50] A claimant does not need to make a claim based on proprietary estoppel if he can succeed in contract.[51] There is a danger that vague statements made by the deceased to the effect that he intends to leave property to a particular person if that person behaves in a particular way will become the basis for a claim.

7.3 Mutual Wills

The Court of Chancery created the doctrine of mutual wills in order to remedy the unconscionable revocation of a will in certain circumstances. There are three requirements which must be satisfied for the doctrine to apply.

The first requirement of the doctrine is that two or more persons make an agreement as to the disposal of some or all of their property on death and execute wills pursuant to the agreement. The persons are often husband and wife but the principle is not restricted to husbands and wives. A relatively straightforward arrangement will be where each will gives the other person a life interest, with remainder to the same beneficiary.[52] Sometimes, each will

---

[46] [1986] 1 W.L.R. 1498.

[47] Sitting as a High Court judge.

[48] [1986] 1 W.L.R. 1498, 1503 H.

[49] *Wayling v Jones* (1995) 69 P. & C.R. 170; *Gillett v Holt* [2001] Ch. 210; *Campbell v Griffin* [2001] W.T.L.R. 981; *Jennings v Rice* [2003] 1 F.C.R. 501; *Grundy v Ottey* [2003] W.T.L.R. 1253

[50] *Re Basham* [1986] 1 W.L.R. 1498 was criticised by Hayton (1987) 215 and Sherrin (1987) 263.

[51] Claims under this heading are particularly likely to be formulated where claims in contract would fail because section 2(1) of the Law of Property (Miscellaneous Provisions) Act 1989 enacts that 'A contract for the sale or other disposition of an interest in land can only be made in writing and only by incorporating all the terms which the parties have expressly agreed.'

[52] *Re Hagger* [1930] 2 Ch. 190.

gives the other person an absolute interest, with an alternative gift to the same beneficiary in case the other dies first.[53] The second requirement is that the parties agree that the survivor shall be bound by the arrangement. The fact that the parties agreed to make, and did make, wills at the same time and in substantially identical terms is not, of itself, sufficient to establish that they agreed that the survivor should be bound.[54] The third requirement is the occurrence of the binding event, the death of the first party.[55]

If the three requirements are satisfied, equity enforces the arrangement against the survivor by treating him as holding the property concerned on a constructive trust,[56] to apply it in accordance with his mutual will.[57] This constructive trust does not stop the survivor from revoking his mutual will which, like any other will, is by its very nature revocable until his death. If the mutual will of the survivor is revoked and he makes a new will, any appointment of executors[58] in his new will is effective (even if the executors are not the executors named in his mutual will), and on his death the new will must be admitted to probate.[59] *But* the survivor's personal representatives[60] take the property concerned subject to the constructive trust, and to that extent the new will is ineffective.[61] In short, equity does not prevent, but frustrates, the unconscionable revocation of a mutual will.

It is rarely sensible for persons to make mutual wills.[62] If they insist on doing so, they ought carefully to consider what provision should be made in their arrangement for possible future events, such as the remarriage of the survivor or the birth of children to the survivor. Again, mutual wills ought clearly to define the property of each person which is intended to be bound by the arrangement and the powers which are intended to be conferred on the survivor to dispose of such property during his lifetime.[63]

---

[53] *Re Green* [1951] Ch 148.

[54] *Re Oldham* [1925] Ch. 75; *Re Goodchild* [1997] 1 W.L.R. 1216.

[55] *Re Dale* [1994] Ch. 31.

[56] Unlike an express trust, which is founded on the expressed intention of the parties, a constructive trust arises by operation of law. Most constructive trusts are imposed to prevent some form of unconscionable conduct.

[57] *Birmingham v Renfrew* (1937) 57 C.L.R. 666; *Re Cleaver* [1981] 1 W.L.R. 939.

[58] For 'executors' see fn. 60 below.

[59] *In the Estate of Heys*, [1914] P 192.

[60] 'Personal representatives' are the persons who, under English law, are responsible for winding up an estate. They consist of 'executors' who are appointed by the will, or 'administrators' who act where there is an intestacy, or where no executor has been appointed. They are called 'personal representatives' because, until 1897, they dealt only with personalty. Since then, they have dealt with realty too.

[61] *Re Cleaver* [1981] 1 W.L.R. 939.

[62] See Law Reform Committee's 22nd Report, *The Making and Revocation of Wills*, Cmnd. 7902 (1980) 26.

[63] In *Carvel Foundation v Carvel* [2007] 4 All ER 81 the parties had specifically agreed that while they were both alive neither should make gratuitous transfers unless the other consented, and that once the first had died the survivor should make no gratuitous transfers.

8 Freedom of Testation in England in the Twentieth and Twenty First Centuries

True freedom of testation became widespread in England during the early years of the twentieth century when, for tax reasons, and for reasons linked with the rights of married women over their own property, both strict settlements and marriage settlements began to die out. Trusts were still created, to avoid tax, but these were most likely to be *intervivos* settlements and were less designed to control the succession to property than to ensure the avoidance of income tax and/or of taxes on death.

The early years of the twentieth century were probably *the* period in English legal history when there was the largest degree of true freedom of testation. The Mortmain Act had been repealed, trusts controlling the destiny of property after death were becoming rarer, and property ownership was becoming more widespread. But then came the Family Provision legislation.

Most British colonies in the nineteenth century adopted the English principle of freedom of testation, but were probably less inclined than England to limit this freedom by the imposition of settlements and trusts. At the end of the nineteenth century, there was a move in New Zealand to limit freedom of testation and to introduce a system based on Scottish law. This was rejected *but* in 1900 the New Zealand Parliament passed the Testator's Family Maintenance Act which enabled a widow, a widower, or child of a testator[64] to apply to the court for provision out of the deceased's estate if the will had made inadequate provision for the 'proper maintenance and support' of the applicant. The system was discretionary and, in developing the jurisdiction, the New Zealand courts developed a 'moral duty' test. Before the Second World War, the New Zealand system was copied by all the Australian jurisdictions and, slightly later, most of the Canadian provinces followed suit.

It was in 1928 that Viscount Astor initiated a debate in the House of Lords suggesting that Family Provision legislation on the New Zealand model should be introduced into England, but he was opposed by Viscount Haldane, the former Labour Lord Chancellor, and by Lord Hailsham, the then Conservative Lord Chancellor. There were then a series of attempts to enact legislation, but it was not until ten years after Viscount Astor's first attempt that the Inheritance (Family Provision) Act 1938 became law. This Act did not have universal support, and its promoters had to accept a number of qualifications to the provisions which they had originally wanted to insert in it. As enacted, the Act applied only to persons who died testate after 13th July 1939, and those who could apply were spouses, infant or incapacitated sons and unmarried or incapacitated daughters. The Act was amended in 1952 following the Report of the Committee on the Law of Intestate Succession.[65] The intestates' Estates

---

[64] The Act applied only if the deceased left a will.

[65] This Committee was chaired by Lord Morton, and is usually referred to as the Morton Committee. Its Report was Cmd. 8310 (1951).

Act 1952 increased provision for widows and widowers on intestacy but, at the same time, it extended the 1938 Act to cover cases of total intestacy. This was to deal with cases where someone left a surviving spouse who was a survivor of a second marriage and there were also children of an earlier marriage. The next change was in 1958, when section 3 of the Matrimonial Causes (Property and Maintenance) Act gave former spouses the right to apply for maintenance from the estates of their ex-husbands and wives and, in 1966, the Family Provision Act greatly enlarged the power of the courts to make awards; in particular, the courts were empowered to award lump sums, rather than merely periodic payments, in estates of whatever size.

In 1973 the Law Commission, which had been set up in 1965, and which had just completed a project involving the substantial reform and codification of divorce law and of property and support rights arising on divorce, produced a Report, *Family Law: First Report on Family Property. A New Approach*[66] in which it considered the possibility of introducing a system under which a surviving spouse would have a legal right to inherit part of the deceased's estate, a form of forced heirship. But, having considered the matter, the Law Commission concluded that it was not desirable to introduce such a principle but that, instead, the claim of a surviving spouse on the family assets under the discretionary system should be increased so that it was at least equal to that of a spouse on a divorce. This led, the following year, to a further Law Commission Report, *Family Law: Second Report on Family Property: Family Provision on Death*[67] which led to the enactment of the Inheritance (Provision for Family and Dependants) Act 1975.

The 1975 Act made a number of important changes to the 1938 legislation. It increased and amended the standard of provision for spouses: it added adult children (even if they were not unmarried or incapacitated) and step-children as applicants; it added to the orders the court could make; it added to the property out of which financial provision could be ordered; and it introduced anti-avoidance provisions. In 1995, in accordance with a recommendation from another Law Commission Report, *Distribution on Intestacy*,[68] section 2 of the Law Reform (Succession) Act amended the 1975 Act by adding cohabitants as a further class of applicants, and in 2004 the Civil Partnership Act put same-sex couples who register their partnerships in the position of spouses.

The 1975 Act, as amended, applies on the death of a person on or after 1 January 1996 and any of the following persons may now apply for provision:
1) a spouse or civil partner of the deceased;
2) a former spouse or former civil partner of the deceased (provided that he or she has not remarried or entered into a new civil partnership);
3) a person who lived in the same household of the deceased as if he or she were the spouse or civil partner of the deceased, for a period of two years, ending immediately before the deceased's death (a cohabitant);

---

[66] Law Com No. 52.

[67] Law Com No. 61.

[68] Law Com No. 187.

4) a child of the deceased;
5) any person treated by the deceased as a child of the family in relation to a marriage or civil partnership (a step-child); and
6) any other person who immediately before the death of the deceased was being maintained, wholly or partly, by the deceased (a dependant).

The 1975 Act applies only if the deceased died domiciled in England and Wales and an application under the Act must be made[69] not later than six months from the date on which a valid grant of probate or letters of administration to the deceased's estate is first taken out. The court may order provision to be made under the Act for an applicant only if it 'is satisfied that the disposition of the deceased's estate effected by his will or the law relating to intestacy, or the combination of his will and that law, is not such as to make reasonable financial provision for the applicant'.[70] There are a number of factors which the court must take into account in every case:

1) the financial resources and financial needs which the applicant has, or is likely to have in the foreseeable future;
2) the financial resources and financial needs which any other applicant has or is likely to have;
3) the financial resources and financial needs which any beneficiary of the estate has or is likely to have;
4) any obligations and responsibilities which the deceased had towards any applicant or beneficiary;
5) the size and nature of the net estate;
6) any physical or mental disability of any applicant or beneficiary; and
7) any other matter, including the conduct of the applicant, which in the circumstances of the case, the court may consider relevant.

There are two standards of provision under the Act, the surviving spouse standard and the maintenance standard. The surviving spouse standard is applicable on an application by the deceased's wife, husband or civil partner, and means 'such financial provision as it would be reasonable in all the circumstances of the case for a husband or wife or civil partner to receive, whether or not that provision is required for his or her maintenance'.[71] This is a particular guideline to which the court must have regard on an application by the deceased's spouse or civil partner and it includes a calculation as to what the applicant might reasonably have expected to receive if, on the day on which the deceased died, the marriage or civil partnership, instead of being terminated by death, had been terminated by divorce. This is known as the 'imaginary divorce' guideline.

The maintenance standard applies to all other applicants and means 'such financial provision as it would be reasonable in all the circumstances of the

---

[69] Either to the Chancery Division or to the Family Division of the High Court, or to the county court.

[70] S.2(1).

[71] S.1(2)(a) and s.1(2)(aa).

cases for the applicant to receive for his maintenance.'[72] It does not mean merely the provision of the bare necessities of life[73] but nor, for example, does it include the provision of a capital sum to assist in paying tax on an earlier gift which has been dissipated in spendthrift living.[74]

9 What Problems Are There Under the 1975 Act?

There are two basic questions which have to be answered when drafting Family Provision legislation. First, who should be able to make a claim, and secondly, how much, or what proportion of the estate should an applicant in a particular category be entitled to expect? The answers to the two questions are inter-linked. There are now six categories of applicant under the 1975 Act, but the categories are set out in the legislation in rather a confusing way and it is simpler to look at spouses, former spouses, co-habitants and dependants together, and then to compare and contrast their treatment with that of children and step-children. On the whole, the group who have fared badly under the legislation have been the children (and, to a lesser extent, the step-children). Those who have gained have been the spouses and, in particular, widows.

There is, on the whole, little difficulty in identifying the spouse of a deceased person[75] and so the only significant question which arises in relation to spouses is the amount of the entitlement. The 'imaginary divorce' guideline means that the deceased's spouse has, since 1975, been entitled to expect to find himself/herself in approximately the position in which he or she would have been had the marriage ended in divorce rather than by death or, as s.3(2)(b) of the 1975 Act puts it, 'the court shall...have regard to the provision which the applicant might reasonably have expected to receive if on the day on which the deceased died the marriage, instead of being terminated by death, had been terminated by.... divorce'. The object of the change, made in 1975, was to ensure that a widow or widower[76] did not find herself or himself worse off on death than she or he would have been on divorce. Having said this, there are a number of differences between divorce and death. In the latter, the deceased has no future earnings, but also no future needs; and there is also less need for a 'clean break' (which is favoured in the case of living former spouses, to keep the parties apart, and to

---

[72] 1975 Act s.1(2)(b).

[73] *Re Coventry* [1980] Ch 461.

[74] *Re Dennis* [1981] 2 All ER 140.

[75] Judicially separated spouses are spouses, so are parties to voidable marriages which have not been annulled, and so also are parties to polygamous marriages. The most tricky category will be someone who in good faith entered into a void marriage – but such cases will be very rare.

[76] The cases appear to say that widowers and widows will be treated in the same way. In fact, claims by widowers are rare, but the recent case of *Re Waite, Baron v Woodhead* [2009] 1 FLR 747 appears to be a move towards equality. An undeserving husband obtained the sort of overgenerous provision which would have been given to an undeserving wife.

prevent bickering). These points were noted by Black J in *P v G*[77] and she also noted that the tax position may differ as between death and divorce.

Given that former spouses have, in England and Wales, until recently, received provision on divorce which appears generous by international standards, it seems unlikely that surviving spouses will have found much to complain about in relation to what they have been awarded under the 1975 Act. Having said this, the allegedly over-generous treatment of divorcees in England has come under the spotlight recently[78] and it seems not improbable that provision for ex-spouses will be less generous in the future than it has been in the recent past. But this takes us into the realms of Family Law, and away from Succession. There is insufficient space in this chapter to discuss, for example, whether pre-nuptial agreements are likely to be recognised soon by the English courts.[79]

Former spouses or civil partners may claim under the 1975 Act, but their chances of success are not particularly good. This is because the English courts have wide powers to make capital adjustments between spouses in matrimonial proceedings, and they tend nowadays to favour a clean break at the time when a marriage or civil partnership is dissolved. If there has been such a clean break, the courts will not favour re-opening it on the later death of one of the parties. This is illustrated by the cases of *Re Fullard*[80] and *Re O'Rourke*[81] in both of which former wives failed in their claims against their former husbands' estates.

Claims by cohabitants and dependants are more problematical. Dependants were added as a class in 1975,[82] opposite-sex cohabitants were added in 1995[83] and same-sex cohabitants in 2004.[84] Although the 1975 Act, as amended, where it sets out the list of potential applicants, puts cohabitants ahead of dependants; and although because of the way the Act is drafted, a dependant can claim only if he or she is not a cohabitant; there is a good deal of potential overlap between

---

[77] [2006] 1 FLR 431.

[78] See e.g. the Gresham Lectures given by Baroness Deech in the winter of 2009/10 and, in particular, her first lecture 'Divorce Law – A Disaster' given on 15 September 2009. The Gresham Lectures are available on the Gresham College website.

[79] In October 2009 the Law Commission began a project involving an examination of the status and enforceability of pre-nuptial and post-nuptial agreements. Such agreements are not currently enforceable in the event of a divorce in England (in contrast to the position in many other jurisdictions) but the Law Commission published a Consultation Paper in January 2011 and responses to it are invited by April 2011. In the meantime, the Supreme Court, in *Radmacher v Granatino* [2010] UKSC 42; [2010] 3 WLR 1367 held that, although a court was not obliged to give effect to ante- or post-nuptial agreements, it should give effect to an agreement which was freely entered into by each party with full appreciation of its implications unless, in the circumstances prevailing, it would not be fair to hold the parties to it.

[80] [1982] Fam 42.

[81] [1997] 1 FCR 188.

[82] By the 1975 Act itself.

[83] By the Law Reform (Succession) Act 1995.

[84] By the Civil Partnership Act 2004.

the categories *and* in a very real sense, cohabitants were added as a class to overcome problems which had arisen over the definition of dependants. When dependants first appeared, in 1975, most of those who discussed the logic, or otherwise, of including them as a class probably thought that dependants would almost all be what used to be called 'mistresses'. One popular newspaper went so far as to describe the 1975 Act as a 'mistresses' charter'.[85] In fact, mistresses were not the only persons who could claim to be dependants, a brother or sister could be a dependant,[86] but that then led to problems where the person who alleged that he or she was a dependant had provided direct or indirect benefits for the deceased. Someone who lives in someone else's house, rent free, is, *prima facie*, a dependant. Someone who pays the going market rate in cash to live in someone else's house is, *prima facie*, not a dependant. Someone who lives in someone else's house, and who provides services, such as cooking and clean-ing, may be hard to classify. This, essentially, is why the class of cohabitants was added in the 1990s. It avoids having to deal with the problem which arises in cases like *Bishop v Plumley*[87] where the deceased had made a substantial contri-bution to the applicant's needs *but* this had allegedly been cancelled out by care provided by the applicant for the deceased during a period at the end of the deceased's life when he had been very ill.

The addition of the class of cohabitants avoids this problem, but it creates two other problems in its stead. First of all, who is to be classified as a cohabit-ant? The Act specifies that this is someone who, during the whole of the last two years of the deceased's life, was living in the same household as the deceased and as his or her husband, or wife, or civil partner. It was established in *Re Watson*[88] that it was not necessary to prove that the couple shared a bedroom, but the essential point appears to be that the relationship is 'openly and unequivo-cally displayed to the outside world',[89] so a secret lover cannot claim to be a cohabitant within the family provision legislation. But that then leads to the second question, why, particularly in this age of growing economic equality between men and women, should someone (who is not a dependant) be entitled to make a claim simply on the grounds that he or she and the deceased lived together as husband, or wife, or civil partner? The potential unfairness becomes especially apparent when it is noted that brothers and sisters cannot bring themselves within this heading; and yet siblings may live together in situations which are, from an economic viewpoint, virtually identical with those involving married couples.[90]

---

[85] See Green (1988) 51 MLR 187, 195.

[86] *Re Wilkinson* [1978] Fam 23.

[87] [1991] 1 WLR 582.

[88] [1999] 1 FLR 878.

[89] *Baines v Hedger* [2008] 2 FLR 1805.

[90] Brothers and sisters may inherit from one another on intestacy, and will often do so in cases where the deceased was unmarried and childless, but there will be particular unfairness if, say, a brother and sister live together and the first to die leaves a will in which he or she leaves all his or her property to charity.

10 Particular Problems with Children and Step-children

On the whole, it is not difficult for an infant child to make a successful claim for maintenance from the estate of a deceased parent, but such claims are likely only where the deceased had a surviving spouse who is not the child's parent.[91] What causes more of a problem are claims by adult children. The courts have not looked favourably on claims by 'able-bodied and comparatively young men, in employment, and able to maintain themselves'[92] and the same is likely to be true of able-bodied young women. On the other hand, there appear to be three groups of cases where adult children are now succeeding. First, there are cases where the child worked for the deceased parent for a low wage, or for no wages, on the understanding that he or she would inherit a business, or some other property, when the parent died.[93] Secondly, cases where the deceased parent had inherited property from the other parent (who had died earlier), and that parent had somehow understood that the deceased would later pass it on to the child.[94] Thirdly, there are the 'lame duck' cases where adult children appear not to be able to cope well with life in general.[95] The problem with this last group is that favouring them may appear unfair to virtuous adult children, who, because they work hard and provide for themselves, end up by being treated less generously than their prodigal brothers and sisters.[96]

Adult step-children will sometimes be able to make successful claims, but such cases will be unusual. There may well be an element of sympathy for an adult step-child if the deceased step-parent inherited property from the step-child's natural parent.[97]

11 Reform of the 1975 Act

At the time of writing, the Law Commission are looking at a project for the reform of the law of intestacy in England and Wales and at reform of the family provision legislation. The last time that the Law Commission looked at reform of intestacy was more than twenty years ago[98] and, at that time, the Commission clearly wanted to favour spouses at the expense of children. This met with opposition and the Commission's proposals were not enacted in their entirety. The Commission published a consultation paper in 2009[99] and,

---

[91] *Re Robinson* [2001] WTLR 267.

[92] *Re Coventry* [1980] Ch 461.

[93] *Re Abram* [1996] 2 FLR 379.

[94] *Re Goodchild* [1997] 1 WLR 1216, such an 'understanding' may create mutual wills (see above) and, if it does, the child will probably have a better claim than he would under this heading.

[95] *Re Hancock* [1998] 2 FLR 346; *Espinosa v Bourke* [1999] 1 FLR 474.

[96] See *Re Jennings* [1994] Ch 286.

[97] *Re Callaghan* [1985] Fam 1.

[98] Law Com No. 187 (1989).

[99] Consultation Paper No. 191 (2009).

when they have looked at the responses to it, they will publish another report. Again, the Commission's instinct is to favour spouses and cohabitants at the expense of children. Apart from suggesting that cohabitants might be given an entitlement on intestacy, the Commission wonder whether they should not be given more generous provision under the family provision rules, i.e. there is a suggestion that cohabitants might be given the same kind of financial provision as spouses, rather than being entitled merely to maintenance. The Commission have also suggested that dependants should be able to make claims without proving that they contributed substantially less to the parties' relationship than did the deceased. But in this case, are they dependants? The thinking behind this seems confused. As to adult children, the consultation paper asks whether they ought to be treated more generously, but appears to suggest that they should not be. The bias of the consultation paper is reasonably clear, and the present writer does not share it. But, just as twenty years ago, the Law Commission failed to obtain implementation of their then suggestions, he hopes that they will fail again this time. In cases where the deceased's spouse is also the parent of his children, it generally makes little long term difference whether, on his death, his property passes to her or to them. If X dies, leaving a widow, Mrs X, and two children, Y and Z, property which passes from X to Mrs X will pass from Mrs X to Y and Z on her later death. This is, of course, on the supposition that Mrs X does not later remarry or form some other relationship. But, if Mrs X is not the mother of Y and Z, it makes a lot of difference whether property passes to her, or to them on X's death. Making over-generous provision for spouses who are not the parents of the children of deceased persons can create a situation which comes to resemble a lottery, and things are only made worse if not only spouses, but also dependants and cohabitants have rights.

Whether it would be better to scrap the discretionary system and move towards a system of forced heirship seems to the present writer to be more of an academic than a practical question in England today. There may be much to be said in favour of forced heirship, but it will not be said by lawyers for whom work is generated by a discretionary system. Having said this, it is worth noting that the number of contested family provision claims coming before the courts in England is not large, and appears to be declining. Family provision claims may be heard in the Chancery Division, or in the Family Division of the High Court, or in the county court. The Law Commission's recent consultation paper notes that there are no statistics for the Family Division or for the county court, but that, in 2007, the Chancery Division was recorded as dealing with only forty three applications, as compared with almost five hundred in 1980.[100] There are various potential explanations for this, including the possibility that most claims are settled before they reach court, but it is likely that some would-be applicants are deterred by the cost of this form of litigation. Forced heirship legislation would avoid this, but the suggestion that forced heirship might be introduced

---

[100] Consultation Paper No. 191 (2009) para 1.9.

into England was made in the 1970s[101] and was not proceeded with. It may have been unfortunate that the suggestion was made at a time when the United Kingdom was in the process of joining what is now the European Union, because forced heirship will be associated in the minds of some with a slightly negative vision of a bullying 'Europe'. Forced heirship is not, of course, un-British, they have it in Scotland. But what may be the real underlying problem is that any attempt to introduce forced heirship into England would provoke an even bigger problem than exists at the present time as to agreeing who are most deserving of protection – spouses, dependants, co-habitants, children? And that involves different visions of what 'the family' consists of, and as to who is entitled to expect what.[102]

---

[101] See fn. 66, and accompanying text, above.

[102] The writer would like to thank his collegue, Gwen Seabourne, for her helpful comments on an earlier draft of this Chapter. The usual disclaimers apply.

CHAPTER 8

Law of Succession and Testamentary Freedom in Germany

A. Röthel

1   Introduction

As is well-known, in the section of the BGB dealing with the law of succession, German law adopted the underlying liberal tendencies of Roman law to a considerable extent. Testators are afforded extensive scope to structure their succession arrangements through the regulation of fideicommissum / reversionary succession (§§ 2100 ff. BGB) and the execution of the will (§§ 2197 ff. BGB).[1] The limits to testamentary freedom arise elsewhere: in the first place in the compulsory portion (§§ 2303 ff. BGB) and otherwise in the judicial understanding of the public interest (§ 138 BGB) as well as in a number of separate testamentary prohibitions.

The following presentation is necessarily cursory and limited to a focus on individual features of particular significance and importance. The emphasis is placed on recent legal developments and tendencies in the current discussions on reform.

2   Testamentary Freedom and Public Policy (§ 138 BGB)

Like all legal transactions, testamentary dispositions are subject to the requirements of "good morals" (§ 138 BGB). Alongside the law on the compulsory portion, good morals constitute the most significant limitation on testamentary freedom.

The view of how testamentary dispositions violate public policy (morals) has naturally changed in the course of 110 years since the BGB came into force. Initially the prime focus was the so-called "mistress" or extramarital will, which was long regarded as immoral and accordingly declared void.[2] Beginning in the 1970s the view changed: initially attitudes changed towards extramarital or "marriage breaking" relationships.[3] Later came the additional insight that § 138 BGB did not entitle judges to gauge the effects of testamentary dispositions according to their own ideas of justice and modify the intentions of the testator.[4] The morality standard was to an extent "legally defined" (brought within the law) – a development which persists until the present day. The decisive standards are now basic rights,[5] and in the process have also become a matter of fundamental law.

---

*   The author thanks Mr. Ulrich Wilke, LL.B, Bucerius Law School, for his help with the necessary details.

1   A comparative law perspective for example in Dutta (2009) 1735-1739 and 1477-1481 respectively.

2   RGZ 166, 395, 399 ; BGHZ 20, 71, 72; BGH FamRZ 1963, 287, 288; analysed in Karow (1997); Falk (2000) 451-494.

3   BGHZ 53, 369, 377 ff. – Will benefiting a mistress ("Geliebtentestament").

4   BGHZ 140, 118, 129 – Hohenzollern.

5   In detail Röthel (2010a) 32-66, 37 ff.

This matter of fundamental rights is in many ways characteristic of present German law as shown in particular in the following groups of cases, which reflect the current state of the debate.

2.1 Conditional Inheritance: "Undue Influence" on Heirs?

The first group of cases concerns testamentary dispositions by means of which the testator through conditional inheritance and other measures attempts to influence or direct the conduct of the heirs after succession. A well-known case is that of the succession to the House of Hohenzollern, which in recent times has engaged courts at all levels up to the Federal Constitutional Court. A significant controversy arose as to whether it is admissible to make the inheritance subject to the condition that the heirs marry "befitting their rank" ["*standesgemäß*"]. This involves the more general question of the extent to which the testator can exert pressure on the exercise of constitutionally protected fundamental freedoms through testamentary dispositions: Is the testator entitled to make the inheritance conditional upon the heirs marrying or not marrying, changing their religious faith, leaving a sect, or giving up alcohol? Is that an inadmissible restriction of fundamental freedom, or is the heir ultimately sufficiently protected by the law on the compulsory portion?[6]

The Federal Supreme Court approved the disputed clause, seeing no "significant interference" in the essential personal freedom of decision.[7] In the view of the Federal Constitutional Court, the Federal Supreme Court had however in this matter chosen too easy a path. The Federal Constitutional Court quashed the decision as the Supreme Court had insufficiently considered whether the blood relation clause was suitable to generate this "unreasonable pressure" on the entry into marriage.[8] This rather narrow understanding of testamentary freedom is in keeping with the overwhelming majority view in scholarly writings.[9]

---

[6] A conditional heir is an heir subject to restrictions (§ 2104 BGB). – Thus it is open to the heir subject to restrictions, provided that person is also entitled to a compulsory portion, to challenge the will and claim the compulsory portion (§ 2306 Para. 1 BGB latest amendment).

[7] BGHZ 140, 118, 128 ff. – Hohenzollern; the lower court held differently, see OLG Stuttgart FamRZ 1998, 260 ff.

[8] BVerfG NJW 2004, 2008 ff. – Hohenzollern.

[9] Thielmann (1973) 122 ff.; Kellenter (1989) 76, 84; Otte (2003) § 2074 No. 31; Lange – Kuchinke (2001) § 27 VI 2; Leipold (2010) § 2074 No. 18. In favour of unrestricted validity of conditional appointment as heirs however Gutmann (2001) 208 f.; idem (2004) 2347-2349, 2348; Muscheler (1999) 151-152, 152; Kroppenberg (2006) 86-105, 103 ff. In my view the formulation "unreasonable pressure" is rather vague. Following the Federal Constitutional Court's jurisprudence on the substantive regulation of sureties and marital contracts, wills should only then be void if the heir is unable to protect his or her own freedom through a disclaimer because of a particular situation of "structural dependence"; in more detail Röthel (2010) 32-66, 50 ff.

2.2 Wills in Favour of Disabled People or of People in Need versus Social Welfare

The second group of cases to have exercised jurisprudence in recent years concerns wills in which the testator seeks to shield the estate from social welfare. This is achieved through a combination of institution as a reversionary heir and testamentary execution. One example is where the testator wishes to name his disabled son as his sole heir but at the same time wishes to avoid his son losing rights to social provision as a disabled person. The solution is to grant his son the position of a fiduciarius heir and at the same time appointing a permanent executor, whereby the payments to the son are limited in such a way that the claims to basic social benefits are preserved. This form of protection of the estate against intervention by social welfare institutions is not seen as contrary to public policy [*sittenwidrig*].[10] In the meantime the so-called "disabled" and "deserving" wills are standard elements in the repertoire of succession arrangements.[11]

However this could change in the future. Increasing doubts have been raised recently regarding whether this mechanism can still be seen as a realisation of testamentary freedom which is worthy of protection.[12] There are particular doubts regarding situations involving the protection of deserving groups other than the disabled, such as the long-term unemployed. In one case the Social Court deemed that such a will was invalid, reasoning largely that it could not be legitimate to provide an heir with considerable advantages from the estate (hobbies, travel), while the taxpayer continued to finance the everyday living of that individual.[13]

2.3 The "Rule Against Perpetuities"

One of the few features common to both continental European and Anglo-American law is the reservation against people binding their assets for too long (the rule against perpetuities). German law also includes provisions which impose limits on testamentary freedom in the form of a "rule against perpetuities". However these limits are drawn relatively generously as can be

---

[10] BGHZ 111, 36 ff.; 123, 368, 378 – This type of will in favour of a disabled person is not contrary to public policy since the subordination principle [*Nachrang*] of social welfare is not consistently implemented, so that the will cannot be tested against a "clear, unequivocal legislative value or general legal conceptions"

[11] Drafting proposals for example in Litzenburger (2009) 278-281; detailed structural proposals by Köss-inger (2008) 936 ff., 950 ff.

[12] See OLG Hamm, decision dated 16 July 2009, ZEV 2009, 471-472 – Disclaimer of a severely disabled social welfare recipient contrary to public policy; a concurring comment by Leipold (2009) 472-473; SG (*Sozialgericht*, Social Welfare Court) Dortmund, decision dated 25 September 2009, ZEV 2010, 54-56 – Will in favour of an indigent contrary to public policy; see the critical comment by Keim (2010) 56.

[13] SG Dortmund, decision dated 25 September 2009, ZEV 2010, 54-56, 55; see the critical comment by Keim (2010) 56.

inferred in detail from the admissibility of contingent substitution (subsequent heirs, §§ 2100 ff. BGB) and permanent execution (§§ 2197 ff. BGB). Compared with the majority of European jurisdictions, German law has opted rather for an emphasis on freedom of testation. The possibility to appoint a fiduciarius or fideicommissary is linked neither to a particular category of persons nor a material interest, and the execution is automatically also admissible as permanent execution.[14]

The BGB draws only time limits. Thus reversionary succession and testamentary execution cease to be effective 30 years after devolution of the succession (§ 2109 Para. 1 phrase 1, § 2210 phrase 1 BGB). However this principle is also subject to certain exceptions (§ 2109 Para. 1 phrase 2, § 2210 phrase 2 BGB).[15] Thus the testator may order that the execution should continue until the death of the heir, or the executor, or until the occurrence of another event concerning either of them (§ 2210 phrase 2 BGB).

Again recently there was a succession arrangement in the House of Hohenzollern, which led to three new judicial rulings.[16] The inheritance contract concluded in 1938 between William of Prussia and his son Louis contained among others the provision that the execution should continue "as long as permissible by law (BGB § 2210), that is at least 30 years after the death of the Crown Prince, at least until the death of the (fideicommissary) heir and at least until the death of the executor or his successor". Further it provided that the President of the German Federal Court should appoint an executor if one of the three named executors or alternatively one of the three named deputy executors ceased to exist, which in the event occurred.[17] On a literal reading of § 2210 phrase 2 BGB, a permanent execution would be possible. The Berlin Regional Court relied on a purposeful reading of the provision: the legislature of the time had been concerned to set a time limit. Thus the provision would have to be corrected in order to avoid perpetual and continuing execution.[18] This raises a fundamental question, namely the validity and scope of the so-called "rule against perpetuities" in the German law of succession. The German Supreme Court has however already interpreted the time limits rather generously and taken the view that the permanent execution would remain valid as long as an executor is in office who was appointed within 30 years of the death.[19] This

---

[14] A comparative law overview in Muscheler (1994) 60 ff.; Zimmermann (1998) 267-304.

[15] On the consequences see Röthel (2010b) forthcoming.

[16] On the order of succession, LG Hechingen, FamRZ 2001, 721; OLG Stuttgart, FamRZ 2002, 1365; OLG Stuttgart, FamRZ 2005, 1863; BGH, NJW 1999, 566; BVerfG, NJW 2004, 2008. On the term of execution, LG Berlin, ZEV 2006, 506; KG, ZEV 2007, 335; BGHZ 174, 346 ff.; BVerfG, 1 BvR 909/08 of 25 March 2009 (rejection of legal remedy).

[17] Cf. LG Berlin, ZEV 2006, 506 f.

[18] See for example Mayer (2008) § 2210 No. 4; Zimmermann (2010) § 2210 No. 3; in a narrower sense, Reimann (2007) 3034-3037, 3037: only the executor appointed first within the 30 year period should be considered.

[19] BGHZ 174, 346 (355 ff.) – Permanent execution of the last will in Haus Hohenzollern.

led in the instant case to the execution continuing, because the appointed and acting executor was appointed in 1975, before expiry of the 30-year time limit. Thus the execution has already taken 60 years and may continue for another 10 to 20 years. With increasing life expectancy, fideicomissa and permanent executions that last for over 100 years will not be rare. In other words, there are rules within German law which serve the function of rules against perpetuities but which are interpreted in an increasingly liberal manner.[20]

In any case, one can still not speak of a true "rule against perpetuities" under German law, because there is still the possibility to establish a private foundation. Thus in the conventional view, foundations are outside the application of time limits for fideicommissum and execution, which in turn enables a perpetual binding of assets to be achieved. Accordingly, one cannot actually speak of a rule against perpetuities in German law.

2.4   Particular Testamentary Prohibitions

More significant in practice in recent times is a particular statutory prohibition to inherit that applies to home operators, home managers, and other care home employees (§ 14 German Care Home Act [HeimG]).[21] This regulation is regarded as a prohibition (§ 134 BGB) on corresponding testamentary gifts,[22] these dispositions thus being void. Its purpose is among others to protect the elderly in that their right to free disposition *mortis causa* is in effect endangered through open or concealed influence (duress).[23]

There is a pronounced tendency towards a liberal interpretation of this regulation in court judgments,[24] from which we may infer corresponding needs in practice where unfortunate circumstances arise. In scholarly writing, however, either the criticism predominates, in the sense that this represents a dispropor-

---

[20] Arguing *de lege ferenda* (what the law ought to be) for a limitation see Röthel (2010c) sub. F. II. 3 b, bb.

[21] Law on retirement homes and nursing homes for adults (HeimG) in the version published 23 April 1990 (BGBl. I 764); see also in the meantime § 10 of the law on home assistance and care (*Wohn- und Teilhabegesetz* – WTG), GVBl. NW 2008, 738; Art. 8 of the law on the regulation of assistance, care and housing quality of the elderly and disabled (*Pflege- und Wohnqualitätsgesetz* – WoqG), BayGVBl. 2008, 346 and § 14 of the law on retirement homes and asylums in Baden-Wuerttemberg (LandesheimG), GBl. BW 2008, 169.

[22] BGHZ 110, 235 (240); BayObLG, NJW 1998, 2369 (2370).

[23] BVerfG, NJW 1998, 2964 – § 14 HeimG.

[24] OLG Düsseldorf ZEV 1997, 459: application to the appointment of children of a home director as heirs; OLG Frankfurt a.M. NJW 2001, 1504: application to a bequest to a home porter and his wife; BayObLG NJW 2000, 1875: application to a bequest to a shareholder / director of a limited company running a home; BayObLG NJW-RR 2004, 1591: application to a member of home staff after the testator's transferral to another ward; OLG München NJW 2006, 2642: application to a bequest to a relative of a home resident; VG Würzburg ZEV 2008, 601: application to a bequest to the home through a donation to an affiliated foundation.

tionate restriction on testamentary freedom,[25] or alternatively there is criticism of the regulation's limited scope: With some justification it is asked why there is a prohibition on dispositions in favour of care home personnel on the one hand but not carers or domestic carers on the other.[26] In any case protecting the testator from undue influence will constitute one of the future tasks of the German law of succession. Whether in substantive terms this is better achieved through further designation of particular occupational groups or rather through a strengthened judicial monitoring is at present unclear. Case law and legal writing are only at a preliminary stage.[27]

3 Testamentary Freedom and the Compulsory Portion (§§ 2303 ff. BGB)

The most apparent limits to testamentary freedom are imposed by the law on the compulsory portion.[28] This law is a constant subject of discussion. For many it appears obsolete.[29] Some have regarded the compulsory portion as an unconstitutional limit on testamentary freedom. However, the Federal Constitutional Court dispelled these doubts in 2005 and instead made clear that the participation of children in their parents' estates regardless of need is guaranteed constitutionally under Article 6 Para. 1 of the German Constitution (protection of marriage and family).[30]

The most recent reform of the law of succession, which entered into force on 1 January 2010[31], does not pose any fundamental challenge to the compulsory portion law, making only marginal changes (see below 3.2). The basic design, however, remains unchanged – particularly regarding the level of, and those entitled to, the compulsory portion. There is also no statutory provision establishing limits, that is upper limits to the compulsory portion or privileges to the benefit of non-profit organisations.[32]

---

[25] Brox – Walker (2009) No. 261; Meyer-Pritzl (2008) 1175.

[26] For example Art. 909.2 of the French Civil Code is seen as exemplary.

[27] In more detail Röthel (2010a) 32-66, 61 ff.

[28] Detailed presentation already in Röthel (2008a).

[29] Especially critical Dauner-Lieb (2001) 460-465; Henrich (2000); idem (2001) 441-452; Beckert (2007) 1-22.

[30] BVerfGE 112, 332 ff. – Right to the compulsory portion.

[31] *Gesetz zur Änderung des Erb- und Verjährungsrechts* (Reform of the Laws of Succession and the Statute of Limitations, dated 24 September 2009, BGBl. I, 3142). See to this regard Reimann (2009) 1633-1636; Muscheler (2008) 105-112; Röthel (2008b) 112-116; Windel (2008) 305-308; Otte (2008) 260-262.

[32] Suggested in Hüttemann – Rawert (2007) 73-90.

3.1 Overview of the Basic Concept

In contrast to the classic civil (Roman) legal system, the German compulsory portion is a claim under the law of obligations. The party entitled to the compulsory portion is not an heir. Those entitled are the children, the parents and surviving spouses as well as civil partners within the meaning of the Civil Partnership Act (§ 10 Para. 6 LPartG). The claim extends to half of the intestate portion.

In particular cases, the amount the surviving spouse or civil partner receives depends on the matrimonial property regime and whether the deceased left children. Normally in practice spouses will have been subject to the statutory matrimonial property system (community of accrued gains) and, if the deceased left children, the surviving spouse would take ½ through intestacy (§§ 1931 Para. 1 and Para. 3, 1371 Para. 1 BGB), which means that the spouse's compulsory portion amounts to ¼ of the estate. If the testator has no children but rather one or two parents, the share in intestacy of the surviving spouse amounts to ¾, and therefore the compulsory portion is ³/₈. Only when the testator has neither children nor surviving parents is the surviving spouse the sole statutory heir; accordingly, the spouse's compulsory portion is ½.

However, it should not be forgotten that in practice the compulsory portion of the surviving spouse does not play an important role because the spouse is rarely disinherited or disclaims the estate. Far more significant is the legal position regarding divorced spouses. To the extent Germany follows the concept of the "clean break" – if the deceased has applied for divorce and provided the requirements for divorce are fulfilled, then the spouse's rights of succession are extinguished (§ 1933 BGB). Thus there is also no compulsory portion. Provision to the divorced spouse is rather a matter of maintenance rights. At times maintenance rights are directed now at the estate of the party subject to maintenance obligations (§ 1586b BGB). The most recent maintenance reform[33] however, has imposed further and stricter limits on maintenance claims. The former perpetual living standard guarantee has been abolished. Also there is a tendency to subject maintenance provisions to time limits (§ 1578b Para. 2 BGB). This is at the same time a weakening of the position of the surviving divorced spouse.

If the divorced party marries again, the new spouse is entitled by law to inherit as a spouse, so that if the spouses were subject to the statutory matrimonial property system and there are children of the deceased, the spouse will take ½ of the estate in intestacy (§§ 1931 Para. 1, Para. 3, 1371 BGB) and the compulsory portion amounts to ¼ of the estate. In calculating the statutory portion quota it is immaterial whether the first or second spouse is concerned. Even so the second spouse may in certain circumstances be obliged to assume responsibility for the maintenance of a divorced spouse. The latest maintenance law reform in 2009 in this regard favours the current over the divorced spouse.

---

[33] *Gesetz über die Reform des Unterhaltsrechts* (Reform of Maintenance Act) dated 21 December 2007, BGBl. I, 3189.

3.2 Reforms in the Law on Compulsory Portion (2009)[34]

3.2.1 Increase of Compulsory Portions Due to *Inter Vivos* Donations (§ 2325 BGB latest amendment)

Where the testator has made a gift to a third-party during his or her lifetime, a person entitled to a compulsory portion may claim, as a complement of the compulsory share, the amount by which the compulsory share would be increased if the donated asset were added to the estate (§ 2325 Para. 1 BGB).

Hitherto however, gifts were not to be taken into account if they were made 10 years or more prior to the death. Since 1 January 2010 a scaled system is in place: gifts made in the first year prior to the demise are taken into account to their full extent, those made two years before are estimated at $9/10$ of their value, and so on (§ 2325 Para. 3 BGB latest amendment).

3.2.2 Deferment (§ 2331a BGB latest amendment)

Equally the law regarding the deferment of payment by the heir was amended as of 1 January 2010. The declared aim of the legislature was to strengthen the right to deferment. Because obligations are due immediately, liquidity problems can arise if the estate does not include cash, but real estate or a company. In the past, it was often criticised that the enforcement of compulsory portion claims led to a splitting of company assets and therefore was prejudicial to companies.[35]

The significant differences to the previous law consist in the fact that in future not only an heir who is entitled to the compulsory portion – that is children or parents of the deceased as well as the spouse or civil partner – but rather any heir is entitled to demand additional time (§ 2331a Para. 1 phrase 1 BGB latest amendment). In substantive terms, however, the grounds for additional time have only been moderately extended. Additional time may be demanded where the immediate fulfilment of the compulsory portion claim would give rise to an inequitable hardship for the debtor (before the reform, deferment would be granted if immediate payment affected heirs in an unusually burdensome and unreasonable way). It now remains to be seen whether in judicial practice the new law will actually lead to a more generous provision of additional time.

3.2.3 Deprivation of the Compulsory Portion (§ 2333 BGB)

Finally the grounds for deprivation of the compulsory portion were changed and "modernised". In particular, the deprivation of the com-

---

[34] By means of the *Gesetz zur Änderung des Erb- und Verjährungsrechts* (Reform of the Laws of Succession and the Statute of Limitations) dated 24 September 2009, BGBl. I, 3142.

[35] Critical Dauner-Lieb (2001) 460-465; reform proposals by Schmidt (2007) 37-56.

pulsory portion due to "leading a disreputable or immoral life" (former § 2335 Para. 5 BGB ff.) has been abandoned. In its place the compulsory portion may be withdrawn because of an intentional criminal offence due to which participation in the estate for the testator has become unacceptable (§ 2333 Para. 1 phrase 4 BGB latest amendment).[36]

4   Testamentary Freedom and Inheritance Agreements

4.1   Overview of the Applicable Law

Alongside the individual will, German law recognises other ways of structuring testamentary arrangements in the form of the joint will (§§ 2265 ff. BGB) or the inheritance contract (§§ 2274 ff. BGB). A significant difference between the joint will and the inheritance contract is that only married partners or civil partners within the meaning of the Civil Partnership Act can execute a joint will, while inheritance contracts can be concluded by anyone. On the other hand, the formalities for joint wills are simplified, since they can be handwritten (as holographic wills), while inheritance contracts must be notarially recorded. However, their effects are very similar; both result in a binding effect on the testators.

4.2   Reform Debate

The coexistence of joint wills and inheritance contracts under German law has long been criticised. Practical experience has shown that the holographic joint will made without legal advice is generally based on false expectations regarding its binding consequences. Thus there are proposals either to do without the joint will entirely or at least to abandon its formal privileges, but at the same time to provide for its being necessarily recorded by a public notary.[37] It has also been suggested that binding effect should only be given to dispositions that expressly designate themselves as binding. Finally there is discussion on the clarification of the binding effects during the decedent's lifetime (§ 2287 BGB). Under existing law (*lex lata*), contractual heirs may reclaim donations which the decedent made with the intent to prejudice the contractual heirs. In practice, this involves cases in which a testator bound by an inheritance contract wishes to leave something to a new spouse or civil partner. Under existing case law, that is only possible where the testator pursues an own personal interest during his or her lifetime, for example where the donation

---

[36]   An exception is made to this unacceptability standard where the testator participates in the offence, such as in joint drugs criminal activity, as mentioned in the preparatory materials, printed matter of the Bundestag No. 16/8954 dated 24 April 2008, 54 ff.

[37]   Cf. Röthel (2010c) sub. E. III. 3.

reciprocates a benefit obtained by the donor, such as care services.[38] This clearly leads to fictive arguments[39] and should be altered in the long-term.

Overall my impression remains that there is a need for a legal institute that binds the decedent. However, in the meantime there is also a clearer awareness of the dangers which such effects involve for testators. Today more care is taken regarding unconsidered inheritance contracts resulting from duress and commercial inexperience.

5 Summary: Requirements of Freedom of Testation Fit for the Present Day

In many European jurisdictions, the law of succession is currently undergoing reforms or has recently been reformed. This applies to Germany, too. In my view, there is also reason to reconsider a number of detailed aspects. An underlying liberal attitude based on trust alone does not allow for an appropriate law of succession. This is shown not least in the increasing significance and range of experience regarding judicial control according to the public policy standard (§ 138 BGB). Further consideration should be given to protecting the ageing and potentially easily influenced testator, to concerns regarding unintended loss of testamentary freedom through the binding effects of succession law and finally the protection of the heirs against disproportionate control by the testator. There is no simple solution. It is neither a matter of extending, nor solely of restricting, testamentary freedom. Rather we need an informed review and reform – the constant task of every jurisdiction.

---

[38] BGH, NJW 1992, 2630 (2631); BGH, FamRZ 1986, 980; Lange – Kuchinke (2001) § 25 V, 490; Ritter (1999) 203 ff.

[39] Röthel (2010c) sub. E. III. 3. d.

CHAPTER 9

The Law of Succession in Hungary

Zoltán Csehi

1 Introduction

Following the Second World War and the Soviet occupation of
the country, owing to the implementation of the socialist type social system, the
Hungarian law of succession has fundamentally changed from the beginning of
the 1950s. Basically, the socialist social system did not acknowledge private property; moreover, both state and the so-called "social property" were declared to be
dominant, and an attempt was made to implement this principle in economic
and legal practice. In legal regulation, distinctions were made at the level of
the Constitution and the Civil Code (CC) between state, social, and cooperative
property, as well as between personal and private property. We do not intend to
present the ideological background, much less the legal review of this approach.[1]
This system was intended to reduce the properties of private individuals to basic
daily necessities. There was a limited amount of properties that was allowed to
be in the possession of individual persons: one apartment or rental apartment,
one holiday home and one automobile. There were no restrictions regarding
cash and other valuable assets, such as shops, factories, enterprises, works of art,
art collections, but these had been nationalized earlier. In the socialist system
private individuals were not allowed to hold shares in companies, and they
could only invest their money in bank deposits, and from the 1980s, in treasury
bonds.

In this social and economic regime private property was only allowed to play
a minor role. Another factor added to this was that the regulations on marriage,
on kinship and on matrimonial property were also changed. The new family law
provisions, implemented since 1952, terminated all legal differences between
legitimate and illegitimate children, all differences between adopted and biological children, all differences between the rights of the husband and those of
the wife, and matrimonial property law provided that assets acquired during a
marriage became the common property of the spouses in an equal ratio. Even
though the spouses were allowed to agree to depart from these rules, at the
beginning, this happened rarely. The relatively early recognition of partnership
(cohabitation) as a form of non-marital partnership also impacted the law of
succession. In the 1960s Hungarian courts acknowledged the effect of informal
cohabitation on property law.[2] This is of significance because if the relationship between a man and a woman is considered an informal cohabitation – the
condition for which is that they have lived in emotional and economic community on a permanent basis – then any assets acquired by either party during the
existence of the community are considered common assets. For example, if one
partner purchased an automobile, then regardless of the fact that the license of
the car had been issued in his or her name, if the automobile was bought during

---

[1] Vékás (1988) 297.

[2] Bírósági Határozatok [Case Law] 1962, No. 382.; opinion No. 827 of the College of the Supreme Court
of Hungary; Bírósági Határozatok 1963, No. 3771; 1965, No. 442. Summarized in Eörsi-Gellért (1981)
2642.

the existence of the community of this kind of non-registered partnership, it was qualified as common property. Therefore when one of the cohabitants died, only half of the title to the vehicle belonged to the estate acquired during the cohabitation. Informal cohabitation affected the extent of the estate.

The CC of the socialist era was enacted in 1959 (Act IV). Prior to that time there had been no private law codex in Hungary; there had been several acts in force, but fundamentally a case law system had applied. The new code was promulgated on 1 May 1960 and provided detailed rules for the private law of succession. It recognized freedom of testamentary disposition, inheritance contracts, testamentary gifts and, as a subsidiary, secondary arrangement, the CC provides for intestacy (legitimate succession). Hungarian law recognizes the concept of compulsory share; it grants a beneficial interest to a surviving spouse regarding the assets that he or she has not inherited and also recognizes the so-called linear or patrimonial inheritance, which substantially means that certain properties are returned to the testator's family if the deceased leaves no children or descendants, instead of going to the spouse. Hungarian law is quite similar to German and Austrian law, but precisely in the law of succession there are several rules that differ from those two systems.

From 1989-1990 the socialist type social system collapsed, the restrictions on private property were removed and a significant part of the assets came into the possession of private individuals. Owing to the social and economic change, the role of the law on succession and on matrimonial property became more relevant. The range of assets that could be held by private individuals also expanded: shares in companies, intellectual property or intangible goods were a novelty, in addition to the usual categories of real property, tangible goods and cash. Despite that, the civil law provisions on succession have remained basically unchanged; neither the provisions on intestacy nor the assets that can be inherited have changed.

The part of the CC on succession has been practically unchanged since its creation, i.e. since 1959. As a result, owing to the notarial and court practice of fifty years, by now this regulation has become a consistent and transparent area with a huge volume of case-law, even though the legislative provisions are relatively scant. Meaningful changes were brought about by the act on registered partnership of same-gender partners,[3] which included the registered partner in the list of beneficiaries in intestacy, in an equal position to that held by the spouse.

2 Freedom of Testation versus *Ordre Public*

It is the basic principle of Hungarian succession law that the testator is free to dispose of his or her estate. The only significant restriction

---

[3]   2009. évi XXIX. törvény [Act No. XXIX of 2009 on Registered Partnership and the Modification of Rules in connection with Registered Partnership and the Facilitation of Cohabitation].

under private law is the institution of the compulsory share, and in the case of contractual testamentary dispositions, the restrictions that derive from contract law. If the testator chooses not to exercise this right, then the law will determine the order of succession (what we call legal succession; i.e. intestacy). There are situations in which part of the estate is settled by the testament, and the remaining estate is subject to the rules of intestacy. In intestacy, the family has an important role, since the decedent's estate will be inherited primarily by his or her next of kin, spouse, registered partner and relatives, in the order defined by law. The institution of the compulsory share reflects the attachment of the estate to the family; certain persons who were the closest to the testator are entitled to the minimum share, to be taken primarily from the estate. We present the rules on compulsory share below. In the following passage we review the restrictions to testamentary freedom as a result of human rights and public and private law restraints.

We have interpreted the term *ordre public* not in the sense it is used in international private law, but rather as the fundamental constitutional order that underlies the Hungarian legal system. There are no court judgments known to affect succession law in the field of the international private law concept of *ordre public*.[4]

2.1 Restrictions Imposed by Human Rights and Fundamental Rights

In this part we shall review the restrictions in terms of human rights and fundamental rights, but basically we shall present the practice and case-law of the Hungarian Constitutional Court over the last twenty years concerning the constitutional law of succession.

2.1.1 Preliminaries on Human Rights

The freedom of testation and the right to inherit do not belong to the scope of human rights, and the Convention for the Protection of Human Rights and Fundamental Freedoms does not recognize those rights either,[5] even though they are closely related to ownership. The succession-related cases in Strasbourg, like that of *Marckx*, deal with discrimination;[6] in the *Pla and Puncernau v Andorra* case there is a reference to Section 8 as well: it was considered a discrimination concerning private and family life to differentiate between adopted children and biological children.[7]

---

4   Raffai (2009).

5   Schilling (2004).

6   *Marckx v Belgium*, judgment 13 June 1979, Strum (1982) 1150-1159; Jayme (1979) 2425-2429.

7   No. 69498/01 based on violation arts. 8 and 14: "43. The Court has had occasion in previous cases to examine allegations of differences of treatment for succession purposes both under art. 14 taken in conjunction with art. 8 [...] and under art. 14 taken in conjunction with art. 1 of Protocol No. 1 [...]. The

However, the right to succession is provided by the various constitutions, thus in Section 14 (1) of the German Grundgesetz; Section 33 (1) of the Spanish Constitution; Section 62 (1) of the Portuguese Constitution; Section 17 (1) of the Bulgarian Constitution; Section 64 (1) of the Polish Constitution; and Section 33 of the Slovenian Constitution, it is mentioned together with property; in the Croatian Constitution both rights are mentioned in relation with one another, but formulated separately in Section 48 (1) and in Section 48 (4); similarly, in Section 20 (1) of the Slovak Constitution and Section 11 (1) of the Czech Constitution.[8] Similar wordings to those contained in the German Constitution can be found elsewhere: "Property and succession are guaranteed."[9] The German constitutional concept deems the right of inheriting to be a fundamental right,[10] which includes the right of inheriting private property, the fact that private property may remain private after the death of the owner, as well as freedom of testation and the family-bound nature of succession. The Hungarian constitutional approach is different, since the right to succession is not protected as a fundamental right.[11]

2.1.2 The Modern Hungarian Constitution

Act XX of 1949, the new Hungarian written constitution, became the symbol of the socialist social and economic regime. In Section 8 (1) the Constitution of the People's Republic of Hungary declared that the Constitution recognizes property acquired through work. Paragraph (2) declared that private property and private initiatives shall not violate public interests. And paragraph (2) declared that the Constitution guarantees the right to succession. This wording still produces a strange impression: the communist – socialist constitution did not guarantee succession, rather it first declared that private property is of secondary importance, and then provided for the right to succession. Although the great constitutional reform of 1972 retained this wording, succession was placed in a stand-alone section, section 12, and by this highlight-

---

Court reaffirms that the essential object of art. 8 is to protect the individual against arbitrary interference by the public authorities [...]. That being said, it does not merely compel the State to abstain from such interference: in addition to this primarily negative undertaking, there may be positive obligations inherent in an effective 'respect' for private or family life [...]. The factor common to those cases was that the difference of treatment of which complaint was made resulted directly from the domestic legislation, which distinguished between legitimate and illegitimate children [...] or between children born of an adulterous relationship and other children, whether or not born in wedlock [...]. The question raised in each of these cases was whether such difference of treatment within the legal system of the respondent States violated the rights of the applicants under art. 14 taken in conjunction with art. 8 of the Convention or art. 1 of Protocol No. 1." (Quotations are deleted).

[8]   Weber (2004) 769.

[9]   Art. 14 (1): Das Eigentum und das Erbrecht werden gewährleistet.

[10] Haumann – Hohloch (2008) 68.

[11] Salát (2009) 14 § 13.

ing the norm became more emphatic. The preceding section 11 of the Constitution declared that the People's Republic of Hungary acknowledges and protects private property.[12] In this way the concept of private property and its protection was recognized at a constitutional level as well, and before the guarantee of the right to succession.

After that, the next major change was only brought about by the Constitution of the political changes (Act XXXI of 1989), with the structure and wording that has remained valid to this day. Section 9 of the Constitution declared the equality of public and private property, and the wording was clarified in section 14: "The Constitution guarantees the right of succession." This is the law to this day. Essentially, constitutional lawyers qualify this norm as one of the aspects of the right to private property.[13]

2.1.3 The Practice of the Constitutional Court Concerning Succession

The right to succession is discussed as a supplementary topic in the individual resolutions of the Hungarian Constitutional Court.[14] From the constitutional point of view the right to succession cannot be considered a "fundamental right", rather a "constitutional right." It is an important tenet that detailed rules on succession cannot be derived from the constitutional right to succession, since its development is subject to the regulatory power of the state.

In connection with the regulation of partial compensation for the nationalization of the socialist-communist era, the issue of compensation and succession was one of the important matters in the practice of the Constitutional Court. The persons identified by the Act on Compensation are to be considered not as heirs, rather as persons entitled to compensation defined by law. According to one constitutional judgement: "[...] there is no relevant relationship between the constitutional right to succession (section 14 of the Constitution) and section 2 of the Act on Compensation."[15]

The applicant, who lost his father in the Second World War, first had to bring litigation for the declaration of filiation, to prove that he was a son of the deceased born out of wedlock. After that, since the father was declared missing in Auschwitz during the Second World War, and at the request of the child, the court declared the father dead, as of January 15, 1945. The son, who was recognized as such in the eyes of the law as well, submitted a claim for succession as a descendant, but his claim was subject to the rules of succession effective in Hungary at the time of the death. Pursuant to the rules in effect at the time, a child born out of wedlock was considered a member of the family of the mother

---

[12] "Private property" is not the exact translation. "Személyi tulajdon" is a "personal property", a property (the asset) which can be owned by individuals.

[13] Sonnevend (2003) 643.

[14] Holló – Balogh (2005) 346-349.

[15] Resolution No. 28/1991 (June 3) of the Constitutional Court.

with full rights, including succession, but the law did not recognize the filiation regarding the father and the father's family, thus the relationship of succession was not recognized, so a child born out of wedlock was not an heir to the father. The father was only bound by the obligation to support the child. The son initiated a Constitutional review of this norm. The family law rule on filiation had been ineffective for over 50 years, so the Constitutional Court saw no possibility for a retroactive Constitutional review, based on the need to protect the rights and legal relationships acquired by other parties earlier, i.e. on the basis of due process of law and the rule of law.[16] In another case, the Constitutional Court also rejected the petition that called for the legal title and inheritability of the place of burial (tomb site). The Constitutional Court declared that the exclusion of the place of burial from the scope of private property does not affect fundamental rights, since the "right to the acquisition of property" is not a fundamental right.[17] Since it began its task, the Constitutional Court has always considered private property to be a fundamental right.[18]

In 1950, in the communist era, a testator was condemned by a criminal court and his assets were confiscated. The sentence was carried out. As a result of a procedure initiated by the heirs, in 1999 the sentence of the penal court was invalidated and the testator, who was no longer alive, was acquitted. The heirs requested that the state should compensate them for the confiscated assets, but the court rejected the petition. They submitted a complaint under constitutional law, which the Constitutional Court rejected. In the justification of its resolution, the Constitutional Court invoked art. 3 of the 7th Supplementary Protocol of the Convention for the Protection of Human Rights and Fundamental Freedoms, which regulated the right to compensation. According to the Constitutional Court, the accused is entitled to the right of compensation, and the regulatory latitude of the individual states lies within that. In its reasoning the Court pointed out that the Constitution protects property already acquired, but this does not extend to the acquisition of assets – in this case meaning the acquisition of assets by the heirs:[19] "The state is not obliged to provide assistance to a private individual with the acquisition of property or the enjoyment of property"; "it is not possible to derive detailed rules from the right to succession concerning the regime of succession." This rather controversial decision mingles the acquisition of property, succession and the right to compensation for the confiscation of acquired property. It genuinely reflects the hesitation of judicature on fundamental rights.

Foreigners shall not acquire arable land in Hungary, including acquisition of title by succession, which is also excluded (Act LV of 1994, Sections 4 and 7). In a case heard by the Constitutional Court, the petitioner requested that this prohibition should be declared unconstitutional. In a first case the Court

---

[16] Resolution No. 65/1995 (November 10) of the Constitutional Court.

[17] Resolution No. 529/B/1999, Section III.1, of the Constitutional Court. Salát (2009) 14 § 2.

[18] Sólyom (2001) 126-140.

[19] Resolution No. 936/D/1997 of the Constitutional Court, passed on January 26, 1999.

declared that the prohibitions do not restrict, unnecessarily, disproportionately and without reasonable justification, the right to succession guaranteed in section 14 of the Constitution[20] and in a second case, the Constitutional Court declared that the prohibition "is not unconstitutional because it is reasonably justified."[21]

To summarize, in the Hungarian approach to constitutional law -in contrast with, for example, German constitutional law-[22] the right to succession is not a fundamental right. The acquisition of property – which includes succession – is not protected as a fundamental right either.

2.2   Public Law Restrictions

Different restrictions imposed by public law may have an impact on the law of succession. These restrictions primarily come under the heading of public law, affecting property right and certain assets. These may include, for example, public rules that qualify certain assets as non-transferable, the prohibition of possession of certain assets, such as illicit drugs, firearms, arable land, etc. It is an absolute prohibition when the asset may not be possessed by private individuals; in other cases, it may only be acquired with a license. Other restrictions can be mentioned as well.

The obligation of paying stamp duty is another restriction on succession; in fact, it is a kind of tax, although it is not called a tax in Hungary. In one of the cases the Constitutional Court assessed the issue of determining the value of the asset used as the basis for the payment of stamp duty, i.e. what date should be taken as the basis for the calculation of the duty. The provisions of Hungarian law on stamp duty identify the day of the testator's death as the date of the payment of duty, and the prevailing value at that time should be used as a basis for calculation; the Constitutional Court did not find these provisions unconstitutional.[23]

2.3   Private Law Restrictions

There are other restrictions to freedom of testation, which are identified by rules of private law. The definition of what assets and claims belong to the estate may be classed in this category. For example, only the affected person, i.e. the injured party, may claim non-pecuniary damages; similarly, the enforcement of privacy rights is also personal. These claims and rights cannot be inherited, but if the beneficiary brought legal action during his or her life, then the heirs may enter the litigation as legal successors.[24] If the lawsuit

---

[20] Resolution No. 35/1994 (June 24) of the Constitutional Court.

[21] Resolution No. 819/B/2006, Section III.3 of the Constitutional Court.

[22] BVerfGE 91, 346.

[23] Resolution No. 210/B/1997 of the Constitutional Court.

[24] BH 1996.639.

is not yet in progress for those claims, only preparations have been made (for example, the debtor has been required to pay with notice), the heir has no right to bring lawsuit.

Indemnification pursuant to a law promulgated after the death of the testator does not belong to the testator's estate.[25]

Wills must be drafted in person (Section 623 (2) CC), not by proxy or authorized representatives.

Wills must be drafted by one person only; joint wills are not allowed (Section 644 CC), with the exception of inheritance contracts, which married couples may enter.

The form of testamentary disposition is subject to strict rules, basically only written testamentary disposition is accepted,[26] oral wills (nuncupative will) being exceptional in Hungarian law.[27] The CC provides several rules on the written form, which the courts interpret strictly. Here we do not present the detailed rules.

The testator must identify the person of the heir. This cannot be left to a third party, to a sweepstake or other similar mechanisms.[28] If the heir is not properly identified, the testamentary disposition is invalid. Hungarian law does not allow fideicommissum; however, substitutional heirs are allowed for cases where the heir appointed in the first place cannot take (*substitutio vulgaris*).[29]

The Hungarian court practice is relatively strict concerning the "participants" in the execution of a will. Testamentary gifts to people who provided assistance to the testator by preparing, drafting and executing the will need to be confirmed by the testator in handwriting, otherwise these parts of the will may become invalid.[30] A person is deemed to have participated in drafting the will if he or she has written down the last will dictated by the testator and then read it back to the testator.[31]

No prohibition on alienation of assets may be declared by testamentary disposition, i.e. the testator may not prescribe that the heir shall not sell the inherited assets. Also, indivisible physical objects must not be divided up by succession (for example, rooms of a house must not be given to separate heirs) and the rules of property law must not be overridden by testamentary disposition.

After the testator's death, the heirs may divide the estate disregarding his or her declared last will, thus neglecting it completely. It is an important condi-

---

[25] BH 1999.23.

[26] Sections 627-632 CC.

[27] Sections 634-635 CC.

[28] BH 1996.425.

[29] Section 640 CC.

[30] Section 632 CC.

[31] BH 1986.418.

tion that after the testator's death all heirs must agree on the distribution of the estate in writing.[32]

There is one more restriction that could be mentioned here: it is not possible to inherit liabilities only, the liability of the heir is limited to the extent of the volume of the assets.

We shall deal with the additional restrictions in the following parts of this paper.

3   Freedom of Testation versus Legally Granted Hereditary Rights

The restrictions on testamentary freedom may be affected by the following rules and facts:
  i) Preliminary facts affecting the size of the estate, deriving from the status of the testator, such as marriage, registered and non-registered partnership; and
  ii) Compulsory share.

The status of the testator (whether he or she is married or cohabiting, for instance) determines the scope and size of his or her assets and thereupon the estate. A couple living together has assets but usually these assets are not divided between them; rather, they are managed and used as common property by the couple. If one of the parties dies the common assets shall be divided first, prior to determining the scope and size of the estate. The detailed rules of the property relations within marriages and non-marital partnerships cannot be dealt with in this paper.

3.1   Preliminaries on Compulsory Share

The compulsory share has existed in Hungarian law since 1852. The Hungarian rules upheld this institution adopted from the Austrian ABGB.[33] The compulsory share has become an integral part of the Hungarian private law culture, insofar as the law of succession is concerned, for over 150 years. The rules on compulsory share are known in the present Hungarian society; this cultural tradition practically survived the modifications of the CC and it will probably remain unaffected by re-codification.

3.2   Functions of the Compulsory Share

The following functions of the compulsory share should be mentioned: a) Guarantee of a minimum amount of assets from the estate for

---

[32] Section 53 (4) of decree on probate procedure – No. 6/1958 (4 July) of the Minister of Justice.

[33] Sándorfalvi (1939) 385.

the next of kin of the testator;[34] b) The testator is bound by a certain obligation to support his or her relatives even after death (the so-called "care" theory)[35]; c) The purpose of the compulsory share is the prevention of abuse, to ensure that the testator should not be able to put the relatives actually dependent on him or her at a disadvantage arbitrarily.[36] Furthermore, it prevents children from being treated arbitrarily by their parents;[37] d) Similarly to the function stated above (b), the compulsory share guarantees a moral duty of support after death as well, since on the one hand, the testator is free to exclude his or her relatives from succession and, at the same time, this freedom is incompatible with the moral social requirement that can be formulated as the obligation of support to the closest relatives by the testator after death;[38] e) Certain authors mention the family solidarity function (the so-called "Solidaritätsbelohnung") as a quasi-primium concerning the compulsory share;[39] f) Others are of the opinion that the compulsory share has a social function, as it guarantees the provision of a minimum amount of assets to the affected relatives from the estate, which means support in the form of assets. In certain cases it may even amount to the assets necessary for starting or continuing an independent life; g) It has also been raised that the compulsory share has a function of support as well, to the relatives who will remain alone or without assistance after the testator's death; h) Certain authors pose the question whether the compulsory share could provide a minimum guarantee for the right to division of the estate; i) According to another approach, the estate should be considered as family assets and the compulsory share protects this familial nature of the assets by its rule of adjustment ("das Gut rinnt wie das Blut"; e.g. it is typical in family enterprises and small farms that the assets are held together), and in a more abstract wording, others argue that the function of the compulsory share is the preservation of the unity of the family and their assets.[40] j) The compulsory share would have the function of the division of assets aimed at the exact opposite of the former theory, and it prevents excessive concentration of assets by requiring the estate

---

[34] Coing (1990) 50: "Ihr Zweck ist, den nächsten Angehörigen eine gewisse Beteiligung am Nachlasse auf alle Fälle zu sichern, auch wenn der Erblasser sie in seinem Testament nicht bedacht hat"; Leopold (2006) No. 72; Viághy (1987) 96-97; Vékás (1995) 116.

[35] Brox (2003) 308, "Sorgetheorie": "Diese Regelung (Pflichtteilsrecht) beruht auf dem Gedanken, dass den Erblasser eine über den Tod hinausgehende Sorgepflicht für seine nahen Angehörigen trifft".

[36] Oechsler (2000) 607, 612: "Sein Zweck besteht vielmehr darin, die (potentiell) vom Erblasser abhängigen Angehörigen vor Willkürakten des Erblassers zu Lebzeiten zu schützen" (prevention of abuse).

[37] Sándorfalvi (1939) 368.

[38] Olzen (2005) No. 1022: "Moralische Sorgepflicht nach dem Tod?"; "Die Testierfreiheit ermöglicht es dem Erblasser, selbst nächste Angehörige von der Erbfolge auszuschließen. Dies erscheint ungerechtfertigt, wenn man den moralischen Standpunkt akzeptiert, dass ihn auch über seinen Tod hinaus eine Sorgepflicht für seinen engsten Familienkreis trifft"(Duty to support).

[39] The so called "Solidaritätsbelohnungsfunktion des Pflichtteils" (Heinrich (2000) 20).

[40] Karpen (2007) 169-184.

to be divided up;[41] k) The Federal Constitutional Court of Germany was of the opinion that the legal institution of the compulsory share, as a constitutional right, is the guarantee of preservation and protection of the constitutional value of family solidarity, and as such, it was pronounced constitutional, together with the constitutionality of the freedom of testamentary disposition, or even as opposed to it.[42]

Many authors argue that the original function of the compulsory share can no longer be justified; its function of supporting the young generation with establishing an independent life has become obsolete by now, owing to the increase in life expectancy. At the time of the testator's death the generation of the children is no longer so much in need of their parents' assets as even 50 or 100 years ago; as for its function of dividing concentrated assets, the compulsory share is not capable of accomplishing a reasonable economic division.[43]

Today in Hungary, 20 years after the downfall of the socialist system, when a process of wealth accumulation began, one of the features of the new regime is that members of a family create jointly owned enterprises and the joint work of the families is concentrated in assets amassed over the years. Therefore, the origin of these assets is the joint work of the family members. Often these family assets are considered to belong to them all, and the surviving family members only become aware of the randomness brought about by the law of succession upon the testator's death: it does not hold together the assets that had been held together while all the family members were alive.

We see something radically different in the existence and fundamental nature of the compulsory share. It is not just a question of the material world, rather the legal mapping of a fundamental anthropological feature of the human being, which derives from the social nature of humans. The basis of society is the family, and not the single individual. The basis of social coexistence is not the unrestricted and unconditional free will of the individual, rather the written, and even more so, the unwritten rules of social life. Human society and life in the material Western civilization are equally destined for social coexistence; this situation of social coexistence is manifested in the compulsory share, and the law confirms and expresses these spiritual, religious and material roots and bases – albeit not always consciously – and sometimes, like in the case of the compulsory share, presents and articulates them.

For this reason, the counterbalance of the individualistic nature of testamentary freedom is expressed in the compulsory share, which is "attached to the family" and to the constraints that the family imposes upon the estate. Therefore, the compulsory share, deriving from the social nature of the human being, can be defined as an entitlement to the testator's assets for the testator's closest

---

[41] Röthel (2007) 807.

[42] "Ausdruck der Familiensolidarität", BVerfG, Beschluss vom 19 April 2005, NJW 2005, 1561.

[43] Röthel (2007) 807.

biological relatives,[44] or persons qualified as such by the law, and for the person the testator has chosen as spouse or partner. The social coexistence cannot be described in a simple system of "give and receive" relations, especially not among the family members. In the same way, the compulsory share cannot be formulated as a simple claim of "I am entitled to", "I receive" or "I need", which the beneficiary of the claim may enforce at will.[45]

3.3   The Rules on Compulsory Share

The compulsory share imposes a private law restriction to freedom of testation. It is a share of assets provided under the law from the estate to certain specified persons, the persons most closely related to the testator, even if the testator bequeaths his or her assets to another person, or if he or she allocates less assets to the persons entitled to the compulsory share than required by the law. In Hungarian law these persons are the descendants, not only children, but also grandchildren and their descendants, spouses, registered partners and parents (Section 661 CC). Among these potential beneficiaries, only those who would take in intestacy if there were not a will are entitled to the compulsory share (CC Section 661). Family law rules define who is to be considered a child, spouse or parent. The concept of registered partner is defined in the act on registered life partners.[46] In all cases, factual relationships are insufficient; a legal relationship is required, i.e. the person has to be a child, a spouse, a parent or a registered partner under the law.

Former spouses or registered partners are not entitled to the compulsory share, nor are those with whom the testator had ceased to cohabit at the time of his or her death, at least when separation was intended to be permanent. In the case of children and parents the matter of living together is disregarded.

3.3.1   Beneficiaries

The right to a compulsory share does not amount to succession, even if it is linked to the testator's death. It is in fact a claim under the law of obligations, which the persons entitled to the compulsory share must enforce; it must be filed at the probate proceedings and enforced against the obligors. Since succession is *ipso iure* in Hungarian law, i.e. the estate of a person devolves upon an heir in its entirety after the person's death (Section 598 CC), the beneficiary

---

[44] At the beginning of the 20th century it was emphasized that the compulsory share fortifies the relationship among relatives. See Tóth (1932) 308.

[45] *Pla and Puncernau v Andorra*, ECHR, 2004 (appl. No. 69498/0): "26. [...] Family life does not include only social, moral or cultural relations, for example in the sphere of children's education; it also comprises interests of a material kind, as is shown by, amongst other things, the obligations in respect of maintenance and the position occupied in the domestic legal systems of the majority of the Contracting States by the institution of the reserved portion of an estate (réserve héréditaire)."

[46] See fn. 3 above.

must make and deliver a statement in order to obtain the compulsory share. Being a claim under the law of obligations, the applicable statute of limitations is five years, unless the beneficiary was not aware of the testator's death and this is excusable.

A beneficiary may be deprived of the compulsory share (section 606 with 600 CC). The rules on deprivation of the heirs apply. Therefore, a person will be deprived of the compulsory share if he or she:
a) dies before the decedent;
b) cannot legally acquire the estate at the time of descent and distribution;
c) is undeserving of the inheritance;
d) has waived his or her right to the inheritance;
e) has been excluded from the inheritance or disinherited by the decedent;
f) has disclaimed the inheritance.

The CC separately defines the concepts of being undeserving of the inheritance (Section 602 CC), waiver (Sections 603-605 CC), exclusion (Section 637 (2)(3) CC) and disclaimer (Section 674 CC), each of which is a separate legal term with further special rules. It is especially important that the law lists the reasons for being undeserving and exclusion; a detailed court practice has evolved around these concepts. The right to the compulsory share can be deprived by the testator only for reasons listed in the CC, as follows (Section 663 CC):
1) Disinheritance can take place if a person entitled to a compulsory share of inheritance
a) Is undeserving of inheritance from the testator;
b) Has committed a serious crime to the injury of the testator;
c) Has attempted to take the life of the testator's spouse, registered partner or his or her next of kin or has committed another serious crime to their injury;
d) Has seriously violated his or her legal obligation to support the testator;
e) Lives by immoral standards;
f) Has been sentenced to five years of imprisonment or longer by final verdict.
2) A testator can also disinherit his or her spouse or registered partner because of a conduct seriously violating matrimonial duties or the duties of registered partners (Section 663 (2) CC).

Special deprivation applies to the spouse and registered partner. If the conjugal community no longer exists at the time of death, i.e. the married couple or registered partners no longer live together, then the surviving spouse or life partner is not entitled to inherit or to the compulsory share. However, this cause of disinheritance can only be alleged by a person who, as the result of the disqualification of the spouse or registered partner, would inherit or would be exempted from an obligation or other burden to which he or she is bound, by virtue of the testamentary disposition.

3.3.2 Extent

The compulsory share in the case of descendants, parents, spouses and registered partners amounts to half of what they would receive in intestacy. In intestacy, if the children or descendants inherit, the spouse or the registered partner is entitled to the usufruct of the entire estate. In some special cases, i.e. when the deceased leaves neither children nor other descendants, assets acquired from his or her ascendants shall pass back to the ascendant of the deceased, and the spouse or the registered partner inherit only a right of usufruct over these assets. According to the rules on the compulsory share, the spouse and registered partner in this case would be entitled only to a restricted usufruct over the asset as compulsory share. The restricted usufruct entails limited use of the asset, to satisfy the everyday needs of the spouse or registered partner. For example, an apartment where the spouse lived together with the testator must not be taken away from the spouse, and the court usually does not restrict him or her in the use of it as beneficiary of the compulsory share if he or she has no other apartments.

3.3.3 Basis

The law is generous when defining the basis of the compulsory share since the net worth of the estate is not the only factor to be considered. The basis for calculation is the net value of the estate, and the net value, at the time of the gift, of the donations made by the testator *inter vivos* over the last fifteen years (Section 666 (1) CC.).

Exceptionally, if the inclusion of a donation at its net value at the time it was made is seriously unjust to any person concerned, the court shall determine the value of the donation in the light of all of the circumstances (Section 666 (2) CC).

The values of assets donated by the testator before the creation of a relationship conveying entitlement to a compulsory share are not included in the basis of the compulsory share. For example, if the testator has a 13 year old daughter, the basis of her compulsory share shall not be increased by donations made 14 years earlier, i.e. before she was born. Customary gifts, support given to spouses, registered partners and descendants who are in need of support and support provided without consideration to other persons in need up to the extent necessary for subsistence do not increase the basis of a compulsory share (Section 667 (1) CC). The testator may decide that a donation made to one of the beneficiaries is not to be counted towards his or her compulsive share, as long as this does not damage any other beneficiary's entitlement to the inheritance (Section 667 (4) and 668 (3) CC).

The CC also determines when eligibility for the compulsory share begins: The date of wedding is the date for eligibility for the compulsory share of children born in wedlock or adopted by the spouses. The date of registration of the registered partnership is the governing date for children of the registered partners. In all other cases the date of conception of the child is the governing date for the compulsory share claim. If a testator was married or engaged in a registered partnership more than twice, the first marriage or registered partnership shall be the relationship conveying entitlement to a compulsory share of inheritance (Section 667 (2) CC).

Only the assets of the estate shall serve as a basis for the compulsory share of inheritance due to a spouse or registered partner in the form of usufruct (Section 667 (3) CC). Therefore, donations *inter vivos* are not taken into account in this case.

3.3.4   Facts Affecting the Allocated Share

Everything received by a beneficiary from an estate under any title as well as any gratuitous donations he or she has received from the testator shall be applied to satisfy the compulsory share (Section 668 (1) CC). If a person entitled to the compulsory share has been disqualified from inheritance, the value of all of the donations received by that person from the testator shall be set off to his or her descendant's compulsory share. Two or more descendants shall set off the donations of their ancestor in proportion to their shares in the estate (Section 668 (2) CC).

3.3.5   Payment

It is the fundamental rule that the compulsory share shall be paid in money.[47] The CC expressly provides that the beneficiary may request dispensation in money (Section 672 (1) CC); if this is unfair to any of the parties involved, the court may order dispensation in kind (Section 672 (3) CC). It will be dispensed in kind if this was the will of the testator (Section 672 (2) CC).

3.3.6   Obligor

The compulsory share may be primarily claimed from persons receiving a share of the estate, such as heirs and legatees. If that does not cover the compulsory share, those who received donations from a testator within fifteen years prior to his or her death shall be responsible for that part of the compulsory share that cannot be satisfied from the estate, irrespective of the date of the donation (Section 669 (1) (b) CC). Hungarian law does not exclude any gratuitous transfer from the basis of calculation of the forced share, so that the establishment of foundations or gifts to charities must also be taken into account.[48] Therefore, the foundation or charity may be obliged to pay the

---

[47]   BH 2001.475.

[48]   About the topic "Law of succession and foundation law" see Csehi (2005) 412; Csehi (1999) 37-61; Csehi (2006) 316.

compulsory share if the estate is insufficient to satisfy the beneficiaries' claims. A different matter is whether the foundation or the charity may be released from paying the compulsory share if it proves that it has already used the donation for charity purposes.[49]

3.3.7 Collisions with Other Rights

When the compulsory share and the usufruct of a surviving spouse conflict, if the estate does not cover both, the right of usufruct of the surviving spouse prevails; it cannot be reduced.[50]

3.3.8 The Future of the Compulsory Share

One of the current issues is the reform or possible elimination of the compulsory share,[51] as has already been raised in the Hungarian legal literature.[52] It has been rightfully suggested that the compulsory share may have lost its original function.[53] In several cases the compulsory share results in the division of large family estates; it may constitute an insurmountable impediment to succession involving companies and enterprises, since the ownership of these has to be split up.[54] This is connected with the possibility of transferring assets to a foundation prior to the demise, so that this does not affect the status of the relevant asset.

According to the preliminary works and the draft for the new Hungarian CC, the compulsory share shall remain in the law of succession basically with the same rules as in force today.[55]

4 Freedom of Testation versus Freedom to Enter into Inheritance Agreements

The power to dispose of assets *mortis causa* may also be implemented in another form, by contract. The CC regulates the inheritance agreement (Sections 655-658 CC) and *donatio mortis causa* (Section 659 CC) as parts of the law of succession, but there are other forms of contracts as well that provide assets to the other contracting party upon death.

---

[49] Section 361 (2) CC states that if the donation, as a special unjust enrichment, has already been spent with good faith, it shall not return; in other words, the payment can be refused.

[50] BH 1988.100.

[51] Martiny (2002) A1-120; Röthel (2007b).

[52] Bessenyei (1998) 38.

[53] Heinrich (2001a); Heinrich (2001b) 447.

[54] Oechsler (2000) 603-626.

[55] Preliminary works: Weiss (2003) 975-999. Summary of the case law, Sőth (1997).

4.1   Contracts Regulated Outside the Law of Succession

4.1.1   Support Contract

Under a support contract one of the parties shall be obliged to provide proper support for the dependant private individual; support shall include general care, medical treatment, nursing, catering and other activities provided for in the agreement between the parties; in exchange, the dependant transfers assets to the provider (Sections 586 and 587 CC). The asset usually means real property, which is generally an apartment or house – quite often the dependant's only asset. The contract shall be terminated upon the death of the dependant. The support contract is basically concluded for valuable consideration, and the CC does not regulate at what date the title to the real property shall be transferred to the provider. It is possible to register the title for the provider upon the conclusion of the contract, in which case the right to obtain support from the title holder shall be recorded in the land registry, as well as the fact that the dependant is the beneficiary of such a contract. The title to the property may be transferred at a later date as well, but if the parties defer it to the time of death, it may pose a real legal risk for the provider. If the parties agree that the provider will acquire the title of the asset upon the dependant's death, on the one hand, the law of succession will apply, and, on the other, the title will only pass to the provider upon registration. Since the heirs acquire title *ipso iure*, the provider is left with only a contractual claim against the heirs.

Substantially, the content of support contracts is the same as the content of inheritance contracts, but while the former can be freely restricted to nursing and care, in the latter the support element is a required part of the contract. One of the subtypes of support contracts is the life-annuity contract, where the provider does not provide support *in natura*, but in the form of money or other periodical payments (Section 591 CC).

4.1.2   Life Insurance

In the case of death the beneficiary will receive the insurance payment, although this is not considered succession, but only a contractual relationship (Section 560 CC).[56]

4.1.3   Savings Deposits

In Hungarian law savings deposits can serve a support function, where the person in need of it provides that in the event of his or her death the bank shall pay the balance to the person designated therein.[57] Here the law specifically provides that this act shall not be considered succession, the amount

---

[56] Opinion of the college of judges of the Supreme Court of Hungary No. 75.

[57] § 10 Law-decree 2 of 1989 on savings deposits.

is not part of the estate and is not subject to the probate procedure. If this money is a gift, then it will naturally be counted towards the base of the compulsory share; in the same way, if the heir receives it, it will be counted towards his or her share.

4.1.4 Copyright

Another example of transfer of assets upon death is a special provision of the Hungarian law on copyright.[58] In the case of copyright the law allows the appointment of a trustee to manage the author's copyright estate. This appointed person will be entitled to exercise the author's moral rights, but he or she is not considered an heir; this appointment is not a case of succession. If the author chooses not to exercise this right, the moral rights will fall to whoever acquired them through succession (Section 14 Copyright Act).

4.2 Contracts Within the Law of Succession

Within the scope of the law of succession, the CC identifies three types of contract. One is a specific contract concluded between descendants concerning the future estate (Section 680), the other two are contracts concluded by the testator.

4.2.1 Inheritance Contracts

In the case of an inheritance contract, the testator undertakes, in exchange for support or a life-annuity, to make the provider his or her heir (Section 665 CC). In an inheritance contract the testator may also make other testamentary dispositions, such as exclusion, disinheritance or otherwise. The other party has no such right. This contract has a fiduciary nature and continuous service must be provided; it must be concluded for a long term. If the provider pays a life-annuity, then the fiduciary, personal relationship is not that important.[59] The strict rules of written form are applicable (Section 656; Sections 627-632 CC).

The number of contractual parties is not restricted to one provider and one dependant. It is an exceptional rule that spouses as testators may conclude an inheritance contract with a third party in the same contract (Section 73 of the Decree-Act No. 11 of 1960). Two or more persons can be providers; it often happens that spouses undertake the obligation of support.[60] A legal entity may also be a provider, which is not very compatible with the requirement of the personal relation between testator and provider.

---

[58] Act No. LXXVI of 1999, as amended.

[59] BH 1996.534; BH 2000.105.

[60] Gellér (2001) 18.

The concept and contents of support is the same as mentioned above concerning the support contract; the CC refers to those rules (Section 658 (1) CC). The scope and extent of support shall be provided matching the state and needs of the decedent,[61] and the provider shall have the appropriate assets for that. However, concerning assets the legal effects vary. The contract on care and nursing only is not sufficient and cannot be considered an inheritance agreement.[62] The testator may no longer dispose over assets encumbered by an inheritance contract; he or she shall not sell the assets and shall not make any further testamentary disposition. Prohibition on alienation and encumbrance must be recorded in the land registry on the real property bound by the inheritance contract. On the one hand, the prohibition on alienation and encumbrance is based on the CC, i.e. the law; on the other hand, once it has been recorded in the land registry, the acquisition of the contractual heir is guaranteed with the effect of property rights. In exceptional cases, the courts acknowledge that the testator may make another last will, if he or she had already started the procedure or lawsuit with the purpose of ceasing or terminating the inheritance contract.[63]

The contract cannot be invalidated or terminated unilaterally; only a court may declare it null and void. Exceptionally, the court will acknowledge that the contract has ceased if there is no performance and the conduct (implication) of the parties demonstrates that this is their unanimous will; then the contract may be declared to have terminated even without the otherwise obligatory written form (Section 658 (1) CC). The fact that the dependent rejects the support or annuity is not sufficient in itself for the contract to be determined.[64]

An inheritance contract may also be concluded with a person who is legally obliged to support the dependant, such as a spouse or a child. In this case the spouse must have assets of his or her own that are sufficient to fulfil the obligation of support.[65] It may be concluded with a foster child, but it is important that the provider should provide actual services,[66] and it may also be concluded with a registered or not-registered partner.[67]

Inheritance agreements have produced a huge amount of case-law. According to case-law, the assets bound by inheritance agreements must be disregarded when claims for compulsory share are brought forward. Therefore, if the testator has concluded an inheritance contract on all of his or her assets, i.e. on the subsequent estate, then even if there is a person entitled to the compulsory share, according to the established court practice, the contractual assets cannot be claimed from the contractual heir for the purposes of the compulsory share.[68] Therefore, often an inheritance contract is concluded with the aim of evading

---

[61] BH 1995.347.

[62] BH 1976.372; Gellér (2001) 28.

[63] BH 1985.232; BH 1994.80.

[64] BH 2008.242.

[65] Gellér (2001) 18.

[66] BH 1989.272.

[67] BH 1990.157.

[68] The opinion of the college of the judges of the Supreme Court of Hungary No. PK 89 subsection c and BH 1980.286.

the compulsory share, which the beneficiaries entitled to compulsory share may later challenge, claiming that it is invalid. The court will primarily assess whether support was provided according to the inheritance contract, i.e. what kind of services were provided by the provider to the testator. If this cannot be determined, the contract may be declared a sham contract and can be challenged, i.e. the contract is invalid.[69] Allegation of a will being invalid can only be made by a person who would inherit or be relieved of a burden if the will is declared invalid, the court must not proceed *ex officio*[70] (Sections 653, 656 CC). This case-law developed further in such a manner that regarding last wills in which the testator identified the heir because the heir supported the testator, that part of the testamentary benefit which corresponds to the value of the support is not counted towards the basis of the compulsory share. The courts will deduct the value of the support from the base of the compulsory share.[71]

In some cases the court may declare the inheritance contract in conflict with common decency, for example, when the contract was concluded at a time of imminent death of the dependent, and with regard to that, it was concluded with the obvious aim of acquiring material benefits, since the provider was aware that the obligation of support was to be fulfilled only for a very short period of time.[72] In another case, however, the Supreme Court declared that the testator must not be deprived of the right to conclude a contract of inheritance and dispose of his or her assets, even when death is imminent due to an incurable disease[73] (especially if the contract is concluded at the request of the dependant and the provider undertakes to provide full care and nursing)[74]. If the testator concludes a sale and purchase contract mingled with donation, it is not incompatible with common decency.[75]

4.2.2 Donatio Mortis Causa[76]

If a donation includes the condition that the donee shall survive the donor, then it is a special *mortis causa* contract, which is regulated in Hungarian law among the provisions of succession law (Section 659 CC). An essential element of the *donatio mortis causa* is that the donor must die first. This contract is subject to the formal requirements of wills and inheritance agreements.

Whilst one of the parties to an inheritance agreement is the heir, the beneficiary of a *donatio mortis causa* must not be heir; the law excludes this option

---

[69] BH 2001.475.

[70] BH 1996.590.

[71] PK 89, subsection a, see BH 1990 157 (fn. 67 above).

[72] BH 1979.12.; more recently BDT 2008.1868 – Decision of the Court of Appeal of Szeged.

[73] BH 1989.230; BH 2004.59.

[74] BH 2002.267.

[75] BDT 2008.1880 – Decision of the Court of Appeal of Pécs.

[76] Excellent paper on the topic by Kegel (1972).

explicitly. The heir under an inheritance agreement is a universal successor; instead, in a *donatio mortis causa* the donee only acquires certain assets. The subject matter of the agreement cannot be the entire estate, or even a substantial part thereof; it is limited, so that it can only operate like a legacy (Section 659 (2) CC). It is difficult to specify what percentage sets the limit, perhaps a donee *mortis causa* cannot receive more than 20 to 25 per cent of the value of the entire estate. If this measure is exceeded, the contract shall be null and void.[77] The Hungarian law recognizes legacies (*Vindaktionslegat*) (Section 641 (1) CC), but legacies are made in a will. It is also permissible to make donations that must be fulfilled by the heir to the beneficiary. The *donatio mortis causa* is not considered a legacy, but the same limitations apply as far as the amount is concerned.

While the inheritance contract is entered into by the parties for a valuable consideration, i.e. the provider is made heir in exchange for consideration, the *donatio mortis causa* is a gratuitous contract, similar to a will. Otherwise the provisions of the contract of donation of the CC shall be applicable to the contract of *donatio mortis causa*.

It is disputed when this contract becomes effective, when fulfilment is required and what is the meaning of the condition that the donee must survive the testator. Some authors qualify this latter as a condition precedent, i.e. the contract of donation becomes effective upon death, before that time fulfilment is excluded by definition. The donor's assets are not reduced during his or her life, but upon the donor's death this part of his or her assets are given to the donee. Otherwise, i.e. if the contract of donation is concluded and the gift is delivered, and death is considered a condition subsequent, it is not a *mortis causa* contract, but rather an *inter vivos* contract. An agreement that imposes the obligation of delivery of the gift upon death is also not considered a *donatio mortis causa*. It should be specifically mentioned that pursuant to a donation the promised or already delivered gift may be reclaimed. These rules are to be applied *mutatis mutandis* and not automatically in the case of *donatio mortis causa*.

4.2.3   Contract Among Descendants on Anticipated Inheritance

As an exceptional arrangement, the testator's descendants may conclude an agreement about their anticipated inheritance, in writing. The CC only allows this contract concerning a limited scope of persons: the testator's descendants (Section 660 (1) CC). The law specifically provides that no other persons may conclude such an agreement (Section 668 (1) CC). The subject of this agreement is the inheritance anticipated in the future, to be received by one or the other; the parties divide it up between themselves in advance. The contract may refer to the entire inheritance or only to a part thereof. This is different from the case mentioned above, when after the death of the testator the heirs, whether or not they are descendants, divide the estate among themselves.

---

[77] BH 1966.4840.

The parties of the contract for anticipated inheritance can mix their agreement with the agreement concerning disclaiming the inheritance of one of the descendants. The disclaimer is a specific contract which the testator may conclude with the descendant (Section 603 CC). In the disclaimer the descendant may partly or entirely disclaim his or her inheritance in advance, contracting with the testator, and usually will receive assets in exchange. The parties may specify the contents of the agreement without restrictions, they may divide up in kind the anticipated inheritance or the assets between them, they may also agree on who should inherit the title to the individual assets, or one party may leave his or her share to the other party. In many cases this contract fails or becomes impossible to fulfil because of unforeseeable future events, the contracting parties may die before the testator, or the subject of the estate does not follow the assumed will of the parties, the asset changes or transforms, or the testator may decide otherwise by will, disregarding the descendant's wishes. The frustration of the contract terminates the agreement.

5 De Lege Ferenda

Today a big challenge to succession is provided by foundations. The testator does not make a last will, rather he or she bequeaths his or her assets or a substantial part thereof to a foundation, and thereby the foundation acquires title to the assets. In Hungarian law, at present, foundations may only be established for public purposes, but it is planned that within a restricted scope so-called family foundations will be authorized.[78] Essentially, this would mean somehow evading the rules of succession.

It is a condition for the establishment of a family foundation that the purpose of the foundation should not be restricted to the implementation of charitable objectives. The current wording of the draft Hungarian CC is intended to authorize the establishment of such foundations whose beneficiary is the founder or a relative of the founder, with the following restrictions:

> "The founder, a person joining the foundation or relatives of these persons may only be beneficiaries of the foundation if the purpose of the foundation is the provision of support to scientific or artistic activity of the founder, the joining person or the relatives thereof, care of the works of art of these persons, or the care, nursing, support and financing of the medical costs of these persons, or the support of their school education by a scholarship or otherwise."[79]

---

[78] Csehi (2006) 289.

[79] Section 2:61 (3) of Act CXX of 2009 on the Civil Code (new CC), which has not entered into force.

CHAPTER 10

Freedom of Testation in Italy

Andrea Fusaro

1   Freedom of Testation and *Ordre Public*

1.1   Freedom To Make a Will: Different Types of Wills

Italian inheritance law offers any person with testamentary capacity, i.e. anyone who is 18 years old or more and of sound and disposing mind (art. 591 CC), the right to make a will disposing of his or her property after death (arts. 587 ff. CC). A will is valid when it is: unilateral (mutual wills are void); individual (joint and mutual wills are void); personal (a will is void if decisions are delegated to third parties); revocable (binding agreements are void); spontaneous (any mutual provision included in a will would be considered void if subject to the condition of being the beneficiary in someone else's will); of economic relevance; of personal relevance (e.g. it may contain the legal recognition of a child); in writing (oral wills are void); and formal (in strict compliance with legal provisions).

Italian law provides for three types of will (arts. 601 ff. CC):

a) Holographic will (art. 602 CC, *testamento olografo*): the document is personally handwritten by the testator, and must be dated and signed. There is no need for witnesses and there is no attestation clause. It can be a simple letter or document. It can be executed at any time using any kind of paper, therefore being inexpensive.

b) Solemn will (art. 603 CC, *testamento pubblico*): it is drafted by an Italian notary following the testator's instructions. The will is executed by the notary in the presence of two witnesses. The will is read out loud by the notary to ensure that it complies with the last wishes of the testator; it is signed by the testator in the presence of witnesses and recorded and lodged by the notary.

c) Sealed will (art. 604 CC, *testamento segreto*): it is drafted by the testator and placed in a sealed envelope which is then delivered to an Italian notary in the presence of two witnesses in compliance with strict formalities laid down by the law. The contents of the will shall remain sealed until after the testator's death, when the sealed envelope will be opened. The requirements for a sealed will are different from those for a holographic will (i.e., it need not be personally handwritten by the testator).

1.2   *Ordre Public*

In spite of the principle of freedom of testation, Italian law provides for certain restrictions. Here we focus on the prohibition of indefinite settlements and on conditions imposed on the heir.

1.2.1   The Prohibition of Indefinite Settlements

The imposition of restraints on alienation in a will are an attempt to prevent the sale or transfer of real property absolutely or for a limited period of time; the will seeks to prohibit the recipient from selling or otherwise transferring his or her interest in the property. Such a restraint on the freedom to transfer property is generally considered unlawful and therefore void if it is to be effective for a long period of time, as it is deemed to infringe the right of owners to freely dispose of their property. However, certain restraints, if considered reasonable, will be given effect. Traditionally these include the prohibition to transfer or split property for a limited period of time.

In a *fideicommissum* property is to be passed over in the same family from generation to generation: the prior or first heir is subject to the obligation of bequeathing it to another, subsequent heir. Art. 692 Italian CC considers *fideicomissum* void, with the exception of allowing a testator to devise his or her property to a legally incapacitated son, grandchild or spouse, so that it is handed over to other issue upon the death of the original beneficiary, and so for the next generations.

In the *fideicommissum de residuo* the original beneficiary is not bound to preserve the estate for a subsequent beneficiary, but merely has to deliver the remaining balance at his or her death. Although the Italian CC fails to mention it, academic (legal) commentators consider it to be void.[1]

1.2.2 Conditions Imposed on the Heir

In the will the testator can insert conditions either precedent or subsequent; the condition must be lawful and feasible. An unlawful condition is one that is contrary to public order, public morals or mandatory rules.

The Italian CC (art. 636) considers any restraint involving marriage void, but if it is the only reason of the bequest, this becomes invalid.[2] Italian commentators also hold void restrictions on: age and marital status, who and when somebody can get married, if and when to have children, the prescription to get married and have children.[3]

2 Intestacy

If the decedent has not left a will or if the will is declared invalid, the Italian general rules on intestate succession apply (art. 565 ff. CC). These rules are based on the relationship between the deceased and the various heirs.[4] Therefore the closest relatives of the deceased are entitled to a share of the assets in compliance with the provisions of Italian law. The beneficiaries in intestacy are the spouse, descendants, ascendants, collateral and other relatives, according to the following rules. Adopted children hold the same position of legitimate and natural children, but they have no rights in the succession of

---

[1]   Talamanca (1978) 287 ff.

[2]   Cassazione civile,15 April 2009, No. 8941.

[3]   Bianca (2005) 806 ff.

[4]   Alpa – Zeno-Zencovich (2007) 73.

the parents and other relatives of the adoptive parent (art. 567 CC). Each level of entitled persons excludes the next one, so that, e.g., if a spouse or direct descendants survive, the ascendants receive nothing.

Partners have no inheritance rights under intestacy, even if they were living together in a joint household at the time of death, and neither of them was then married to someone else. In Italy, during the last ten years, several bills have been discussed for the introduction of contracts between cohabitants, entitling them to inheritance rights, as this is deemed to be their will, but none were approved by the legislator. At present, partners only benefit under a will.[5]

The main persons involved in intestacy are the forced heirs: the spouse, the legitimate, natural and adopted children, and the ascendants. The first persons called to inherit are the children and their descendants, in equal shares. The surviving spouse is entitled to take if he or she was still married to the deceased or if they were legally separated at the time of death; a divorced spouse does not have a share in the estate. The spouse has the right of occupation of the family home, and the use of its furniture.[6]

If the spouse and one child survive the deceased, half the estate goes to the surviving spouse and the other half goes to the child. If there is a surviving spouse and two or more children, one third of the estate goes to the spouse and two thirds to the children. Where there are no legitimate, adoptive or natural children, parents or ascendants, brothers and sisters, the spouse inherits the entire estate. If the deceased does not leave any children, his or her parents, ascendants, brothers and sisters receive the estate, but 2/3 go to the surviving spouse. If there is no surviving spouse, nor legitimate and natural children, the following are entitled to inherit: parents, siblings and their descendants; uncles, aunts and other collateral relatives (nieces, nephews) and so on, the relatives from the first to the sixth degree included. Where there are no spouse, parents or ascendants, brothers and sisters, or any of the relatives entitled to inherit, the estate is assigned to the State.

3   Freedom of Testation and Hereditary Rights Legally Granted

3.1   Forced Share

Italian law (art. 536 ff. CC) provides that a minimum statutory share of the estate is reserved/can be claimed by the main family members before the remainder may be freely disposed of: some members of the family are

---

5   Ferrando (2007) 47 ff.; Barbiera (2010) 8 ff.

6   Art. 540 Italian CC relates to forced share, but it is also applied to intestacy. See Corte costituzionale, ord. 5 May 1988 No. 527. See Cassazione civile, Sez. II, 6 April 2000 No. 4329, in: *Giustizia Civile* (2001/I) 2198; *Giurisprudenza Italiana* (2001) 33; *Notariato* (2001) 357; notes, Cicariello (2001) 440; Mosca (2001) 141.

entitled to receive a fixed portion of the estate,[7] even if a will provides otherwise. In Italy, the forced share is the right to a fixed share of the deceased's estate; this compulsory share is called *legittima*. Disinheritance is not allowed in the Italian legal system.

The Italian CC provides that parties entitled to the forced share cannot waive their right to reduce gifts whilst the donor is still alive, either by express declaration or by accepting a gift. In any case, the right to reduce gifts can be waived after the donor's death.

A few years ago, some legal commentators discussed a bill for the reform of the forced share,[8] in order to abandon the civilian layout and adopt the English one, based on the concept of "dependants",[9] but few agreed to that idea, and there have been no further proposals after that.[10]

3.2   Subjects

The Italian CC gives qualified status to some family members by granting them a forced share (arts. 536 ff. CC): the surviving spouse, even if separated from the decedent, providing the judge has not declared him or her responsible for the separation; the children (legitimate, legitimated, illegitimate, or adopted); and the ascendants, when no children (or their descendants) are alive at the time of the deceased's death. They are entitled to a fixed portion of the deceased's net estate; the law provides them with this right, regardless of their wealth or need.

Neither partners and cohabitants nor divorced partners have any right to the *legittima*.

3.3   Quotas and Rights

To the spouse is reserved half of the estate, unless children survive the deceased. If only one legitimate or natural child survives the deceased, to him or her is reserved half of the estate. If more than one child survives, the children receive two thirds of the estate, divided equally between them; their descendants take *per stirpes*. If only legitimate ascendants survive the deceased, they are entitled to a third of the estate. If a spouse and one single child survive the deceased, both are entitled to a third of the estate. If a spouse and more than one child survive the deceased, the spouse is entitled to a quarter of the estate and the children are jointly entitled to half of the estate. If the deceased leaves only legitimate ascendants and a spouse, the ascendants are entitled to a fourth of the estate, and the spouse to half. Art. 540 CC provides the spouse with the

---

7   *Legittima* is the right to a fixed portion, not to specific assets: Cassazione civile, Sez. II, 12 September 2002 No. 13310, in: *Famiglia e diritto* (2003) 79.

8   Amadio (2007) 803; Delle Monache (2007).

9   Fusaro (2010) 559 ff.

10   Fusaro (2009) 427 ff.

right of occupation of the family home,[11] and the use of its furniture, even if there are other heirs.

3.4   Calculation of the Forced Share

In order to calculate the "reserved quota" we must take in consideration not only what remains after death (*relictum*), but also donations made whilst the deceased was alive (*donatum*); indeed, property may be donated during the lifetime of the owner (art. 769 ff. CC), but sums received during the testator's lifetime are considered to be advances of the inheritance. Any debts are deducted from the sum. This procedure goes under the name of calculation of a fictitious hereditary estate (*riunione fittizia*). To assess the quotas attributable to the beneficiaries of forced shares, donations and testamentary gifts made to them are taken into account (*imputazione ex se*).

3.5   The Reduction of Testamentary Dispositions and Donations

Gifts and wills that do not comply with the forced share are not void. If the testamentary dispositions or donations exceed the portion that the testator can legally dispose of, then each forced heir can file a claim for reduction (*azione di riduzione*). Donations are reduced after legacies; starting from the most recent right back to those made previously. Legacies are reduced starting from the last testamentary disposition. The "*azione di riduzione*" must be filed within ten years from the devolution of the estate.[12]

3.6   The Circulation of Assets

In Italy, the forced share is not just a credit, as in Germany.[13] As in France before 2007,[14] and other legal systems influenced by the French CC, in Italy the legitimate portion is the right to a share of the deceased's estate. Immoveables restored as a consequence of reduction are free from any lien or mortgage taken out on them by the deceased, except where an action for reduction has been filed after ten years from the devolution of the estate.

[11]   Only if the other spouse is the owner of the house: Cassazione civile, Sez. II, 23 May 2000, No. 6691, in: *Giustizia Civile* (2000/I) 2911; *Studium Juris* (2000) 1137; *Rivista del Notariato* (2000) 1499; *Vita notarile* (2000) 1458. If it belongs to both of them, and the division cannot be done conveniently, the right becomes a claim for compensation. See Cassazione civile, Sez. II, 30 July 2004, No. 14594, in: *Giustizia Civile* (2005/5, I) 1263.

[12]   Cass. civ., sez. un., 25 October 2004 No. 20644, in: *Giurisprudenza italiana* (2005) 1605, *Vita notarile* (2005) 855: "Two different situations must be taken into account in order to determine when the period of prescription for the *azione di riduzione* begins to run: a) if the forced share is affected by donations, the period runs from the devolution of the estate; b) if, on the other hand, testamentary provisions affect the forced share, the period begins to run from the moment when the heir accepts."

[13]   Frank (2007) 255 ff.

[14]   Leleu (1997) 81.

This solution hinders the circulation of assets disposed of by will or intestate succession, or by gift, to counter the risk of claims filed against them by
members of the family that hold the special status provided to them by the rules
on the forced share.

According to a statute enacted in 2005[15] where a donee transfers an immoveable to a third party and twenty years have elapsed since the registration of the
title in implementation of the donation, the forced heir cannot pursue the third
party for recovery of the property. This period may be extended for a further
(renewable) 20 years where the spouse or heir registers a notice of intent to
challenge the gift. The same rule applies to liens and mortgages, which remain
valid if the reduction is claimed after twenty years since the registration of the
donation.[16]

4 Freedom of Testation versus Freedom to Enter into Inheritance Agreements

Our succession law reserves a dominant role to the will: article
458 CC denies validity to succession agreements.

The Italian civil law forbids succession agreements, that is, agreements
between two parties for the transfer of assets after the death of one of them. The
ratio legis of this prohibition is first of all to safeguard the choice made by the
legislators who established that inheritance follows from the law or from a testament, excluding contracts or negotiations. Moreover, it fulfils the need to comply
with the settlor's will.[17]

Art. 458 CC prohibits all agreements by which a person disposes of his or
her own estate, as well as agreements by which a person alienates his or her
potential rights upon succession of a living person, or renounces such rights. An
example of prohibited agreements is the sale of future property considered to be
part of the succession of a living person, or a division which includes property
that is part of the succession of a living person.

Hereditary business ownership transfers have been thoroughly analyzed in
Italy in recent years, relative to the use of legal instruments alternative to gifts
and wills.

It is well known that according to the 1994 Recommendation of the European Commission on the transfer of small and medium-sized enterprises,
Member States should consider allowing the conclusion of agreements on future
succession.[18] Italian scholars have urged the legislature to introduce a new legal

---

[15] *Decreto-legge* 14 March 2005 No. 35, converted into Law 14 May 2005 No. 80.

[16] Gabrielli (2005) 1129 ff.

[17] Palazzo (2003) 41 ff.

[18] OJ L 385, 31 December 1994, 14 (see also the communication containing the motivations of the recommendation: OJ C 400, 31 December 1994, 1), followed by the Communication from the Commission on
the transfer of small and medium- sized enterprises (98/C 93/02).

instrument, following the model of family agreement used in legal practice to transfer ownership and management to one or more heirs, developed so as to avoid the risk of *azione di riduzione*, the procedure by which those entitled to a forced share can file a claim for the reduction of legacies or donations.

Italian legal tradition provides for some similar schemes, especially the "division by the testator", where the testator directs the division, specifying how the portions are to be made; he or she can also state that the division be carried out according to a valuation drawn up by a neutral third party.[19] But it comes into effect under the provisions of a properly executed will, so that the transfer of the firm is postponed until after the testator dies.

In order to facilitate the transfer of enterprises, though, succession rules have been amended,[20] introducing family agreements under which title passes immediately to the transferee.[21]

According to the new articles of the Italian CC, a family agreement is a contract through which, under the rules governing family firms and relative to the different company types, the entrepreneur transfers the firm, wholly or partially, and the stakeholder transfers, wholly or partially, his or her stake to one or more descendants. It must be executed before a public notary.

All forced heirs and the entrepreneur's spouse must participate in it, to give their consent to the assignment of ownership. They receive an equal value through the transfer of apartments or other assets as compensation, or they must waive any assignment in their favour (this is what the surviving spouse often does). They lose the chance to file an *azione di riduzione* later on.

Payment to other beneficiaries of the forced share is made by the recipient of the firm or by the settlor (by making a further gift to the transferee of the firm). The entrepreneur cannot revoke the transfer, unless entitled to withdraw by the contract. The family agreement can also provide for the recipient of the firm to withdraw, e.g. if the business activity should not provide an average income in the years to come.

The entrepreneur can retain the right of life usufruct. Normally, transfer of title is immediate, but according to a (learned) doctrinal opinion it can be postponed by the introduction of conditions or dates; e.g. providing that it is conditional upon, and takes effect upon, death.

---

[19] Salerno (2004) 371.

[20] Through Law No. 55, 14 February 2006.

[21] And adding paragraph V bis to Title IV of Book 2 of the Civil Code: articles 768-bis ff.

Annex: Draft of a Family Agreement[22]

ITALIAN REPUBLIC

On the year .., day... month,...In ...., piazza ..., before me .., notary in... (With the assistance of the witnesses...) [The presence of witnesses is not required for validity, as it is not strictly a donation]:

1) [...]

2) [...]

At the presence of:

1. Rossi Nicola, born in [...], date: [...], tax code [...];

2. Bianchi Irene, born in [...], date [...], tax code [...]; married in regime of separation as to property,

domiciled in [...], in [...], n. ......;

3. Rossi Carlo, born in [...], date [...], domiciled in [...], address [...], tax code [...] married in regime of separation as to property;

4. Rossi Marco, born in [...], date [...], domiciled in [...], address [...], tax code [...], single; whose identities the notary confirms:

whereas:

a) Rossi Nicola and Bianchi Irene are Rossi Carlo and Rossi Marco's parents;

b) Apart from Bianchi Irene, Rossi Carlo and Rossi Marco, there is no other individual who can be defined as legitimate heir in case of a succession to Rossi Nicola;

c) Rossi Nicola is the sole owner, having founded it, of the firm managed under the form of the homonym individual firm (address...., registered....with code n°), described in the assessment here after;

d) The above-mentioned business activity is not carried out in the form of a family firm as described in article 230-bis of the Civil Code;

e) Rossi Nicola is the sole owner (having bought it) of the estate (address) and precisely: the entire building, from ground to roof, used for habitation, with annexed appurtenances, adjoining ..., and registered at the land Office as follows ...;

f) Rossi Nicola, with the consent of Bianchi Irene, Rossi Carlo and Rossi Marco, retaining the right to life usufruct, under articles 768-bis and ff. of the Civil Code, intends to transfer the remainder interest of the above mentioned firm to his son Rossi Carlo and simultaneously settle the other son Rossi Marco, attributing him an equal value through the assignment of the ownership of the above mentioned building and an amount as compensation;

g) Mrs Bianchi Irene consents to the above mentioned attributions and waives any attribution in her favour;

h) for the above mentioned purposes the appearing parties by common consent (committing jointly the task to a business consultant [...]), have proceeded to the inventory and financial position of the abovesaid firm, with reference to February 28, 200n; and, again with reference to that date, have proceeded by common consent (committing jointly the task to a surveyor [...]), to an assessment of the aforesaid building;

---

[22] See Vallone (2006) 15-16.

i) these documents (enclosed under the letter "A") show that the value of the remainder interest amounts to € 800.000 and that the value of the ownership of the building amounts to € 650.000;

Therefore, they agree and contract as follows:

Art 1 *Attribution of the remainder interest of Rossi Carlo's firm*

1.1 Under articles 268-bis and ff of the Civil Code, Rossi Nicola, with the approval of Bianchi Irene and Rossi Marco, retaining the right to a life usufruct, transfers to his son Rossi Carlo the remainder interest of the firm above mentioned at point c).

1.2 The appearing parties assign unanimously to the transfer the value of € 800.000.

Art 2 *Settlement of Rossi Marco*

2.1 Under article 768-quater of the Civil Code, Rossi Nicola, with the approval of Bianchi Irene and Rossi Marco, transfers to Rossi Marco the ownership of the building (above mentioned at point e) of the recitals.

2.2 The appearing parties assign unanimously to this transfer the value of € 650.000.

2.3 In order to equalize the attributions in favour of Rossi Carlo and Rossi Marco, Mr Rossi Nicola, with the approval of Bianchi Irene and Rossi Marco, transfers to Rossi Marco the amount of € 150.000 presenting a registered non-transferable cheque of this amount issued by the Bank [...] in date [...], with the number [...].

Art 3 *Waiver of Mrs Bianchi Irene*

3.1 Under article 768-quater of the Civil Code, Mrs Bianchi Irene consents to the above mentioned attributions and waives any right in her favour.

Art 4 *In case of heirs at law*

4.1 Rossi Carlo and Rossi Marco agree to consider themselves as joint debtors for the settlement of any possible sum due, under article 768-sexies of the Civil Code, to those not included in the present contract, who can qualify as legitimate heirs at the moment of the succession of Rossi Nicola.

Art 5 *Withdrawal*

5.1 In case the business activity in the next five years should not reach an average income after taxes superior to € [...], Rossi Nicola can exert the right to withdraw from this contract.

5.2 The withdrawal mentioned in the preceding paragraph can be exerted through public act sent as registered letter to all contracting parties, as below indicated, by the last day of the sixth month following the closing date of the fifth year succeeding the current year.

5.3 In case of withdrawal:

5.3 a) the ownership of the firm mentioned in point c) of the premises will be returned to Rossi Nicola (or his assignees);

5.3 b) the ownership of the building mentioned in point 2) of the premises will be returned to Rossi Nicola;

5.3   c) Rossi Marco will have to pay back to Rossi Nicola (or his assignees) the amount of
€ 150.000 plus the monthly interests equal to points [...].

*Art 6 Statements under the law 47/1985 and Dpr 380/200 (this article should include
all references to the ordinances enabling the construction of the mentioned building).*

Art 7 Delivery – inventory and caution money

7.1   The contracting parties agree and acknowledge that the transfer of the rights transferred with this contract takes place with the signature of this same contract; and that
the delivery of the assets takes place as well at the signature of the contract.

*Art 8 Guaranties (this article includes the guaranties offered by the contracting
parties: freedom from mortgage, immunity to defects, in addition to the typical guaranties of corporate transfers, solidity of business wealth)*

Art 9 Legal mortgage

9.1   The transferor, if necessary, renounces the registration of the legal mortgage that can
originate from the present contract.

Art 10 Domicile of choice

10.1   The contracting parties, as regard this contract and the communications among
themselves connected to the contract, chose as domicile: [...]

10.2   Any communication connected to the present contract must take place through registered letter to all contracting parties.

10.3   Any communication that is not sent according to the above mentioned terms can be
considered invalid.

10.4   Any change to the above mentioned domiciles and terms of communication will
not come into effect unless communicated through registered letter to all contracting parties; in such case, the change will come into effect on the 30th day after the
receipt of the abovesaid registered letter by the receiver.

CHAPTER II

Acquisition of Property by Succession in Dutch Law

Tradition between Autonomy and Solidarity in a Changing Society

J. Michael Milo

1 Introduction[1]

Dutch succession law has been recently renewed, and the new legislation took force on January 1, 2003 within the Dutch civil code – as its Book 4. The process towards this part of the codification has taken a decade longer than it took for the mainframe of the Dutch civil code. Changes of primary social policies have been achieved: the positions of the partner, the children and forced heirs have been readjusted, in testate as well as intestate succession. Freedom of testation is the starting point – yet other principles serving public policies have been interfering in the distribution of property upon death. Intestate succession is relevant as it shows the relative importance of the involved interests, as it illustrates the changing position of families as a social and economic entity, and, moreover, as present Dutch law regarding intestate succession developed to a large extent from testamentary practice.

In the following I will place the development of Dutch succession law in its context of formative aims, principles and characteristics (2), proceed with systematics and contents in contemporary law (3) and pay particular attention to the readjusted positions of partner, children and forced heirs (4). History, tradition, custom and comparative law play an important role. Freedom of testation and its limitations can only be understood in these perspectives.

2 Principles and Developments in Dutch Succession Law

2.1 Principles and Other Determining Factors

Succession law in The Netherlands starts unsurprisingly from the principle of the autonomy of the testator.[2] Transfer of property upon death – just like transfer of property *inter vivos* – depends upon the will of the testator. It may be founded as well in the powers contained in ownership rights – the most extensive right a person can have in property.[3] Succession law therefore stands also in the perspective of property law, often matrimonial property law. The Netherlands still has a universal community of property scheme as default law.[4]

---

[1] Dutch succession legislation, or inheritance law has been translated by Sumner and Wahrendorf (2005). Descriptions and analyses in English have been published by Nuytinck (2002); Gerver (2006); Reinharz (2006); Van Erp (2007).

[2] Huijgen (2000) 85-92.

[3] Art. 5:1 BW. The article deals with tangible objects, things, but it can be applied by analogy to the entitlement to rights, or the holding of rights such as (intellectual) property rights, or personal rights such as claims.

[4] Already in Grotius' *Inleidinge*, published first in 1631, and translated as *Jurisprudence of Holland* by Lee (1977); see volume I (text) 120-121, particularly in Book II, Chapter 9, Paragraph 8, hereafter II.9.8; see particularly the study by Roes (2006) with an English summary, 303-315.

Succession law is also instrumental in socially and economically safeguarding the social structure of the family as well as to safeguard interests of those individuals like partners and children who are entitled to care, maintenance, upbringing or education. Particularly these latter principles have become enshrined in the new organization of Dutch succession legislation. These fundamental values impose the first category of limitations on the freedom of testation.

The principles of property law form a second category. As succession deals with acquisition of property, property rights in their framework of often mandatory principles and rules in a free market economy come to the forefront of the solutions provided by the law of succession. They set limits to the rights of the acquirers by succession. Some property law principles play an important role as they prescribe and often limit acquisition. The principle of *numerus clausus* of property rights finds itself explicitly in article 3:81 BW:

> "A person entitled to an independent and transferable right may, within the limits of that right, establish the limited rights recognized by law".

Two aspects of the *numerus clausus* are apparent. Only the recognized property rights may be established; and the contents of the established property rights should be within the boundaries set by mandatory rules.[5] It would thus be void under Dutch law to transfer ownership in a fiduciary way, *cum amico* or *cum creditore*.[6] In other principles and rules these two aspects of the *numerus clausus* take shape. The principle of specificity entails that objects of property rights need to be specific. Property law follows the principle of causality. This means that defects in the underlying cause of the transfer influence retroactively (*ex tunc*, art. 3:53 and 3:84 BW) the transfer of property. The principle of publicity means that all legal acts to have effect in property matters are accompanied by mandatory rules concerning publicity. While publicity is strictly observed in case of registered property,[7] movable property and claims may be transferred or burdened in a way which nears a consensual system.[8] The transferability of property is the starting point, which reflects a free market economy; only law or the nature of the right itself may impose untransferability and, remarkably, in

---

[5] In German literature these aspects are known as Typenzwang and Typenfixierung. Baur – Stürner (2009) § 1 No. 7. On the *numerus clausus* of Dutch property law see Struycken (2007); Akkermans (2009).

[6] Art. 3:84 section 3 BW. This prohibition has been mitigated in case law.

[7] Art. 3:10 and 3:89 BW – for registered property transfers and charges or encumbrances need to be registered. Important categories of registered property are immovable property, airplanes and ships, and limited property rights burdening registered property.

[8] Though movable property requires delivery of possession (art. 3:90 BW), this may be accomplished by mutual declaration (art. 3:115 BW); assignment of claims requires a notice to the debtor, but may – since 2004 – be accomplished without. The burdening of a movable or claim with a limited property right follows the same lines of the transfer (art. 3:98 BW).

the case of claims, parties are also allowed to make them untransferable with proprietary force.[9] Expectations of third party acquirers in good faith and therefore the contemporary public interest in a free market economy prevail over the interest in protecting successors.

The mentioned principles and their concrete arrangements in specific rules need to be in conformity with constitutional and supranational fundamental rights contained in the European Convention of Human Rights. The Dutch Constitution (*Grondwet*, GW) itself provides for similar rights, but cannot be easily applied by the judiciary, as there is a formal ban on constitutional testing of parliamentary legislation (art. 120 GW).[10] The international norms have direct force – art. 94 GW. Particularly the right to family life (art. 8 ECHR) and to property (art. 1 First Protocol ECHR) safeguard content and extent of the (national) private law solutions, and thus the law of succession. It is not the family as such whose interests are guarded, but family *life*. Related to this formal infraposition is the receptiveness of Dutch law to developments elsewhere. This is, however, not a recent phenomenon, but has been a standard argumentation technique since the exclusive codification shaped Dutch positive private law from 1809 onwards.[11] This technique of comparative law has always been used, even in periods where textual and systematic interpretations had their heyday in the era of legal positivism.[12] These days are gone and legal argumentation, though still grounded in textual and systematic interpretation, has become more eclectic. Today, the use of foreign law is accepted in legal argumentation, the more so in literature, in legislation as well as – but less explicit – in case law.[13] It has no formal authority, but it may convince.

An important characteristic is the firm alignment of the law of succession to tradition. In the law of succession, the national solutions have shown themselves to be strongly determined by their history – yet not necessarily immune to change. Unlike in many other handbooks on other private law topics, succession law is accompanied by an extensive expose of its history – the contrast is remarkable. While handbooks on property law show a nearly complete lack of historic developments and sources, an important handbook on the law of succession is the opposite.[14]

---

9   On this position see critically Beekhoven Van den Boezem (2003).

10 This is divergent from most jurisdictions, but subject to possible constitutional reform.

11 See on the use of foreign law in the recodification process of private law Sütő (2004); Milo (1997).

12 See e.g. the treatise of Diephuis, 13 volumes on Dutch civil law, of which the 8th (1883) and the 9th volume (1884) deal with the law of succession, and argue constantly and extensively under reference to the French (e.g. Toullier, Demolombe, Aubry et Rau) and Belgian (Laurent) authors.

13 See on comparative law in Dutch case law Asser – Vranken (1995) Nos. 198-216; see also Smits (2009) on – much more but also – comparative law as an ingredient in the methodology of law, particularly Nos. 39 and 41.

14 Asser – Mijnssen – Van Velten – Bartels (2008) on real property rights, makes hardly any use of the historic foundations in Roman-Dutch law; in Asser – Perrick (2009) historic descriptions and analyses

These principles and characteristics do shape the law of succession, and at the same time impose restrictions to the individual's freedom of testation. These limitations are embodied in various parts of the legal framework, and can be systematically organized in various ways. E.g. by the aim (social or economic) of the restriction;[15] by distinguishing the type of restriction: limits to the form of the will, limits to the nature of the disposition; limits to the persons in whose favor the disposition is; limits to the property subject of the disposition.[16] Restrictions to the freedom of testation may be systematized according to their source: constitutional, mandatory national legislative or judicial rules, (unwritten) principles.

Characteristics and principles obviously may vary in their relative importance over time. Societies and their economy change. Supranational human rights took over constitutional protection of fundamental values that earlier national law, canon law and natural law provided. The principle of freedom of testation had a different content at the turn of the 16th and 17th centuries to what it does now. The principle of *numerus clausus* has only gradually taken shape in Dutch property law.[17] Principles of publicity and specificity seem to be declining in importance. Principles may even not exist at all. The *numerus clausus* entered the law of succession only in 2003. Individuals in the earliest days of Dutch legal history were first and foremost a member of a family – and had no freedom of testation at all. At least, that is, in Tacitus' Germania.

2.2   Developments in Precodified Dutch Law

Heredes tamen successoresque sui cuique liberi: et nullum testamentum. Si liberi non sunt, proximus gradus in possessione fratres, patrui, avunculi.[18]

Tacitus' Germania is the first source used by contemporary Dutch authors,[19] but also by Grotius – *as Tacitus testifies*.[20] Tacitus' description of savages from the edges of the classical world should be read with caution, as they are known to

---

make up for a substantial part of the book. Nearly every chapter starts with an historic introduction and in the contemporary analyses historic comparisons appear frequently.

[15]   Du Toit (1999) 232-243; De Waal (1997).

[16]   See Asser – Perrick (2009) Chapter 6.

[17]   Von Savigny (1840) I 372-374 was certainly of importance in the reception of the *numerus clausus*. See Nève (1996) 223-232, 228 ff.; Feenstra (1982) 106-120; Smits (1996) 41-64; Bartels – Milo (2004) 13. But particularly Struycken constructs a detailed description of the making of the *numerus clausus* principle. Struycken (2007) 121-240.

[18]   Tacitus (1869) § 20: "A person's own children, however, are his heirs and successors; and no wills are made. If there be no children, the next in order of inheritance are brothers, paternal and maternal uncles."

[19]   Asser – Perrick (2009) § 4. Also in De Blecourt-Fischer (1969) 329.

[20]   Grotius (1977) II.27.19, 190-191

be often stereotypic. Besides, the territory was "half submerged", and "a race of wretched ichthyophagi dwelt upon terpen, or mounds, which they had raised, like beavers, above the almost fluid soil".[21] Yet Tacitus' citation may reflect more than a grain of truth as the later legal developments in the area of family, property and succession show the strength of family ties and a strong conception of common property,[22] as well as a social reluctance to accept freedom of testation:[23] *Deus solus heredem facere potest, non homo;*[24] *institution d'heritier n'a point de lieu.*[25] The holding of property in common by families or tribes precludes the need for a regulation on individual testamentary succession;[26] quite unlike Roman law, in which (testamentary) succession is qualified as the heart of the law of succession.[27] However, Grotius denies Tacitus' statement as being descriptive of the old Dutch situation: the freedom of testation was always present, *so far as memory extends.*[28] Grotius' stance may be more politically correct than historically in the first decades of the young Dutch republic's independence.

Appearances of private property open the road to individual acquisition by succession, from the 12th century onwards. Testaments were introduced by canon law,[29] but Roman law exercised the largest influence. "No department of the Roman Dutch law is more thoroughly penetrated by the Roman tradition than that of testamentary succession."[30] Huizinga mentions the very common practice to dispose of individually specified property in the 14th and 15th century.[31] Grotius, Van Leeuwen,[32] Voet,[33] all start from the individual's freedom, or at least primacy of testation. Why? The reason is given according to Grotius by natural law – *aengeboren wet* – and the analogy with the freedom to dispose of property *inter vivos* to anyone he pleases – *aen wie hy wil.*[34] The freedom of testation is accompanied by intestate succession, which shows diversity in sources and contents. All writers make a distinction between *aasdoms* law – from Frisian origin and probably with more Roman law influences than other provinces[35]- and

---

[21] Motley (1870) 2.

[22] See the examples that Fockema Andreae (1906) 261 provides, in which consent of all family members is needed for a transfer.

[23] De Blecourt-Fischer (1969) 330.

[24] Coing (1985) 560.

[25] Merlin (1827) at *Héritier.*

[26] Fockema Andreae (1906) 313; see also Lee (1953) 352.

[27] See D. 28.1.1. Coing (1985) 559: "das Herzstück des Erbrechts".

[28] Grotius (1977) 129, II.14.2.

[29] De Blecourt-Fischer (1969) 354.

[30] Lee (1953) 352. Also Coing (1985) 596: "so läst sich sagen, daß das Erbrecht der früher gemeinrechtlicher Länder weitgehend auf das römisch-gemeinen Recht beruht."

[31] Huizinga (1950) 289.

[32] Van Leeuwen (1664) III. 1.4 (Book, chapter and paragraph respectively).

[33] Voet (1736) 2.14.16; Lee (1953) 237-238.

[34] Grotius (1977) 2.14.2, 128-129.

[35] Lokin – Brandsma – Jansen (2003) 11.

schependoms law, from Frankish origin.[36] The first did not accept representation – the latter did.[37] The first eventually accepted some representation on grounds of fairness.[38] The latter did know representation and had a system of classes of heirs, and was used by political ordenance of April 1, 1580 to promulgate a unified law of succession for the Province of Holland.[39] But a lot of diffe-rences remained in some municipalities and other provinces.[40] Succession was accepted to be a form of direct acquisition: *as a universal successor to his rights and burdens.*[41] No subsequent legal act, such as delivery, is needed.

There were limitations, on the basis of social and economic considerations.[42] Forced heirship was important in Holland[43] as well as in the other provinces.[44] Wills disregarding forced heirs could be annulled.[45] Law and *bonos mores* provided other restrictions to wills and testamentary provisions.[46] Mutual wills were allowed, but restricted the revocability by the surviving spouse.[47] Persons not allowed to take by last will were teachers, guardians and administrators of minor's property; children born from adultery were prohibited to take;[48] those married under age without consent of parents were not allowed to take from each others' will.[49] Fideicommissum was allowed, but knew restrictions over

---

[36] According to Meijers (1928) to be traced back to a Ligurian origin.

[37] Grotius (1977) II.28.3.

[38] For Utrecht amended in 1545 with a possibility of representation. E.g. children of a predeceased child would not inherit from the deceased grandparent; but the uncle-surviving child would take it all.

[39] De Blecourt-Fischer (1969) 343; Roes (2006) § 3.3.8.

[40] E.g. the case of *Elandsz v N.N.* in J. Coren (1633) No. 1, 1-11. It dealt with the unifying force of the Politi-cal Ordinance. Is the *politieke ordonnantie* valid in the municipality of Brielle and the Land van Voorne? Yes, as it had not explicitly been requested and argued to derogate therefrom – as in Leyden, Haarlem, Amsterdam and the northern region of the Noorderkwartier. Therefore the Schependomsrecht applied, and representation was allowed.

[41] Grotius (1977) II.14.7; Voet (1736) 41.1.41.

[42] Du Toit (1999) 232-243.

[43] But there are some persons who not only may, but must be appointed heirs: namely children, parents, brothers and sisters, Grotius (1977) II.18.5; Van Leeuwen (1686) III.5.1.

[44] See, particularly for Roman-Frisian law: Lokin – Brandsma – Jansen (2003) especially Chapter 8: The disappointed heir: the unwilling victim of the *cautio Socini*, 141-157. On forced heirship, see also Coing (1985) 610-618.

[45] Grotius (1977) II.18.10.

[46] E.g. determining the form of a will, or regarding the mandatory heirship of orphanages and weeshui-zen, to the extent of the economic value of the expenses paid for their upbringing, see Van Leeuwen (1686) 3.3.6; feudal property cannot be subject to free testamentary disposition, Van Leeuwen (1686) 3.3.7.

[47] Grotius (1977) II,15.9. See on the subject of mutual wills in a comparative perspective, but also on Roman-Dutch law, Braun (2007) 208-225, particularly 210-212.

[48] Grotius (1977) II.16.6.

[49] Grotius (1977) II.16; see also Lee's comment (1953) II, 140-141.

time – to the fourth generation.[50] The fiduciary was under Roman-Dutch law entitled to a share of 25%.[51] The widow often had protection through the matrimonial property schemes,[52] which were frequently a universal community of property. The reception of the edict *unde vir et uxor*, that in the absence of children the widow would inherit (and not "the state") did take place in some parts, but not quite as clearly in Holland.[53] Second marriages had mandatory restrictions regarding matrimonial property law and succession protecting children from the first marriage.[54]

2.3   From the First Codification Onwards

In 1809 the first civil law codification, the *Wetboek Napoleon, ingerigt voor het Koningryk Holland* (WNH), took exclusive force in the Netherlands, under the authority of the first king of Holland, Lodewijk Napoleon.[55] He aimed – contrary to what his brother, the emperor of France, wished – to provide for a Dutch codification, not for the promulgation of the French *Code civil.* It built further on Roman-Dutch law in some parts, other parts were influenced or were mere translations of the French *Code civil*. The law of succession seems to be at least partially a continuance of Roman-Dutch law, through the preceding draft of a civil code by Joannes van der Linden. Its matrimonial property arrangement was either a universal community of property, or a limited community, unless otherwise agreed.[56] Mutual wills were prohibited.[57] The law prohibited illegitimate children to take over 50% of the share of legitimate children in the inheritance of their father.[58] It provided for the inheritance of the widow, if no blood relations closer than the 12th degree were present – counted from

---

[50] Voet (1736) 36.1.33, and Van Leeuwen (1686) 3.8.7, deal with the clause not to remove property from the family; both restrict such a clause to the fourth generation, unless the testator explicitly wanted it to extend further: "Ten waar den Erf-maker uitdruklijk had gewilt."

[51] Grotius (1977) II.20.6.

[52] Roes (2006) 38-47, distinguishes between the acquisition by the widow of specific property if no community was present; the acquisition of a part of the property; and situations where the the widow takes it all (sporadically).

[53] Grotius (1977) II.30.2, is clear: For, though by the Roman law husband and wife and some others not being blood relations were admitted to the succession of the deceased to avoid a destitution of the inheritance, in these Provinces such successions have never been known. See also De Blecourt-Fischer (1969) 352.

[54] Grotius (1977) II.16.7.

[55] See Brandsma (2006) 221-247; Lokin – Milo – Van Rhee (2010). This is not the French *Code civil*, but a code, specifically designed for the Kingdom of Holland (1806-1810), under Louis Napoleon, the emperor's brother. In its systematics it follows the French code, but in contents it is often Roman-Dutch. It was only in force for one and a half years.

[56] Art. 172 and 179 Wetboek Napoleon, ingerigt voor het Koningrijk Holland (WNH).

[57] Art. 653 WNH.

[58] Art. 613 WNH.

the deceased "upwards", to the common ancestor and then "downwards" to the person in question.[59] It protected the children against second marriages.[60] There was forced heirship, but only for descendants and, if no children were present, parents.[61] Illegitimate children were excluded from forced heirship in their father's estate.[62] This codification was replaced by the French *Code civil* in 1811 and by the Dutch *Burgerlijk Wetboek* in 1838. The 1838 legislator built further on the principles laid down in the French codification, thus explicitly Asser,[63] but a lot of Roman-Dutch aspects are similarly present. It knew a universal community of property,[64] and it provided for intestate inheritance rights of the spouse, also in case no blood relations closer than the 12th degree were present.[65] Children and ascendants were considered forced heirs.[66] In 1937, the Hoge Raad held that infringements of the forced heir positions were not to be considered void *ab initio*, but could be annulled by the disappointed forced heir.[67] Mutual wills were prohibited.[68] Clauses aiming to exclude the beneficiary's power to transfer were not allowed (art. 931). Fideicommissum was forbidden, except when legislation explicitly allowed it. The fideicommissum *de residuo* was allowed (art. 928) under all circumstances. A fideicommissum with a duty to keep the property intact was restricted – only allowed to favour the deceased's grandchildren, or his o her brothers' or sisters' children.[69] The Justinian and Roman-Dutch share of 25% was not received in the 1838 codification.

In 1938, in a publication celebrating the centenary of the 1838 Dutch civil code, Eggens concluded that not much had taken place in the law of succession since 1838, with the exception of a legislative change in 1923.[70] The right to inherit was limited after 1923 to the sixth degree.[71] Secondly, the position of the spouse improved and was put on an equal footing with the children.[72] Meijers, the codificator of the new Dutch civil code, expressed in his comments to the draft bill his dismay at various aspects of the bill; among many points of critique

---

[59] Art. 880 and 876 WNH. Only afterwards the State would be entitled to the estate.

[60] Art. 614 WNH.

[61] Art. 695 WNH.

[62] Art. 699 WNH.

[63] Asser (1838) § 435.

[64] Art. 174 BW 1838. The French code knew a community system arranged in more detail (art. 1399 ff) – which differentiated also between movable and immovable objects , this being one of the reasons for the legislator of 1838 to opt for a more uniform solution. See the long legislative debate on this topic by Voorduin (1838), part 2, 292 ff.

[65] Arts. 879 and 908 BW 1838; art. 723 CC.

[66] Arts. 960 and 961 BW 1838.

[67] HR 4 June 1937, NJ 1937, 979.

[68] Art. 968 Code civil; art. 977 BW.

[69] Art. 1020-1023 BW 1838.

[70] Eggens (1938) 425-436, at 426.

[71] Art. 908 BW 1838.

[72] Eggens (1938) 426.

was the lack of argumentation by the legislator as to various other proposed constructions to protect the spouse, such as usufruct or fideicommissum *de residuo*; to put the spouse's right on equal footing with the children was far from in conformity with authoritative foreign legislators, e.g. Germany; only in Bulgaria and some American states would one find a similar solution; it would furthermore negatively influence large families – and punish fertility, thus remarkably Meijers.[73]

Case law shows the tendency towards an increasing social importance of the spouse's interest compared to the children's interests. *Visser/Harms* is one of the key cases.[74] It concerns a conflict between children from the deceased's previous marriages and the widow. There was a matrimonial arrangement which precluded property to be held in common between the spouses. The question was raised whether the payment received by the widow from a life insurance was to be considered a gift, in the sense of article 960 (old) BW. In that case it could be taken into account in the estate and thus in computing the legitimate portion of the children. The widow argued it was the performance of an obligation to take care of her, and should not be considered a gift, and therefore not as a part of the estate. The latter position prevailed as the HR argued – following the advisory opinion of the Advocate-General – that on the basis of morality the payments needed to be considered as the performance of a natural obligation to take care of the widow. This case was particularly formative for the notarial practice in designing wills aiming to protect the spouse. By will a distribution of property was constructed, according to art. 1167 (old) BW, in which the surviving spouse received the estate, and all the children a (conditional) claim to their share, which became only payable after the death of the spouse. This so-called *ouderlijke boedelverdeling* was not contrary to the mandatory rules of forced heirship, as it could be underpinned by the existence of a natural obligation of the children towards the surviving spouse.

The connection between matrimonial property, succession, overriding interests of others, and the technique using morality or reasonableness and fairness can be seen in the case of the murdered spouse.[75] A 38-year old male nurse, L., took care of the 72 year old widow Van Wylick. He managed to marry her without any matrimonial property agreement –thus the *ex lege* community of property applied (art. 1:93 BW). Five weeks later Van Wylick died, under circumstances which led to criminal prosecution. L. was found guilty of murder and convicted to 12 years imprisonment. Was L. entitled to Van Wylick's estate and to the 50% share of the community of property? No. Had there been a testament,

---

[73] Meijers (1920) 118.

[74] HR 30 November 1945, NJ 1946, 62 (Visser – Harms).; Asser – Perrick (2009) No. 6.

[75] The civil case, HR 7 December 1991, NJ 1990, 593 and its criminal corollary in HR 24 June 1986, NJ 1987, 177.

he would have been unworthy (art. 885 BW (old) – art. 4:3 BW) to inherit.[76] His entitlement to the 50% share in the community (art. 1:99 and 100 BW) was denied on the basis of the overarching principle of reasonableness and fairness (then unwritten, but since 1992 in art. 6:2 and 248 BW). The interests of Van Wylick's children thus prevailed.[77]

The 1979 ECHR cases of *Winterwerp v The Netherlands*[78] but particularly *Marckx v Belgium*[79] were of relevance to the development of Dutch law. The latter induced the Dutch legislator to remove the distinction in the law of succession between legitimate and illegitimate children, a distinction which had been denounced as contrary to articles 1 first protocol, 8 and 14 ECHR.

These decisions illustrate the changing techniques in legal methodology which took place in the first half of the twentieth century. A textual and systematic interpretation of the legal provisions were strengthened by interpretation techniques (e.g. teleological interpretation) which were receptive to changing family relationships, in a now mandatory and supranational framework of constitutional principles. Case-law illustrates the interests at stake and the trends which Dutch law shows in its development of the law of succession as it stands today.

3 Contemporary Succession Law in General

3.1 Succession and Matrimonial Property Law

Spouses have their property in common unless a different arrangement has been chosen.[80] In these different arrangements, particularly

---

[76] In accordance with tradition. See e.g. Digest 34.9.3 (Marcianus); Grotius (1977) II.24.24; in the first Dutch codification (1809) in art. 615 WNH.

[77] It was argued that the marriage was null and void, since there obviously cannot have been any will on the side of the spouse to be murdered. Yet marriage is considered an abstract juridical act, so the absence or defects in the will do not bring about nullity, and the community will consequently subsist – although this last consequence does not necessarily have to follow, as a causal connection in the case of acquisition would be more in line with causal transfers.

[78] ECHR 24 October 1979, NJ 1980, 114 (*Winterwerp*). This case dealt with the position of those placed in a mental hospital under Dutch law, which was considered to be a ground for incapacity in itself. In a later case the question whether this incapacity also included the incapacity to make a will was answered affirmatively. HR 12 November 1993, NJ 1994, 230. In art. 4:55 the capacity to make wills by those with a mental disorder is made possible with judicial consent.

[79] ECHR 13 June 1979, NJ 1980, 462 (*Marckx*).

[80] Art. 3:93 BW: "A general community of property exists between the spouses by operation of law from the time of the solemnization of the marriage insofar as no derogation is made therefrom by a marriage contract". Art. 3:94, 1 BW: "The community comprises, where its assets are concerned, all present and future property of the spouses, with the exception of property as regards to which it was provided by last will of the testator or when a gift was made stating that it would fall outside the community of property".

when a complete absence of community has been chosen, case law has applied many techniques, particularly the open norm of reasonableness and fairness, to correct unjust dissolutions.[81] A bill, still pending in parliament,[82] aimed originally to mitigate the total community to a limited community. It has been substantially amended[83] in the meantime, and will have gifts and bequests also included in the common property.[84]

3.2   Succession, Systematization, and Acquisition of Property

The law of succession has found a place in Book 4 of the Dutch civil code,[85] after natural persons (Book 1 – in force since 1970, with many changes since), juristic persons (Book 2 – in force since 1976) and the general part on property law (Book 3, *vermogensrecht in het algemeen* – 1992) and preceding the law of things (Book 5 – 1992), the law of obligations (Book 6 – 1992), specific contracts (Book 7 – 1992 and later) and transport (Book 8 – 1991). Succession is considered one of the ways to acquire property. Dutch law adheres to a closed system, a *numerus clausus* for acquisition of property. It is acquired by "general" or "particular" title[86] (art. 3:80 section 1 BW), and one of the ways to acquire by general title is succession (art. 3:80 section 2 BW). It does thereby – even though the law of succession forms a separate book in the civil code – not depart from the French tradition (art. 711 CC), which found a place in article 639 of the BW of 1838 (a partial translation of the French rule).

Therefore, there has been a slight systematic change affecting the law of succession, compared to the context of the traditional framework of the civil code of 1838, dealing with persons, things and obligations,[87] in which the law

---

In 2003, different arrangements were chosen in 25% of marriages and registered partnerships. In 1900, 3.7% of marriages had a different arrangement. See for these and more statistics Asser – De Boer (2010) No. 381. Publicity is taken care of by a matrimonial property register (art. 1:116 BW), but this is in practice not easily accessible as it is held by the district court of the district were the marriage was entered into. The external force of this registration is debated. See Asser – De Boer (2010) No. 419 ff.

[81]   See for an overview Asser – De Boer (2010) Nos. 453-454. Particularly to apply the rules on reasonableness and fairness in art. 6:248 BW, written for contractual relationships, but also to be applied (art. 6:216 BW) in other juridical acts.

[82]   In November 2010; bill No. 28867.

[83]   See Van Erp (2007) 194-195.

[84]   The legislative debate has been subject to a lot of critique. See Verstappen (2010). See also Asser – De Boer (2010) Nos. 289-291c, Nos. 377-379 ae.

[85]   Inheritance law in the translation of the Dutch civil code by Warendorf – Thomas – Curry – Sumner (2009).

[86]   General title (*algemene title*): the position of the predecessor is continued by the acquirer and consequently all the deceased's property and debt (*vermogen*) are acquired; no juridical act is necessary. See Meijers (1954) explanatory report to art. 3:80, art. 3.4.1.1 of the Draft civil code, 209. Particular title: acquisition of specific property.

[87]   Book 1 on persons; Book 2 on property; Book 3 on obligations; and Book 4 on evidence and prescription.

of succession was a part on the 2nd Book, dealing with property.[88] This former systematization has been criticized[89] particularly by Meijers: the French *Code civil* did not do a great systematic job; its third book is a hotchpot in which the most differing subjects – among which the law of succession – are dealt with.[90] The German model in which the law of succession was the last subject dealt with in the civil code was first followed, but quickly gave way, and the law of succession finds itself in the place where it is now, following systematics of the Italian civil code, as Meijers explicitly pointed out.[91]

Book 4 deals with the following aspects: general provisions (title 1); intestate succession (title 2); intestate succession of a spouse who is not judicially separated, of the children and other statutory rights (title 3); last wills (title 4); various types of testamentary dispositions (title 5); consequences of the succession (title 6).

Property is directly acquired *ex lege* by the heirs, and also the deceased's debts (art. 4:7 BW) are included (art. 4:182 BW) in the estate: *le mort saisit le vif*.[92] Heirs are held in principle to perform the obligations of the deceased.[93] The estate forms a separate patrimony. The estate is held in common by the heirs and needs to be distributed.[94] In case the estate includes registrable property like immovable property[95] this acquisition is a registrable fact and may be entered in the public registers of immovable property.[96] Not having it registered renders the register incorrect, and consequently may mislead an acquirer of immovable property. Article 3:24 BW protects an acquirer of registered property: a registrable fact which has not been entered in the public registers, cannot be held against the acquirer, unless he or she was aware of it. The principle of alienability of property prevails. However, in case of successions and testamentary dispositions the third section of art. 3:24 BW allows a three month time span in which the acquisition can be held against third parties even though it has not yet been registered. The reason given in the legislative history leading to this article is that it may take some time until it is clear who will be entitled to the registered property.[97] Protection of third party-acquirers in case of movable

---

[88] Also in accordance with Grotius' systematization, who dealt with succession in the second book, but different from Van Leeuwen, who provides for a separate book on succession – Book 3. In the old civil code of 1838 it was contained in title 11-17 BW.

[89] See e.g., Eggens (1838) 425.

[90] Meijers (1954) 16.

[91] Meijers (1954) 17.

[92] An heir may accept or disclaim a deceased's estate. Acceptance may take place unconditionally or subject to the privilege of an inventory of the estate (art. 4:190 BW).

[93] HR 23 June 1989, NJ 1989, 732 (*Gaasbeek*); Asser – Perrick (2009) No. 256.

[94] Art. 4:13 BW or – in case of testamentary succession, 3:182 BW on property held in common.

[95] Art. 3:10 BW, property for the transfer of which registration is required, e.g. article 3:89,1 BW immovable property.

[96] Art. 3:17 BW.

[97] *Parlementaire Geschiedenis* (Legislative history, PG) Boek 3 (1981) 136.

property is even more facilitated, for cases where the transferor was not privileged to dispose and the acquirer bought the movable and was in good faith (art.
3:86 BW). Mandatory laws concerning the protection of third party acquisitions
prevail therefore over succession law. The public interest regarding the free
movement of property prevails over the principle of freedom of testation.

The rules on intestate succession law apply by default, in the absence of a
will. Is intestate succession reflecting a presumed intention? It at least reflects
the pre-2003 testate practice or custom, in which testaments were used to
balance the interests of surviving spouse and children as was stated *supra* in
section 2.3; it may very well be that a choice is made not to make a will, as the
intestate arrangement is thus reflecting the intention of the deceased.

3.3   Intestate Succession

Intestate succession law is regulated in accordance with family
relations, as recognized by law (art. 4:10 BW). Mere biological relations do not
suffice. In order to establish this family relation with children, fathers who are
not married to the mother may need to recognize the child,[98] and if they refuse
to do so, since 1 April 1998, the mother or the child may request a judicial declaration of paternity (art. 1:207 BW). The former solution was probably contrary
to the constitutional protections (particularly art. 8, family life) of the European
Convention of Human Rights.[99] Same-sex marriages have been made possible;[100] registered partnership is put on an equal footing with marriage (art. 4:8
BW). As family relations are socially and economically evolving, succession law
needs to adapt.

Four classes of heirs are recognized, the former excluding the latter: 1.
Children and surviving spouse; 2. Parents, siblings, brothers and sisters; 3.
Grandparents; 4. Great-grandparents. Offspring will take the place of the heir
when he or she either dies before the deceased, is unworthy, is disinherited, has
disclaimed the benefit, or the right to succeed has lapsed (art. 4:12 BW).

All the heirs receive equal parts (art. 4:11 section 1 BW). But half-siblings
receive half the share of a full sibling (art. 4:11 section 2 BW) and the deceased's
parents will each receive a minimum of 25% (art. 4:11 section 3 BW). In the
first category of heirs, the division will be in accordance with the provisions in
article 4:13 BW. The spouse will acquire *ex lege* the property and the debts of
the deceased. Though in conformity with art. 4:11 BW spouse and children will

---

[98] Art. 1:198 BW.

[99] The absence of family life was one of the reasons the appeal to the ECHR by a non-recognized child
was denied (ECHR 13 January 2004, *Haas – The Netherlands*). See Asser – Perrick (2009) No. 56; Van
Mourik (2008) No. 4; Huijgen – Kasdorp – Reinhartz – Zwemmer (2005) No. 22. The former Dutch
solution has been declared unconstitutional on the basis of art. 8 and 14 ECHR, see: ECHR 3 October
2000 *(Camp and Bourimi – The Netherlands)*, also published, NJ 2001, 258.

[100] Since April 1, 2001. See art. 1:30 BW. A marriage may be entered into by two different persons of a
different or of the same sex.

receive equal parts, the children do so in the form of a monetary claim, which only becomes payable after the death of the spouse. It is an important deviation from the old solution. The balancing of interests between spouse and children becomes visible (see further under the next section 4). In the absence of heirs, the state will receive the property (art. 4:189 BW). By will a testator is able to deviate from the intestate arrangement, thus explicitly article 4:13 section 1 BW.

3.4 Testamentary Dispositions and Restrictions

A testamentary disposition (art. 4:42 BW) is a unilateral juridical act (a declared intention, art. 3:33 and 4:42 BW) that may be revoked at any time, and is subject to grounds for annulment. One needs to be 16 or older to have the capacity to make a will (art. 4:55 BW). The general grounds for annulments of juridical acts are found in the general part of property law, in article 3:40 and 44 BW, but are amended by the law of succession in art. 4:43 and 44 BW.[101] Duress, fraud and mistake are possible grounds for annulment, under the conditions set forth by art. 4:43 BW, but abuse of circumstances has been excluded (art. 4:43 section 1 BW).[102] A will should be within the limits of art. 4:44 BW, in accordance with *bonos mores* and public policy.

Dutch law follows a closed system of testamentary dispositions according to the wording of art. 4:42 BW:

> "A testamentary disposition is a unilateral legal act whereby a testator makes a disposition which will become operative only upon his or her death and which is regulated in this Book or is so considered by legislation".[103]

It has been argued that the rigidity of a closed system is mitigated as the content of the bequest, in particular, would provide sufficient room for flexibility, and would thus be more similar to the open system of the law of contracts than the closed system of the law of property.[104]

But this organization has also been criticized as posing an inconvenient bar to legal development.[105] Possibilities offered are: the appointment of heirs (*erfstellingen*, art. 4:115 ff. BW) which does not automatically bring about representation; bequests (*legaten*, art. 4:117 ff. BW); testamentary obligations (*testamentaire last*, art. 4:130 ff. BW); the appointment of an executor (*benoeming van executeur*, art. 4:142 ff. BW); the testamentary administration (*bewind over goederen*, art.

---

[101] Asser – Perrick (2009) No. 125-127; Van Mourik (2008) No. 24; Huijgen – Kasdorp – Reinhartz – Zwemmer (2005) No. 22.

[102] Why? Meijers remarked in his explanatory report that a provision on abuse of circumstances might cause a flood of procedures, and that absence of such an option would not cause a serious disadvantage to the testator, see Meijers (1954) 322.

[103] Explicitly also in the parliamentary history. *PG Invoeringswet Boek 4* (2003) 1773.

[104] Van der Burgt – Ebben (2004) No. 220.

[105] Van der Burgt – Ebben (2004) No. 220; Nuytinck (2006).

4:152 ff. BW). Legislation mentions, for example, the exclusionary clause according to which the inherited property will not fall into the matrimonial community property of the heir (art. 1:94 BW); the exclusion of a netting or set-off clause in a matrimonial property agreement (art. 1:134 BW);[106] the clause regarding fiduciary administration of a child's inherited property by someone other than the parents (art. 1:253 i section 4 BW); the exclusion of the right of the parents have to use and benefit from property inherited by the child (art. 1:253 m BW); the appointment of a guardian over the child (art. 1:292 BW). The new legislation in force since 2003 acknowledges the validity of wills made under the pre-2003 situation (art. 79 OW, *Overgangswet*, transition law).

There are provisions concerning the form of the disposition, imposed by law. In a continuous tradition since 1809, Article 4:93 BW forbids mutual wills by establishing that a last will made by two or more persons in the same instrument shall be null and void.[107] Notarial deeds containing last wills should not contain other juridical acts (Art. 20 a WNa, *Wet op het Notarisambt*, Notary Act) which seeks to prevent circumventions of this prohibition). There is no such thing as a *Gemeinschaftliches testament* (§ 2265 ff. BGB) or an *Erbvertrag* as in § 2274 ff. BGB.[108] The reason was the classical argument that revocability of a last will should always be clear to the testator.[109] The *numerus clausus* organization implies that contractual constructions can no longer be considered valid, as was allowed under pre-2003 law in art. 1:146 ff. BW (these articles were abrogated in 2003). Old contractual arrangements[110] and donations *mortis causa* shall be considered bequests, with which the joint heirs are burdened.[111] Donations *mortis causa* will lapse on the death of the donor, *unless* he or she personally entered into the donation and it was made in the form of a notarial deed, or by codicil.[112]

A disposition needs to be made either in the form of a notarial deed or as a holographic testament (art. 4:94 and 4:95 BW). The latter, which is rarely used[113], needs to be deposited with the notary. Bequests may be in holographic form without having it deposited, if in its entirety written by hand, dated and signed, regarding clothing, personal property and jewellery, household effects

---

[106] Art. 1:134. It may be provided by testament of the testator or when a gift is made, that no netting is permitted of capital acquired pursuant to hereditary succession, bequest or gift and of benefits thereof, if the matrimonial property arrangement provides for netting.

[107] HR 19 June 1939, NJ 1939, 848 dealt with a German *Erbvertrag* and ruled that art. 977 BW (old) contains a formal requirement, so that recognition was possible.

[108] See on the subject of mutual wills in a comparative perspective, Braun (2007) 208-225.

[109] Asser – Perrick (2009) No. 319.

[110] Through the immediate force of the new law of succession, art. 68 a Ow.

[111] Art. 4:126 BW.

[112] Art. 7:177 BW.

[113] And never was, according to Asser (1838) 333-334.

and books (*codicil*).[114] The fact that a will has been made shall – but only *as soon as possible* – be registered in the central register of testaments (art. 4:106 BW).

The notarial deed needs to be in conformity with mandatory requirements like place, year, date and time of the deed. What is the consequence when a notarial deed containing a last will does not mention the year? Not observing formalities does not necessarily lead to nullity – an *ex lege* consequence which would have been the result according to the text of the pre-2003 legislation. It leads at most to the option of annulment, which would protect the involved interest sufficiently, as held by the HR.[115] Why? It is an error, which might have been corrected by the notary; place and time may be quite easily found out by other means; it is a reasonable interpretation, fitting into the system of the law, and in conformity with the majority of opinions in literature and would above all anticipate the new 2003 legislation (art. 4:109 section 4).

Some persons are not allowed by law to inherit from certain decedents and under certain circumstances. These are the usual suspects: guardians, teachers, healthcare providers and notaries of the testator (artt. 4:57-62 BW). In these cases, the consequence is the option to annul.

Testamentary dispositions may be made conditional or unconditional. Both types of clauses may be against public provisions, public order or *bonos mores*. A judgment of the Alkmaar District Court ruled that a clause in a will which arranged that the usufruct of the surviving spouse would end in case of remarriage and that thus the children could effectuate their claim against the surviving parent was not against *bonos mores*.[116] This may surprise, as it influences the personal freedom of the heir too much,[117] but it would have been possible to disinherit the spouse, with the lower limit of the mandatory rights to care in art 4:29 ff BW (see below in the next section).

Clauses which aim to exclude the power to dispose of the property are held to be unwritten (art. 4:45 section 2 BW). These clauses would undermine the principle of the *numerus clausus* of property rights, as ownership without the power to dispose is not a recognized construction; furthermore they would undermine the principle of transferability of property as laid down in art. 3:83 BW. It has been defended (and practice favours this opinion) that such clauses or similar constructions[118] would be acceptable, if serving a public interest, such

---

[114] Art. 4:97 BW.

[115] HR 5 October 2001, NJ 2002, 410. Earlier cases have appeared which mitigated the pre-2003 nullity consequence. For example, the court of appeal in The Hague decided that a wrong date on a testament by notarial deed does not bring about nullity if the parties agree on the date on which the testament was made. Hof Den Haag, 6 December 1984, NJ 1986, 61.

[116] Rb Alkmaar May 4, 1994, NJ 1995, 281.

[117] According to Asser – Perrick (2009) No. 152.

[118] Appointment of a foundation whose purpose is to protect and preserve in the public interest. See art. 2:285 ff BW. Careful scrutiny seems in place here.

as the protection or preservation of cultural or natural property.[119] As claims may be contractually made untransferable,[120] this will also be possible by testament. Furthermore restrictions on transfer, e.g. by requesting consent of others to transfer will be possible.[121] Such a restriction is in essence not affecting the transferability of property, but amending the powers of the heir to dispose of the property. It is therefore legally possible to perform a transfer, according to art. 3:84 BW. Third party acquirers will be easily protected against the absence of this consent, against these clauses in general – and thus, the absence of the privilege to dispose – on the basis of their good faith (art. 3:86 or 88 BW), or on the fact that this clause does not appear in the public registers in case of registered property (art. 3:24 BW).

The fideicommissum is still allowed, in the form, however, of (resolutive in combination with suspensive) conditional dispositions. The restrictions are set in article 4:56 BW, which stipulates in section 1 that in order to inherit the beneficiary must exist. Exceptions to this requirement of existence are set forth in the next three sections for descendants of the deceased's parents. Sections 2 and 3 deal with the fideicommissum, containing a duty to keep the property intact. Section 2 deals with dispositions to relatives, section 3 to others; section 4 allows the fideicommissum *de residuo*. The acquisition takes place under the resolutive condition of the heirs' death; the condition is at the same time the fulfillment of the suspensive condition to receive unconditionally by the then living descendants of the deceased's parents. The condition means that property rights in the individual assets are conditional as well. This implies that a transfer of the property can only take place under the same condition (art. 3:84 section 4 BW). Third party acquirers, however, may take free of the condition, provided they were in good faith (art. 3:86 and 88 BW). The fideicommissum involves only one generation. The *numerus clausus* of property rights and its cornerstone, the prohibition of fiduciary transfers (art. 3:84 section 3 BW), is thereby infringed to a minimal level.

Bequests may be restricted in case of unforeseen circumstances (art. 4:123 BW), and testamentary obligations may be changed or ended on the basis of

---

[119] Asser – Perrick (2009) No. 175. It would seem to me that such clauses in order to be acceptable, should be in conformity with the present legislation concerning cultural property, e.g. the ratified conventions Unesco 1954 and 1970, EU directive 93/7, and national legislation, particularly the *Wet Behoud Cultuurbezit*. On the Dutch and Belgian legislation regarding cultural property, see Milo and Sagaert (2008) 468-491.

[120] Art. 3:83 BW: [1] "Ownership, limited rights and claims are transferable, unless this is precluded by law or by the nature of the right [2]. Transferability of claims can also be excluded by agreement between obligor and obligee [3]. Other rights are only transferable where the law so provides." This arrangement of making claims contractually untransferable or unpledgeable has been criticized. It provides no protection of acquirers at all and thus undermines the economic value of claims as assets in factoring or security constructions. The disadvantages become clear in HR 17 January 2003, NJ 2004, 281 (*Oryx – Van Eesteren*), and have been extensively dealt with by Beekhoven Van den Boezem (2003).

[121] Asser – Perrick (2009) No. 175.

personal or societal interests involved (art. 4:134 BW). In both cases (see section 2 of both articles) the court will as much as possible safeguard the intent of the testator. A case in which this option was used, under old legislation, concerned an important art collection of 18th and 19th century catchpenny prints, reproductions and catalogues.[122] The testator bequeathed it to the Dutch state, under the condition that it should not be removed from the *Rijksprentenkabinet* of the Rijksmuseum.[123] The Rijksmuseum wanted to make use of the objects for study purposes and to be able to have objects from the bequest contribute to expositions elsewhere and it made clear that that the collection was visible only after request, that there was not enough room to have it on display, that catchpenny prints needed to be given more attention in art, and that the collection had been carefully restored. The testamentary disposition could be changed, following the intention of the testator. This was twofold, on the basis of the wording of the will. First to keep his collection available to the public by the *Rijksprentenkabinet*; second, to have sufficient care provided. The latter was an important reason why the prohibition to remove was included, but due to the fact that the provided care since the 1930s has increased, a changing of the clause would quite likely have been in conformity with the intention of the testator. An additional argument was that an improvement of the public accessibility of the collection would also be in accordance with the testators' will.

The technique of interpretation of wills has been the subject of legislation and case law. The interpretation technique of wills deviates from contractual interpretation techniques, which adhere less to the text of the contract and allow contextual aspects to be of influence in determining the meaning. Yet recent cases have illustrated and underpinned the importance of the text.[124] The text is of more importance in a last will. Art. 4: 46 BW is central:

> "[1] In interpreting the meaning of a testamentary disposition, attention shall be given to the relationships for which the last will manifestly intended to provide and to the circumstances under which the last will was made. [2] Acts or statements of the testator outside the last will may only be used for the interpretation of the meaning of a disposition if it would clearly not make sense without such acts or statements. [3] When a deceased obviously made a mistake in the indication of a person or asset, the disposition shall be executed in accordance with the testator's intention if such an intention can be unambiguously determined with the aid of the last will or with other information".

---

[122] HR 10 January 1997, NJ 1998, 397.

[123] See http://www.rijksmuseum.nl/collectie/prenten?lang=en

[124] Contractual interpretation has developed through case law – the statutory rules were considered superfluous, too general and at the most mere guidelines. Particularly HR 13 March 1981, NJ 1981, 635 (*Haviltex*) and HR 20 February 2004, NJ 2005, 493 (*DSM – Fox*) are seminal, and illustrate the evolution towards a more objective, textual interpretation.

An example of the interpretation technique is the case whereby in a will the testator did not include an exclusionary clause as provided by art. 1:94 BW. The inherited property would therefore fall into a community of property of the testator's niece and her husband. The testator did not include such a clause as – so it became clear from a testimony of the involved notary on statements made by the testator – she thought at the moment of making the will that her niece and her husband were already divorced, but they were not. Can this information be used to interpret the will so as to include an exclusionary clause? The Court of appeal answered affirmatively, but the HR annulled the decision and decided differently: the absence of such a clause does not have any meaning by itself, in which case the testator's acts or statements cannot be used.[125] This case anticipated art. 4:46 BW.

Art. 4:46 BW prompts to take into account "the circumstances under which the last will was made." This is of interest in the context of the *Pla and Puncernau* decision of the ECHR,[126] in which the majority expressed the – not undisputed- opinion according to which an interpretation of a will shall not be "exclusively in the light of the social conditions existing when the will was made (...). Where such a long period has elapsed, during which profound social, economic and legal changes have occurred, the courts cannot ignore these new realities". Art. 4:46 BW needs to be applied in the context of this constitutional decision.

As already discussed, wills were used under the old law to create mechanisms to protect the spouse: the so-called *ouderlijke boedelverdeling*, which found its basis in the decision regarding natural obligations of *Visser-Harms*.[127] This provided practical fundaments, from which the now legal provisions were taken,[128] concerning the balancing of the interests of the partner and the children. These bring about important limits to the freedom of testation.

4 Position of the Spouse and the Children

4.1 Intestate Positions of Spouse and Children

The interests of the spouse and children in the first class of relatives called to intestacy have been balanced in such a way to, on the one hand, make sure that the interests of the surviving spouse are taken care of so that he or she may continue as much as possible the way of life led prior to the demise.[129] On the other hand, legislation aims to protect the children's expecta-

---

[125] HR 17 November 2000, NJ 2001, 349. See Asser – Perrick (2009) No. 132.

[126] ECHR 13 July 2004, NJ 2005, 508. See on this decision and Dutch decisions regarding testamentary dispositions, Nieuwenhuis (2007).

[127] Huijgen (2005) 326; Huijgen – Kasdorp – Reinhartz – Zwemmer (2008) Nos. 366-379; Van Mourik (2008) No. 40.

[128] Asser – Perrick (2009) No. 60; Van Mourik (2008) No. 40.2.

[129] As made explicit in parliamentary history; see Asser – Perrick (2009) Nos. 59 ff.

tion to eventually receive the deceased's property. The spouse's interest ranks first, however. The spouse acquires the property *ex lege* – as a corollary he or she also receives the debts of the estate. The children do not acquire property, but only a monetary claim, equal to their share in the estate. This claim[130] only becomes payable on certain conditions: when the spouse dies or is subject to insolvency or debt-rescheduling proceedings[131] and in cases stipulated in the will. Examples of the latter may be that the spouse no longer needs this protection, or that he or she remarries or emigrates – but these latter conditions may very well be held *contra bonos mores*.[132]

For the children there is an economic disadvantage on the horizon. The children's claims may be at risk when the surviving spouse remarries. The law then provides remedies for the children to prevent specific property form deviating towards the step-parent. The children may express their will to demand property of the estate, to the maximum of the value of the claim, in four situations: from the spouse, in case the spouse has declared the intention to remarry (art. 4:19 BW); from the step-parent in case the remarried spouse passed away and the claim in the estate of the first deceased parent becomes payable (art. 4:20 BW); from the step-parent in case the remarried spouse passed away and the child gets a non payable claim from the step-parent (art. 4:21 BW); from the heirs of the deceased step-parent when the claim on the estate of the spouse becomes payable (art. 4:22 BW).[133]

The transfers to the child shall be arranged under reservation[134] of a usufruct in favor of the parent or step-parent in the cases mentioned under art. 4:19 and 4:21 BW respectively. A usufruct (*vruchtgebruik*) is one of the property rights (art. 3:201 BW) that Dutch law recognizes in its closed system of property rights, and thus insolvency proof.[135] Mandatory requirements need to be observed in order to have a valid usufruct established. These depend on the type of property in which a usufruct is reserved.[136] However, these rights of the child only partially influence the possibility for the parent or step-parent to transfer property to third parties – they will not be privileged to dispose of the property and may thus not validly transfer in accordance with the requirements laid down in

---

[130] With interest unless otherwise stipulated or agreed, see art. 4:13-4 BW.

[131] In accordance with the rules on debt relief of natural persons (*Wet Schuldsanering Natuurlijke Personen*, WSNP) incorporated in the insolvency act (art. 284-362 FW).

[132] Asser – Perrick (2009) No. 152.

[133] Asser/Perrick (2009) No. 90; Van Mourik (2008) Nos. 28 ff. Huijgen – Kasdorp – Reinhartz – Zwemmer (2005) Nos. 74-115; Van Mourik (2008) Nos. 53-65.

[134] Property rights may be created or reserved in the context of a transfer of the property, see article 3:81, 2 BW.

[135] On the *numerus clausus* of Dutch property law see Struycken (2007); Akkermans (2009).

[136] In case of movable property a transfer of possession is needed (art. 3:98 and 3:90 BW); in case of immovable property a notarial deed and registration are necessary (art. 3:98 and 3:89 BW); in case of claims a deed in specific form is necessary (art. 3:98 and 3:94 BW).

article 3:84 BW,[137] but third party acquirers of movable property are protected if they are in good faith and for value. This has been criticized as the children may thus see their expectation to receive specific movable property become illusory.[138]

4.2   Testate Position of Spouse and Children

Freedom of testation allows to deviate from the intestate arrangement, but this freedom has restrictions. The interest of being taken care of – as shown by the developments which led to the practice of the *ouderlijke boedelverdeling* and case law such as *Visser-Harms* that found their way into the law of succession as mandatory law – cannot be deviated from through a will (art. 4:41 BW). These rights are regulated in detail, and have priority over the rights of forced heirs. In particular, they concern partners and children in different situations. Children do have rights with regard to their care and upbringing, if under age, or maintenance and education until the child has turned 21 (art. 4:35 BW). The spouse, but also those who shared a household with the deceased for a long period of time, have the right to continue in the use of the house for a period of six months. The spouse has, under certain circumstances, the right to claim from the heirs the establishment of a usufruct on the house and its household effects, if he or she so requests (art. 4:29 BW) and any other property, if he or she needs it (art. 4:30 BW), but not if within a year before the death divorce proceedings had started (art. 4:32 BW). While the spouse has the claim to demand a usufruct, the heirs are not privileged to dispose of the property (art. 4:29 section 2 BW) – as we have seen the absence of the privilege to dispose does not provide an absolute guarantee that a transfer to a third party acquirer will not take place, yet in the present situation the fact that the transferor is not in possession of the asset will make it difficult for the third party to be in good faith.

The duty to establish a usufruct may be lifted by the court, if having regard to all the circumstances, the spouse has no need for the usufruct for his or her care (thus article 4:33 section 2 BW). In the case leading to HR 8 June 2007[139] (the first Hoge Raad case on the new law of succession) this right of the spouse to have a usufruct established has been given a limited interpretation, in conformity with, and under reference to, parliamentary history.[140] The usufruct is meant to serve as a safety net, and there is only a right to it if there are no other means available.

---

[137] Dutch law adheres to a causal delivery system; in order to transfer a delivery is needed, based on a valid *causa*, by somebody privileged to dispose of the property. See Van Vliet (2000).

[138] Van Erp (2007) 202.

[139] NJ 2008, 220.

[140] HR 8 June 2007, NJ 2008, 220, No. 3.3.1. *PG Invoeringswet Boek 4*, 1723-1724. Asser – Perrick (2009) No. 286.

4.3   Forced Heirship

Freedom of testation sees its limits also in the legal protection of descendants by forced heirship, on the basis of arguments like protection of family relationships, a duty to take care of descendants, common opinion, tradition and comparative law. But it is hotly debated and arguments against are at least as powerful: arguments for are not convincing; autonomy is to be preferred nowadays; justice; the right to care is effectuated by other means; simplicity.[141]

Ascendants were already no longer forced heirs since 1996. Article 4:63 BW protects descendants by reserving for them a part of the value of the estate they may not be deprived of, by gifts or by wills. This part amounts to half of the part they would have been entitled to in case of intestacy (art. 4:64 BW). Gifts and debts are taken into account (art. 4:65 ff. BW) in computing the value of the *legitieme portie*. But forced heirs are no longer considered heirs as such, but merely creditors of the estate (art. 4:80 BW), and only entitled to a monetary claim. The claim is not exigible before six months have lapsed since the death, and it is not enforceable to the detriment of a usufruct established according to art. 4:29 and 30 BW (art. 4:81 BW). By testamentary disposition the claim of the forced heir may be made payable only after the death of the spouse (art. 4:82 BW). Hence, the position of the forced heir has been substantially diminished compared to the pre-2003 regulation. Also here the overarching principle of reasonableness and fairness may correct in extreme circumstances. Under explicit referral to the case of the murdered spouse, the district court and the court of appeal decided that a child who had killed his parents was not allowed to receive by representation his father's legitimate portion from his grandmother's estate. Whether it is desirable to impose forced heirs on the autonomy of persons and their freedom of testation is still the subject of a continuing discussion.[142]

5   Concluding Remarks

Dutch succession law adheres to the principle of freedom of testation, as it always did, if we are to believe Grotius. Yet in its solutions and developments it of course needs to take other private and public interests into account, and it has thus developed under various other formative influences. In contemporary succession law the positions of the partner and children have been strengthened, due to new legislation and the supranational and constitutional family-life concept. The position of the forced heir is but a shadow of what it was under the pre-2003 legislation, and it now struts and frets its hour upon the stage.

---

[141] Asser – Perrick (2009) Nos. 235 ff. Huijgen – Kasdorp – Reinhartz – Zwemmer (2005) Nos. 74-115; Van Mourik (2008) Nos. 53-65. Van Mourik (1995) 60 ff.; Verbeke (2000) 1111-1236.

[142] Asser – Perrick (2009) No. 237. See also the recent publication Castelein – Foqué – Verbeke (2009).

The present solution is firmly anchored in its tradition, yet developments and transformations did not happen in national isolation, not even under the exclusive codifications since 1809. Dutch law shows that it is receptive to changing societies and economies.

In the course of development, techniques of legal argumentation have changed enormously, from traditional and European authoritative doctrine of Roman-Dutch law to exclusive national codifications since 1809, and afterwards, subject to explicit supranational legislation. Yet the different tools did not influence substantive development too much, so it seems. Natural law provided a safety net for Roman-Dutch writers, as reasonableness and fairness, or morality, or human rights provided at later moments in this evolution. Developments under our codifications have sprung mainly from judicial decisions, with the exceptions of 1923 and 2003. The precise position freedom of testation takes on the scale between individual's autonomy and solidarity depends on the relative importance of the involved formative interests, principles and characteristics.

Property law principles have been formative as well. Property rights entail the freedom to transfer, thus also the freedom to transfer upon death. Yet as property law also serves the public interest of a free market economy and the transferability of goods, the fideicommissum has been restricted, as well as clauses aiming to restrict transferability. Third party acquirers in good faith are protected – but to a lesser extent in case of registered property.

Depending on the interests at stake, freedom of testation was more or less limited and shows different substantive levels and developments. It has been increasing from the early days of the Dutch Republic onwards to contemporary days regarding the persons allowed to receive by succession (e.g. the inclusion of illegitimate children and the decreasing importance of forced heirship). But the freedom of testation has been decreasing regarding fideicommissary substitutions: these have been gradually restricted. Freedom of testation is furthermore underpinned by a decrease of nullities (e.g. formal deficiencies). The changing legal positions reflect and illustrate changes in society: it moved away from a religious organization towards a more secular one; it shows a development from social towards individualistic orientations; traditional families were replaced by family life, all in a society where a free market economy became more important. Freedom of testation and its limitations can only be understood in these perspectives. It is a living concept.

The Norwegian Approach to Forced Share, the Surviving Spouse's Position and Irrevocable Wills

Peter Hambro

1 Introduction

The purpose of this article is to give a brief presentation of
three subjects covered by the Norwegian Act on succession and two other acts.
These are the freedom of testation, certain rights of the surviving spouse and
the possibilities of securing irrevocable rights for an heir. As a rule, a person
may freely decide in a will how his or her estate is to be divided. The only important limitation to this right is that certain heirs have what is usually called a protected right to inherit. In addition there are certain restrictions as to what may
be determined in a will, but these are of minor importance. The most relevant
right for the surviving spouse is the right to keep the entire estate in *uskifte*,
which could be translated to *usus fructus*, but which gives the spouse more freedom than *usus fructus*. Wills may be made irrevocable and similarly a beneficiary clause in an insurance policy may be made irrevocable. Pre- or postnuptial
agreements can of course not be changed merely by one party to the agreement.

2 The Forced Share Inheritance

In the legal area of inheritance law we have in Norway three
main sources of law: Firstly we have the Act of Succession (AS) dated March 3,
1972. Our first Act of Succession was from 1854 and this law was subsequently
revised and changed several times. Secondly we have a large amount of Supreme
Court decisions and finally we have legal theory. The law from 1972 is divided
into two main parts: The title of its first part is *Inheritance according to Law
and the Right of Usus Fructus* (uskifte). The title of the second part is *Inheritance
According to Wills*. The second part of the law starts with § 48, where the wording in the first paragraph is as follows: "A person who has reached 18 years of
age may in a will decide how his estate shall be divided when he dies." This right
is limited as in most European countries when a person has direct descendants;
that is children, grandchildren and further issue.

The title of Chapter 4 of the AS is *Forced Inheritance*. According to the first
sentence in AS § 29 two thirds of the deceased's estate is forced inheritance for
his or her descendants. This means that when one has children (or grandchildren) one may only dispose by will over the so-called free third. This 1/3 of the
estate one leaves can by will be given to whoever the testator desires. If a person
has two children he or she can give 1/3 to one child in addition to this child's
share of the forced inheritance of 2/3. Up until 1937 the forced inheritance was
3/4. This rule of forced inheritance applies to children born in wedlock, out of
wedlock and adopted children (and the descendants of these children). Of course
it does not cover step-children or foster children. Adopted children have the
right to inherit from their adoptive parents but also lose all rights to the estate of
their biological parents.

The rule of forced inheritance gives protection only against dispositions *mortis causa*. By lifetime dispositions – dispositions *inter vivos* – a person with children can give away the entire estate to whomever he or she wishes. One can therefore transfer one's entire estate by lifetime gifts to one of several children thereby disinheriting the other children. The only requirement is that a disposition is fulfilled during one's lifetime. Such gifts are furthermore not taken into consideration when dividing the estate between the children. *Inter vivos* gifts to one child are only taken into consideration when an estate is settled if the donor – in other words the deceased person – has made it clear that this is his or her wish (AS § 38). If a person makes a substantial donation in favour of one of his or her children without giving the other children a corresponding amount, the donor may, in writing or orally, decide that this gift shall be equalized after death. One can use as an example a case where a father has given one of his children 100,000 Euros. He leaves a written statement where he expresses his wish that this gift be equalized after his death. He leaves three children and an estate of 800,000 Euros. This means that each of the other children first receives 100,000 Euros from the estate. The remaining 600,000 are divided into three parts. Such a decision about equalizing may be made without fulfilling the formal requirements for a will.

The rule of forced inheritance has been interpreted as being both a quantitative and a qualitative limitation to freedom of testation.[1] This means that when a person has descendants a will must be limited to 1/3 of the net estate that that person leaves. In addition it is not possible to dispose over individual assets worth more than this 1/3 even if the beneficiary pays an amount to the estate. For example, let's take a person who leaves an estate of 375,000 Euros and owns a residence worth 187,500 Euros. This person can in a will give 125,000 Euros to whoever he or she wishes, but cannot devise the residence even if the beneficiary is willing to pay 62,500 Euros to the estate, since the residence is worth more than 125,000 Euros.

Until 2007 Norway was I believe the only country in Europe with a specified maximum amount on the size of the forced inheritance. A special rule for large estates was introduced in 1918 and has gradually become very important since this maximum amount has only been increased a few times. According to AS § 29 the forced inheritance cannot exceed 1 million Kroner (125,000 Euros) for each of the testator's children or their descendants. This means that if the testator has an estate of 1,250,000 Euros and two children, he or she can dispose over 1 million through a will. This amount can be left to whomever the testator wishes – a friend, a cohabitant or one of the two children. Through a will, the testator can leave 9 million to one child and 1 million to the other. 1 million Kroner is merely 125,000 Euros and this means that rich and wealthy people can dispose over most of their estate fairly freely. Transferring a family business from one generation to the next can simply be done by will. Obviously a testator owning a family business has sufficient funds to satisfy the maximum of 1

---

[1]   References in legal theory, Lødrup (2008) 111; Hambro (2007) 198-200 and Rt (1948) 359.

million Kroner if he or she wishes to do so. In the new Danish inheritance law
from 2007 the same system has been adopted and the maximum sum is also
1 million Kroner. If the testator has children from a previous marriage and has
remarried he or she can use the 1 million maximum to secure the accustomed
standard of living for the surviving spouse.

In the preliminary materials to a change in the law made in 1985 it is stated
that this maximum amount must regularly be increased by Parliament or else
the system will have unintended consequences.[2] Since 1972 the sum has been
increased only once – from 500,000 to 1 million in 1985 – so obviously, at
present, the system of a maximum sum is far more important in practice than
originally intended. There are no current plans to increase the sum or change
the system.

We also have a form of forced inheritance for the surviving spouse which,
however, is only used when the deceased's estate is fairly small. The surviving
spouse inherits a share of the deceased's estate (AS § 6). This so-called "regular"
inheritance is *not* a forced inheritance and may be reduced or eliminated by a
will. This share is: a) 1/4 if the deceased person had direct descendants, b) 1/2 if
the deceased had as closest relatives parents or descendants from them, and c)
the entire estate if the closest relatives are grandparents or their descendants. If
the spouses were under a community property system the surviving spouse of
course keeps half of their net estate as his or her share. If the "regular" inheritance results in a small amount, the surviving spouse as an alternative has a
minimum inheritance and this minimum inheritance is a forced inheritance.
The amount of this minimum inheritance is tied to the so-called basis amount
which is used to calculate benefits under our social security system. This basis
amount is increased by Parliament every year and is currently roughly 10,000
Euros. If the deceased person has direct descendants as heirs, the surviving
spouse has a minimum inheritance of 4 times the basis amount, in other words,
40,000 Euros. This amount cannot be reduced by a will and prevails over the
forced inheritance of children. If the deceased person leaves an estate of 60,000
Euros, the surviving spouse will inherit 40,000 and the children the remaining
20,000. If the deceased person left as closest heirs parents or descendants from
them, the minimum inheritance for the surviving spouse increases to 6 times
the basis amount – 60,000 Euros. If a person leaves an estate of 120,000 euro
and has children and a spouse, 2/3 of the estate or 80,000 Euros is the forced
inheritance for the children and 40,000 Euros is the minimum inheritance for
the surviving spouse. In other words, when the estate is below this level there is
nothing left for testamentary gifts.

---

[2]   Innst. O. No. 80 (1984-85) 3.

3 The Contents of Wills

As a rule, a testator can decide how the estate is to be divided. The decisions made in a will may be based upon prejudices that most people find distasteful, but that would have no consequences for the validity of the will. The testator may decide that a certain amount shall be divided between his or her grandchildren provided they are born in wedlock and exclude adopted children. The testator can exclude a sibling as an heir because he or she is homosexual or has converted to a religion the testator dislikes. The only general prohibition in our law is contained in AS § 64, the wording of which is as follows: "A disposition in a will is invalid if it stipulates a use or destruction which obviously serves no meaningful purpose." This paragraph is hardly ever applied in practice. Firstly, the requirement is that the decision contained in the will is *obviously* meaningless. Secondly, more than 90% of all estates are settled privately by the heirs without interference from the courts. Clauses in a will which could violate AS § 64 will simply be ignored by the heirs.

In addition to AS § 64, in Norway we have a general principle which is not codified in law that dispositions made in a will must not be in violation of "law and common sense of decency". This expression was first used about contracts in a 1687 act, which is still partly in force. Applying this principle, it would be invalid to establish a foundation to encourage racial discrimination, for example. "Common sense of decency" is obviously a very vague phrase. A disposition is invalid if its contents is contrary to our general moral and cultural values or if it is clearly contrary to our general legal feelings and beliefs. In legal theory, classical examples are wills where the testator gives X a sum contingent upon X marrying a specified person or getting a divorce.[3] Similarly, a clause where the inheritance is contingent upon the heir converting to another religion would not be accepted. These are personal affairs that according to legal feelings and beliefs in Norway are private matters that should not be influenced by external factors, such as wills. In some cases it can be uncertain whether a gift is totally invalid or whether only the part that is in violation of "law and common decency" should be considered invalid. This would be a question of interpretation, but I believe that in most cases the whole clause would be invalid.

The Norwegian Constitution from 1814 includes one paragraph concerning inheritance. § 108 prohibits the creation of fideicommissum/family foundations. The purpose with this rule was to avoid the creation of an aristocracy with inherited privileges. The point with a fideicommissum is that the capital may not be used by any individual. People within the family have the right to use the income from the fideicommissum and the founding documents decide who shall have the right to receive the income. A testator may of course by will establish a foundation which will benefit future generations. If the income is reserved for people belonging to a specified family the will would violate § 108. There are similarities between § 108 in the Constitution and AS § 71. AS § 71 regulates how

---

[3] Lødrup (2008) 151.

far in the future a testator can determine the distribution of his or her estate. The testator can include one unborn generation. In other words, the testator can benefit, firstly, a living friend; then this friend's children that are already born and finally the children that a living person may have in the future.

According to court decisions and legal theory there are strict limitations on the right to delegate authority in a will.[4] A clause giving a named person the right to settle the testator's estate as the former deems fit, would clearly be invalid. A testator may, however, include in the will a person who shall have the right to supplement the will. The testator may, for example, donate a sum to medical research and include a clause giving a medical professor the right to decide which causes shall benefit from the will. A relevant factor in court practice has been whether such a clause covers a small part of the estate and whether the testator had an acceptable reason to formulate the will in this fashion. Furthermore, the will has to be formulated in such a manner that a third party, in practice the courts, can determine whether the person given the delegated authority has acted within the testator's wishes.

4 The Position of the Surviving Spouse

The title of Chapter III AS could be translated as *Right to Usus Fructus Due to Marriage.* However, *usus fructus* is not the word used in the act. The Norwegian term is *uskifte*, which quite simply means that the estate is not settled when one spouse dies. Directly translated *uskifte* means "not settled." The surviving spouse keeps the entire estate without paying out any inheritance and with the right to dispose over the estate as an owner. This system is unique for Norway and Denmark and is the most important and commonly used right for the surviving spouse upon the death of the other spouse. Obviously it is better to keep the entire estate rather than receive part of the estate as an inheritance. The *uskifte* consists of the assets and liabilities of the deceased spouse and the surviving spouse. The assets and liabilities of both merge together in one estate. Therefore, upon using the right to *uskifte* the surviving spouse automatically becomes liable for all the debts of the deceased spouse. This right to *uskifte* dates back several hundred years and has gradually increased in importance.

According to AS § 9 the surviving spouse has the right to keep in *uskifte* the community property assets belonging to the deceased spouse. Until 2008 spouses were a couple consisting of a husband and wife. In 2008 the Marriage Act was changed so couples of the same sex can be formally married and have the same rights as husband/wife couples.

If the spouses have a pre- or postnuptial agreement establishing separate property, the surviving spouse may only keep such assets in *uskifte* as follows from the agreement or if the other heirs give their consent. In other words, the spouses can agree to separate property but maintain the right of *uskifte* for the

---

4   Lødrup (2008) 153; Hambro (2007) 341; Frantzen (1997) 950 and Rt (1912) 162.

surviving spouse. Thereby the surviving spouse can keep the entire estate in *uskifte* and when the surviving spouse dies the heirs of the spouse who died first receive his or her separate property.

The surviving spouse has the right to keep the estate in *uskifte* if the heirs are descendants of the deceased or parents of the deceased or descendants from them. If the heirs are more distant the surviving spouse inherits the entire estate (see above). There is one limitation to this right of *uskifte* which has become very important in, roughly, the last 20 years. If the deceased spouse leaves children or more distant descendants from a previous marriage or relationship, the surviving spouse needs consent from such heirs for *uskifte*. These heirs, in other words, may demand that their inheritance be paid out immediately. Given the high divorce rate we have in Norway – and the large number of people living together without being married – a deceased spouse quite frequently these days leaves heirs from a previous relationship. Often the spouses also have children together. In such cases the surviving spouse may keep the estate in *uskifte* with the joint children, but will have to pay out the inheritance to the other children. AS § 12 specifically states that partial *uskifte* is a right for the surviving spouse. Given the frequency of marriages with so called "separate" children, estate planning has become very important in many marriages.[5]

One way to secure the surviving spouse's position is to obtain consent to *uskifte* from the separate children while their father or mother is still alive. Such consent may be combined with specific clauses to protect the future inheritance of the children. This was determined by the Supreme Court in an important decision from 1992.[6] A typical example would be that the agreement with the children includes a clause whereby the surviving spouse accepts that he or she may not in the future sell or mortgage real estate in the *uskifte*. Consent may be "encouraged" by a "threat" to write a will in favour of the spouse if consent is not given.[7] Spouses can also secure each other through a prenuptial agreement. If one spouse has far more assets than the other, they can make an agreement about separate property but also include a clause to the effect that the separate property shall be transformed to community property if the marriage is dissolved by death. When one spouse dies, the surviving spouse then automatically receives half of the total net assets held by the spouses. A prenuptial agreement can be combined with a will giving the surviving spouse the free 1/3 or everything above 1 million Kroner for each child. Obviously, given the 1 million Kroner limitation of the forced inheritance, wealthy spouses can freely write a will covering most of their estates.

The right to *uskifte* gives no protection against a will from a spouse (AS § 7). Unless otherwise specified a will is to be fulfilled when the testator dies. If a spouse in a will has given most of his or her estate to a friend, this will must

---

[5] This is the theme I was able to analyze in 2006 in *Avtalt uskifte* (contractual "*uskifte*").

[6] Rt (1992) 374. Reference also in: Hambro (2007) 62; Hambro (2006) 180-191; Asland (2008) 132.

[7] Hambro (2006) 100-101.

be fulfilled upon death and the surviving spouse can only keep the remaining estate in *uskifte*. The sole protection given to the surviving spouse is that a testator, while alive, has to notify his or her spouse of a will which reduces the spouse's rights.

Everything the surviving spouse acquires during the *uskifte* period automatically becomes part of the estate (AS § 17). This includes income, gifts and inheritance. If the surviving spouse has a high income this could result in the *uskifte* increasing in value. In such cases the surviving spouse would often be better off settling the estate immediately when the other spouse dies. In the case of gifts or inheritance the surviving spouse can avoid this becoming part of the *uskifte* by deciding to terminate the *uskifte*. If the inheritance is large compared to the size of the *uskifte*, this could be a sensible decision for a surviving spouse who wishes to secure his or her own heirs.

AS § 18 provides that a surviving spouse may dispose over the *uskifte* as an owner. This means that the surviving spouse can use the estate as freely as if he or she owned the whole estate. The income can be spent, assets can be sold – including real property – and the surviving spouse can improve his or her standard of living. The surviving spouse has the right to spend the whole estate during his or her lifetime with no consideration to the future inheritance of the other heirs. There are only two limitations on what the surviving spouse may do: One is that the surviving spouse has no right to give away real property and other gifts which represent a substantial part of the estate. The other limitation is that the surviving spouse is not entitled to pay out inheritance to one of the heirs without giving a proportional amount to the other heirs (of the deceased spouse) (AS §§ 19 and 21).

Mortis causa the surviving spouse may dispose by will over his or her share of the *uskifte* (AS §18). If the *uskifte* consists of community property this means half of the total estate. If the *uskifte* consists of separate property assets the system is more complicated; upon establishing the *uskifte* one calculates the percentage of the *uskifte* represented by the assets of each spouse. The surviving spouse may by will dispose over his or her percentage of the remaining estate.

The *uskifte* has to be terminated when the surviving spouse remarries unless the heirs consent to a continued *uskifte* (AS § 23). The surviving spouse can also at any time decide to settle the estate with the heirs of the deceased spouse.

Upon death the remaining *uskifte* is divided between the heirs of both spouses. If the heirs are solely joint children, they simply divide the estate. If there are other heirs, half of the estate – assuming community property – goes to the heirs of the first deceased spouse and the remaining half to the heirs of the last deceased spouse. If the *uskifte* consists of separate property assets the division is as mentioned based on the percentage of the assets which originally belonged to each spouse.

In 2008 an addition was included to Chapter III about *uskifte*. During the last 20 years there has been a substantial increase in the number of people living together without being formally married. Therefore, it has been discussed for many years whether laws should be made to give legal rights to cohabit-ants. The law from 2008 gives a limited right to *uskifte* to cohabitants who fulfil certain criteria. The main criterion is that this addition to the law only applies to cohabitants who have children together. The right to *uskifte* for cohabitants includes the main residence, household goods, cars and second homes intended for joint use. Financial assets such as stocks, bonds or bank accounts are not included in the right to *uskifte* for cohabitants. If the deceased cohabitant had children from a previous relationship, they can as in the case of "regular" *uskifte* demand their inheritance immediately upon the death of their father or mother.

5   Irrevocable Wills

Whether or not a will may be made irrevocable seems to be a question which is solved differently even in countries with very similar laws and legal traditions. One description of the nature of a will is as follows:

> "A will is an ambulatory instrument; that is, it walks with the testator during his life but has no legal effect until the testator's death. As long as the testator has mental capacity, the testator has full authority to change or revoke a will. Only upon the testator's death does the will become irrevocable".[8]

In some countries this description of wills has as a consequence that wills may not be made irrevocable. In Norway, ever since our first law of succession in 1854, it is taken for granted that a testator may enter into a so called inherit-ance contract whereas in Sweden this is unacceptable according to § 10:5 of the Swedish law of succession from 1958. According to AS § 56 a testator may, through an inheritance contract, give up the right to make, change or revoke a will. This is called *arvepakt*, which means inheritance pact or agreement. Of these alternatives certainly the most practical would be not to change or revoke a will.

The formal requirements for an irrevocable will are the same as for regular wills. In addition there are two criteria which must be fulfilled. Firstly, the will must contain a phrase making it quite clear that the will is irrevocable. Secondly, the testator must inform the beneficiary that he or she has irrevocably been included as an heir. Giving the beneficiary a copy of the will does not in itself make the will irrevocable. In legal theory and court practice the question has been posed whether irrevocability can result from an interpretation of the will. Courts have been very reluctant to accept implied irrevocability.[9]

Irrevocable wills can be divided into two categories. On the one hand we have what could be called "pure" irrevocable wills. This is a will where a person

---

[8]   Beyer (2007) 153.

[9]   Agder appeals court 9 October 2007 and in legal theory Lødrup (2008) 197; Andenæs (1985) 34; Frantzen (1996) 85; Hambro (2010) 52.

is named as an heir and the testator for some reason makes the appointment irrevocable. The other category is cases where the will is part of a contract between the testator and a third party. An example would be that the testator needs substantial personal care in his or her old age. He or she makes an agreement with a person that in return for extensive care for the rest of his or her life, this person will be his or her sole heir. In order to make this an attractive agreement the testator makes an irrevocable will. As pointed out in legal theory by Torstein Frantzen such wills are in reality dispositions *inter vivos*, that is, regular lifetime agreements.[10] Frantzen argues convincingly that most irrevocable wills are dispositions *inter vivos* and thus binding regardless of the wording of the will. Whether a disposition is *inter vivos* or *mortis causa* is determined by the contents and not the title given to the document.

An irrevocable will means that the testator may not by a later will cancel, or alter, the first will. However, as a rule, the testator may dispose of his assets freely through subsequent *inter vivos* gifts. For example, if the testator irrevocably names a person as sole heir and later, say at the age of 80, decides to give away most of his or her belongings, because the testator feels he or she does not need them anymore, these gifts would be valid even if they affect most of the estate. The testator may promise to respect the contents of the will by limiting this right to make dispositions *inter vivos*. This would be a promise where the formal requirements for a will would be unnecessary. In certain cases an irrevocable will may be interpreted as a limitation also to the testator's right to make *inter vivos* dispositions. For example, legal theory mentions cases where the testator has given an heir specified property irrevocably in the will.[11]

6   Other Irrevocable Instruments

6.1   Insurance Policies

In Norway, as in most European countries, a large number of people have purchased insurance policies where a specified amount of money is paid out upon death. According to the Act on insurance agreements from 1989 (§ 15-1), if no beneficiary has been named in a policy, the stipulated amount is paid to the surviving spouse. According to § 15-2 the person who purchases a policy may appoint a specified person as a beneficiary. Such an appointment may later be revoked unless the policy owner has informed the beneficiary that the appointment is to be viewed as final. The agreed upon sum in the policy is paid to the beneficiary regardless of the size of the estate and whether the owner of the policy has direct descendants or not. The rule of forced share in the Act of succession does not limit the right to name a beneficiary in an insurance policy. The person who purchases a policy may, for example, appoint only one of his or

---

[10]   Frantzen (1996) 85.

[11]   Lødrup (2008) 202; Hambro (2010) 56.

her children as the sole beneficiary. Purchasing an insurance policy and including a beneficiary clause is therefore a practical way of securing the position of a
cohabitant or a spouse if there are children from a previous relationship.

6.2 Pre- and Postnuptial Agreements

The Norwegian marriage act is dated July 4th, 1991. The law
specifies which types of marital agreements spouses may enter into. Some of
these agreements are in reality dispositions *mortis causa* in the sense that the
agreement has consequences only upon the death of one of the spouses. The
most obvious example is an agreement of separate property which upon death
is transformed into (deferred) community property. The purpose of such an
agreement is to offer protection for a spouse in case of divorce, but also to secure
the surviving spouse's positions upon death. Such an agreement may be limited
to applying only if for example the husband dies first or if it stipulates that the
wife's assets are to remain separate property regardless of who dies first.[12] Such
pre- or postnuptial agreements are obviously binding and can only be revoked
by agreement between the spouses. Again, the rule of forced share inheritance
does not limit the right to enter into such agreements. Pre- or postnuptial agreements can therefore be used as an effective way of reducing the inheritance of
children. Agreements of this type are especially practical in cases where one
of the spouses has children from a previous relationship and wishes to provide
primarily for his or her surviving spouse. For example, the husband has remarried and has grown-up children from a previous marriage or relationship. He
makes a premarital agreement with his spouse according to which they have
separate property. If the husband dies first, his property is to be transformed
into community property whereas the wife's property shall remain separate
property. Assuming the husband dies first, his surviving spouse will receive half
of his estate as her share of the community property. In addition she will inherit
her share according to the Act of succession or a larger share according to her
husband's will.

---

[12] § 42 in the Marriage act and Lødrup – Sverdrup (2009) 179.

CHAPTER 13

Restraints on Freedom of Testation in Scottish Succession Law

Eric Clive

I Underlying Values

The fundamental values underlying succession law are hard to pin down. Probably it is largely a matter of customary expectations. However, it can be argued that the values of freedom, security, justice and efficiency identified in the DCFR as underlying many areas of European private law also underlie succession law.

Freedom is very commonly stressed in relation to freedom of testation. Subject to certain limitations, a person should be free to leave his or her property as he or she pleases. Why this should be so is rarely explored. The basic idea of personal autonomy is there but is less strong in relation to what is to happen after the person is dead. Ideas of incentives to work and save probably play a role. As often happens, ideas of freedom and ideas of general economic efficiency may overlap.

Security requires that there should be some system of orderly succession which commands broad support. Insecurity would be fostered if a person's property became ownerless and subject to a free-for-all on his or her death. So far as the content of the succession rules is concerned, security is most commonly stressed in relation to the position of the surviving spouse (and those in a similar position) who could be left vulnerable and insecure if not given at least some share of the deceased spouse's property. The Scottish Law Commission in its 2009 *Report on Succession* reflected this consideration when it said that it seemed important:

> that the surviving spouse's or civil partner's share of the intestate estate should generally be sufficient to ensure that she does not have to leave the former matrimonial or family home.[1]

In relation to children, the security of the right to aliment may also be regarded as a relevant consideration: it would seem unfortunate if this right were to be cut off by the death of the alimentary debtor. In Scotland children have a right to aliment against their parents until the age of 18 or, if the child is undergoing further education, 25. Ascendants have no right to aliment against descendants.

Justice is more difficult. It would generally be agreed that the rules on succession should be perceived as fair. Indeed the Scottish Law Commission has said that 'the primary purpose of any reform of the law of intestate succession should be to ensure that the estate is fairly distributed'.[2]

What is seen as fair may depend on rather large questions of how society is organised or perceived as being organised. In a kinship-based social system, succession rights for family members may be seen as a simple *quid pro quo* for the support furnished by the kinship group. In a state-based social system a

---

[1]   *Report on Succession* (2009) Scot Law Com No. 215 at para. 2.4. Civil partnerships for same sex couples were introduced in Scotland by Part 3 of the Civil Partnership Act 2004.

[2]   Scot Law Com No. 215 at para. 2.3.

share for the state via inheritance tax or similar mechanisms could be justified in a similar way. In other words there are solidarity aspects to justice to be balanced against individual freedom of testation. The claims of relevant social groupings, whether family, kin or state, are however rather vague and do not tell us much about what the content of succession laws should be. Nor do they help to resolve conflicting claims from within a social group such as the family, particularly when changes in social conditions have meant that that group is much more fluid and diverse than it used to be.

What is just or fair in this area often seems to boil down to what is customary and therefore expected. For example, children may expect to inherit from their parents. It may therefore seem unjust to the children of a man's first marriage if his whole estate passes to his second wife (who has no means of her own) and then on her death to her child by an earlier marriage. The Scottish Law Commission gave this as an example of a result which some commentators considered unjust[3] but it is not entirely clear where the injustice lies if it does not simply lie in disappointed expectations.

Some minimum requirements of justice in succession law can be based on the principle of non-discrimination. The succession law should not discriminate on objectionable grounds. It should not, for example, prefer males to females. It should not prefer first-born children to later-born children. It should not prefer children born in wedlock to children born out of wedlock. These things seem clear now but fifty years ago Scottish succession law offended against all these requirements of justice.[4]

Other questions of justice in succession law are much more difficult. What weight should be given to such matters as rewarding the deserving and not rewarding the undeserving? Suppose one of four children has looked after the deceased parent for years and the other three, although in a position to do so, did nothing? Is justice served by giving all four equal succession rights? And how does justice help a legislator to decide between a deserted wife (still undivorced) of twenty years standing and a cohabitant of ten years standing?

Efficiency is most commonly mentioned in debates on Scottish succession law in relation to the question whether the claims of certain people should be protected by means of a fixed share (the traditional Scottish way) or by means of the English system of allowing courts to award a discretionary payment. The latter system is said to be relatively more inefficient and expensive. Efficiency also crops up every time a simpler mechanism is preferred to a more complicated one. For example, the Scottish Law Commission has argued that a simple set of rules on intestate succession will make it easier for people to see whether it is desirable to make a will.[5]

---

3   Scot Law Com No. 215 at para. 2.26.

4   The Succession (Scotland) Act 1964 abolished the rule that the eldest son inherited the immoveable estate on intestacy. The Law Reform (Miscellaneous Provisions) (Scotland) Act 1968 gave children born out of wedlock equal succession rights.

5   Scot Law Com No. 215 at para. 2.30.

It is a characteristic of underlying values such as those just mentioned that they often conflict with each other and have to be balanced against each other in the actual legal rules. In the ensuing pages this will be illustrated in relation to the principle of freedom of testation.

2   Freedom of Testation and Protection of Certain Claimants

The most controversial question in Scottish succession law is currently the place which should be given to fixed legal shares (known as 'legal rights' in Scotland) for a surviving spouse, or civil partner, and children. This will be addressed here only in relation to testate succession where there is an obvious conflict with the principle of freedom of testation. Another controversial question is how far a surviving cohabitant should be protected when the deceased cohabitant has left his or her estate to someone else.

The current law is that the surviving spouse or civil partner has a right to a half of the deceased's movable estate if there are no surviving issue or a third if there are surviving issue. The children or other surviving issue have a right to a half of the movable estate if there is no surviving spouse or civil partner or a third if there is a surviving spouse or civil partner. Only the remaining half or third (as the case may be) can be disposed of by the deceased's will. Cohabitants are currently not protected at all when the deceased died testate.

Where a person who is entitled to 'legal rights' is left something by the deceased's will that provision is deemed to be in satisfaction of legal rights, unless it contains an express provision to the contrary.[6] So the beneficiary must normally renounce the testamentary provision if he or she wishes to take the legal rights.

The deceased is free to dispose of immovable property as he or she wishes: it is not affected by these 'legal rights' of spouse, civil partner or issue.

The present law on legal rights is not regarded as satisfactory. So far as the surviving spouse is concerned there is general agreement that a fixed share is justifiable ('security', 'justice', 'societal expectations') but the content of the law, and in particular the fact that only movables are affected by the fixed share, is thought to be in need of reform. It is worth mentioning in this connection that the basic Scottish matrimonial property regime is separate property, with a norm of equal division of matrimonial property on divorce but with the division on death being left to succession law. This, clearly, strengthens the argument

---

[6]   Succession (Scotland) Act 1964 s. 13 and Civil Partnership Act 2004, s. 131(4). There are also rules which require a child or remoter descendant claiming legal rights to collate *inter vivos* gifts of movable property received from the deceased unless the deceased made it clear that the gift was to be received in addition to legal rights on death. This doctrine is known as collation *inter liberos*. The effect is that the person receiving the gift must bring it into the fund available for satisfying the legal rights of issue. The donee can avoid collation by renouncing legal rights. The doctrine is referred to in the Succession (Scotland) Act 1964 s. 11(3).

for giving the surviving spouse a guaranteed fixed share: the fixed share can be regarded as a sort of surrogate for matrimonial property rights. So far as issue are concerned there is an acute division of opinion as to whether they should be entitled to anything more than a commutation of their right to aliment (which would mean that adult children over the age of 25 would have no fixed share and could be completely disinherited). Even those who think that something more than a commutation of the right to aliment is justified consider that the content of the law needs to be reformed. Again a major criticism is the limitation of the fixed share to movable estate. This produces arbitrary results which cannot be justified on any view.

It is worth noting, however, that in practice the 'legal rights' of spouse or children are rarely claimed.[7] The reasons for this are not too difficult to understand. First, those who could claim legal rights are often provided for by the deceased's will in any case. Secondly, at the time of the death of a family member the surviving relatives generally want to respect the wishes of the deceased, or at least to appear to do so, even if they have got little or nothing themselves by the will. In particular adult children may not wish to claim legal rights where everything has been left to the surviving spouse. Even where the will's provisions may on their face seem to omit a spouse or child unfairly there will very often be good reasons for the deceased's choice which will be well-recognised within the family. For example, there may have been some form of *inter vivos* provision for the omitted person. A claim for legal rights could risk family opprobrium.

The law has been reviewed twice in recent years by the Scottish Law Commission.[8] In its most recent report the Commission found opinion to be so divided on the question of legal share for issue that it was unable to make a recommendation either way and put forward two options for consideration by the Scottish Parliament. The Commission was, however, able to make a recommendation on the question of a fixed share for the surviving spouse or civil partner and that matter may therefore be considered first.

2.1 Fixed Share for Spouse or Civil Partner

The Scottish Law Commission gave as one justification for the rights of the surviving spouse or civil partner the attempt by the law

to ensure that the surviving spouse or civil partner will not be destitute if the deceased had decided not to make provision for the survivor in the will.[9]

---

[7] See Reid (2008) 399 fn.7.

[8] See the Commission's *Report on Succession* (1990) Scot Law Com No. 124; *Report on Succession* (2009) Scot Law Com No. 215.

[9] Scot Law Com No. 215 at para. 3.2.

However, this is not in itself a sufficient justification because the rights exist even if the spouse is nowhere near destitution. A better rationale is probably the notion of spousal solidarity which is often reflected in matrimonial property regimes. The surviving spouse's guaranteed share can be seen as a sort of crude surrogate for his or her share of the matrimonial property. It is a status-based right, not one based on indigence or relief of the public purse. It reflects the idea of marriage as a partnership: an idea which in the case of civil partners is present in the very name 'civil partnership'.

Whatever the rationale behind the legal rights of the surviving spouse or civil partner, the Commission found on consultation that most respondents supported the view that spouses and civil partners should continue to be protected from disinheritance.[10] Moreover a large majority thought that this protection should take the form of a fixed share rather than an allowance at the discretion of a court.[11] And there was unanimous support for the view that the fixed share of the surviving spouse or civil partner should be based on the value of the whole of the deceased's estate, not just movables as at present.[12]

Beyond this point all sorts of schemes are possible. One idea, not considered by the Commission in its Report, would be to follow a deferred community of acquests approach and give the spouse a half share of the property built up by the joint efforts of the spouses during their marriage. That would be a principled approach but it would also be complicated and difficult to operate, because a lot would depend on the history of what had happened before and during the marriage. Moreover the analogy with divorce is not so sound because on death there is not such a pressing case for recognising the claims of the deceased spouse. It is not surprising therefore that the Commission did not go down this route. What it recommended was that the surviving spouse or civil partner's fixed share should amount to 25% of what he or she would have inherited if the deceased had died intestate.[13] The Commission saw this as a simple approach which achieved a reasonable balance between protection of the surviving spouse or civil partner and the deceased's freedom of testation.[14] As the rules on intestacy, both under the existing law and under the reformed scheme proposed by the Commission elsewhere in its report, would give the surviving spouse or civil partner the whole of the estate in a large majority of cases, the result is that the fixed legal share, except in very large estates where the deceased is also survived by issue,[15] would amount to a quarter of the estate. It should be mentioned that

---

[10]   Scot Law Com No. 215 at para.3.4.

[11]   Ibid.

[12]   Scot Law Com No. 215 at para.3.6.

[13]   Ibid.

[14]   Ibid.

[15]   The threshold figure would be fixed by Parliament and could vary over time. The Commission proposed a figure of £300,000. Below this, even if there are issue, the surviving spouse or civil partner would take all the intestate estate. Above this, if there are issue, the surviving spouse or civil partner would

the fixed share would take the form of a sum of money, not a right to particular assets or a share of them.

This scheme is to be commended. It is simple and balanced. Of course, the figure of 25% is to some extent arbitrary, but it is also easy for the legislature to modify upwards or downwards if it wishes. The basic scheme remains the same whether the share is fixed at, say, 20% or 30% or anything in between. It is to be hoped that the Commission's recommendations are quickly implemented but there could well be opposition to them.

What sank the Commission's earlier proposals to extend legal rights to the whole estate is believed to be opposition from the farming and land-owning community which disliked the idea of legal rights being exigible out of land. The freedom to leave a farm to, say, a son who had been working it would be destroyed. There often would not be enough cash to buy out the surviving spouse or civil partner without selling all or part of the farm. The Commission in its 2009 report dealt with this question to some extent by stressing that the surviving spouse or civil partner could renounce his or her legal share either before the deceased's death or afterwards and that such a renunciation should not enlarge the share of the deceased's issue.[16] This would enable the farmer, for example, to come to an arrangement with the spouse *inter vivos* and to ensure that the testamentary provision was not disturbed. This is a fair point but it does not provide cash where there is none. The Commission therefore also recommended that the executor should be able to apply to a court for an order as to the time of payment of the legal share. This would enable a deferred payment, or payment by instalments, to be ordered in appropriate cases.[17] The Commission also considered, but rejected, suggestions that agricultural land, landed estates and agricultural businesses should be excluded from the deceased's estate for the purpose of fixed legal shares. The Commission observed that the existing law sometimes required payments of a similar kind to be made out of mainly agricultural property (e.g. on divorce) and this did not seem to cause insuperable problems. It also pointed out that under the existing law agricultural property is often held via shares in a company or partnership. Such shares will be movable and thus already subject to legal rights on death and yet this does not seem to cause insuperable problems. Whether such arguments, convincing though they seem to an observer, will be sufficient to deflect opposition to the Commission's proposals from landed interests remains to be seen. They were not sufficient before. It is to be hoped that politicians will be prepared to face down any opposition there may be because it would be unprincipled to give an exemption for agricultural businesses but not other businesses. The contribution made by the agricultural sector to the economy and life of the country should certainly not be undervalued and there may well be good arguments for special treatment to take

---

take the first £300,000 and half the rest. If there are no issue the surviving spouse or civil partner would take the whole estate whatever its amount.

[16] Scot Law Com No. 215 at para 3.8.

[17] Scot Law Com No. 215 at para 3.11.

account of special difficulties or problems but such special treatment should not be at the expense of fair provision for surviving spouses and civil partners.

2.2   Fixed Share for Issue

The fixed share for issue under the existing law is called legitim. As noted above, the legitim fund is a third of the movable estate if there is a surviving spouse or civil partner and a half if there is not. The surviving children of the deceased, and the issue of any predeceasing child, have a right to legitim. The system comes from the ancient customary common law of Scotland. It developed at a time when life expectancy was much lower and when social and economic conditions were very different to what they are today. It is not surprising that the question of its justification in present conditions should come up for consideration.

The Scottish Law Commission was clear that the right to legitim in its present form should be abolished. The limitation to movable property gives rise to completely arbitrary results, depending on the composition of the deceased's estate at the time of death. Where the estate is mainly movable the rather severe restraints on the testamentary freedom of a widow or widower can be hard to justify. Why, it might be asked, should the deceased in such a case not be free to leave everything to one child who might be particularly in need of support (e.g. because of mental incapacity) or particularly deserving of reward for having looked after the deceased for many years? Why should other adult children, perhaps in late middle-age and well-established in life, be able to claim a share contrary to the deceased's wishes? On the other hand, if the deceased's estate at the time of death consists almost entirely of a house, if the surviving children are still dependent, and if the deceased has left everything to, say, a cohabitant or second spouse who is not the parent of the children, then legitim may be completely inadequate for the support of the deceased's children. The status quo is indefensible.

One option for replacing the present law would be a system whereby children or other issue could apply to a court for a provision out of the deceased's estate. The amount would be at the court's discretion although it could be directed to have regard to various factors. There was no support for this solution on consultation and the Commission rejected it.[18] It was right to do so. Recommending such a system would have been a failure to face up to the question of why any fixed provision for children is justified.

The Commission did, to its credit, face up to this question. It put forward for consideration two options. I will call them the 'aliment-based scheme' and the 'status-based scheme'.

The aliment-based scheme proceeds on the idea that a child who is entitled to aliment should not be deprived of that entitlement by the death of a parent, at least if that parent's estate is not inherited by someone who is also under an

---

[18]   Scot Law Com No. 215 at paras. 1.18 and 3.36.

obligation of aliment to the child. For practical reasons, and in order to enable estates to be wound up efficiently and finally, the child's right should take the form of a capital sum representing, in a rough way, a commutation of the right to aliment. A very young child might therefore receive a substantial capital sum: a child in his or her last year of education would receive enough to see him or her through to the end of the course or to the age of 25 whichever came first. The legal share would, however, not be characterised as an alimentary right. It would be a succession right based on the notion of security of the right to aliment. It would be exigible out of the whole estate including any passing under the rules on intestacy. It would not, however, be exigible out of estate passing to a person (normally the other parent of the child) who himself or herself is obliged to aliment the child. The rationale for the fixed share ceases in such a case.

The status-based scheme was based on rather less clear notions of tradition and family solidarity. A child of any age would, simply by virtue of his or her status as a child of the deceased, be entitled to a fixed share of the deceased's whole estate. For simplicity, this would be 25% of what the child would have obtained if the deceased had died intestate. The issue of a predeceasing child would have the same claim. It will be apparent that in its essentials this second scheme is just a modernisation of legitim. The significant changes would be that the legal share would be exigible out of the whole estate and that the method of calculation would be different. The justification, or rather the lack of justification, would be the same.

As between these two schemes the aliment-based scheme seems to me to be clearly preferable. It is worked out in considerable detail in the Commission's report and there seems to be no reason to suppose that it would not be entirely workable. It is based on the identifiable principles of security and efficiency. A dependent child's alimentary right is secured against the death of a parent and this is done by the provision of a capital sum – a method which favours the efficient winding up of estates. The second scheme is based on notions of family solidarity which are of no help when problems arise *within* a family. It would limit, for no detectable reason, a testator's freedom to favour a dependent child over non-dependent children, or to favour a deserving non-dependent child over an undeserving non-dependent child. Above all, it would not provide any secured continuance of support for a dependent child. This is because 25% of what a child would receive on intestacy will often be absolutely nothing. This would be of most relevance in practice in the case of a reconstituted family. Consider the following example.

X is killed in a road accident. He had two children by a first marriage which was ended by divorce five years before his death. Neither spouse claimed any financial provision on the divorce. The children lived with their mother but X contributed to their support. After an intervening cohabiting relationship, which also broke down, X has recently remarried. He left all his property, worth some £250,000, by will to his second wife. The two children of the first marriage are in secondary education. One is about to go to university.

On the status-based scheme X's children would have a right to 25% of what they would have received on intestacy. However, as X's estate is under the threshold sum of £300,000 and as he has a surviving spouse, the whole estate would pass on intestacy to the surviving spouse. So the children have a right to 25% of nothing. On the aliment-based scheme they would have a right to a capital sum calculated by reference to what their future right to aliment would have been worth if their father had not been killed.

The wording of the Commission's report suggests that it regarded the arguments in favour of the aliment-based scheme as more persuasive and that it was not too impressed by the arguments in favour of the status-based scheme. Nonetheless it concluded that, because public opinion surveys had shown continuing support for the idea of legitim and because the views of consultees and its advisory group were divided, it was better for it not to make a firm recommendation either way but to leave the matter for political decision. Accordingly it put forward two fully-worked out schemes, with draft legislation for both, in its report. This was a proper and understandable way of proceeding but, to my mind, it is unfortunate that the Commission did not simply go with the balance of the arguments and recommend the aliment-based scheme. The results of public opinion surveys depend on the questions put. In this area of public policy there is a big danger that rather general questions about legal shares for children will be answered in the light of rather general feelings about what the respondent would want himself or herself or would do himself or herself. If a question can be interpreted as meaning 'Would you like to be disinherited by your father or mother' then the answer is likely to be 'No' and the same applies if the question can be interpreted as meaning 'Would you want to be able to disinherit your children or one or more of them'. Most people would have no reason to do that. Legal shares would be of practical relevance only in unusual situations and a public opinion survey would have to focus on such situations if it were to lead to useful results. In the public opinion surveys cited by the Commission the respondents could not be made fully aware of the implications of the different options in specific situations where they would lead to different results because the details of the two schemes had not been fully worked out. What is needed now is a new, large-scale public opinion survey focussing not only on particular situations but also on the cases where legal share might be a live issue. The two schemes presented by the Commission in fully worked out form are at least a useful way of testing opinion.

2.3   Protection of Cohabitants

The incidence of cohabitation without marriage has greatly increased in Scotland in recent decades. It is not only young people who are choosing to cohabit without getting married – or to cohabit for an extended period before getting married. It is also older people, particularly those who have been widowed or divorced. Scottish law has made provision for some protection for a surviving cohabitant when the other dies but, arguably, it does not go far enough.

The present law is contained in section 29 of the Family Law (Scotland) Act 2006. The surviving cohabitant has a right to apply, within certain time limits, to a court for an award out of the deceased cohabitant's intestate estate. Although Scottish lawyers are not too keen on discretionary systems of this kind there is really no alternative in the case of cohabitation. The nature and duration of cohabitational relationships vary too much to justify a fixed legal share approach of the type suitable for spouses and issue. The 2006 Act was therefore an important step forward. Before that the surviving cohabitant had no rights at all on the deceased cohabitant's estate and had to rely on a will being made in his or her favour. However, the scheme of section 29 has been criticised on two main grounds. First, it gives too wide and unguided a discretion to the courts. There is no indication of the underlying principle or policy. Secondly – and this is the point of interest here – it does not apply where the deceased died testate. It provides no protection where the deceased left the whole of his or her property by will to someone other than the cohabitant. In this respect the scheme of section 29 departed from the recommendations of an earlier report by the Scottish Law Commission on which it was generally based.[19]

The Scottish Law Commission endorsed these criticisms and responded to them by recommending, first, a tightening up of the rules on the court's exercise of discretion and, secondly, an extension of the discretionary system to testate estate. The underlying principle should be the extent to which the cohabitant deserves to be treated as a surviving spouse for succession purposes. In assessing that (as a percentage) the court should have regard to only three matters – the length of the cohabitation; the interdependence, financial or otherwise, between the cohabitant and the deceased during the period of the cohabitation; and what the cohabitant contributed to the relationship.[20] So, in a case of a long, stable cohabitation where the woman had stayed at home for many years to look after children of the relationship she might be entitled to be treated as if 100% a spouse. In a case of a short cohabitation where both parties had lived more or less independent lives the percentage might be 25% or even less. Once the percentage was fixed, the surviving cohabitant would be entitled to that proportion of the intestate succession rights or legal share which a surviving spouse would have.

The Commission's attempt to introduce more principle into the determination of a surviving cohabitant's succession rights is commendable, even if the idea of assessing a cohabitant's 'succession-worthiness' as a percentage of a spouse's seems at first sight to be a bit strange and to involve a sort of ideal

---

[19] Report on Family Law (Scot Law Com No. 135) (1992).

[20] Scot Law Com No. 215 at para. 4.14.

spouse as the point of comparison. For the purposes of a discussion on limitations on freedom of testation, however, the important development here is not
so much the attempt to limit the court's discretion but the renewed recommendation that the surviving cohabitant should be protected even in cases where
the deceased died testate. This can be justified on the view that if the surviving cohabitant is to be treated as if he or she were, to a greater or less extent,
in the position of a spouse then he or she should have the same protection as a
spouse against disinheritance. The policy considerations are the same. It will be
remembered that under the Commission's recommended scheme for surviving
spouses the legal share would be 25% of the deceased's estate. So if a cohabitant
were regarded as being entitled to say 50% of what a spouse would receive then
he or she would get only 12.5% of the estate. In the case of a short and rather
non-intense cohabitation the share might be only a fraction of that.

A difficult situation arises if the deceased is survived by both a spouse and
a cohabitant. Here the Commission proposes that if the deceased died intestate
the value of the surviving spouse's entitlement on intestacy should be split
between the surviving spouse and the cohabitant. The cohabitant would take the
appropriate percentage of half that value and the spouse would take the rest. If,
for example, the estate is worth £200,000 the surviving spouse would normally
take it all on intestacy. So a cohabitant who was 100% succession-worthy would
take a half of the estate and the rest would go to the spouse. A cohabitant who
was adjudged to be 25% succession-worthy would take a quarter of the estate and
the spouse would take three-quarters. If the deceased died testate the cohabitant
would take the appropriate percentage of what the surviving spouse could have
claimed by way of legal share. This would apply whether the estate was left to
the spouse or to someone else. If, in the latter case, the spouse also claimed legal
share the two claims would just be cumulative.

Under section 29 of the Family Law (Scotland) Act 2006 a claim by a surviving cohabitant must be made within 6 months of the deceased's death. The
Commission received evidence that this short time-limit posed problems in
some cases. It recommended a time limit of one year which could be extended
by the court on cause shown.[21]

3   Other Restraints on Freedom of Testation

3.1   Inheritance Tax

At certain times inheritance tax has been seen as a major
restraint on freedom of testation but much depends on exemption levels and
reliefs and the availability of simple avoidance measures, all of which vary from
time to time. For some time now, exemption levels have been rather high in the
United Kingdom and inheritance tax has been rather easy for the well-advised

---

[21] Scot Law Com No. 215 at para. 4.32.

to avoid (mainly by giving assets away or putting them into a trust in good time before death). So it is not in practice a major restraint on freedom of testation. In so far as it is a restraint it can clearly be justified by the same sort of arguments used to justify kinship-based restraints on freedom of testation. It is the claim of solidarity against the claim of individual freedom. And the claim of solidarity can itself be based on ideas of rough reciprocity – support in exchange for support.

3.2   Limitations on Accumulation of Income

It is very common in Scotland for testators to set up a testamentary trust and to direct the assets to be held for various beneficiaries and purposes. For a long time there have been limitations on the extent to which income can be accumulated in such trusts. The idea behind these statutory limitations is that long accumulations of income can freeze up assets excessively and allow the hand of the dead to unduly control the activities of the living. In the case of testamentary dispositions the law of Scotland currently permits income to be accumulated for one of a number of periods – e.g. 21 years from the death of the granter of the disposition; or the minority of any beneficiary living or *in utero* at the date of the granter's death.[22]

The rationale of such restrictions has recently been examined by the Scottish Law Commission.[23] The Commission criticises the current law on a number of grounds. First the restrictions produce unreasonable restraints on ordinary commercial practices (e.g. in the field of pension provision or insurance) which use trusts as a mechanism. This is not relevant to the present discussion of restraints on testamentary freedom but it may be noted that the Commission suggested removing all restrictions on accumulation of income in commercial trusts. Secondly, the rules are unduly complex and produce arbitrary results.

In relation to ordinary family situations the Commission considered that the main justification for restrictions was simply the need to strike a balance between testamentary freedom and the claims of succeeding generations. The latter claims are fortified by an argument that 'it is socially desirable that the wealth of the world be controlled by its living members and not by the dead'.[24] The Commission thought that it was indeed necessary for the law to strike a balance between the truster's freedom to dispose as he or she wishes and the freedom of (usually) the truster's descendants 'to make use of the family patrimony in a manner that is suited to contemporary conditions'. However, it did not consider that fixed limits were a good way of striking this balance.[25] Instead it

---

[22]   See the Trusts (Scotland) Act 1961 s. 5 and the Law Reform (Miscellaneous Provisions) (Scotland) Act 1966 s. 6. There is another restriction in the Accumulations Act 1892 which applies where accumulated income is to be invested in land.

[23]   Discussion Paper on Accumulation of Income and Lifetime of Private Trusts (DP No. 142, 2010)

[24]   DP No. 142, 2010 at para. 5.16 quoting Simes (1955) 707.

[25]   DP No. 142, 2010 at para. 5.23.

suggested that the Court should have a power to vary any trust which had lasted for more than a certain period (say, 25 years) 'to the extent that such alteration is clearly expedient in order to take account of any material changes in circum-stances that had occurred since the trust was created'.[26]

The Commission's criticisms of the rigidity, complexity and arbitrary results of the existing law are undoubtedly well-made and the suggested solution seems sensible. It might be little used, because family trusts of excessively long duration are not generally considered desirable anyway, but that is no objection to it. It is interesting to note that the DCFR adopts a similar solution.[27] This is referred to by the Commission in its Discussion Paper.[28]

3.3   Limitations on Future Liferents

The current law of Scotland prevents a testator from leaving property to a succession of liferenters. The policy is achieved by a rule which provides that if a person of full age becomes entitled to a liferent of any prop-erty, that person acquires the fee of the property if he or she was not living or *in utero* at the date when the deed creating the liferent came into operation.[29] In other words the effect is that 'an interest may validly be created only in favour of a person alive (or in the womb) at the time when the deed creating the interest comes into operation'.[30]

The Scottish Law Commission subjected this rule to criticisms similar to those directed, with justification, at the rule against excessive accumulation of income in family trusts. The law had given rise to difficulties. It produced arbitrary results. The current rules did not seem to be a good way of balancing the freedom of testation against the legitimate claims of descendants and other future beneficiaries. In addition the Commission noted that the historical justi-fication for the restriction on successive liferents (a desire to prevent avoidance of legislation passed against entails) had ceased to be important. The Commis-sion's suggestion was that the rules restricting the creation of liferents in favour of those not alive or *in utero* should be repealed and that the necessary balanc-ing of interests should be secured, as noted above, by ensuring that a court had power to vary trusts of long duration.[31]

---

[26] DP No. 142, 2010 at para. 5.25.

[27] X.–9:203 DCFR (Variation by court order of trusts for beneficiaries).

[28] DP No. 142, 2010 at para. 4.16.

[29] Law Reform (Miscellaneous Provisions) (Scotland) Act 1968 s. 18. Different restrictions apply in relation to deeds executed before the Act came into operation.

[30] DP No. 142, 2010 at para. 3.32.

[31] DP No. 142, 2010 at para. 5.25.

3.4   Purposes Otherwise Contrary to Public Policy

Under the common law of Scotland a bequest may be struck down on the ground that it is contrary to public policy. The law was developed in a series of cases concerning bequests by testators who wished great monuments to be erected to themselves or members of their family.[32] Although this rather vague and general rule can be difficult to apply, it is not in practice a significant restriction on testamentary freedom. Only the most outrageous cases will fall within it. The Scottish Law Commission surveyed it but recommended no change.[33]

Inheritance agreements (*pacta successoria*) are not regarded as contrary to public policy in Scottish law but do not seem to be used in practice. For estate planning purposes a trust would be the more usual mechanism.

---

[32]   See e.g. *McCaig's Trs v Kirk-Session of United Free Church of Lismore* 1915 SC 426; *Aitken's Trs v Aitken* 1927 SC 374; *Sutherland's Tr v Verschoyle* 1968 SLT 43.

[33]   DP No. 142, 2010 at para. 5.74. The DCFR tackles this problem by requiring, in the definition of a trust, that the trust fund must be 'to benefit a beneficiary or advance public benefit purposes'. See X.–1:201 (Definition of a trust). The bizarre Scottish bequests which have been struck down under the common law rules could equally have been struck down under this provision.

CHAPTER 14

Freedom of Testation in Slovenia

Suzana Kraljić

1 Introduction

In the Republic of Slovenia (RS) the right to private property and inheritance is guaranteed in the Constitution (art. 33 CRS).[1] It is interesting that in the same article, and even in the same sentence, the right to personal property and the right to inheritance are provided for. There is an immediate connection between property and the right to inheritance. Namely, inheritance is one of the ways to obtain ownership. The death of an individual leads to a mutation of the title holder. Thus, as a rule property relations and the rights and obligations deriving from these relations of a dead person pass to another natural or legal person.

In addition, art. 67/2 CRS expressively provides that the modalities and the conditions of inheritance are regulated by law. The basic legal act for succession is the Inheritance Act,[2] enacted in 1976 and in force since 1 January 1977. The specialties of the inheritance of protected farmlands are regulated by the Inheritance of Agricultural Holdings Act 1995.[3] Provisions referring to inheritance can also be found in numerous other acts, as for example:

a) Registration of a Same-Sex Civil Partnership Act;[4]
b) Marriage and Family Relations Act;[5]
c) Denationalization Act;[6]
d) Act on Reestablishment of Agricultural Communities and Restitution of Their Property and Rights (e.g. acquisition of property rights that had been taken from ancestors);[7]
e) Inheritance and Gift Tax Act;[8]
f) Copyright and Related Rights Act (e.g. inheritance of economic copyrights);[9]

---

[1]   Ustava Republike Slovenije (Constitution of the Republic of Slovenia: CRS): Uradni list RS, No. 33/91-I, 42/97, 66/00, 24/03, 69/04, 69/04, 69/04, 68/06.

[2]   Zakon o dedovanju (Inheritance Act: IA): Uradni list SRS, No. 15/76, 23/78, 17/91-I; 13/94; 40/94; 82/94; 117/00; 67/01; 83/01.

[3]   Zakon o dedovanju kmetijskih gospodarstev (Inheritance of Agricultural Holdings Act: IAHA): Uradni list RS, No. 70/95, 54/99.

[4]   Zakon o registraciji istopolnih partnerskih skupnosti (The Registration of a Same-Sex Civil Partnership Act (RSSCPA): Uradni list RS, No. 65/05; 55/09.

[5]   Zakon o zakonski zvezi in družinskih razmerjih (Marriage and Family Relations Act: MFRA): Uradni list RS, No. 69/04 (official consolidated version: OCV – 1); 101/07; 122/07.

[6]   Zakon o denacionalizaciji (Denationalization Act: DA): Uradni list RS, No. 27/91-I s številnimi spremembami.

[7]   Zakon o ponovni vzpostavitvi agrarnih skupnostih ter vrnitvi njihovega premoženja (Act on Reestablishment of Agricultural Communities and Restitution of Their Property and Rights: ARACRTPR): Uradni list RS, No. 5/94; 38/94; 69/95; 22/97; 79/98; 56/99; 72/00; 51/04.

[8]   Zakon o davku na dediščine in darila (Inheritance and Gift Tax Act: IGTA): Uradni list RS, No. 117/06.

[9]   Zakon o avtorski in sorodnih pravicah (Copyright and Related Rights Act: CRRA): Uradni list RS, No. 16/2007 (OCV – 3); 68/08.

g) Companies Act (e.g. consequences of the death of an entrepreneur or an associate in a personal or capital company);[10]

2 Freedom of Testation

A testament enables the testator to freely dispose of his or her property in case of death. Freedom of testation is one of the principles of inheritance law and enables the testator to decide on the destination of his or her property in a different way to that foreseen in intestate succession. Because of this, testamentary succession prevails over intestate succession.

The testator may regulate inheritance according to his or her personal wishes, needs and designs by means of a will. Property may be left to a natural or even legal person; the will may cover the entire estate or only a share thereof. In spite of this, it cannot be claimed that freedom of testation in the RS is absolute, as there are certain limitations to the ancestor's power to dispose of his or her estate by testament. I will focus on questions of *ordre public* (e.g. admissibility of certain conditions), reciprocal testaments and forced share.

2.1 *Ordre public*

The IA does not determine when the content of a will is admissible. This is left to the Code of Obligations (CO). According to the latter, the content of a will is inadmissible if it conflicts with the Constitution, mandatory rules or moral principles (arts. 37 and 39 CO). Compliance with moral principles is analysed from the point of view of social and personal moral principles. Inadmissibility leads to the testament being null and void (art. 35 CO). An example of inadmissible content would be when the testator provides in favour of someone so that this person does not press charges against the testator for a criminal offence. A prohibition can also be found in art. 79/3 IA: Slovenian law forbids fideicommissum or successive appointment of heirs.[11]

On the other hand, the content of a will needs to be determinable; i.e. it must be possible to find out who the beneficiaries are (art. 83 IA) and what assets are the subject matter of the gifts included in the testament. When interpreting a will, the testator's intention is paramount. If this cannot be discovered, the rule is to construe the testator's words in the most convenient way for the intestate beneficiaries or for the beneficiary who is burdened with a charge or obligation.

2.2 Forced Share and *Exheredatio*

Freedom of testation is not absolute. Making a will does not allow an ancestor to completely avoid the intestate order. The forced share is a

---

[10] Zakon o gospodarskih družbah (Companies Act: CoA): Uradni list RS, No. 65/09 (OCV – 3); 83/09.

[11] See VSK Conclusion I Cp 388/2003.

clear restraint on testamentary freedom. The IA provides a list of people who are entitled to a forced share, even if the testator did not mention them in the will.

According to the IA, forced heirs may be:

a) absolute forced heirs (art. 25/1 IA): the testator's descendants, his or her adoptee and their descendants, his or her parents and his or her spouse or civil partner;

b) relative forced heirs (art. 25/2 IA) – grandparents, brothers and sisters of the deceased, who may have the right to a forced share only if they are permanently incapable of work and have no means of living.[12]

The forced share is an aliquot share of the deceased's estate. The forced heir has the right to a share of each asset belonging to the deceased's estate.[13] The share of absolute forced heirs is half of what they would be entitled to under the rules of intestacy; for relative forced heirs, the share is a third of their intestate stake (art. 26/2 IA). Only people who could take under intestacy can be forced heirs and the rule according to which relatives of a closer order exclude further removed relatives also applies in this instance.

The institute of forced share limits a person's privilege to dispose *mortis causa*, but also *inter vivos*, for gratuitous (lucrative)[14] transfers. If the testator has not respected the forced share by disposing of his or her assets by will or by means of gifts *inter vivos*, the forced heir may demand that the gifts made in the will are reduced; if this is not sufficient to cover the forced share, he or she may seek the restitution or reduction of *inter vivos* donations (arts. 35, 36 and 38 IA).

Slovenian law separates the reasons for disinheritance in two groups. The first group includes reasons based on the violation of personal relations between the heir and the decedent (e.g. marriage, adoption), i.e. the forced heir has acted immorally in not behaving according to the values of mutual respect and support that underpin these relationships. The second group includes criminal offences as well as socially unacceptable acts.[15] Disinheritance essentially shows the testator's disapproval of an heir's behaviour by depriving him or her of the share or a part thereof that he or she would otherwise be entitled to.[16] Grounds for disinheritance are laid down by the law; the mere fact that the testator dislikes the forced heir or his or her behaviour is not sufficient to justify disinheritance, unless it falls within one of the grounds provided for in the IA. The following are valid grounds for disinheritance:

---

[12] VSL sklep II Cp 1502/93 – "A sister of a decedent being in need for support in a home for elder people and paying the care partly from her pension and partly from social support, has sufficient means for living. Therefore, she has no right to a forced share."

[13] Kraljić (2005) 22.

[14] VSL sodba II Cp 1660/98; VSL sodba II Cp 780/2009.

[15] Blagojević (1964) 224.

[16] Smole (1965) 126.

a) Severe violation of some legal or moral duty of the heir towards the deceased.

Not every violation of moral duties is sufficient for disinheritance: it has to be severe, not only by criteria ruling in the relation between the testator and the forced heir, but according to criteria of a wider social morality. Examples of these reprehensible behaviours are neglect of due respect,[17] bad behaviour,[18] failure to help in times of illness and trouble, failure to visit an elder testator and similar actions and omissions.[19] But the heir must be able to fulfil the duties towards the deceased without endangering his or her own life or health.[20] If the reasons for an interruption of mutual relations are on the side of the deceased, the heir cannot be expected to permanently try to make contact with somebody who does not wish to keep in touch.[21] The concrete reasons for disinheritance must be stated in the will. It must be noted that other areas of the law include obligations towards the decedent and that acting in breach of these duties may also constitute a solid ground for disinheritance. This is the case of obligations deriving from a family relation.[22] The law specifically sets the duty of parents to maintain their children,[23] but they are also obliged to represent them and to manage their assets for their benefit. For the children, it sets the duty to respect their parents[24] and to offer help.[25] Spouses also have duties towards each other.[26] Minors cannot

---

[17] VSL Verdict I Cp 3723/2008 – "In spite of the relations between the decedent and the defendant that were not model-like, as it was already established by the court of justice, but all the contrary, since the accused and the decedent even had conflicts in front of the court of justice, this does not yet represent a fulfilment of the legal conditions for disinheritance."

[18] VSL Verdict II Cp 3204/2007 – "The defendant acted in an extraordinarily aggressive manner towards the decedent. He repeatedly hit her, dragged her by the hair, destroyed her sleep by banging the doors and entering her bedroom. Such behaviour is in line with the term of bad behaviour being a reason for disinheritance."

[19] Šorli (1982) 27.

[20] Kreč – Pavić (1964) 138.

[21] Verdict of Supreme Court RS: II I ps 233/98 from 13 March 1999, published at: http://www.ius-software.si/baze/sovs/b/vs04490.htm; 27 August 2009.

[22] Kreč – Pavić (1964) 136.

[23] See arts. 102, 103, 123 and 125 MFRA.

[24] The defendants, by not visiting and trying to help the decedent in his illness, did not violate any legal or moral duties, which would represent a reason for disinheritance after art. 42/1/1 IA – Verdict II I ps 983/93; Supreme Court of RS; No. VS01053; published at http://www.sodisce.si/znanje/sodna_praksa/vrhovno_sodisce_rs/2660/; 30 October 2009.

[25] (1) A mature child is obliged, in line with his possibilities, to maintain its parents, if they do not have enough means for living and are not able to get any. (2) A mature child is not obliged to maintain the parent, who for unjust reasons did not fulfil the duty to maintain him before (art. 124 MFRA).

[26] A spouse is obliged to maintain the other spouse without means only if he or she does not have means for living, if he or she is unemployed or incapable of work or unintentionally unemployed. In these cases a spouse has to be capable of maintaining the other without endangering his or her own maintenance or that of other dependants.

be disinherited on the grounds of violating a moral duty.[27] When the reprehensible act is a severe violation of the duty to maintain the deceased it amounts to the unworthiness of the heir.

b) Grave criminal offence with intent against the deceased, or his or her spouse, child, adoptee, or parents or adoptive parents

As well as the close relatives of the deceased, due to the personal and familiar connection, also cohabitants, same-sex partners in a registered same-sex partnership and the adopting person belong here. Whether a criminal offence is a reason for disinheritance is judged according to the rules of Criminal Law. The fact that an heir has been found guilty of a concrete criminal offence does not automatically deprive this person of the forced share; disinheritance must be expressed clearly in the testament.[28] It is irrelevant whether the heir was convicted of a criminal offence or not. It is sufficient that the act has been committed, and so even a statute-barred crime or a severe criminal offence with amnesty is a valid reason for disinheritance. The existence of a criminal offence may also be determined by a civil court of justice as a preliminary issue that has effect only in the concrete dispute, except if a criminal court has already delivered a verdict, in which case the civil court is bound by this verdict.[29]

c) Idleness and other reprehensible conducts

Actions of the heir, such as drunkenness, laziness, immorality, hazardous behaviours, begging or violence are judged in each individual case; the court decides whether the conditions for disinheritance are met. This category also includes dishonest and illegal activities; the cultivation and distribution of drugs, arms dealing or trafficking people. Therefore, this category differs from the previous (b) in that there the heir acts against the decedent or his or her relatives, whilst in this case the listed actions are considered immoral, unjust or unethical by the society in general. The law considers that those who severely damage society also violate their duties towards the deceased and thus do not deserve the forced share.[30] Idleness in this context is defined as a permanent and unfounded avoidance of work.[31] This reason for disinheritance must also exist at the time of the demise.[32]

The first condition for the validity of disinheritance is the validity of the will that contains it. The mere fact of not mentioning a forced heir in the will does not amount to valid disinheritance; this needs to be clearly expressed in the

---

[27] Verdict of Supreme Court RS II Ips 415/98 from 26.5.1999; published at IUS INFO, Database, http://www.ius–software.si/baze/sovs/b/vso4894.htm; 30 October 2009.

[28] Kreč – Pavić (1964) 138.

[29] Gavella (1986) 145.

[30] Smole (1965) 127.

[31] Kreč – Pavić (1964) 139.

[32] The other grounds have to be present at the time when the will was made.

will.[33] There is no presumption of disinheritance. However, the decedent can also disinherit a forced heir in a non-testamentary document (i.e. a document where no heir is appointed) as long as it fulfils the conditions for a valid will.[34] Stating the ground for disinheritance is not a prerequisite for valid disinheritance, but art. 43.1 IA provides that it is useful; it facilitates proving the reason. Sometimes the deceased does not wish to make the reason for disinheritance public, either for his or her own sake or for the heir's. In these cases, the testator may express the existence of the grounds for disinheritance in a mediate way; it is sufficient if he or she makes it clear that there is a legal reason for disinheritance. Expressing more than one reason is irrelevant, since the court will not analyse other reasons as soon as one of them has been established.[35] The grounds for disinheritance must exist at the time when the testator makes the will,[36] and for idleness or other reprehensible acts (above, b), also at the time of the demise.[37] If there is a conflict on the foundation of disinheritance, the court of justice interrupts the probate hearing and directs the heirs to a contested matters proceeding, which is in line with art. 213.1 IA. According to art. 43.3 IA, the burden of proof shifts to whoever defends the validity of the will; this party needs to prove the existence of the ground for disinheritance.

When a forced heir is validly disinherited, other people may occupy his or her position (right of representation). In cases of full disinheritance, the disinherited heir loses his or her status and is treated as if he or she had died before the testator (i.e. as if he or she had never had the right to a forced share). Therefore, the disinherited heir cannot demand the reduction of testamentary or non-testamentary gifts. These rights pass to those who would have been forced heirs if the disinherited heir had not existed.

Partial disinheritance is also possible. The testator leaves the forced heir less than would be due according to the rules on forced share, clearly expressing that partial disinheritance is intended. The disinherited heir does not lose his or her status, but the amount to be received is reduced.[38]

---

[33] Thus, a written declaration on disinheritance in a donation contract without respecting the formalities prescribed for a testament is not valid. – VSH Rev 1786/85, 3 December 1985, Pregled VSH 30/86 p.88, obr., 3 December 1985, Croatia; published at http://www.sodisce.si/znanje/sodna_praksa/32135/; 30 August 2009.

[34] Šinkovec – Tratar (2005) 186.

[35] Verdict of the Higher Court in Ljubljana VSL sodba II Cp 3204/2007 from 12 March 2009; published at IUS INFO, Database, http://www.ius.software.si/baze/iesp/b/574757.htm; 4 September 2009.

[36] This provision does not encompass only acts at the time when the testament was made, but the heir's actions through a certain period of time. Thus, the relation between the heir and the decedent has to be shattered even before the testament is made, but it is not determined how long the conflict has to have lasted: verdict of the Higher Court in Ljubljana, VSL sodba II Cp 3204/2007 from 12 March 2008; published at IUS INFO, Database, http://www.ius-software.si/baze/iesp/b/574757.htm; 8 September 2009.

[37] Žnidaršič (2000) 13.

[38] Šinkovec – Tratar (2005) 190.

A disinherited heir will not personally receive anything from the deceased (the exclusion operates both for testamentary entitlements and for intestacy). The disinherited heir is treated as if he or she had died before the deceased. The descendants of the disinherited heir will receive his or her share by right of representation.[39]

Revocation of disinheritance is possible and valid, if it is made by the testator in a testament or if the disinherited is named heir in a new testament.

Also the institute of deprivation of forced share for the benefit of the successors (*exheredatio bona mente*) increases freedom of testation. There is a fundamental difference between this and disinheritance. By means of the latter, the testator punishes the forced heir because of reprehensible conducts towards the decedent or towards society in general. Instead, *exheredatio bona mente* protects the rights of the testator's descendants who have the right to a forced share. It must also be grounded in one of the reasons strictly laid down by the IA; i.e. the forced heir is in such a financial position (debts and overspending)[40] that creditors would seize the forced share or he or she would spend it, to the detriment of his or her descendants. In these circumstances, the testator may chose to deprive the forced heir of his or her share, totally or partially, as long as the legal conditions are respected.[41] But it must be noted that *exheredatio bona mente* is aimed at protecting the descendants, so deprivation is only possible for the benefit of minor grandchildren or minor grandchildren of a passed child or if they are adults, but incapable of work. They will have the right to the forced share by right of representation.[42]

3 Especial Limitations for Agricultural Holdings

The IAHA, as *lex specialis*, also limits freedom of testation. According to the IAHA, a testator may name just one person or exceptionally two persons as heirs, if these persons are spouses/cohabitants or parent/adoptive parent and child/adoptee. Any different provision would lead to the invalidity of the will and the rules on intestacy would apply. The main principle of the IAHA is to prevent the division of protected farms in case of intestate and testamentary succession.

The IAHA sets special conditions besides general conditions to be met by any heir, whether succession is testate or intestate. In intestacy, only one heir may inherit. If the decedent is the sole owner of the protected farm and there are several potential heirs belonging to the same order, the "criteria for exclusion" laid down by art. 7 IAHA apply. First, the farm will pass to the intestate heir that has been selected by the other potential heirs and who has the inten-

---

[39] Šinkovec – Tratar (2005) 190.

[40] Šinkovec – Tratar (2005) 194.

[41] Smole (1965) 133.

[42] Zupančič – Žnidaršič Skubic (2009) 105.

tion to work on the farm. If this still leaves more than one potential heir, the rule is that closer relatives exclude farther removed ones and, among relatives of the same order, the farm will go to the heir who is most capable of running the farm or proves he or she is better qualified to do so; when possible, the surviving spouse's wishes will be respected. If a farm is owned by both husband and wife, the surviving spouse will be the heir (art. 8 IAHA). If the protected farm was co-owned by a parent and a child (whether adopted or not), the surviving co-owner will receive the farm, as long as he or she may take under intestacy. Otherwise, we revert to the rules explained above.

Art. 11 IAHA contains further "exclusion criteria" that will only be used if after applying these rules there are still several potential heirs. They may be excluded if:

a) due to mental illness, mental disturbance or physical impairment, the potential heir is obviously not capable of managing the protected farm permanently;

b) due to an obvious and permanent tendency towards over-spending, alcoholism or drug abuse, there is a risk that the potential heir is not going to manage the protected farm well;

c) there has not been news of the potential heir for several years, leading to the conclusion that his or her return cannot be expected within a reasonable time. Absence due to war or captivity in war is not such a case.

A further restraint on the freedom of testation pursuant to IAHA can be found in the special regulation of the forced share for those who do not receive the farm. The list of forced heirs after IAHA (spouse/cohabitant; descendants; adoptee and their descendants; parents/adoptive parents) is shorter than in IA (spouse/cohabitant; descendants; adoptee and their descendants; parents/adoptive parents; grand-parents; brothers and sisters). This sets a double limitation on freedom of testation, i.e. by the institute of forced share and by the limited circle of forced heirs after IAHA. The amount of the forced share is determined in accordance with the provisions of the IA, i.e. half of the intestate share for the spouse/cohabitant and descendants/adoptees, and a third for parents and adoptive parents.

There are also limitations on the legacies that the testator may choose to leave. If the subject matter of the legacy is part of a protected farm, the legacy is only valid if the economic potential of the farm is not damaged, and this is deemed to occur whenever the legacy is of a piece of farmland. If this is not the case, individual legacies that do not exceed 2% of the value of the farm are considered valid, as long as all the legacies contained in the will do not exceed 10% of that value (art. 22 IAHA).

4 Inheritance Agreements

Inheritance agreements are agreements by which one of the parties is in some way bound regarding the privilege to dispose *mortis causa*. Slovenian inheritance law forbids this type of agreements, when they refer to assets that a person may have at the time of his or her death (arts. 7 and 103 IA), but the law of obligations accepts contracts that will be effective at the time of death, but that refer to assets that a party owns when entering into the agreement.

Slovenian law does not allow *simultaneous wills* –where two or more people execute mutually connected or interrelating last wills. But case law considers a testament valid, where two people (usually spouses) reciprocally name each other heirs.[43] These schemes are obviously very close the forbidden inheritance agreements,[44] although the difference lies in the fact that a testament is revocable.

The CO recognizes the validity of different contracts with *mortis causa* effects. It accepts contracts between a person and his or her descendants by which the latter disclaim the future and expected inheritance; unless otherwise stated, the disclaimer is also binding for the descendant's issue. Art. 546 CO provides for a contract between an ancestor and all of his or her issue by means of which the ancestor transfers assets owned at the time of the contract to one or more of them; if the spouse or cohabitant does not consent, the contract is valid but may be challenged and the assets transferred *inter vivos* are considered gifts when calculating the forced share. This contract may only be determined by the ancestor due to severe ungratefulness shown by the beneficiary, failure to maintain or assist the ancestor or someone else as agreed in the contract or failure to pay the ancestor's debts as agreed in the contract.[45] Another contract regulated by the CO which will have *mortis causa* effects is the contract of annuity for life; a person undertakes to take care of another person (and/or of his or her estate or funeral) in exchange for the latter's disposition of property (including real estate) in favour of the former; delivery is postponed until the person to be maintained dies.[46] A similar goal of providing care for the person who undertakes to transfer assets presides the regulation of the usufruct contract (art. 564 CO), although it differs from the contract of annuity for life in many other aspects. Finally, Slovenian law also recognizes the validity of *donationes mortis causa*. All these contracts are subject to formalities, generally involving a notarised deed.

---

43 See VSL Conclusion II Cp 755/2001: "It is in the nature of the matter that a holographic testament can not be valid, if it contains the will of two decedents in one act".

44 Zupančič – Žnidaršič Skubic (2009) 128.

45 Šinkovec/Tratar (2005) 671; Plavšak *et al* (2003) 506; Zupančič – Žnidaršič Skubic (2009) 193.

46 Zupančič – Žnidaršič Skubic (2009) 196; Kraljić (2006) 9.

Freedom of Testation, Legal Inheritance Rights and Public Order under Spanish Law

Sergio Cámara Lapuente

1 Overview

The tension between the freedom to make a will and its legal restrictions affects virtually all institutions of succession law. The degree of legislative intervention by reducing or extending this autonomy varies, in Spain and elsewhere, according to the socio-cultural conceptions of different times and groups of people. The Spanish case is particularly illustrative of the diversity of possible solutions even among neighbouring regions, and of the mutable nature of the law in every legal system; it also offers a wide scope for legal comparison due to the coexistence, in Spain, of seven different systems of succession, each being applicable depending upon the region. To address this matter we will proceed (section 2) to describe and assess the legal limits on testamentary freedom both in the Spanish Civil Code (CC) and in the laws of the six autonomous communities with competence to legislate in this area. To this end, an analysis will be made of the main institution limiting free disposal, the forced share for certain relatives, and the rights of the widowed spouse and civil partnerships in both testate successions and in intestacy. The following section (section 3) shows the lively current debate about the configuration of the *'material' freedom* to make a will, i.e. whether to keep, eliminate or reduce the forced shares, primarily in the context of the Spanish Civil Code, in the light of the legislative and practical experiences of the regulations in force in the Autonomous Communities and comparative law. It is also necessary to establish (section 4) the degree of *'formal' freedom* to make a will under the existing Spanish laws, that is, the instruments or channels that are permitted or prohibited to organize *mortis causa* succession. This study concludes (section 5) with the analysis of the relationship between the limits of testamentary freedom and the concept of *'public order'* and, in particular, examining the question of whether the forced share is a matter included in that concept.

2 Limits on the Freedom to Dispose *Mortis Causa* in the Spanish Civil Code and in the Autonomous Communities

2.1 Legal Frame

The rules on *mortis causa* successions contained in the Spanish Civil Code of 1889 are not directly applicable in all parts of Spain, but rather, only in 11 of the 17 Autonomous Communities (plus Ceuta and Melilla) into which the Spanish territory is divided. The other six autonomous communities have their own civil law with peculiarities on succession law, in a phenomenon which stems from the so-called *Derecho foral* (local Law) existing in these territories since the Early Middle Ages. The special laws for certain regions of Spain were approved between 1959 and 1973 and are currently deemed as second or third generation laws or codes which have been revised several times and which combine respect for historic tradition with the modernization of inheritance law. In their most recent version, said regulations exist in Navarre (1973), the Balearic Islands (1990), the Basque Country (1992 and 1999), Aragon (1999), Galicia (2006) and Catalonia (2008).[1] In contrast, the Spanish Civil Code (which is only applied in some issues as supplementary or subsidiary law in those regions) remains the same in most of its key features as it was enacted in the nineteenth century; having been reformed 15 times, only a quarter of its original articles have been amended.[2] Except for concrete institutions, mainly amended to bolster freedom of testation in favour of some social groups or certain purposes (see *infra* 2.3 and 3.3.1), the system of forced shares in the CC is simply as it was 120 years ago.

2.2 Description of the *ex lege* Rights in Favour of the Deceased's Family

In general terms, it can be stated that the systems of the autonomous communities enjoy greater formal freedom (because they allow instruments prohibited under the Spanish Civil Code, such as inheritance agreements, joint wills, certain fiduciary schemes, etc.; see *infra* 4) and greater material freedom. In this respect, though, they differ enormously, ranging from absolute material freedom in Navarre and in the territory in the Basque Country where the *Fuero de Ayala* [Ayala Laws] is applicable, in which cases testators are allowed not to leave anything to their children, to little material freedom in other areas, as occurs when the *Fuero de Vizcaya* [Vizcaya Laws], relevant to another Basque area, governs a succession: in this case, testators are obliged to leave four-fifths of their inheritance to their children.

---

[1] In *Navarre*, Law 1/1973, of 1 March on the Compilation of the Civil Foral Law of Navarre or *Fuero Nuevo de Navarra* (modified by Law 5/1987). In the *Balearic Islands*, Legislative Decree 79/1990, of 6 September (which consolidates the text of the Law 5/1961). In the *Basque Country*, Law 3/1992, of 1 July of the Civil Regional (*Foral*) Law of the Basque Country (formerly in Law of 30 July 1959 and Law 6/1988) plus the Law of the so-called *Fuero* of Guipúzcoa of 30 December 1999 (only for the succession to *caseríos*, or rural traditional houses/farms). In *Aragon*, Law 1/1999, of 24 February on *Mortis Causa* Successions (formerly, within Law 15/1967 as amended by Law 3/1985). In *Galicia*, Law 2/2006, of 14 June on the Civil Law of Galicia (formerly in Law 4/1995 and before then in Law 147/1963). In *Catalonia*, Law 10/2008, of 10 July on 'Book IV of the Civil Code of Catalonia, dealing with succession' (formerly Law 40/1991 and previously in Laws 13/1984 and 40/1960). Quotation of article numbers in brackets throughout the text are referred to the corresponding Law of the autonomous community cited in each case.

[2] For an account of those reforms and the trends regarding legislation and case law on succession contained in the Spanish Civil Code, see Cámara Lapuente (2007) 7 ff.

The following tables show the differences between the seven succession systems with regard to forced shares and legally established inheritance rights, as major restrictions on the testamentary freedom:[3]

Table 1 Descendants' Forced Share ('Legítima')

Spanish Civil Code	2/3 'long forced share' *[legítima larga]* (1/3 'short' forced share, 1/3 'betterment' or *mejora*)	Children (other descendants in the absence of children or subject to representation)
Catalonia	1/4 (credit in value or money, not in kind)	Children (other descendants subject to representation)
Galicia	1/4 (credit in value or money, not in kind)	Children (other descendants subject to representation)
Balearic Islands	1/3 if there are 4 or less 1/2 if there are more than four	Children (other descendants subject to representation)
Aragon	1/2 'collective *legítima*' (equal, unequal or individual distribution)	All descendants at any level
Basque Country	4/5: 'collective *legítima*': F. Vizcaya **Nothing**: all can be excluded: F. Ayala 2/3: areas without their own law (*fueros*) = Spanish Civil Code	Descendants Descendants Children (other descendants...)
Navarre	**Nothing**: formal *legítima*, without economic content	Children (other descendants subject to representation)

A *summa divisio* can be drawn between Spanish systems which set a fixed share for the children and descendants that the testator cannot dispose of in favour of other people (Spanish Civil Code, Catalonia, Galicia, Balearic Islands, Aragon and part of the Basque Country),[4] and those systems (Navarre and the *Fuero* of Ayala in the Basque Country) that give absolute freedom to the testator to exclude these forced heirs and appoint only the heirs he or she wishes. Both Navarre and the *Fuero* of Ayala nevertheless retain the Roman concept of 'formal forced share',[5] so it is necessary to mention the forced heirs in the will

---

[3] These tables do not follow a chronological or alphabetical internal order, but are based on similarities between systems, to highlight these as well as the differences that can be found in relation to each right studied.

[4] The Basque Country legislation, contained in Law 2/1992, is divided into four different regimes that apply to the citizens of different areas: a) Jurisdiction of Biscay (*Fuero de Vizcaya*, applicable in the province of Biscay, except in certain villages and the capital, Bilbao), traditionally with greater restrictions on testamentary freedom; b) Jurisdiction of Ayala (*Fuero de Ayala*, applicable to part of the province of Álava), which provides the system with the greatest testamentary freedom in Spain; c) Jurisdiction of Guipúzcoa (*Fuero de Guipúzcoa*, applicable in that province), where the Spanish Civil Code governs, except for certain special rules for the undivided transmission of farmhouses in rural areas (art. 153); d) In areas excluded from these regional jurisdictions (e.g. in the three Basque capitals, Bilbao, San Sebastian and Vitoria, in all urban areas of Guipuzcoa, etc.) the forced share system of the Spanish Civil Code applies.

[5] See Miquel González (2009) 495 ff.

to exclude them from the succession; this rule is designed to protect the testator from making mistakes concerning the existence of descendants (arts. 271 and 136-139, respectively). Once this requirement is fulfilled, the forced share has no economic or material content in Navarre (art. 267), although it should be noted that there is a limit on testamentary freedom to protect children born from previous marriages, who cannot receive from their parents less than the most favoured among the children or spouses of subsequent marriages (art. 272). Regarding the Jurisdiction of Ayala, the forced heirs and their shares are the same as in the Spanish Civil Code, but as explained, they may all be freely excluded without cause and without other restrictions.

As for the systems that reserve a fixed share of the estate for children or descendants – i.e. the testator may only disinherit them based on a limited list of serious reasons–, it is possible to propose a subdivision into three groups, depending on the degree of freedom of disposal granted by law for such shares: *(i)* first, there are systems that recognize a single share to be distributed equally among all the children or, failing that, the descendants: it is the case of Catalonia (arts. 451-3, 451-5 and 451-6), Galicia (art. 243) and the Balearic Islands (arts. 42, 65 and 79, where shares vary depending on the number of descendants); *(ii)* Second, the Spanish Civil Code (arts. 808 and 823-833) – even if the forced share covers a large part of the estate, namely two thirds – makes the system of equal distribution more flexible through the mechanism of 'betterment' *(mejora)* whereby the forced share is divided into two equal parts, so that a third of the estate ('short forced share') should be distributed among all children equally, without the possibility of imposing burdens, conditions or substitutions (art. 813), while the other third ('betterment') can be distributed at the testator's own choice between some (or even only one) of the children and also, even where there are children, among other more remote descendants. This formula guarantees a certain testamentary freedom making it possible to leave to one child two thirds of the estate ("betterment" plus the third that is not part of the forced share) plus the result of dividing the other third ("short forced share") among his or her siblings: *(iii)* The third system extends the testator's power of choice among his or her issue beyond 'betterment': the law designates a share called 'collective forced share' that the testator can distribute among his or her descendants at will in equal or unequal amounts, or even leaving the entire quota to only one person, without the others being entitled to claim anything whatsoever. This is the system of the *Fuero* of Biscay in the Basque Country (arts. 54 to 55, without compensation for those excluded) and in Aragon (art. 171, but with maintenance rights for those excluded where necessary, as provided by art. 200).

Moreover, there is another difference between the various systems of forced shares in Spain, because while some, as paradigmatically occurs with the Spanish Civil Code, maintain the rule that the receipt of the property by the heirs should be *in natura,* i.e. in kind or in hereditary assets *(pars hereditatis,* see art. 806 CC), with some exceptions (arts. 815, 831, 841-842, etc.; see *infra* 3.3.1),[6]

---

[6]   See Domínguez Luelmo (1989); Torres García (2006) 191 ff. and (2009) 307 ff.

other systems have designed the heirs' right as a mere personal right (*pars valoris*) against the heir reaching a quarter of the value of the net inheritance which, therefore, may be paid in extra-hereditary assets, so that the forced heir is not necessarily a part of the hereditary community; this is the system established in Catalonia (arts. 451-5 and 451-11),[7] and, since 2006, also in Galicia (arts. 243 and 246).[8]

The possibility that more remote descendants should inherit the forced share in place of the predeceased, disinherited or unworthy children (right of representation) is a rule, with different nuances, in the Spanish laws which set a forced share of equal sharing, including the Civil Code, at least where betterment or *mejora* have not been used by the testator (arts. 761, 814 and 857).

Table 2 Ascendants' Forced Share ('Legítima')

Spanish Civil Code	Basque Country	Catalonia	Balearic Islands	Aragon	Navarre	Galicia
Yes	Yes	Yes	Yes	No	No	No
Ascendants	Ascendants	Only parents	Only parents			
1/2 if alone	F. Vizcaya: 1/2	1/4	1/4 (other shares in Ibiza and Formentera)			
1/3 with a surviving spouse	F. Ayala: No					
	F. Guipuzcoa = CC					

As for the ascendants' forced share, there are three approaches in the Spanish laws: *(i)* The recognition of forced shares, in the absence of descendants, in favour of all sorts of ascendants, those closest (parents, for example) excluding the more remote ones (grandparents, great grandparents), who are appointed on a subsidiary basis. This is what happens in the Spanish Civil Code (arts. 807 and 809-810) and in Biscay in the Basque Country (arts. 53, 56-57); *(ii)* To ensure a minor forced share only for the parents, not other ascendants, where there are no descendants, as in Catalonia (art. 451-4) and the Balearic Islands (arts. 41, 43, 65 and 79):[9] *(iii)* Not to consider either parents or more remote ascendants forced heirs in any case; this is the option chosen in Aragon (art. 171) and Navarre (art. 268), which renders these systems faithful to their historical tradition and is provided for, respectively, in their Laws of 1967 and 1973; and recently, modifying earlier legislation that recognized rights to the ascendants as in the Spanish CC, Galicia has also adopted this solution in its 2006 reform (art. 238). It can be concluded that there is a legislative trend in Spain tending to abolish or diminish ascendants' rights, according to the proposal of the majority

---

7   For comparison, see Arroyo Amayuelas (2007) 268 ff.

8   See Carballo Fidalgo (2009) 139 ff.

9   Only 1/4 (as in Catalonia) in Mallorca and Menorca (arts. 41, 43, 65); in contrast, the same shares as in the Spanish Civil Code in Ibiza and Formentera (art. 79). For details and criticism, Grimalt Servera (2006) 1611.

of the doctrine[10] (see *infra* 3.2) and in line with the trend detected in comparative law.[11]

Table 3 Legal Rights of the Surviving Spouse and Cohabitant

	Surviving Spouse			Cohabitant
	Alone	With Descendents	With Ascendants	
Spanish Civil Code	2/3 usufruct	1/3 usufruct	1/2 usufruct	**No rights**
Galicia	1/2 usufruct	1/4 usufruct	1/2 usufruct	= spouse
	Voluntary universal usufruct is also lawful			
Basque Country	2/3 Usufruct (Vizcaya) Voluntary universal usufruct is lawful 2/3 Usufruct (Ayala) but non mandatory.	1/2 usufruct (F. Vizcaya) 1/3 usufruct (Ayala) but removable	1/2 usufruct (F. Vizcaya) 1/3 usufruct (Ayala) but removable	= spouse **(No rights** in areas without their own law)
	Voluntary universal usufruct is also lawful (Vizcaya and Ayala)			
Balearic Islands	Mandatory Universal Usufruct (Mallorca-Menorca)	1/2 usufruct (Mallorca-Menorca). In Ibiza-Formentera, 1/2 if intestate	2/3 usufruct (Mallorca-Menorca). In Ibiza-Formentera, 2/3 if intestate	= spouse
Navarre	Mandatory universal usufruct ('*fealdat*') [effects from the death of the spouse onwards]			= spouse
Aragon	Mandatory universal usufruct ('*viudedad*') [special effects while alive, from the date of marriage onwards]			**No rights**
Catalonia	1/4 ownership only in case of need ('*cuarta vidual*')			= spouse

Regarding the legal rights of the surviving spouse, all succession laws in Spain, except the Catalan Law 10/2008, recognize a portion in usufruct. In some laws the share varies depending on who is involved in the succession, being reduced when there are descendants (Spanish Civil Code, arts. 834, 837 and 838; Galicia, arts. 253-254; Basque Country, art. 58; Balearic Islands, arts. 45, 65), while in other systems there is a mandatory usufruct over the whole estate, whether or not there are descendants or ascendants (Navarre, arts 253-266; Aragón, art. 72 ff. Law 3/1985), thus making an effort to strengthen the surviving spouse's position. The laws of Galicia (arts. 228-237) and the Basque Country (arts. 61 and 140 relating to the jurisdictions or *Fueros* of Vizcaya and Ayala) allow the testator to surpass the mandatory share and give the spouse the universal usufruct over the entire estate, which entails encumbering the forced share of descendants or ascendants. The existing rule in Catalonia (arts. 452-1 to 452-6)

---

[10] Against, Moreu Ballonga (1997) 98 ff. and (2006) 164.

[11] Cámara Lapuente (2003) 1221; Vaquer Aloy (2009) 566; see these works also for further comparison of Spanish Law with other legal systems within the European Union.

differs from all others by granting the surviving spouse up to a quarter of the estate in full ownership, rather than a usufruct, but provided that the spouse 'does not have sufficient financial means to meet his or her needs'. Regardless of the legal nature of this 'widow/er allowance', halfway between the right to maintenance (although a periodic pension is not provided for and its amount is limited) and a forced share (although financial need is required and other conditions must be met to keep it),[12] it should be noted that the fraction of a quarter of the liquid estate is the maximum that can be reached depending on the surviving spouse's needs; it is not a set share.

Table 4 Rights of the Surviving Spouse and the Cohabitant in Intestacy

	Surviving Spouse			Cohabitant
	Preference	Quantum	Forced share (in intestacy)	
Spanish Civil Code	1. Children/descendants 2. Ascendants 3. Spouse	– – All	1/3 1/2	**No rights**
Galicia	1. Children/descendants 2. Ascendants 3. Spouse	– – All	1/4 1/2	= Spouse
Basque Country [F. Vizcaya]	1. Children/descendants 2. Ascendants 3. Spouse	– – All (excluding some patrimonial assets – *bienes troncales*)	1/2 1/2	= Spouse
Balearic Islands	1. Children/descendants 2. Ascendants 3. Spouse	– – All	1/2 2/3	= Spouse
Navarre	1. Children/descendants 2. Brothers/Sisters 3. Ascendants 4. Spouse	– – – All (excluding some patrimonial assets – *bienes troncales*)	Universal usufruct Universal usufruct Universal usufruct	= Spouse
Aragon	1. Children/descendants 2. Ascendants 3. Spouse	– – All (excluding some patrimonial assets – *bienes troncales*)	Universal usufruct Universal usufruct	**No rights**
Catalonia	1. Children/descendants 2. Spouse	– All, but forced share for parents	Universal usufruct 1/4 ownership	= Spouse

---

12   Del Pozo Carrascosa – Vaquer Aloy – Bosch Capdevila (2009) 417-418.

The surviving spouse's position in intestacy completes the design of the legal rights granted to him or her. In all inheritance laws existing in Spain, except two, the spouse takes in the third place in intestate succession, after the descendants and ascendants. When not appointed as a legal heir due to there being other relatives of the deceased, he or she is entitled to the forced share (or other legal rights), which operates in both testate successions and in intestacy.[13] This weak protection is compensated in some autonomous laws by the mandatory universal usufruct (Navarre, Aragon and Catalonia). In areas where there is still a special destination established by law for the so-called 'patrimonial, family or core assets' (*bienes troncales*), real estate reserved for certain blood relatives of the testator's family line, even when the spouse becomes intestate successor in the absence of descendants or parents, he or she will not receive all the inheritance because these goods are reserved for collateral relatives of the deceased (in Navarre, Aragon and Biscay). The two exceptions to the system of appointing the spouse in third place are, first, Navarre, where the spouse takes in fourth place in the order (therefore, after the deceased's siblings), and second, with a very different result, Catalonia, where the spouse takes in second place, only behind the descendants and, if the deceased also left issue, the surviving spouse has the right to the universal usufruct.

2.3 Assessment of the Main Legislative Trends

2.3.1 Strengthening the Legal Position of Surviving Spouses

Under Spanish testamentary practice there is a significant tendency to try to favour the spouse beyond the statutory rights recognized in the Spanish Civil Code, and even beyond that permitted by the rules on the descendants' or ascendants' forced shares;[14] it is common for spouses (90%) to attend the notary's office together and make similar wills, each leaving the other the universal usufruct over all the estate, against the limit established in the Spanish CC, which does not allow the forced share (of descendants or ascendants) to be encumbered by charges or burdens, such as it is by a usufruct. One of the usual channels to try to expand the testamentary freedom of the deceased is the so-called *Socini clause* whereby the testator gives a forced heir an amount of money or assets exceeding the forced share, stating that if the burdens or limitations imposed are not accepted (these often being the universal usufruct for the spouse) his or her right will be reduced to the legally established minimum; this enables the forced heir to choose between accepting the gift as established in the will or taking the exact forced share without burdens (*plus quantum, minus quale*). The usual procedure is to designate the spouse as a legatee of the usu-

---

[13] Espejo Lerdo de Tejada (1996) *passim*.

[14] In a survey conducted in early 2009 among nearly 400 notaries practicing in the 11 Autonomous Communities where the Spanish Civil Code governs in the field of inheritance law, 93% of respondents answered affirmatively when asked about the existence of this practice: Rebolledo Varela (2010) 32-33.

fruct of the entire estate and the descendants as bare owners. Although these clauses are not foreseen in the Spanish Civil Code, case law has recognized their validity through a broad interpretation of art. 820.3.[15] The clause is expressly deemed valid in the Law of Catalonia (art. 451-9.2), Mallorca and Menorca (art. 49) and Aragon (art. 185.1). A similar result is reached in certain regions by means of a provision allowing the testator to voluntarily assign the universal usufruct to the surviving spouse, as in the *Fueros* of Vizcaya and Ayala in the Basque Country (arts. 61 and 140) and Galicia (arts. 228 and 241).

As can be seen, the autonomous civil laws have tried to accommodate their legislation to the testators' usual wishes of favouring their spouses, either by increasing the legal quota of their share (e.g. the Basque Country in 1992) or by expressly permitting the testator to voluntarily establish a universal usufruct over the entire estate in their favour (e.g. Galicia in 2006) or by reducing the descendants' forced share to allow a greater freedom of disposal (e.g. Aragon in 1999 or Galicia in 2006); likewise, in some cases these laws have improved the surviving spouses' position in intestate succession, either by giving them preference over certain relatives, or by a broadening their forced share in such cases of absence of a will.

However, within the sphere of the Spanish Civil Code, the clear guidelines in testamentary practice have had little legislative implementation, as shown by the fact that the preference given to spouses over collateral relatives was introduced in 1981 (and no subsequent reforms have been enacted), and that their legal share as special forced heirs (this qualification is debated as it is not subject to exactly the same rules as descendants and ascendants) has not changed since 1889. By contrast, many reforms have imposed on surviving spouses additional burdens or a prominent role with respect to the testator's relatives (maintenance, guardianship, etc.), which have not been accompanied by an increase in their rights, something widely criticized by the doctrine.[16] However, the rights of surviving spouses have been strengthened by the Spanish Parliament as for the testators' inheritance ruled by the Spanish Civil law mainly through different laws that establish special succession rights on certain property items or rights and thus give preference to the spouse over all the deceased's relatives: this is the case with the Urban Rent Act of 1994 (art. 16), the Rural Rent Act of 2003 (art. 24), different indemnities awarded under obligatory insurance covering travel, death in road accidents or when the deceased is a victim of violent or terrorist crimes.[17]

2.3.2   Legal Rights in Favour of a Cohabitant

There are clear contrasts between the six autonomous communities with competence on succesion law and the Spanish national legislation,

---

[15]   STS 10 July 2003. See also STS 3 December 2001 and STS 29 December 1939. See Real Pérez (1988); Cabezuelo Arenas (2002); Ragel Sánchez (2003).

[16]   On this criticism, see e.g. Carrancho Herrero (2006) 733 ff.

[17]   Martínez Martínez (2006) 438 ff.

which still does not regulate in general terms, either through an *ad hoc* law or in the Civil Code, the succession rights of non-married cohabitants. In the areas governed by the provisions on succession of the Civil Code, cohabitants do not have reciprocal succession rights; only spouses have these rights, whether they are in a same-sex marriage or not. National case law has not extended the rights to forced share[18] or to intestate succession of spouses[19] to cohabitants by analogy. Among academics, there is an intense debate on whether it is possible and feasible to extend the spouse's *mortis causa* legal rights to cohabitants.[20] Meanwhile, in everyday testamentary practice a notable increase has been detected in the number of wills made by cohabitants granting each other rights, although the content of these provisions is not uniform: especially when the couple has no children, the ascendants of the testator are usually appointed as his or her forced heirs, whereby legally the partner has no inheritance rights *ex lege*.[21]

In the civil laws of the autonomous communities two different approaches can be found: most of the laws envisage full equalization in succession with the spouse in a marriage (Balearic Islands, Basque Country, Galicia, Navarre and Catalonia),[22] whereas other laws opt not to grant the cohabitant succession rights in the strict sense of the term, although they do grant some other advantages under Public, Family or Maintenance Law (namely in Aragon). Given this second alternative, doctrine is divided between the school of thought that

---

[18] The judgment of the Provincial Court of Malaga of 12 November 1999 can be cited as an example of an exceptional and incorrect decision, which contravenes existing legislation. In this case the court granted by analogy a forced share to a same sex partner who had lived with the deceased for 30 years; this recognition of rights reduced the decedent's mother's forced share from a half to a third. However, for a favourable comment on this judgment, see Nieto Alonso (2010) 122-124.

[19] However, sometimes the Supreme Court, which has never recognised the analogy with the status of spouse as for inheritance rights, has found other equitable solutions in specific cases: for instance, in the well known judgment of 17 June 2003, the Supreme Court granted compensation of a quarter of the estate in favour of the cohabitant who took care of the deceased for years, in a case where the intestate inheritance of the latter was assigned by law to a collateral relative. The Court's decision rested on the doctrine of unjust enrichment.

[20] Recently, in favour, for instance, Pinto Andrade (2008) 150-151. Against, Amunátegui Rodríguez (2002) 276; Cuena Casas (2005) 1571. The different grounds that justify forced shares and intestate rights may explain why some scholars against the equalization in the first case support the extension of intestate rights to cohabitants: see Nieto Alonso (2010) 125 ff.; Fernández Campos (2010) 291.

[21] According to the above-cited survey among notaries – Rebolledo Varela (2010) 30 – while 92% of notaries responded affirmatively to the question of whether cohabitants show more interest in leaving a will, only 58% did so to the question of whether cohabitants without children are concerned about leaving their partners in a solid position, to the detriment of their own ascendants.

[22] In Catalonia, until the Law 10/2008, which has recognised full equalization to marriage for all kinds of stable couples (regardless of their homosexual or heterosexual profile), the Law 10/1998 granted more legal succession rights to the surviving cohabitant in same sex couples. For comparative details, see Gete-Alonso – Ysàs – Navas – Solé (2006) 362 ff.

considers this lack of full equalization to be a reactionary approach,[23] and those
who feel this decision stems from greater freedom of disposal for those who do
not want to marry and, therefore, represents a more modern and liberal view of
the function of the law of succession.

2.3.3 Scarce Enlargement of the Grounds of Disinheritance and Unworthiness

One of the obvious ways to extend the testamentary freedom
within systems that recognize forced share rights is to allow a greater number
of grounds for the testator to disinherit his or her forced heirs or for them to be
unworthy to succeed even if the testator does not expressly disinherit them. In
the field of the Spanish Civil Code these grounds have only undergone minor
amendments (Laws 22/1978, 20/1981 and 11/1990) as a consequence of the legal
changes on marriage breakdown, some penal reforms (adultery, abandonment,
prostitution or corruption of children) or the strengthening of the protection of
disabled people. Neither have the autonomous laws made profound changes in
this area, with two exceptions: first, under the Balearic Islands legislation, introduced by Law 3/2009 of 27 April, two new articles (arts. 7 bis and 69 bis) clarify
the typical grounds of disinheritance and unworthiness provided in the Spanish
Civil Code (that governs on a supplementary basis) to ensure the exclusion of
the spouse or cohabitant who has committed acts of domestic violence against
his or her spouse or partner. On the other hand, Catalonia, in the Law 10/2008,
of July 10, has extended the causes of indignity to various criminal offences, in
particular to family or gender-based violence offences or those against sexual
freedom committed against the testator or other people in his or her household.
In addition, the Catalan law has considered as a cause of unworthiness the
non-payment of financial relief granted in matrimonial proceedings, as well as
including the infringement of custody obligations, abduction of minors or other
forms of family abandonment other than the non-payment of pensions (art. 412-
3). Another important novelty of this Law 10/2008 – in this case formally but not
materially limiting the freedom of the testator to ensure the proper formation of
his or her will – has been the provision (art. 412-5.2) stating that gifts to natural
or legal persons who have provided care, residential facilities or other services to
the testator under a contractual agreement have to be laid down in an open will
or inheritance agreement drafted by a notary. In these cases, although the law
does not declare these potential beneficiaries unfit to succeed, in order to avoid
injustice on the one hand and on the other, the suspicion of undue influence on
the testator, arrangements in their favour are not allowed to be made by means
of a holographic or closed will.

---

[23] For instance, see Merino Hernández (2000) 655 ff., regarding Aragon.

2.3.4 Special Protection for Certain Social Groups

Although any new recognition of legal rights for certain groups of people seems to inexorably curtail the testator's freedom to dispose of his or her assets, not all reforms have led to this conclusion. This has in fact been the result of Law 13/2005 of 1 July, which allowed same-sex marriage, thus granting homosexual spouses the same inheritance rights as heterosexual spouses; testamentary freedom has also been limited based on other legislative policy when in the five autonomous regions the cohabitant has been recognized the same inheritance rights as a spouse.

In a similar way, when the Spanish Civil Code was adapted to the 1978 Constitution by Law 11/1981 of 13 May, equal legal rights (forced share and intestate) were recognized to children born in wedlock and those born out of wedlock and adopted children (art. 108). Thus, regarding deaths occurred after the entry into force of the Spanish Constitution, although the testator's will may have been executed earlier, the *natural children and adopted children* came to enjoy the same inheritance rights that up until then only children born in wedlock enjoyed. However, under the 8th transitional provision of the Law 11/1981 (according to the Supreme Court's until now uniform interpretation), if the father of a child born out of wedlock (or 'illegitimate' child, in pre-constitutional terminology) died before the entry into force of the Constitution, for reasons of legal certainty, his estate is governed by the laws in force at the time of death, so the 'illegitimate child' would have no legal rights *mortis causa*.[24] The child is entitled to the recognition of the real filiation throughout his or her life, but this will not affect the father's succession. However, a recent and controversial Constitutional Court ruling of 27 May 2010,[25] following to some extent the doctrine contained in the judgment of the European Court of Human Rights of 13 July 2004 (Case *Pla and Puncernau v Andorra*),[26] understood that the term 'legitimate children' in a will executed in 1927, by a testator who died in 1945, but one of the provisions of which was applied in 1997[27], must be interpreted

---

[24] SSTS 17 March 1995, 28 July 1995, 15 October 1997, 17 March 2005 and 31 July 2007.

[25] BOE No. 129, of 27 May 2010, p. 28 ff.

[26] For critical comments, Arroyo Amayuelas – Bondía García (2004) 7 ff.; Marsal Guillamet (2005) 477; Vaquer Aloy (2009) 574. On the topic of the *Drittwirkung* and Succession Law, which underlies on this judgment, see De Vos (2008) 801.

[27] In particular, the testator had ordered that all his estate should be transmitted to the eldest of his five sons; and if that son died without heirs, the estate would pass to the following child in order of age or in the absence of any of these, to their 'legitimate children' instead of their predeceased parents. The firstly appointed heir in this *fideicommissum* (fiduciary substitution) died single and childless in 1997; the second son in line had died in 1940 without children, and the third died in 1995 with two adopted daughters of full age, who claimed the inheritance. Registration of ownership on the inherited properties was denied by the Land Registry on the grounds that the heiresses were not 'legitimate daughters' according to the parameters of the will. These two adopted daughters lost the lawsuit in all the

in accordance with the constitutional principle of equality and non discrimination based on filiation. The judgment recognizes the rights of two adopted
daughters, who, according to the wording of the will, would not have been
able to inherit. Thus, the Constitutional Court arguably introduced a different
approach to that handled so far by the Supreme Court, in establishing that the
testamentary provisions should not only be interpreted in accordance with the
existing legislative framework in force at the time of the testator's death, but that
when they are sufficiently ambiguous to uphold two interpretations, it should be
understood that 'it is not the testator's will to make distinctions that counter the
grounds of the legal system in force at the time the condition is fulfilled and the
relevant testamentary provisions should be implemented'.

Despite all this, the Spanish Civil Code has also known reforms to protect
certain groups that have reinforced the testamentary freedom. Without changing the legal share limiting the freedom of disposal, in 2003 the legislator (Law
41/2003) allowed the testator to dispose of his or her entire estate in favour of
a *legally incapacitated descendant* (appointing him or her as fiduciary heir for
life), even if the testator had other children, who would receive nothing until
the death of the incapacitated descendant (arts. 782, 808 and 813 CC). The same
year, for the benefit of business people and to facilitate the undivided transmission of family businesses and other economic exploitations and capital companies, Law 7/2003 amended art. 1056 CC, with two very important developments
affecting other principles contained in the Spanish Civil Code: it allows payment
of the forced share with money, even in the absence of such money in the estate
and, above all – through a unique rule in the Civil Code, waiving the principle of
qualitative inviolability of the forced share of art. 813 CC – it allows the testator
to postpone payment of the forced share credit for five years from the testator's
death. These two reforms benefit disabled individuals and business people,
extending the margin of testamentary freedom for these purposes. There is not
an equivalent provision in the autonomous civil laws to date.

3   Material Freedom of Testation

3.1   The Current Debate Regarding the Suppression or
Modification of the Forced Share ('Legítima')

In recent years, and particularly in the last five or six, an
interesting debate has re-emerged in Spain among notaries, academics and
practitioners on the appropriateness of suppressing forced shares or making the
regime governing them more flexible. A similar dispute took place in the 19th

---

procedural stages, pursuant to case law of the Supreme Court. Even the judgment of the High Court of
Justice of Catalonia of 22 January 2004, which ended the case, upheld the decision of the lower courts.
This judgement was later revoked by the Constitutional Court.

Century before the Spanish Civil Code was approved. The arguments then were the same as they are now but the underlying factors fuelling controversy were different, since in the 19th Century a single Civil Code for the whole of Spain was at stake and there was a struggle to reflect the irreconcilable traditions of Spanish Law and the different 'foral' regions in this Code regarding the issue of testamentary freedom. Today, few voices dare to propose a harmonised system of forced shares throughout Spain, which would delete the differences among regional systems and that are grounded on historical reasons.[28] The reopening of the debate is focused more on the system of *legítimas* provided in the Spanish Civil Code and is closely related to social, family and economic changes. We will now examine in detail the arguments in favour and against greater testamentary freedom in order to be able to sketch a summary of the main proposals for reform.[29]

3.1.1 Arguments in Favour of Forced Shares ('Legítimas')

a) *Legal arguments*: (i) existence of a sort of family co-owner-ship of property; (ii) the *mejora* (one third of the inheritance) already allows for a more flexible system of forced shares, albeit only in favour of descendants; (iii) it is a matter of public order that cannot be suppressed (as affirmed by the Supreme Court in STS 23 October 1992, but overruled by STS 15 November 1999, see *infra* 5); (iv) it is an equivalent or surrogate of the maintenance rights of certain relatives; (v) fixed shares protect the freedom of forced heirs avoiding undue influence or threats of free disinheritance by the testator; (vi) in foreign systems with freedom of testation (such as England or USA) some voices claim for the introduction of schemes similar to forced shares so as to provide more legal certainty, since the courts tend to grant rights to a wide number of persons, even beyond the circle of near relatives, via the so called 'family provisions', so that judges exercise a sort of moral control.[30]

b) *Ethical-family arguments:* (i) the equality of all the children before the law makes equal treatment obligatory in the law of succession; (ii) children are the clear successors of the physical and spiritual personality of their parents, hence they should also be the successors of their wealth; (iii) a moral duty exists towards descendants, ascendants and spouses both during life and after death in accordance with the minimum established by law; (iv) forced shares derive from Natural Law, on the same grounds as the duty of support and maintenance;

---

[28] Such a proposal in Bercovitz Rodríguez-Cano (2010) 1121.

[29] For further information on the reasons and references to (old and recent) authors, see mainly Arroyo Amayuelas (2007) 257; Barrio Gallardo (2008) 15; Bermejo Pumar (2005) 21; Calatayud Sierra (1995) 241; Carrancho Herrero (2006) 733; Carrasco Perera (2003) 11; Cobas Cobiella (2006) 49; De la Esperanza Rodríguez (2002) 1097; Delgado Echeverría (2006) 122; Magariños Blanco (2005) 3; Moreu Ballonga (1997) 98 ff. and (2006) 164; Parra Lucán (2009) 481; Torres García (2006) 214; Rivas Martínez (2009) 1406; Valladares Rascón (2004) 4893; Vaquer Aloy (2007) 3.

[30] Further on this comparative argument, Parra Lucán (2009) 487.

(v) the suppression of forced shares would infringe family unity and increase litigation, particularly if strangers would benefit at the expense of more direct relatives; (vi) the current status promotes family values in a context of liberalism and individualism and in the case of the ascendants' share represents a 'weak compensation to the sacrifices already made' for children. To sum up, the bases of forced share are not to be found in guaranteeing maintenance for relatives, but in the ethical right to participate in the wealth of the deceased.

c) *Economic arguments:* (i) forced shares favour property transfers and avoid the permanent entailment of assets; (ii) reciprocal family support in the acquisition of property requires family members to participate in its distribution after the death of the title holder.

d) *Other arguments:* the long historical tradition gives rise to a strong inertia that is difficult to depart from immediately and in the plea for suppressing the forced shares the testator's voice is the most clearly heard (mainly via the Notaries that receive people's last wishes and wills), but neither the voice of the beneficiaries of the *legítima* nor that of the society as a whole are taken into account.

3.1.2 Arguments in Favour of Testamentary Freedom

a) *Legal arguments:* (i) the family as such does not own an estate and, hence, at least a distinction would have to be made between assets received from the family itself through a lucrative title and assets acquired by the testator's own efforts; (ii) it is incoherent to allow owners total freedom in life with respect to their transfers and contracts and restrict them with respect to their *mortis causa* transfers; (iii) although the duty to support and maintain and the forced share are based on the common principle of the duty to protect the family, the former is based on the real need of the beneficiary, whereas the latter is an arbitrary fixed share, which does not take into account the real economic needs of the forced heirs; (iv) the example of some autonomous community systems that allow maximum testamentary freedom and the trend shown by comparative law in this area are worth imitating; (v) there are various examples in daily practice that prove that the legal system governing forced shares fails to cater for the needs and desires of most testators: thus, the frequent usage of wills to try to modify the distribution of the Spanish Civil Code, the regular use of the 'Socini clause', the huge number of lawsuits concerning the disinheritance of relatives outside the scope of legally accepted grounds or the changes in 'legal residence' to take advantage of a system allowing greater testamentary freedom (see *infra* 5); (vi) various legislative changes have shown that the primary functions of forced shares have disappeared: equal treatment of all children born in and outside marriage, and the rights of non-relatives such as the spouse, today question the historical roots whereby the forced share system tries to maintain property within the lineage or original family; and forced shares are no longer used to ensure that all children receive the so-called production assets because the share can be paid with money, and the exceptions continue (Law 41/2003); (vii) the regime protecting forced shares has become so technically complex that it exceeds practical needs; (viii) the suppression of forced shares would not violate the Spanish Constitution (see *infra* 5).

b) *Ethical-family arguments:* (i) only testamentary freedom can do justice to relatives who depend on the testator, because not all of them have the same needs or merits; the mechanical, egalitarian and abstract application of the law does not allow testators to fairly privilege minors, disabled people, poorer relatives, etc.; the same goes for the faculty to favour just the children who take care of old and ill parents; (ii) greater freedom will strengthen the authority of parents at the helm of family life; (iii) the forced share system is an obstacle to the satisfaction of socially legitimate interests, such as the spouses' capacity to guarantee the well-being of their partners.

c) *Economic arguments:* (i) the absence of forced shares would make it easier to maintain family estate and its productivity intact; (ii) it also makes it easier for testators to be sure they choose the best successor for this purpose and it also favours succession within the company; it should be noted that 80% of Spanish companies are family companies, which produce 60% of GDP (gross domestic product) and generate 80% of private employment in Spain, so there is a social interest in ensuring their continuity, for which it is said that the rigidity of the forced shares regime can be a hindrance.[31]

d) *Sociological arguments*: today different changes, such as greater life expectancy or the very absence of the transfer of economic and social power through inheritance,[32] are altering the need for, and the efficiency of, the forced shares system; changes in the structures of families and estates corroborate this hypothesis.

3.2   Proposed Solutions

In Spain, during the last decade, a tendency in favour of reforming the forced share system and expand testamentary freedom can be detected in most legal writings, particularly in those produced by notaries and scholars, who have criticized the current system. Notwithstanding, the solutions proposed are not uniform. Five possibilities can be found:

---

[31]   On this point, Parra Lucán (2009) 484, 505 ff. and, especially, 541-542, who invokes interesting counter-arguments that reduce the value of the objection. For example, the different effect of the forced share depending on the volume of the company, or the possibilities of payment of the forced share in money, which along with good succession organization and where appropriate, legislative flexibility, may make unnecessary the removal of forced shares to transfer the company.

[32]   According to statistics (see Vaquer Aloy (2007) 8-11) in 2003, life expectancy was around 80 years (whereas at the time of the Spanish Civil Code, at the end of the 19th century, it was 35), the average age of descendants at the time of death of their ascendants is between 40 and 55 years old, which coincides with the average age when people are wealthier. Inheritances (and forced shares) arise when then the beneficiaries' economic position is at its best.

a) *Elimination of the forced share and recognition of full testamentary freedom.*
To date, no-one backs this extreme solution. There is, however, a broad consensus on the need to eliminate the forced share for parents and ascendants[33] (which does not necessarily entail their elimination from intestacy, in line with the existing rule in Aragon, Navarre, in Galicia since 2006, and also in France).

b) *Elimination of the forced share and creation of a new maintenance right against the estate or the heirs.* It should be noted that, today, the legal obligation to provide maintenance (art. 142 CC) disappears when the debtor dies (art. 150 CC). The creation of this new *mortis causa* alimony to replace the forced share would be based on the need to protect those depending on the deceased only when in real need.[34] To a certain extent, something similar already exists in the Basque Country (arts. 66 and 158) regarding children who are excluded from the succession to the farmhouse and in Aragon (art. 200) in favour of the forced heirs excluded from inheritance due to the testator not having included them among the beneficiaries of the collective forced share. Likewise, the maximum quarter of the estate that the surviving spouse can claim in Catalonia is granted for care purposes (i.e. only if it is needed) (art. 452-1). A recent proposal to regulate succession in Valencia also follows this system concerning the surviving spouse.[35] Several Latin American countries with systems that guarantee testamentary freedom grant *mortis causa* maintenance rights to certain relatives and to the spouse.[36] Contrary to the implementation of this system in the Spanish Civil Code, it has been argued that an excessive confrontation with the traditional system of fixed shares would entail high transaction costs (litigation, reports and consultations), and could produce unjust situations if the situation of necessity is only considered at the time of the testator's death, whilst taking other moments into account could prove to be problematic.[37] Another criticism

---

[33] Most of the works cited in previous notes support this solution. It was also one of the conclusions of the XII Seminar of the Association of Professors of Civil Law held in Santander in 2006, dedicated to the reform of the law of succession: see Delgado Echeverría (2006) 170: Conclusion 12: 'Deleting the ascendants' forced share may be suggested, except welfare or alimony provisions, as well as the reduction of the descendants' forced share and the generalization of its payment in money, even if non-hereditary.' Against it, Moreu Ballonga (1997) 98 ff. and (2006) 164. Miquel Gonzalez (2009) 499 defends this elimination only when ascendants concur with the widowed spouse.

[34] In favour, Notaries De la Esperanza Rodríguez (2002) 1116, Gomá Lanzón (2005) 934-935 and Magariños Blanco (2005) 27-29; also professors Delgado Echeverría (2006) 119-131 and Valladares Rascón (2004) 4902. Against this 'quasi-maintenance', Parra Lucán (2009) 503-505; Torres García (2006), 224; Vaquer Aloy (2007) 220-224 and 227.

[35] In the blueprint or draft of Valencian Law on *mortis causa* succession (2009), not yet public, usufruct up to one half of the estate if needed (art. 8): see Montés Penadés (2009) 14.

[36] Thus, according to Barrio Gallardo (2008) 22 ff. (who also offers an overview of the special maintenance system in Aragon), in Mexico, Costa Rica, Honduras or Panama. See also Cobas Cobiella (2007) 61 ff. (quoting the Cuban CC) and Azcárraga Monzonís (2007) 56 (who quotes art. 1198 ff. of the Civil Code of Nicaragua).

[37] On those arguments, mainly, Vaquer Aloy (2007) 14.

against those who defend maintenance rights for ancestors is that they are not fully consistent with strengthening the position of the spouse or cohabitant, regardless of his or her needs.[38]

c) *Reduction of the legal share of the descendants*, while maintaining the structure and functions of forced shares. This occurred in Aragon in 1999, where descendants went from being entitled to two thirds of the estate, to only half; or in Galicia in 2006, from two thirds to a quarter (*supra*). In this vein, some authors suggest reducing the descendants' forced share to a third or a quarter of the estate.[39]

d) *Extension of the rights of the surviving spouse (and, where appropriate, of the cohabitant)*. A general consensus exists that the minimum rights in usufruct acknowledged today are advocates for extending their legal rights (as done in the Basque Country in 1992), either by increasing their share in usufruct or by granting them a share in property or equivalent to the value of this property.[40] The second line of thought proposes a reduction of the legal share of children to allow testators to freely dispose of a larger part of the estate in favour of the spouse (as was done in Aragon in 1999 or in Galicia in 2006). The doctrinal proposals have been very varied, because there are authors who defend, from a more generous conception of testamentary freedom, either the reduction of the amount of the spouse's forced share, or making its implementation more flexible according to the circumstances of each family (reducing rights only to certain assets, allowing cash payments at the request of the widower in any case, etc.) or even granting those mandatory legal rights only for marriages that have lasted a certain number of years (e.g. from 3 or 5 years' duration and cohabitation).[41] Practical unanimity is reached concerning the improvement of the position of the surviving spouse in intestate succession,[42] due to the disparity between its grounds (subsidiary application and design according to the more sociologically extended order of affection) and those of forced share rights.

e) *Maintenance of the forced share system as it is, but reforming its technical deficiencies and relaxing some aspects*. This option, continuist yet reforming, has many supporters, although the specific aspects to change in order to achieve the aforementioned flexibility are not always explained. At other times, a list of proposals is offered combined with a reduction in the amount of the forced shares.[43] To explain this last option – which may be the most reasonable even taken as a cautious first step before perhaps considering formulas that result in a greater testamentary freedom in a more distant future – the pre-existing relaxing reforms made in the Spanish Civil Code should first be noted, before

---

[38] Parra Lucán (2009) 505.

[39] For instance, Miquel González (2009) 499 (1/3 or 1/4, elimination the betterment or *mejora*) or Vaquer Aloy (2007) 15 (a half or less if there is also a surviving spouse).

[40] Thus, for instance, Carrancho Herrero (2006) 747-750.

[41] See those three last proposals by Fernández Campos (2009) 289-293.

[42] See especially Corral García (2007); Pérez Escolar (2003) and (2007) 1641 ff.

[43] E.g. Miquel González (2009) 499-500.

suggesting other possible reforms for which the legal comparison with the
models offered by the legislation of some autonomous communities and other
countries is valuable.

3.3 Channels for Relaxation without Eliminating the Forced Share

3.3.1 Reforms Already Implemented in the Spanish Civil Code

Four noteworthy changes have been introduced in the Span-
ish Civil Code:[44] a) Law 11/1981, of 13 May, authorised the payment of the forced
share in money and not in hereditary assets in case all or part of the estate is left
to any of the deceased's children or descendants; the beneficiary of the estate
should pay the other children or descendants' forced share in cash. This is one
of the exceptions in the Spanish Civil Code to the rule providing that payment
of the forced share should be made in kind, *in natura* (see mainly arts. 821, 929,
831, 829 and 1056.2 CC); b) Law 7/2003, of 1 April, reformed art. 1056.2 CC,
which now provides that testators who, in order to preserve the company or in
the interests of their families, wish to preserve an economic activity undivided
or maintain control over a corporation or group of companies, may decide to
pay the forced share corresponding to the other interested parties in cash, even
if there is none in the estate. This cash may originate from sources other than
the estate itself; moreover, payment of the forced share may be deferred – for
up to five years following the testator's death. This derogates from the general
rule that no encumbrances or conditions can be imposed on forced shares nor
can their payment be postponed (article 813.2 CC). If the form of payment
was not established in the will, the forced heir may demand his or her forced
share in assets from the estate; c) Law 41/2003, of 18 November, reformed art.
831 CC,[45] which now allows the testator to confer to his or her spouse or to the
other parent of their common children (not necessarily a partner in a registered
couple) broad powers to improve and distribute the estate of the predeceased
among the common children or descendants. This kind of *fiducia sucesoria*
or *mortis causa* trust follows the pattern of the provisions already established
in various autonomous community laws. The same Law 41/2003 introduced
reforms to improve the position of disabled people, in the areas of unworthiness to inherit, forced share and collation; for instance, it is now possible to
encumber the entire forced share of the other forced heirs with a fideicommissum ('sustitución fideicomisaria') to favour children or descendants incapacitated by a court (arts. 782 and 808); art. 822 also establishes a new *mortis causa*
right to inhabit the habitual residence in favour of disabled forced heirs. d) Law
15/2005, of 9 July on separation and divorce, clarified the contradictory rules

---

44 More details in Cámara Lapuente (2007) 7 ff.

45 See García Rubio (2008) 57; Rivas Martínez (2007) 1629 and (2009); Rodríguez Yniesto (2005) 169;
Rueda Esteban (2005) 155.

existing in the Spanish Civil Code on the succession rights of spouses when a marriage breakdown procedure is taking place at the time of death, both with respect to forced shares and intestate inheritance rights; according to the new rules contained in arts. 834 and 945 CC, spouses only hold such rights if they are not separated legally or *de facto* when their spouse dies. The express mention of separation – even if not certified by a court – means an enlargement of the freedom of disposal of the deceased when compared with some unclarified situations existing before this legislative change.

3.3.2 Other Reforms that Might be Suitable in View of Comparative Law (Both Interregional and International)

The following aspects, either most of them jointly or only some of those reforms combined, could be helpful to achieve greater testamentary freedom without dismantling the traditional system of fixed legal shares (thinking of the descendants in particular). It is worth reflecting on these changes in the context of the Spanish Civil Code in the light of the experiences of other jurisdictions:

a) *Transformation of the Spanish Civil Code's forced share into a 'collective' forced share*, in line with the model provided in Aragon and some areas of the Basque Country, so that the testator, where there are multiple forced heirs, may choose to leave that share to only some or one of them at his or her choice. In some ways, it could be understood that this change expands the existing mechanism of 'betterment' to all forced shares.

b) *Establishment of a variable amount depending on the number of forced heirs* in order to reduce the restraints on free disposal when the testator only has one or two children. Though the following shares do not necessarily have to be maintained, it is the system of the Balearic Islands (arts. 42, 65 and 79: a third if there are four children or fewer, half if there are more); it is also proposed in the succession Bill for Valencia[46] and was introduced in Louisiana in 1995 (a quarter if there is one child, half if there are more than two);[47] it is also the system of the French and Belgian Civil Codes (art. 913).

c) *Limitation of the age or establishment of conditions for the descendants to be entitled to a forced share*. In this regard, in 1990 Louisiana passed a law to limit within the Civil Code (art. 1493) the descendants' right to a forced share to 'descendants of the first degree who, at the time of death of the decedent, are twenty-three years of age or younger or descendants of the first degree of any age who, because of mental incapacity or physical infirmity, are permanently incapable of taking care of their persons or administering their estates at the

---

[46] Art. 6 of the Draft of Bill enshrines a share of one third for one or two children and half of the estate if there are more than two children.

[47] This article formulates the rule with this wording: "Gratuitous transfers, either by *inter vivos* acts or by wills, may not exceed half of the property of a disposing person, where he leaves only one child at his death; one-third, where he leaves two children; one-fourth, where he leaves three or a greater number".

time of the death of the decedent'; after a 1993 ruling of the Supreme Court of
Louisiana considering the rule to be unconstitutional, the Constitution of this
State was reformed in 1995 (art. 12.5) to approve the rule currently in force.[48] In
Spain, similar proposals have been made suggesting that the maximum age of
the forced heirs be reduced to 25 or 26 years of age.[49]

d) *Acceptance of the anticipated waivers of the forced share while the testator is
alive*, with or without *inter vivos* compensation, which would have to be agreed
with the testator. These waivers, forbidden by art. 816 CC, are allowed by most
autonomous laws. Another formula, somewhat more restricted in scope but also
worthy of consideration, would be to admit an inheritance agreement whereby
the forced heirs waive in advance any actions to reduce donations, as currently
provided for in art. 929 of the French Civil Code after its reform in 2006.

e) *Express recognition of the possibility to encumber the descendants' forced
share* (or the ascendants', where sustained) *in favour of the spouse*, in one of the
following two ways: either by legally admitting the '*Socini clause*' (*supra* 2.3.1)
where the value of the burden exceeds the forced share and, therefore, the forced
heir has an option to compensation, – as has happened in Aragon, Mallorca,
Menorca and Catalonia –, or allowing, by law, the universal voluntary usufruct,
where there is no compensation or option for the forced heir if the testator has
expressly stipulated so – as established in Galicia and, in the Basque Country,
in the *Fueros* of Vizcaya and Ayala, ibidem –. For its part, the Belgian Civil Code
(art. 745 octies), according to the amendment made by the law of 28 March
2007, provides that the testator may order that all his or her estate belongs to the
spouse when there are no descendants, only ascendants.[50]

f) *Granting the forced share the status of a personal right* against the heir (*pars
valoris*), also payable with money that is not part of the estate, generalizing some
exceptional solutions that now exist in the Spanish Civil Code. This configuration for forced shares exists in Catalonia, and Galicia also adopted it in 2006.
This trend is also found in comparative law, as such a personal or credit-related
aspect is typical of German law, French law (after the 2006 reform) and in the
Netherlands.

g) *Allowing payment deferral* not only to keep family businesses undivided
(as permitted by art. 1056 CC as of the 2003 reform), but for other purposes,
such as *keeping the family home* when the assets received by the heir (e.g. spouse
or partner or a son) – who must pay the forced share in money – are the family
home, as is expressly provided for in the reform of the German Civil Code that
entered into force in 2010, expanding the former provisions of § 2331a BGB.[51]

---

[48] See Azcárraga Monzonís (2009) 56; Parra Lucán (2009) 503.

[49] Respectively, Vaquer Aloy (2007) 17 and Magariños Blanco (2005) 28.

[50] The Belgian Civil Code compensates this detriment in the rights of ascendants with alimony when
needed at the time of the death of the descendant.

[51] At present such a postponement may be requested by any heir and not only by forced heirs and also in
cases of 'unfair burden' provided the interests of the forced heir are reasonably accounted for. In this
respect, *vid*. Arroyo Amayuelas (2010) 9-10.

h) *Extension or relaxation of the grounds for disinheritance* to adapt to new family realities. However, the reforms so far undertaken in jurisdictions that have updated their disinheritance causes except in Catalonia (on the Balearic Islands and Germany after the reform implemented in 2010 *vid. supra* 3.3.2), have not gone so far as to include the deprivation of the forced share based on the mere fact that family relations have deteriorated or broken, which is one of the main factors in litigation. For example, the German Constitutional Court does not admit this fact as a ground for disinheritance;[52] neither does the Spanish case law, at least if it has not materialized in refusing to comply with maintenance obligations for no legitimate reason (art. 853.1 CC).

i) *Reform of some rules on the calculation, allocation and reduction of bequests, as well as collation (clawback clause).* Upon analysis of comparative law, three rules may be useful in the context of the Spanish Civil Code: 1) *Restriction of the donations that are to be added to the estate to calculate the forced share.* At least two methods have been tried in some legal systems: firstly in Italy since 2005 and in Catalonia since 2008 (art. 451-5 b) only donations made by the deceased in the ten years prior to death count; on the other hand, in Germany since 2010 (§ 2325.3 BGB) contrary to the system previously in force, still only donations made in the last ten years are counted, but the count is progressively reduced at a rate of 10% of the value of the gift for each year that has elapsed since it was made. Thus, only donations made the year before the death count 100%; if the donation was made two years before that time, it counts 90% and so on up to 10 years, since donations beyond this period are not taken into consideration; 2) *Establishment that the reduction of donations or bequests due to them exceeding the available amount may be performed by giving money* rather than necessarily returning property. This rule would be in line with the changing nature of the forced share, since the action for reduction, currently with a rescinding nature under the Spanish Civil Code, would no longer be a real action for a *pars hereditatis,* but the action resulting from a personal right. A transformation of the donation reduction action in this regard occurred in Galicia in 2006 (art. 251) and in the same year, in French law (art. 924 and CC 924-1). 3) *Relaxation of the collation rules,*[53] at least reversing the rule of art. 1036 CC, so that the donations made to the forced heirs are only taken into account as an advanced payment of the forced share if expressly provided by the testator. In the reform of the Spanish Civil Code by Law 41/2003, a similar reversal of the rule has been effected in art. 1041, but only in relation to the costs of the special needs of disabled descendants, so that the proposed rule[54] would only generalize the exception for the sake of a greater testamentary freedom.

---

[52] Arroyo Amayuelas (2010) 11. Art. 451-17 e of the Law of Catalonia does allow the "evident and continuous lack of relationship" as a ground for disinheritance insofar as attributable to the forced heir. On it, see in this volume Vaquer Aloy.

[53] For instance, in the Draft of a Bill on Succession Law for Valencia (2009) collation is eliminated: see Montés Penadés (2009) 14.

[54] Also Miquel González (2009) 500.

j) *Reduction in the time limit for exercising the claim of the forced share or its complement* in the event of an insufficient allocation by the testator. Thus, the legal uncertainty produced by the Spanish Civil Code by not expressly setting a statute of limitations (whereby it is argued if it is 15 or 30 years)[55] would disappear. In this sense, Catalonia (art. 451-27) in Law 10/2008 has reduced this limit from 15 to 10 years, and Galicia in 2006 (art. 252) fixed it *ex novo* at 15 years.

3.4   Other Possible Enlargements of Material Freedom of Testation

Although forced shares are the main constraint to material testamentary freedom, it is possible to trace other manifestations of the latter that perhaps merit further consideration based on their absence in the Spanish Civil Code, but for now we should note, for example, that material freedom of testation would increase if the legislator were to *(i)* clarify that the partition made by the testator cannot be altered by the heirs (or the opposite, if testator's autonomy at this point is restricted, as recently done by art. 464-1 Catalan Law 10/2008), as there is contradictory case law and varying opinions about art. 1056.1 CC (*vid.* STS 4 February 1994); *(ii)* regulate *post mortem* mandates and powers (as in Navarre, art. 151.2); *(iii)* permit and lay down rules on the testamentary exclusion of the intestate heirs (*Enterbung*, as has happened recently in Aragon and Catalonia, and partially in Galicia);[56] *(iv)* redesign and, where appropriate, reduce the scope of special hereditary reserves (arts. 811 and 968-980);[57] (v) reinforce the use of various fiduciary figures allowed in some regional laws as a sort of *mortis causa* trust (see *infra* 4.3).

4   Formal Freedom of Testation

4.1   Testamentary Forms

Another manifestation of the degree of testamentary freedom granted by the law is the number of formal instruments or mechanisms through which the last wishes of the deceased can be properly translated. Sev-

---

[55] Similarly, there are different opinions, arguments and judgments on the statute of limitations that applies to the action to reduce bequests – the legislative determination of which would also be appropriate– ranging from 15 years (art. 1964 CC), to 5 years (art. 646 CC, STS 4 March 1999), or 4 years (art. 1299 CC).

[56] In 1999 Aragon (arts. 198-199), in 2006 Galicia (art. 226) and in 2008 Catalonia (art. 423-10). See Cámara Lapuente (2000) *passim*.

[57] In this regard, the Supreme Court interprets that, given the exceptional nature of the so-called 'linear reserves,' the judicial interpretation should be as favourable as possible to the testamentary freedom of the deceased (the person whose freedom of disposal is limited by the reserve), thus restricting as much as possible the scope of art. 811 CC: among others, STS 13 March 2008.

eral data suggest that Spain is one of the countries of the world where wills are used most to organize succession (about 50% of inheritances).[58] Of all testamentary forms, the one most overwhelmingly used is the open will executed before a Notary. Although the autonomous laws also contain some special rules on the formalities of individual wills (e.g. Catalonia does not support any form of parol testament made only before witnesses, art. 421-5.3; or the number or need of witnesses in notarized wills varies),[59] the bulk of regulation on this matter rests with the Spanish Civil Code.

4.2 Inheritance Agreements, Joint Wills and Other *Mortis Causa* Instruments

On the other hand, it is worth noting that there are several succession instruments prohibited by the Spanish Civil Code, which are however allowed and regulated in some of the civil laws of the autonomous communities. These include *inheritance agreements* and joint wills. The former are allowed in the form of positive agreements for the appointment of heirs in the six autonomous communities with competence in the field, in some cases limited to the family environment (e.g. Catalonia), in others without such limits (e.g. Aragon); the autonomous laws also foresee anticipated succession waiver agreements, including the forced share waiver, although the structure is also somewhat uneven, as some systems are based on a prohibition with exceptions (e.g. Catalonia, art. 451-26, Galicia, art. 242), while others barely set restrictions (e.g. Balearic Islands, arts. 50-51, 77). In the Spanish Civil Code, the inheritance agreements, both for the appointment of heirs and for waivers, are prohibited (art. 658, 1271.2, 816), although there are a few exceptions[60] and case law that understands that positive agreements are valid in some cases, but only when they deal with assets that are known and existing when the contract is executed; this is accepted by interpreting the prohibition on agreements about 'future inheritance' on a restrictive basis, as referring only to agreements on the entire estate.[61] Today a debate has started in the Spanish doctrine on the possibility and convenience of allowing inheritance agreements in the Spanish Civil Code following the model of some autonomous laws.[62] Contrary to the arguments used against them in the nineteenth century during the codification procedure (fear of pressure or undue influence on the testator's will, avoiding the desire

---

[58] See Delgado Echeverría (2006) 103; Zoppini (2002) 125. In 2008 in Spain 570,044 testaments were authorized by a public notary, whereas only 91,901 decrees pronouncing the beneficiaries in intestacy in the Probate Registry were recorded in the same year: see *Anuario DGRN* (2010) 508.

[59] For a comprehensive survey on the topic of testamentary forms and formalities in the different Succession Laws in Spain, see Cámara Lapuente (2011).

[60] See Espejo Lerdo de Tejada (1999) and Sánchez Aristi (2003).

[61] SSTS of 4 May 1902, 8 October 1915, 8 October 1916, 26 October 1926, 16 May 1940, 12 June 1956, 24 January 1957, 3 March 1964, 22 June 1997.

[62] In favour, with arguments, for instance Sánchez Aristi (2006) 477 and Herrero Oviedo (2009) 199.

to advance the testator's death, breach of public order), it is noted that several agreements of this type have already been temporarily admitted in the Spanish Civil Code (regarding the succession of adopted children under a 1958 Act or the succession in agricultural businesses between 1981 and 1995) and may be a suitable vehicle for the transmission of family businesses.

The *joint will* is also forbidden by the Spanish Civil Code (arts. 669 and 773) and, instead, is allowed in Galicia (arts. 186-195), Aragon (arts. 91.3, 94-95 and 102-107), the Basque Country (arts. 49-52 and 172) and Navarre (arts. 199-205); in these legal systems the future legislative trends go from allowing it only between spouses (even today in the Basque Country and Galicia from 1995) to allowing anyone to make a joint will (Navarre and, since 1999, Aragon). The joint holographic will is not allowed in the Basque Country or Navarre. Also in recent years there has been a doctrinal movement in favour of its regulation in the Spanish Civil Code,[63] even stronger than in relation to inheritance agreements; this is based on several reasons: the successful experience in the four regions where it has been used and is regulated; a confirmed everyday practice in the context of spouses under the Spanish Civil Code who go to the notary together to draw up two wills with an identical (and reciprocal) content and in favour of the children;[64] the disappearance of the 19th century arguments against it (influence over the testator's will, fraud based on unilateral repeal, a reduced testamentary freedom) which also exist in some cases of unilateral wills and in any case can be prevented by using legal guarantees (only revocable while both testators are alive, notifications), etc.

Other instruments that allow a greater flexibility at the time of *mortis causa* disposal, forbidden by the Spanish Civil Code and allowed in some autonomous laws are: *codicils* (allowed in Catalonia, art. 421-21/22 and 422-4; Mallorca and Menorca, art. 17; and Navarre, arts. 194-195) and the will before a parish priest (now recognized only in Navarre, arts. 186, 189 and 191).[65] As for testamentary memorandums (*schedulae testamentariae*) and *mortis causa* donations, they are allowed in the Spanish Civil Code (arts. 672 and 620) but are treated as other figures (holographic wills and *mortis causa* disposals such as legacies), so that in this legal text they have practically lost their uniqueness, although *mortis causa* donations continue to enjoy a widespread use; in contrast, testamentary memorandums or informal notes have their own regulation and genuine characteristics in Catalonia (articles 421-21/22 and 422-4) and Navarre (arts. 196-198), while *mortis causa* donations are comprehensively regulated alongside with inheritance agreements in all autonomous civil laws.

---

[63] Arjona Guajardo-Fajardo (2008) 6; Castiella Rodríguez (2001) 9; García Vicente (2006) 289.

[64] Rebolledo Varela (2009) 40-41.

[65] Also until 1999 in Aragon and until 2008 in Catalonia.

4.3 Delegation of the Power to Make a Will, Appointment of Representatives with the Power to Choose Beneficiaries or to Distribute the Estate, or Appointment of Trustees ('fiducia sucesoria')

The weight of two features originating in the Roman wills, that is, its personalism and its formalism, has led to very different prohibitions, exceptions or admissions regarding the devices included in the category of *mortis causa* trust or "successory fiducia", for the first time designated as a single category in the famous STS 30 October 1944. It is dealt with from very different approaches by the Civil Code and in the context of other Succession Laws in force in Spain.

Contrary to institutions representing the delegation of *mortis causa* disposing powers in another person, to a greater or lesser degree, in addition to the fear of abuse and fraud, the Civil Code of 1889 understood that wills were the sole channel to organize succession. The main grounds for this decision were the rigor of the classical conception of wills, with the two features mentioned, the aversion to the entailment of assets and to perpetual burdens and the legislator's scarce sympathy for interim or pending legal situations and, in particular, testamentary secrecy and uncertain beneficiaries and aims.[66] The testamentary personalism, which was foreseen with different nuances in most European codes, implies that a will is a personal act of the testator which should not depend on the discretion of others.

Today, art. 670 of the Spanish Civil Code provides:

'A will is a strictly personal act: its preparation cannot be left, in whole or in part, to the discretion of a third party or made by a commissioner or representative. Neither can the subsistence of appointment of heirs or legatees be left to the discretion of third parties, or the designation of the portions to which they are heirs when they are appointed nominally.'

There are, however, some exceptions,[67] most notably art. 671 (the testator may entrust to a third party the distribution of quantities left to certain groups, such as relatives, the poor or charitable institutions, and the choice of individuals or establishments to whom they are delivered) and, especially art. 831 (delegation of distribution of the estate on the spouse, partner or the person with whom the deceased had children; on it see *supra* 3.3.1). Apart from the important art. 831 (which, however, limits the subjects in whom disposal can be delegated as well as the beneficiaries), the scope of the prohibition contained in art. 670 CC is vast: it excludes the testament made by a commissioner or proxy (formal personalism) and also to leave the preparation of the will to the discretion of a

---

[66] Fernández del Pozo (1987) 1751.

[67] Arts. 671, 747, 749, 775-776, 831, 875-876 and 1057. *Vid.* Asúa González (1992) 96 ff.

third party so that the latter may fully or partially complete the contents of the disposal (material personalism). The Spanish doctrine offers two interpretations of the provision: a stricter one, understanding that virtually any interventions by a third party in the succession of the testator breaches the principle of personalism: all *mortis causa* content should be determined by the testator and only he or she may draft the will, thus not even the figure of the *nuntius* is possible.[68] A second interpretation believes that the personalism in art. 670 forbids the discretion of others, a third party's intervention in the preparation of the will or its provisions, so *nuntius* mechanisms would not be prohibited due to this cause (but they would be by formalism);[69] and, to try to make sense of the various exceptions of the Spanish Civil Code, a major part of the doctrine even distinguishes between the preparation and the performance of the will, so that an intervention by a third party at the stage of implementing or fulfilling the testator's intention would be admissible, because the testator would have already made the relevant disposing provisions in the form of a will.

To classify the various types of the testamentary *"fiducia"* (close to trust) that are allowed in Spain, especially in certain areas, it is useful to take as a starting point the classification made in the 17th century by Cardinal De Luca based on the degree of confidence, from more to less:[70] a) when the testator entrusts to another full powers to dispose at will; b) where the testator foresees as beneficiary a certain group of people, leaving the concrete specification to the trustee, who is empowered to choose or distribute among the individuals belonging to the group designated by the testator; c) where the testator entrusts to another person the interpretation of his or her full and public will; d) where the testator has completely determined his or her testamentary will but does not wish to publish it and secretly communicates its contents to a trustee for it to be revealed or executed in due course. By reducing these to three categories (a, b, d) and combining them with the factor of the extent of discretion of the trustee defined as the degree of freedom that is left to determine the fate of the estate, it is possible to outline a picture of the law currently in force in Spain:

a) The full delegation of the powers to choose heirs and order the succession of the deceased, with *broad boni viri discretion*. This would encompass both the figure of the *'power of appointment'* (as in English and South African law) and the so called 'will executed by a commissioner', when the trustee himself or herself uses such powers to formally execute a will on behalf of the deceased, breaching both the formal personalism (to test) and the material formalism (deciding on the fate of the inheritance). These institutions are forbidden by art. 670 CC and are only explicitly allowed in the Basque Country.[71]

b) Delegating the power to appoint heirs or distribute the inheritance among

---

[68] Asúa González (1992) 13 ff.

[69] Cámara Lapuente (1996) 1202 ff. *Vid.* STS 30 May 1978.

[70] De Luca (1696) 182-183 and 192. On it, *in extenso*, Cámara Lapuente (1996) 233 ff.

[71] Art. 32-48 Law 2/1992 (cf. art. 164-171).

the persons designated by the testator, with a restricted discretion.[72] With many different names, there are many institutions that allow this *electio certis de incertis* limited to the scope of the family (by the spouse, partner or certain relatives in favour of the deceased's descendants), as established in Catalonia, the Balearic Islands (Ibiza and Formentera), Galicia[73] and in art. 831 itself of the Spanish Civil Code, or even beyond family ties (since both delegate and beneficiaries can be completely unrelated to delegator/testator), as in Navarre, Balearic Islands (Mallorca and Menorca) and, since 1999, in Aragon.[74] In such cases the trustee usually has powers of administration and not only the power to appoint successors, but he or she does not hold the title of heir for his or her own benefit of the property that he or she must dispose of. Based on admitted exceptions in Roman law for the fideicommissa there is, however, in Navarre and Catalonia, the possibility to grant powers of distribution and even selection of fideicommissary heirs in a fideicommissum ('sustitución fideicomisaria').[75]

c) Entrusting an heir or legatee, *without giving him or her free discretion or decision powers*, to take charge of the property as a pure intermediary in order to dispose of it as secretly entrusted to him or her by the testator, through written or verbal instructions that are not included in the will (*herencia de confianza*). In this case there is a secrecy, but no discretion in the hands of the the trustee; discretionary powers are not given to someone else to decide on the inheritance. Instead, the trustee is granted the power to perform the *mortis causa* orders secretly communicated, either through acts of disposal, or by disclosing the identity and appointing the real heirs, as intended by the testator. This figure is similar to the Common Law secret trusts (and half-secret trusts) and is at the moment expressly forbidden in the Spanish Civil Code (art. 785.4, although case law has been more flexible sometimes) and in Aragon (art. 127 Law 1/1999). Along with other factors, the erroneous belief that this mechanism is a type of fideicomissum or that it breaches the personal nature of a will was decisive in the Spanish Civil Code; in fact, it does not infringe either formal or material personalism, but it does infringe strict formalism, because it is based on the will of the deceased, which is expressed in two times, remaining partially secret and not complying, for this part, with the solemn formalities of wills.[76] It is however allowed, according to historical precedent (*supra*) and is thoroughly regulated

---

[72] On those institutions, in history and in current practice, Asúa González (1992); Cámara Lapuente (2001) 321 ff.; Fernández del Pozo (1987); Merino Hernández (1994); Núñez Iglesias (1991); Puig Ferriol (1964) 14 ff.

[73] Art. 424-1 to 424-10 Catalan Law 10/2008, art. 71 Balearic Islands LD 79/1990 and art. 196-202 Galician Law 2/2006.

[74] Art. 281-288 Navarre Law 1/1973, art. 18 Balearic Islands LD 79/1990 and (the most detailed ones so far) art. 124-148 Aragon Law 1/1999.

[75] Art. 235 Navarre Law 1/1973 and art. 426-11 Catalan Law 10/2008. In the *Digest*, D. 31.77.25 (Pap. 8 *resp*), D. 31.67 pr. 1-8 (Pap. 19 *quest*) and D. 34.5.7(8).1 (Gai. 1 *de fideic.*).

[76] STS 2 November 1944.

both in Catalonia and Navarre;[77] in this latter territory it is even admitted that
the trustee heir can be a legal entity that may operate for an unlimited time,
keeping the secret or not, with successive substitutes in this position.

4.4   Notaries' Plea for Further Reforms

As a final consideration it is interesting to bear in mind one of
the conclusions reached in the 9th Congress of Spanish Notaries, held in Barcelona between 12 and 14 May 2005, where this measure was proposed: 'to take on
legislative reforms that, based on the principle of civil liberty, provide mechanisms for legal auto-regulation. For this purpose, *it is considered very useful to
review the rigid aspects of the system of forced shares* and to enable the development of legal formulae to control the creation, organization and transmission of
family companies, such as *joint wills, inheritance agreements and fiduciary institutions*, provided that these comply with our public economic order'.[78]

5   Freedom of Testation and Public Order

5.1   Is the Forced Share a Matter of Public Order?

Traditionally, public order (or public policy) is understood as a
set of principles underlying a system that reflect the core values of a society at a
particular time.[79] Today, a restrictive interpretation of this concept is favoured,
linking it to constitutional principles, so that one can only speak of a rule being
contrary to the Spanish public order if it is inconsistent with the Constitution.[80] From this perspective, rules that are more favourable to the testamentary
freedom comprised in some autonomic laws, as opposed to the more restrictive
system of the Spanish Civil Code, cannot be considered contrary to public order.
Thus, there is no doubt about the constitutionality of provincial or autonomous
forced heir systems, including those in which the testator can freely leave children and descendants without any proprietary right whatsoever, as in Navarre or
in the *Fuero* of Ayala.
The same is true for other institutions resulting in a greater testamentary
freedom than that contained in the Spanish Civil Code, such as joint wills,
inheritance agreements, *mortis causa* trusts or *fiduciae*, etc., allowed in various
autonomous laws. And, hence, the logic leads to believe that it is not possible to

---

77   Arts. 424-11 to 424-15 Catalan Law 10/2008 and arts. 289-295 Navarre Law 1/1973. Analysis in: Cámara
Lapuente (2009) 394 ff. and (2001) 537 ff. respectively.

78   See http://www.onpi.org.ar.

79   De Castro y Bravo (1982) 1293 describes it as the 'principles or guidelines which at all times inform the
legal institutions, whether to attribute primacy to one rule over another, whether underlying the changing sense of each institution within the changing leading ideas of the legal system.'

80   Calatayud Sierra (2009) 94.

use the concept of 'public order' for the non-application of foreign laws recognizing a greater freedom than that established in the Spanish Civil Code (or a different forced share system). Thus STS of 15 November 1996, in the *Lowenthal case* (refuting the erroneous approach contained in the STS of 23 October 1992), expressly noted that 'the forced share is not a protected issue of internal public order' in relation to the succession of a citizen of the United States. Subsequently, courts have not applied the notion of 'public order' to the forced share regime and several judgments of the Provincial Courts have referred to the argument of the diversity of systems in Spain to reach this result,[81] to the extent that recent case law sometimes does not even approach these considerations permitting, when allowed by art. 9.8 CC (nationality of the deceased at the time of death) and other normative referral or *renvoi* criteria, the full implementation of foreign laws establishing a greater freedom than the Spanish Civil Code, an example being the STS of 10 July 2009.[82]

5.2 Does the Spanish Constitution Guarantee the Forced Share?

So far, this has not been carefully studied by the Spanish doctrine, though in the light of the German Federal Court judgment of 19 April 2005 – which considered that the children's forced share is a constitutional requirement that cannot be repealed by the ordinary legislator – and despite the lack of rulings on the subject in Spain, authors have begun to pay attention to this issue. Some authors consider that total testamentary freedom would be fully in line with the Constitution, deriving from the fundamental right to the free development of personality (art. 10), as well as due to the lack of a real social function of forced shares, which are now seen as an obstacle to that function: testamentary freedom would improve the protection of the family and the Constitution only recognises 'the right to private property and to the inheritance' (art. 33).[83] Other scholars deny the possibility to abolish the forced share due to constitutional reasons,[84] mainly quoting art. 39 of the Spanish Constitution

---

[81] Thus, SAP Málaga 13 March 2002 (English testator), SAP Alicante 27 February 2004 (German testator), SAP Tarragona 13 May 2004 (Belgian testator), SAP Granada 19 July 2004 (Irish testator) and SAP Barcelona 28 September 2004 (Swiss testator). On the topic, see Aguilar Benítez de Lugo – Aguilar Grieder (2005) 873; Castellanos Ruiz (2007) 304.

[82] The Supreme Court acknowledged the validity of testamentary provisions of a testator of Spanish origin who acquired the Mexican nationality, without losing the Spanish nationality as this was not recorded. In his will he invoked the Mexican system of testamentary freedom, without applying the forced share regime of the Spanish Civil Code. Likewise, *vid.* STS 13 October 2005 on the implementation of the Italian forced heir system (in intestate succession) by the Spanish court.

[83] In favour of the abolition of the forced share, arguing the constitutionality of that reform: De la Esperanza Rodríguez (2002) 1115; Magariños Blanco (2005) 25; Valladares Rascón (2004) 4901.

[84] López López (1994) 35; Moreu Ballonga (2006) 167; Torres García (2006) 220.

on the protection of the family and the recognition of the right to inheritance
in art. 33, together with the fact that all succession systems in Spain recognise
different kinds of forced share, albeit sometimes with no economic content, in
favour of some relatives or persons close to the deceased. The main argument
is, therefore, that whereas the Constitution orders protection for the family, no
constitutional rule guarantees freedom of testation, but only the right to inherit,
and this limited by the social function of property.

In my opinion it is better grounded to understand that the forced share
is just one possible way to fulfil the constitutional mandate of protecting the
family and, of course, the cited constitutional provisions do not prevent its modification, reduction or even elimination, as long as other means of protection of
the testator's family are foreseen[85] (and, as an hypothesis, a *mortis causa* right to
maintenance, whether or not, as explained above, this system presents perhaps
too many problems). Reforms such as the proposals above (3.3.2), including a
reduction of the descendants' rights to a forced share or the suppression of the
ascendants' forced share, should not be constitutionally hindered. A different
question is their suitability or the need for other protection mechanisms. On the
other hand, in the scenario of a total abolition of forced shares it should be noted
that at least all[86] the forced heir systems in Spain, including those that do not
preserve legal rights of economic content for the descendants (Navarre and the
Fuero de Ayala) defend the formal forced share – in a wide sense – through the
testator's obligation to mention the children in the will or at least, to state that
he or she knew of their existence upon drawing up the will, to ensure that his
or her testamentary will has been formed properly and without defects due to
ignoring the existence of relatives. Perhaps one might think that, whichever the
system of family protection designed to comply with art. 39 of the Constitution
after the testator's death, at least one formal guarantee of this kind should be
present.

5.3   Scope of Spanish Public Order in International Succession

According to art. 12.3 of the Spanish Civil Code 'under no
circumstances shall foreign law be applied when contrary to the public order.'
Consequently, if a conflict of laws rule refers to a foreign norm contrary to
public order, this will not apply, but will be replaced by the corresponding Spanish rule. Traditionally the possible intervention of the Spanish public order has

---

[85] See Miquel González (2009) 498; Parra Lucán (2009) 500; Vaquer Aloy (2007) 14.

[86] Although nominally the law in Aragon, through its latest reform, expressly dispensed with the obligation to comply with the 'formal forced share' (Preamble VI § 6 of Act 1/1999), it continues to regulate
the consequences of the testator's failure to include descendants in the will due to mistake, so the statements in the text can be maintained.

been approached in three types of cases:[87] a) regarding Germanic-inspired legal systems that allow joint wills or inheritance agreements, b) in respect of the Common Law systems that support the testator's absolute freedom to dispose of his or her property, c) with respect to Islamic legal systems that support polygamous marriages and discriminate in inheritance rights on the basis of religion, gender or filiation. According to the findings studied in previous sections and given the current concept of constitutional 'public order' in matters of inheritance, this cannot he used in the first two cases cited, both because of the existing internal legislative diversity in Spain (with systems that support inheritance agreements, joint wills or the testamentary freedom) and because the Constitution does not guarantee forced shares.

In contrast, both the doctrine and the (still limited) case law have considered contrary to Spanish public order – due to the violation of fundamental rights enshrined in the Spanish Constitution – certain rules that are typical of Islamic countries governed by Sharia law, such as the following:[88]

a) The rule whereby women receive half the share taken by men in cases of equal relationship; Spanish courts equal the shares (*ex* art. 14 Constitution), as does the case law of Germany or France.

b) The requirement of a legitimate filiation link with the deceased to have succession rights, as contrary to the constitutional principle of equality of the children regardless of whether they are legitimate (born in wedlock) or illegitimate (born out of wedlock), established in arts. 14, 16 and 39 of the Constitution.

c) The absolute impediment to inherit based on the potential beneficiary not professing the Muslim religion (e.g. art. 332 of the Moroccan *mudawana*, contrary to arts. 14 and 16.1 of the Constitution). In this sense, the SAP Barcelona of 28 October 2008 deems both this rule (c) and the above rule (b) to be contrary to Spanish international public order.[89]

d) More controversial is the application of constitutional public order in relation to the possible inheritance rights of several widowed spouses when the polygamous spouse dies. It is clear that polygamy is contrary to public order in assuming the inequality between men and women and the subjection of women to men (STS 19 June 2008), so that a foreigner can never formalize a polygamous marriage in Spain even though his personal law allows him to. When a polygamous spouse dies Spanish case law tends to attribute social rights to all widows who prove to be such according to their personal law in order to avoid any of them being left in a state of neglect. The doctrine is divided, however, about whether to grant rights in the *mortis causa* succession to all the widows

---

[87] Aguilar Benítez de Lugo – Aguilar Grieder (2005) 856.

[88] For further explanations see Garrote Fernández-Díez (2009) 149 ff. and especially 184 ff.

[89] See commentary by Oró Martínez (2009) 287, who underlines that this is the first and sole judgment in Spain on the application of the exception of public order to the *mudawana* in the field of Succession Law (p. 289).

(as recognized by Sharia law), or just to the first of them: for some authors only the first marriage is valid (art. 32.1 Constitution, art. 42.2 Civil Code and art. 217 Criminal Code), so only the first wife may be entitled to the forced share or intestate succession; otherwise Spain would be granting civil effects to a polygamous marriage.[90] according to another school of thought, which follows the example of the French doctrine (and the ruling of the Court of Cassation of 3 November 1980, the *Bendeddoche case*) it is consistent with the constitutional principles to recognize equal rights to all the widows.[91]

5.4 Public Order and Fraud to the Law of Succession

Art. 12.4 of the Spanish Civil Code provides that 'the use of a conflict of laws rule in order to avoid a Spanish mandatory provision will be deemed *fraus legis*.' In principle, it is understood that this rule also applies to interregional law (i.e. the relationship between the various autonomous civil laws, so as to avoid the fraudulent evasion of an autonomous rule by applying other rules in force in Spain), under art. 16.1 CC. The situation would be as follows: In order to obtain a greater testamentary freedom, the testator would change the connection – the nationality if he or she wishes to make his or her will according to the rules of another country or 'civil neighbourhood/citizenship' (*vecindad civil*) based on one's habitual residence if intending to make one's will in accordance with the rules of a Spanish succession system other than the one applicable until then – to circumvent the applicable mandatory law. This would apply, for instance, to a Catalan testator or to a testator subject to the Spanish Civil Code who changes his or her usual residence (for at least two years, art. 14.5 CC) for the sole purpose of freely making a will without being subject to the forced share of the descendants; this would be the result if the testator acquires the personal statute (neighbourhood/citizenship) of Navarre or of a person subject to the jurisdiction, or *Fuero,* of Ayala.

The mechanism of *fraus legis* has only been used in private international law in connection with the Spanish concept of public order.[92] Therefore, since public order is not concerned with the forced share, some judgments, such as STS 5 April 1994, have been criticized in finding internal or interregional fraud of law declaring void two wills made under the law of Biscay by two spouses normally resident outside the territories subject to that law, but who registered and resided there for two years and later made a will declaring their grandsons as their heirs to the total exclusion of their children. With better reasoning, the Spanish doctrine has taken one of the following two paths to deny the existence of an interregional fraud of law: a) There are authors who deny that *fraus legis*

---

[90] Calatayud Sierra (2009) 95.

[91] Garrote Fernández-Díez (2009) 188, who supports the application by analogy of the rules on putative marriage, as it is promoted by part of the French doctrine.

[92] Fernández Rozas – Sánchez Lorenzo (2007) 132.

303

can be applied to interregional law based on various grounds:[93] the equality of all Spanish Civil laws (Civil Code and regional laws on succession), the freedom to choose a "neighbourhood" (*vecindad civil*) after a period of residence, which is recognized in the Spanish Civil Code so that the application of the different laws that coexist in Spain is not seen as a privilege attached to beign born in a certain place; the intention to be subject to another law could never be fraudulent. b) For other authors, although the wording of the Spanish Civil Code may lead to understand that *fraus legis* may also occur at the interregional level, this will almost never be declared as it is not possible to evidence the intent to defraud, which is one of the necessary requirements (subjective condition), especially in the cases of two years residence in the territory whose law the testator wishes to be governed by, where there are signs of real links with the new territory of residence.[94] A different matter is the allegation of false residency by the testator (SAP Biscay 15 June 2001) or the drawing-up of a will in accordance with a residency that was never taken up for failure to comply with formal requirements (effective residence) as required by the Spanish Civil Code.

Recently, the Supreme Court in its judgment of 14 September 2009[95] has sought to clarify the case law in relation to interregional fraud of law, reaching the following conclusions:

'It may be that the change of residence is a fraud, but this must always be proved and cannot be merely inferred from the simple fact of the acquisition of a citizenship (*vecindad*) other than the one previously held. This is because: 1. The change of regional citizenship must always be formalized by one of the means provided by law in article 14 CC; these are rules which, as noted above, establish mandatory requirements. 2. Clearly, the change of citizenship will involve a change in the legal regime applicable to the relations of the person making the statement [after two years residence] or after 10 years residence have elapsed without making any statement to the contrary. But that does not mean that all changes should be considered fraudulent, but only those pursuing a proven purpose of defrauding the applicable rule. 3. The equality between the Spanish legal systems means the coverage law is equal to the law originally applicable; therefore an argument related to the problem of varying legitimacy of the autonomous rights cannot be used for the consideration of a fraud when using a law allowing citizenship changes to alter the connection factor and allow the application of another law more favourable to the interests of the person who makes the statement'.

---

[93] Calatayud Sierra (2009) 95, 111-112; Delgado Echeverría (2000) 429-430, who also adds the technical argument that although art. 16 CC does not exclude art. 12.4, neither does it exclude art. 12.6.2 and yet there are no doubts about the fact that it is not applicable in interregional law.

[94] Pastor Ridruejo (1966) 40; Zabalo Escudero (1995) 399. Cf. Calvo Caravaca and Carrascosa González (2007) 244.

[95] See commentary by Bercovitz Rodríguez-Cano (2010) 1093.

This type of action (fraudulent or not) should lead to not only a legal debate but a general debate of the whole of society about the limits to testamentary freedom and the most suitable design in tune with the times. Within Spain, the testators' 'foot voting', even facing a change of residence for more testamentary freedom, together with notaries' statements leave no doubt about the wishes of those who are in the process of making a will, yet we are still to hear the opinion of those made beneficiaries by operation of the law, the same people who will one day become testators.

Bibliography

Bibliography Chapter 1 (Walter Pintens)

M. Antokolskaia, "Would the harmonisation of family law in Europe enlarge the gap between the law in the books and the law in action?" (2002) *FamPra.ch* 268 ff.

Àrea de Dret Civil Universitat de Girona (Coord.), *Nous reptes del Dret de familia* (Girona 2005)

E. Arroyo i Amayuelas – D. Bondia García, "¿Interpretación de testamento contraria a los derechos humanos? El caso Pla & Puncernau vs Andorra" (2004/18) *DPyC* 7 ff.

E. Arroyo i Amayuelas, "Pflichtteilsrecht in Spanien", in: A. Röthel (Ed.), *Reformfragen des Pflichtteilsrechts* (Cologne *et al.* 2007) 257 ff.

P. Badura, "Testierfreiheit und Schutz der Familie", in A. Röthel (Ed.), *Reformfragen des Pflichtteilsrechts* (Cologne *et al.* 2007) 151 ff.

BBE-Unternehmensberatung, *Branchereport Erbschaften* (Cologne 1999).

B. Beignier, *La réforme du droit des successsions. Loi du 3 décembre 2001: analyse et commentaire* (Paris 2002).

K. Boele-Woelki, *Perspectives for the Unification and Harmonisation of Family Law in Europe*, in: European Family Law Series, No. 4 (Antwerp 2003).

A. Borkowski, *Textbook on Succession*, 2nd edn (Oxford 2002).

M. Brandon, "UK Accession to the Convention on the Establishment of a Scheme of Registration of Wills and the Convention providing a Uniform Law on the Form of an International Will" (1983) *ICLQ* 742 ff.

S. Cámara Lapuente, "Derecho europeo de succesiones? Un apunte", in: S. Cámara Lapuente (Ed.), *Derecho Privado Europeo* (Madrid 2003) 1185 ff.

C. Castelein – R. Foqué – A. Verbeke (Eds.), *Imperative Inheritance Law in a Late-Modern Society*, in: European Family Law Series, No. 26 (Antwerp *et al.* 2009).

H. Collins, *The European Civil Code. The Way Forward* (Cambridge 2008).

M. G. Cubeddu Wiedemann, "Italien", in: R. Süß – U. Haas (Eds.), *Erbrecht in Europa*, 2nd edn (Angelbachtal 2008) 853 ff.

Z. Csehi, "Plichtteilsrecht in Ungarn", in: A. Röthel (Ed.), *Reformfragen des Pflichtteilsrechts* (Cologne *et al.* 2007) 277 ff.

N. Dethloff, "Europäische Vereinheitlichung des Familienrechts" (2004) *AcP* 544 ff.

M. De Waal, "Comparative Succession Law", in: M. Reimann – R. Zimmermann (Eds.), *The Oxford Handbook of Comparative Law* (Oxford 2006) 1071 ff.

M. De Waal, "A Comparative Overview", in: K. Reid – M. De Waal – R. Zimmermann (Eds.), *Exploring the Law of Succession. Studies National, Historical and Comparative*, in: Edinburgh Studies in Law, vol. 5 (Edinburgh 2007) 1 ff.

A. Dutta, "Succession and Wills in the Conflict of Laws on the Eve of Europeanisation" (2009) *RabelsZ* 547 ff.

A. Fusaro, "Legitimate Portion and other Techniques of Protection of Surviving Spouses and Children. A Comparison between Civil Law and Common Law Systems", in: B. Verschraegen (Ed.), *Family Finances* (Vienna 2009) 751 ff.

M. Ferid – K. Firsching – H. Dörner – R. Hausmann (Eds.), *Internationales Erbrecht*, 78th edn (Munich 2010).

R. Gaier, "Pflichtteil und grundrechtliche Freiheit", in: A. Röthel (Ed.), *Reformfragen des Pflichtteilsrechts* (Cologne *et al.* 2007) 161 ff.

L. Garb – J. Wood (ed.), *International Succession*, 3rd edn (Oxford 2010).

J. Harris, "The Proposed EU Regulation on Succession and Wills: Prospects and Challenges" (2008) *Trust Law International* 181 ff.

D. Hayton (ed.), *European Succession Laws*, 2nd edn (London 2002).

M. Heggen, "Europäische Vereinheitlichungstendenzen im Bereich des Erb- und Testamentsrechts" (2007) *RNotZ* 1 ff.

D. Henrich – D. Schwab (Eds.), *Familienerbrecht und Testierfreiheit im europäischen Vergleich* (Bielefeld 2001).

Chr. Kohler – W. Pintens, "Entwicklungen im europäischen Familien- und Erbrecht 2008-2009" (2009) *FamRZ* 1531 ff.

Chr. Kohler – W. Pintens, "Entwicklungen im europäischen Familien- und Erbrecht 2009-2010" (2010) *FamRZ* 1481 ff.

J.H. Langbein, "The Non Probate Revolution and the Future of the Law of Succession" (1984) *Harv Law Rev* 108 ff.

P. Legrand, *Fragments of Law-as-Culture* (Deventer 1999).

D. Leipold, "Europa und das Erbrecht", in: *Festschrift Söllner* (Munich 2000) 647 ff.

Y.-H. Leleu, *La transmission de la succession en droit comparé* (Antwerp 1996).

D. Lehmann, *Die Reform des internationalen Erb- und Erbprozessrechts im Rahmen der geplanten Brüssel-IV Verordnung* (Angelbachtal 2006).

P. Lokin, "De unificatie van het conflictenrecht in de toekomstige Verordening inzake erfrecht" (2009) *WPNR* 54 ff.

P. Lødrup, "Pflichtteilsrecht in Norwegen und in den Nordischen Staaten", in: A. Röthel (Ed.), *Reformfragen des Pflichtteilsrechts* (Cologne *et al.* 2007) 235 ff.

K.- H. Nadelmann, "The Formal Validity of Wills and the Washington Convention 1973 providing the Form of an International Will" (1974) *Am. J. Comp. L.* 365 ff.

R. Nave-Herz, "Vermögensnachfolge im gesellschaftlichen Wandel" (2009) *ErbR* 202 ff.

K. Neumayer, "Einheit in der Vielfalt. Bewegung und Bewahrung im Erbrecht der Nationen", in: *Festschrift Ferid* (Munich 1978) 659 ff.

K. Neumayer, "Eigenartiges und Altertümliches aus dem vergleichenden Erbrecht", in: *Mélanges Piotet* (Bern 1990) 485 ff.

D. Parry – R. Kerridge, *The Law of Succession*, 12th edn (London 2009).

P. Pestiau, *Héritage et transferts entre générations* (Brussels 1994).

W. Pintens (Ed.), "Family and Succession Law", in: R. Blanpain (Ed.), *Encyclopaedia of Laws* (Alphen aan den Rijn 1997 ff.)

W. Pintens, "Die Europäisierung des Erbrechts" (2001) *ZEuP* 628 ff.

W. Pintens, "Europeanisation of family law", in: K. Boele-Woelki, *Perspectives for the Unification and Harmonisation of Family Law in Europe*, in: European Family Law Series, No. 4 (Antwerp 2003) 3 ff.

W. Pintens, "Das Erbrecht in der Rechtsprechung des Europäischen Gerichtshofs für Menschenrechte", in: *Festschrift Ress* (Cologne 2005) 1074 ff.

W. Pintens, "Family Law – A Challenge for Europe?", in: Àrea de Dret Civil Universitat de Girona (Coord.), *Nous reptes del Dret de familia* (Girona 2005) 21 ff.

W. Pintens – Ch. Declerck – J. Du Mongh – K. Vanwinckelen, *Familiaal vermogensrecht*, 2nd edn (Antwerp 2010).

W. Pintens – D. Pignolet, "L'influence de la Cour européenne des droits de l'homme sur le droit successoral" (2005) *Lex Familiae* 21 ff.

W. Pintens – S. Seyns, "Compulsory Portion and Solidarity Between Generations in German Law", in: C. Castelein – R. Foqué – A. Verbeke (Eds.), *Imperative Inheritance Law in a Late-Modern Society*, in: European Family Law Series, No. 26 (Antwerp 2009) 167 ff.

W. Pintens – N. Torfs – R. Torfs, *Internationaal Testament* (Antwerp 1984).

K. Reid – M. De Waal – R. Zimmermann (Eds.), *Exploring the Law of Succession. Studies National, Historical and Comparative*, in: *Edinburgh Studies in Law*, vol. 5 (Edinburgh 2007).

G. Ring – L. Olsen-Ring, "Dänemark", in R. Süß – U. Haas (Eds.), *Erbrecht in Europa*, 2nd edn (Angelbachtal 2008) 451 ff.

A. Röthel (Ed.), *Reformfragen des Pflichtteilsrechts* (Cologne *et al.* 2007).

K. Schurig, "Das internationale Erbrecht wird europäisch – Bemerkungen zur kommenden Europäischen Verordnung", in: *Festschrift Spellenberg* (Munich 2010) 343 ff.

H.- P. Schwintowski, "Auf dem Wege zu einem Europäischen Zivilgesetzbuch" (2002) *JZ* 210 ff.

U. Spellenberg, Vorbemerkung zu Art. 1 EheGVO, in: *J. von Staudingers Kommentar zum Bürgerlichen Gesetzbuch. Internationales Verfahrensrecht in Ehesachen* (Berlin 2005).

U. Spellenberg – C.N. Himonga – K. Adjamagbo-Johnson, "Recent developments in succession law", in: R. Blanpain (Ed.), *Law in Motion* (Antwerp 1997) 711 ff.

A. Staudinger, "Die Europäische Menschenrechtskonvention als Schranke der gewillkürten Erbfolge" (2005) *ZEV* 140 ff.

R. Süß – U. Haas (Eds.), *Erbrecht in Europa*, 2nd edn (Angelbachtal 2008) 451

P. Terner, "Perspectives of a European Law of Succession" (2007) *MJ* 147 ff.

S. Van Erp, "The New Dutch Law of Succession", in: K. Reid – M. De Waal – R. Zimmermann (Eds.), *Exploring the Law of Succession. Studies National, Historical and Comparative*, in: Edinburgh Studies in Law, vol. 5 (Edinburgh 2007) 193 ff.

M.J.A. Van Mourik, "De legitieme portie: weg ermee" (1991/6018) *WPNR* 621 ff.

A. Verbeke – Y.-H. Leleu, "Harmonisation of the Law of Succession in Europe", in: A. Hartkamp *et al.* (Eds.), *Towards a European Civil Code*, 3rd edn (Nijmegen 2004) 335 ff.

R. Zimmermann, "The Present State of European Private Law" (2009) *Am. J. Comp. L.* 479 ff.

Bibliography Chapter 2 (Andrea Bonomi)

A. Bonomi, "Choice-of-Law Aspects of the Future EC Regulation in Matters of Succession – A First Glance at the Commission's Proposal", in : *Liber Amicorum Kurt Siehr* (The Netherlands, Eleven International Publishing, 2010) 157-171.

A. Borrás, "L'approche du renvoi dans un système d'unité de la succession", in: *Liber amicorum Mariel Revillard* (Paris, Défrenois, 2007) 23-34.

S. Cámara Lapuente, "New Developments in Spanish Law of Succession" (2007/4) *InDret* (www.indret.com)

H. Dörner, "Comments to Arts. 25, 26 EGBGB (Internationales Erbrecht)", in: *J. von Staudingers Kommentar zum Bürgerlichen Gesetzbuch, Einführungsgesetz zum BGB* (Berlin, Sellier – de Gruyter, 2007)

M. Ferid, "Die gewillkürte Erbfolge im internationalen Privatrecht", in: W. Lauterbach, *Vorschläge und Gutachten zur Reform des Deutschen Internationalen Erbrechts* (Berlin – Tübingen, De Gruyter-Mohr, 1969) 91-120.

German Notary Institute, *Conflict of Law of Succession in the European Union. Perspectives for a Harmonisation* (2004).

M. Goré, "De la mode ... dans les successions internationales: contre les prétentions de la professio juris", in: *Mélanges en l'honneur de Y. Loussouarn* (Paris, Dalloz, 1994) 193-201.

P. Kindler, "Vom Staatsangehörigkeits– zum Domizilprinzip: das künftige internationale Erbrecht der Europäische Union" (2010) *IPRax* 44-50.

E. Lein, "A Further Step Towards a European Code of Private International Law – The Commission's Proposal for a Regulation on Succession" (2010) *Yearbook of Private International Law* 107-141.

Y. Lequette, "Comments to *Cassation Civile* 20 March 1985 *(Caron)*" (1986) *RCDIP* 66 ff.

M. L. Niboyet-Hoegi "Comments to *Cassation Civile* 20 March 1985 *(Caron)*" (1987) *JDI* 81 ff,.

E. Rodriguez Pineau "Comments to STS 15 novembre 1996 *(Lowenthal)*" (1998) *IPRax* 135 ff.

Bibliography Chapter 3 (Esther Arroyo i Amayuelas – Miriam Anderson)

N. Álvarez Lata, "Empresa familiar y planificación sucesoria. Un acercamiento a los protocolos familiares como instrumentos de ordenación", in: Á. Rebolledo Varela (Ed.) *La familia en el Derecho de sucesiones: cuestiones actuales y perspectivas de futuro* (Madrid, Dykinson, 2010) 555-602.

M. Anderson, "Comments to Arts. 442-6 and 442-9 CC Cat", in: J. Egea Fernández – J. Ferrer Riba (Dirs.), *Comentari al Llibre quart del Codi civil de Catalunya, relatiu a les successions*, I (Barcelona, Atelier, 2009) 286-290, 296-301 (cit. 2009a).

M. Anderson, "La capacitat per a testar de qui té habitualment disminuïda la capacitat per a testar" (2009/3) *Indret* (www.indret.com) (cit. 2009b).

M. Anderson, "Hacia una flexibilización del fenómeno sucesorio: El problema de la legítima y la posición del cónyuge viudo en la sucesión intestada", in M. A. Carregal – G. De Reina Tartière (Dirs.), *Planificación Sucesoria (Estate Planning)* (Buenos Aires, Heliasta) (forthcoming).

E. Arroyo Amayuelas – C. González Beilfuss, "Die katalanische Rechtsordnung und das Zivilrecht Kataloniens" (1995/3) *ZEuP* 564-575.

E. Arroyo Amayuelas, "Le pluralisme de l'ordonnancement civil en Espagne et le droit civil en vigueur en Catalogne" (1998/4) *RGD* 411-447.

E. Arroyo Amayuelas, "Matrimonio e coppia in Diritto espagnolo", in: F. Brunetta d'Usseaux (Dir.), *Matrimonio e coppia in Diritto europeo* in: M. Lupoi, *Formazione, vita e crisi della coppia nei Paesi dell'Unione Europea* (Padova, Cedam, 2005) 373-435.

E. Arroyo Amayuelas, "Pflichtteilsrecht in Spanien", in: A. Röthel (Ed.), *Reformfragen des Pflichtteilsrechts* (Cologne, Heymanns, 2007) 257-276.

E. Arroyo Amayuelas, "La reforma del derecho de sucesiones y de la prescripción en Alemania" (2010/1) *Indret* (www.indret.com).

F. Badosa Coll, "... Quae ad ius Catalhanicum pertinet. The Civil Law of Catalonia, ius commune and legal tradition", in: H. L. MacQueen – A. Vaquer – S. Espiau (Eds.), *Regional Private Laws and codification in Europe* (Cambridge, Cambridge University Press, 2003) 136-163.

F. Badosa (Dir.) – J. Marsal (Coord.), *Manual de Dret Civil català* (Barcelona *et al.*, Marcial Pons, 2003).

J. Beckert, *Inherited Wealth*, English translation by T. Dunlap (Princeton, Princeton University Press, 2008).

F. Bellivier – J. Rochfeld, "Droit successoral – Conjoint supervivant – Enfant adultérin (Loi n° 2001-1135 du 3 décembre 2001 relative aux droits du conjoint survivant et des enfants adultérins et modernisant diverses disposicions de droit successoral, JO 4 déc. 2001, 19279)" (2002) *RTDC* 156 ff (http://www.dalloz.fr/)

E. Bosch Capdevila, *L'acreixement en el Dret successori català* (Barcelona, Generalitat de Catalunya, 2002).

E. Bosch Capdevila, *El principio* nemo pro parte testatus pro parte intestatus decedere potest. *Evolución y significado* (Madrid, Dyckinson, 2006).

B. Bouckaert, "The Post Mortem Homo Economicus: What Does He Tell Us?", in: C. Castelein – R. Foqué – A. Verbeke (Eds.), *Imperative Inheritance Law in a Late-Modern Society*, in: European Family Law Series, No. 26 (Antwerp *et al.*, Intersentia, 2009) 91-106.

J. M. Bustos Lago "Limitaciones dispositivas del causante: legítimas y reservas", in: R. Bercovitz Rodríguez-Cano (Coord.), *Derecho de sucesiones* (Madrid, Tecnos, 2009) 414-529.

A. Calatayud Sierra, "Comments to Art. 154 CS", in: L. Jou Mirabent (Coord.), *Comentarios al Código de Sucesiones*, vol. I (Barcelona, Bosch, 1994) 600-607.

S. Cámara Lapuente, "New Developpments of the Spanish Law of Succession" (2007/4) *Indret* (www.indret.com).

S. Cámara Lapuente "Testamento negativo, memoria de confianza y otras especialidades del Derecho sucesorio catalán. A propósito de la STSJ Cataluña de 23 de abril de 1998" (2000/4) *RJC* 743-778 (cit. 2000a).

S. Cámara Lapuente, *La exclusión testamentaria de los herederos legales* (Madrid, Cívitas, 2000) (cit. 2000b).

A. Casanovas Mussons, "Comments to Art. 461-12 CC Cat", in: J. Egea Fernández – J. Ferrer Riba (Dirs.), *Comentari al Llibre quart del Codi civil de Catalunya, relatiu a les successions*, vol. II (Barcelona, Atelier, 2009) 1491-1493.

A. Casanovas Mussons, "Entorn de la Llei 9/1987, de 25 de maig, de successió intestada: aspectes problemàtics" (1987) *RJC* 297-324.

H. Casman, "Comparative Law – Belgium", in: C. Castelein – R. Foqué – A. Verbeke (Eds.), *Imperative Inheritance Law in a Late-Modern Society*, in: European Family Law Series, No. 26 (Antwerp *et al.*, Intersentia, 2009) 153-166.

C. Castelein, "Introduction and Objectives", in: C. Castelein – R. Foqué – A. Verbeke (Eds.), *Imperative Inheritance Law in a Late-Modern Society*, in: European Family Law Series, No. 26 (Antwerp *et al.*, Intersentia, 2009) 1-38.

S. Cavanillas Mújica, "La herencia no aceptada: apuntes de derecho comparado", in: J. M. González Porras – F. P. Méndez González (Eds.), *Libro homenaje al profesor Manuel Albaladejo García*, vol. II (Murcia, Universidad de Murcia, 2004) 1003-1015.

F. Cerdà Albero, "La successió en l'empresa familiar", in: Àrea de Dret Civil Universitat de Girona (Coord.), *El nou Dret successori del Codi civil de Catalunya* (Girona, Documenta, 2009) 181-206.

I. Corpart, "L'amélioration de la protection *post mortem* des conjoints par la loi n° 2001-1135 du 3 décembre 2001" (2002) *Recueil Dalloz* 2952 ff. (http://www.dalloz.fr/)

E. Corral García, *Los derechos del cónyuge viudo en el Derecho civil común y autonómico* (Barcelona, Bosch, 2007).

M. J. De Waal, "A Comparative Overview", in: R. Kenneth – M. J. De Waal – R. Zimmermann (Eds.), *Exploring the Law of Succession. Studies National, Historical and Comparative*, in: Edinburgh Studies in Law, vol. 5 (Edinburg, University Press, 2007) 1-26.

J. Delgado Echeverría, "Objetivos de una reforma del derecho de sucesiones", in: *Derecho de sucesiones. Presente y Futuro. XII Jornadas de la Asociación de Profesores de Derecho Civil* (Murcia, Universidad de Murcia, 2006) 85-171.

J. Egea Fernández, "El nou règim jurídic de la successió contractual" (2009/1) *RJC* 11-58.

S. Espiau Espiau, "El usufructo vidual y la legítima de los descendientes" (1996/3) *RJC* 629 – 642.

T. Facal Fondo – Mª P. Torrens Calle, "Cambios sociológicos de la familia con repercusión en el Derecho de sucesiones", in: Á. Rebolledo Varela (Ed.) *La familia en el Derecho de sucesiones: cuestiones actuales y perspectivas de futuro* (Madrid, Dykinson, 2010) 43-82.

F. Ferrand, "Comparative Law – France", in: C. Castelein – R. Foqué – A. Verbeke (Eds.), *Imperative Inheritance Law in a Late-Modern Society*, in: European Family Law Series, No. 26 (Antwerp *et al.*, Intersentia, 2009) 189-202.

J. Ferrer Riba, "Tradició heretada i innovació en el nou Llibre Quart del Codi Civil de Catalunya", in: Àrea de Dret Civil Universitat de Girona (Coord.), *El nou Dret successori del Codi civil de Catalunya* (Girona, Documenta, 2009) 15-32.

R. Foqué – A. Verbeke, "Conclusions. Towards an Open and Flexible Imperative Inheritance Law", in: C. Castelein – R. Foqué – A. Verbeke (Eds.), *Imperative Inheritance Law in a Late-Modern Society*, in: European Family Law Series, No. 26 (Antwerp *et al.*, Intersentia, 2009) 203-221.

E. Gacto Fernández, *Temas de Historia del Derecho: Derecho del constitucionalismo y de la codificación*, vol. II (Sevilla, Publicaciones de la Universidad, 1981).

R. Gaier, "Pflichtteil und grundrechtliche Freiheit", in: A. Röthel (Ed.), *Reformfragen des Pflichtteilsrechts* (Cologne, Heymanns, 2007) 161-168.

Mª P. García Rubio – M. Herrero Oviedo, "Las disposiciones generales sobre pactos sucesorios en el Libro IV del Código civil de Cataluña. Apertura, Innovación y alguna perpejlidad", in: Àrea de Dret Civil Universitat de Girona (Coord.), *El nou Dret successori del Codi civil de Catalunya* (Girona, Documenta, 2009) 465-483.

M. Garrido Melero, *Código civil de Cataluña. Libro IV, relativo a sucesiones (Ley 10/2008, de 10 de julio* (Barcelona *et al.*, Marcial Pons, 2008).

Mª. C. Gete-Alonso Calera, "La sucesión intestada incorporada al Código civil de Cataluña (Principios – Innovaciones)", in: Àrea de Dret Civil Universitat de Girona (Coord.), *El nou Dret successori del Codi civil de Catalunya* (Girona, Documenta, 2009) 209-261.

Mª E. Ginebra Molins, "La parella de fet: estudi comparatiu dels aspectes civils de la regulació autonòmica" (2006/6) *RCDP* 91-165.

Mª E. Ginebra Molins, "Comments to Arts. 441-6 CC Cat", in: J. Egea Fernández – J. Ferrer Riba (Dirs.), *Comentari al Llibre quart del Codi civil de Catalunya, relatiu a les successions*, vol. II (Barcelona, Atelier, 2009) 1240-1244.

J. C. Ginisty, "La reforma del Derecho de sucesiones en Francia", *El Notario del siglo XXI* (2010/34) (http://www.elnotario.com/egest/noticia.php?id=1921&seccion_ver=0.

F. Gómez Pomar, "Comments to Arts. 412-3, 412-5 CC Cat", in: J. Egea Fernández – J. Ferrer Riba (Dirs.), *Comentari al Llibre quart del Codi civil de Catalunya, relatiu a les successions*, vol. II (Barcelona, Atelier, 2009) 102-116; 120-124.

E. González Bou, "Los heredamientos como forma de ordenación de la sucesión por causa de muerte de la empresa", in: M. Garrido Melero – J. Mª Fugardo Estivill (Dirs.), *El patrimonio familiar, profesional y empresarial. Sus protocolos*, vol. II (Barcelona, Bosch, 2005) 733-766.

M. Grimaldi, "Droits du conjoint survivant: brève analyse d'une loi transactionelle" *AJ Famille* (2002) 48 ff. (http://www.dalloz.fr/).

A. Guitián Rodríguez, *La capacidad de testar: especial referencia al testador anciano* (Madrid, Civitas, 2006).

M. Herrero Oviedo, "El renacer de los pactos sucesorios", in: S. Álvarez González (Ed.), *Estudios de Derecho de familia y sucesiones (dimensiones interna e internacional)* (Santiago de Compostela, Imprenta Universitaria, 2009) 199-217.

L. Jou Mirabent, "Los heredamientos y la transmisión del patrimonio familiar", in: M. Garrido Melero – J. Mª Fugardo Estivill (Dirs.), *El patrimonio familiar, profesional y empresarial. Sus protocolos*, vol. IV (Barcelona, Bosch, 2005) 359-382.

L. Jou Mirabent, "Comments to Arts. 421-7, 421-14 CC Cat", in: J. Egea Fernández – J. Ferrer Riba (Dirs.), *Comentari al Llibre quart del Codi civil de Catalunya, relatiu a les successions*, vol. I (Barcelona, Atelier, 2009) 172-180; 209-215.

U. Karpen, "Das Pflichtteilsrecht im Spannungsfeld von Einzelnem, Familie, Gesellschaft und Staat", in: A. Röthel (Ed.), *Reformfragen des Pflichtteilsrechts* (Cologne, Heymanns, 2007) 169-184.

I. Kroppenberg, "Pflichtteilsrecht", in: J. Basedow – K. Hopt – R. Zimmermann (Eds.), *Handwörterbuch des europäischen Privatrechts*, vol. II (Tübingen, Mohr, 2009) 1156-1160.

I. Kroppenberg, "Testierfreiheit", in: J. Badedow – K. Hopt – R. Zimmermann (Eds.), *Handwörterbuch des europäischen Privatrechts*, vol. II (Tübingen, Mohr, 2009) 1481-1485.

I. Kroppenberg, "Universalsukzession", in: J. Badedow – K. Hopt – R. Zimmermann (Eds.), *Handwörterbuch des europäischen Privatrechts*, vol. II (Tübingen, Mohr, 2009) 1560-1564.

A. Lamarca Marquès, "Relacions familiars i atribucions successòries legals. Llegítima i quarta vidual al llibre IV del Codi civil de Catalunya", in: Àrea de Dret Civil Universitat de Girona (Coord.), *El nou Dret successori del Codi civil de Catalunya* (Girona, Documenta, 2009) 263-307 (cit. 2009a).

A. Lamarca Marquès, "Erbrecht in Katalonien", in: R. Süß – U. Haas (Eds.), *Erbrecht in Europa*, 2n edn (Angelbachtal, Zerb, 2008) 899-934.

A. Lamarca Marquès, "Comments to Art. 451-8 CC Cat", in: J. Egea Fernández – J. Ferrer Riba (Dirs.), *Comentari al Llibre quart del Codi civil de Catalunya, relatiu a les successions*, vol. II (Barcelona, Atelier, 2009) 1340-1348 (cit. 2009b).

A. Lamarca Marquès, "Successió intestada a Catalunya. De la Compilació al Codi civil i els cinquanta anys entre dues lleis (1936-1987)" (2010/4) *RJC* 1169-1214.

J.J. López Burniol, "Comments to Art. 67 CS", in: L. Jou Mirabent (Coord.), *Comentarios al Código de Sucesiones*, vol. I (Barcelona, Bosch, 1994) 328-336.

J. Marsal, "La ineficàcia dels actes i disposicions d'última voluntat", in: Àrea de Dret Civil Universitat de Girona (Coord.), *El nou Dret successori del Codi civil de Catalunya* (Girona, Documenta, 2009) 129-147.

J. Marsal, *El testament* (Barcelona, Generalitat de Catalunya, 2000).

J. Marsal, "La institució d'hereu", in: F. Badosa (Dir.) – J. Marsal (Coord.), *Manual de Dret Civil català* (Barcelona *et al.*, Marcial Pons, 2003) 687-694.

J. Marsal, "La introducción del testamento común ológrafo y su consolidación en el Derecho civil de Cataluña", in: J.M. Scholz (Ed.), *Fallstudien zur spanischen und portugiesischen Justiz 15. bis 20. Jahrhundert* (Frankfurt a.M., Klostermann, 1994) 459-484.

J. Martí i Miralles, *Principis de Dret successori aplicats a fórmules d'usdefruit vidual i d'herència vitalícia* (Barcelona, La Renaixença, 1925; reprint Barcelona, Textos Jurídics catalans series, Departament Justícia Generalitat de Catalunya, 1985).

P. Matthews, "Comparative Law – United Kingdom", in: C. Castelein – R. Foqué – A. Verbeke (Eds.), *Imperative Inheritance Law in a Late-Modern Society*, in: European Family Law Series, No. 26 (Antwerp *et al.*, Intersentia, 2009) 123-151.

J. Miquel González, "Legítima material y legítima formal" (2009/40) *AAMN* 493-560.

S. Navas Navarro, "El pacto sucesorio de atribución particular en el Código civil de Cataluña" (2009/2) *Indret* (www.indret.com).

J.C. Ollé Favaró, "La reforma del Derecho de Sucesiones en Cataluña" (2009/40) *AAMN* 443-491.

G. Otte, "Comments to BVerfGE 19 April 2005" (2005/20) *JZ* 1007-1010.

M. Á. Parra Lucán, "Legítimas, libertad de testar y transmisión de un patrimonio", in: Consejo General del Poder Judicial (Ed.), *Reflexiones sobre materias de Derecho sucesorio* (Madrid, Consejo General del Poder Judicial, 2009) 469-599.

M. Pereña, "La reforma del Derecho sucesorio francés llevada a cabo por la Ley 3 de diciembre de 2001" (2003/679) *RCDI* 1-22 (http://vlex.com/vid/329597)

M. Pérez Escolar, *El cónyuge supérstite en la sucesión intestada* (Madrid, Dykinson, 2003).

M. Pérez Simeón, "Incompatibilidad entre las sucesiones testada e intestada en el Codi de Successions de Catalunya" (1999/10) *La Notaria* 15-50.

W. Pintens – S. Seyns, "Compulsory Portion and Solidarity Between Generations in German Law", in: C. Castelein – R. Foqué – A. Verbeke (Eds.), *Imperative Inheritance Law in a Late-Modern Society*, in: European Family Law Series, No. 26 (Antwerp *et al.*, Intersentia, 2009) 167-187.

L. Puig Ferriol, "Els principis successoris catalans: present i futur", en *La reforma de la Compilació: el sistema successori. Materials de les III Jornades a Tossa de Mar* (Barcelona, Edicions de la Universitat de Barcelona, 1984) 39-59.

L. Puig Ferriol – E. Roca Trias, *Fundamentos de Derecho civil catalán*, vol. III-2 (Barcelona, Bosch, 1980).

L. Puig Ferriol – E. Roca Trías, *Institucions del Dret Civil de Catalunya*, 7th edn (València, Tirant lo Blanch, 2009).

Á. Rebolledo Varela, "La actualización del Derecho sucesorio español ante los cambios sociológicos y jurídicos de la familia", in: Á. Rebolledo Varela (Ed.) *La familia en el Derecho de sucesiones: cuestiones actuales y perspectivas de futuro* (Madrid, Dykinson, 2010) 23-41.

D. S. Reher, *La familia en España. Pasado y Presente* (Madrid, Alianza editorial, 1996).

J. Ribalta Haro – E. Arroyo Amayuelas, "Dels donats als acollits. La Llei 22/2000 d'acolliment de persones grans", in: A. Vaquer Aloy (Coord.), *El Dret Privat del Pallars Sobirà* (Lleida, Pagès ed., 2001) 33-80.

J. Ribot Igualada, "Comments to Art. 451-17 CCCat", in: J. Egea Fernández – J. Ferrer Riba (Dirs.), *Comentari al llibre quart del Codi civil de Catalunya, relatiu a les successions*, vol. II (Barcelona, Atelier, 2009) 1393-1402.

R. Mª Roca Sastre, "Los elementos componentes de la Compilación", in: *Estudios sobre sucesiones*, vol. I (Madrid, Instituto de Estudios Políticos, 1981) 99-120.

A. Röthel (Ed.), *Reformfragen des Pflichtteilsrechts* (Cologne, Heymanns, 2007).

V.D. Rougeau, "No Bonds but those Freely Chosen: An Obituary for the Principle of Forced Heirship in American Law" (2008/3) *Civil Law Commentaries* (http://papers.ssrn.com/sol3/papers.cfm?abstract_id=1396678).

R. Sánchez Aristi, "Propuesta para una reforma del Código civil en materia de pactos sucesorios", in: *Derecho de sucesiones. Presente y Futuro. XII Jornadas de la Asociación de Profesores de Derecho Civil* (Murcia, Universidad de Murcia, 2006) 477-541.

J. M. Scholz, "Spanien", in: H. Coing (Ed.), *Handbuch der Quellen und Literatur der neueren europäischen Privatrechtsgeschichte*, vol. III-1 (Munich, Beck, 1982) 397-687.

J. Solé Feliu, "Comments to Art. 422-4 CC Cat", in: J. Egea Fernández – J. Ferrer Riba (Dirs.), *Comentari al Llibre quart del Codi civil de Catalunya, relatiu a les successions*, vol. I (Barcelona, Atelier, 2009) 222-233.

J. C. Sonnekus, "Freedom of testation and the Ageing Testator", in: K. Reid – M. De Waal – R. Zimmermann (Eds.), *Exploring the Law of Succession. Studies National, Historical and Comparative*, in: Edinburgh Studies in Law, vol. 5 (Edinburgh, University Press, 2007) 78-98.

T. F. Torres García, "Legítima, legitimarios y libertad de testar (síntesis de un sistema)", in: *Derecho de sucesiones. Presente y Futuro. XII Jornadas de la Asociación de Profesores de Derecho Civil* (Murcia, Universidad de Murcia, 2006) 173-277.

B. Trigo García, "Pactos sucesorios y empresa ¿familiar?", in: Àrea de Dret Civil Universitat de Girona (Coord.), *El nou Dret successori del Codi civil de Catalunya* (Girona, Documenta, 2009) 499-512.

E. Valladares Rascón, "Por una reforma del sistema sucesorio en el Código Civil", in: J. M. González Porras – F.P. Méndez González (Eds.), *Libro Homenaje al Profesor M. Albaladejo García*, vol. II (Murcia Universidad de Murcia, 2004) 4893-4902.

S. Van Erp, "The New Dutch Law of Succession", in: R. Kenneth – M. J. De Waal – R. Zimmermann (Eds.), *Exploring the Law of Succession. Studies National, Historical and Comparative*, in: Edinburgh Studies in Law, vol. 5 (Edinburg, University Press, 2007) 193-207.

M. J. A. Van Mourik, "Comparative Law – The Netherlands", in: C. Castelein – R. Foqué – A. Verbeke (Eds.), *Imperative Inheritance Law in a Late-Modern Society*, in: European Family Law Series, No. 26 (Antwerp *et al.*, Intersentia, 2009) 107- 122.

A. Vaquer, "Introduction", in: S. Van Erp – A. Vaquer (Coords.), *Introduction to Spanish Patrimonial Law* (Granada, Comares, 2006) 1-17 (cit. 2006a).

A. Vaquer Aloy, "Spain", in: J. M. Smits (Ed.) *Elgar Enciclopedia of comparative law* (Cheltenham, Edward Elgar, 2006) 672-676 (cit 2006b).

A. Vaquer Aloy, "Reflexiones sobre una eventual reforma de la legítima" (2007/3) *Indret* (www.indret.com).

A. Vaquer Aloy, "El Derecho civil catalán: presente y futuro" (2008/46) *RJ Navarra* 69-108.

A. Vaquer Aloy, "Comments to Art. 442-4 CC Cat", in: J. Egea Fernández – J. Ferrer Riba (Dirs.), *Comentari al Llibre quart del Codi civil de Catalunya, relatiu a les successions*, vol. II (Barcelona, Atelier, 2009) 1267-1272.

A. Verbeke – Y.H. Leleu, "Harmonisation of the Law of Succession in Europe", in: A. Hartkamp *et alii* (Eds.), *Towards a European Civil Code*, 3rd edn (Nijmegen, Ars Aequi Libri-Kluwer, 2004) 335-350.

R. Zimmermann, "The Present of European Private Law" (2009/2) *Am. J. Comp. L* 479-512.

R. Zimmermann, "Erbunwürdigkeit. Die Entwicklung eines Rechtsinstituts im Spiegel europäischer Kodifikationen", in: P. Apathy *et al*. (Eds.), *Festschrift für Helmut Koziol zum 70. Geburtstag* (Wien, Jan Sramek Verlag, 2010) 463-511.

Bibliography Chapter 4 (Esteve Bosch Capdevila)

E. Arroyo Amayuelas – D. Bondia Garcia, "¿Intepretación de testamento contraria a los Derechos humanos? El caso Pla & Puncernau vs. Andorra" (2004/18) *DPyC* 7-88.

A. M. Borrell i Soler, *Derecho civil vigente en Cataluña* vol. V, 2nd edn (Barcelona, 1944).

M. Duran i Bas, *Memoria acerca de las Instituciones del Derecho Civil de Cataluña* (Barcelona, 1883).

J. Marsal Guillamet, "Els fills posats en condició: interpretació del testament i discriminació" (2005/2) *RJC* 477-496.

Bibliography Chapter 5 (Antoni Vaquer Aloy)

G. Amenta, "La successione necessaria: essere o non essere?" (2009) *Rassegna di Diritto Civile* 605-633.

E. Arroyo Amayuelas, "La reforma del derecho de sucesiones y de la prescripción en Alemania" (2010/1) *Indret* (www.indret.com).

E. Arroyo Amayuelas, "Pflichtteilsrecht in Spanien", in: A. Röthel (Ed.), *Reformfragen des Pflichtteilsrechts* (Cologne *et al*. 2007) 257-276.

P. Badura, "Erbrecht, Testierfreiheit und Schutz der Familie", in: A. Röthel (Ed.), *Reformfragen des Pflichtteilsrecht* (Cologne *et al*. 2007) 151-160.

G. Bonilini, "Sulla possibile riforma della successione necessaria", in: G. Bonilini (Dir.), *Tratatto di diritto delle successioni e donazioni*, vol. III, *La Successione legitima* (Milano 2009) 729-748.

B. Bouckaert, "The Post Mortem Homo Economicus: What Does He Tell Us?", in: C. Castelein – R. Foqué – A. Verbeke (Eds.), *Imperative Inheritance Law in a Late-Modern Society* in: European Family Law Series, No. 26 (Antwerp *et al*. 2009) 91-106.

S. Cámara Lapuente, "New Developments in the Spanish Law of Succession" (2007/4) *Indret* (www.indret.com).

R. Chester, "Disinheritance and the American Child: An Alternative from British Columbia" (1998/4) *Utah Law Rev* 1-35.

P. Del Pozo Carrascosa – A. Vaquer Aloy – E. Bosch Capdevila, *Derecho civil de Cataluña. Derechos reales* (Barcelona *et al*. 2009).

P. Del Pozo Carrascosa – A. Vaquer Aloy – E. Bosch Capdevila, *Derecho civil de Cataluña. Derecho de sucesiones* (Barcelona *et al.* 2009).

M. Dossetti, "Concetto e fundamento della successione necesaria", in: G. Bonilini (Dir.), *Tratatto di diritto delle successioni e donazioni*, vol. III, *La Successione legitima* (Milano 2009) 5-43.

J. Dukeminier – R.H. Sitkoff – J. Lindgren, *Wills, Trusts, and Estates*, 8th edn (Austin *et al.* 2009).

J.M. Fontanellas, *La professio iuris sucesoria* (Madrid 2010).

R. Foqué – A. Verbeke, "Toward an Open and Flexible Imperative Inheritance Law", in: C. Castelein – R. Foqué – A. Verbeke (Eds.), *Imperative Inheritance Law in a Late-Modern Society* in: European Family Law Series, No. 26 (Antwerp *et al.* 2009) 203-221.

F. H. Foster, "Linking Support and Inheritance: A New Model from China" (1999) *Wisconsin LR* 1199-1258.

F. H. Foster, "Towards a Behavior-Based Model of Inheritance? The Chinese Experiment" (1998) *U. Cal. Davis LR* 77-126.

I. Gliha, "Croatia", in: *International Encyclopaedia of Laws* (The Hague 2005).

F. Gómez Pomar, "Comments to Art. 412-15 CC Cat", in: J. Egea Fernández – J. Ferrer Riba (Dirs.), *Comentari al llibre quart del Codi Civil de Catalunya, relatiu a les successions*, vol. I (Barcelona 2009) 120-124.

A. J. Hirsch, "Freedom of Testation /Freedom of Contract" (2009) (http://www.ssrn.com).

M. Hrušáková, "Czech Republic", in: *International Encyclopaedia of Laws* (The Hague 2002).

K. S. Knaplund, "Grandparents Raising Grandchildren and the Implications for Inheritance" (2006) *Arizona Law Rev* 1-22.

W. Kopcuk – J. P. Lupton, "To Leave or not to Leave: The Distribution of Bequest Motives" (2007) *RESL* 207-235.

K. N. Korpus, "Extinguishing Inheritance Rights: California Breaks New Ground in the Fight Against Elder Abuse But Fails to Build an Effective Foundation" (2000-2001) *Hastings Law J* 537-578.

A. Lamarca Marquès, "Relacions familiars i atribucions successòries legals. Llegítima i quarta vidual al Llibre IV del Codi Civil de Catalunya", in: Àrea de Dret Civil Universitat de Girona (Coord.), *El nou Dret successori del Codi Civil de Catalunya* (Girona 2009) 263-307.

J. H. Langbein, "The Twentieth-Century Revolution in Family Wealth Transmission" (1988) *Mich Law Rev* 722-751.

C. Lasarte Álvarez, "Abandono asistencial de la tercera edad y desheredación de los descendientes en la España contemporánea", in: C. Lasarte Álvarez (Dir.), *La protección de las personas mayores* (Madrid 2007) 363-397.

B. L. Liebman, "Legitimacy through Law in China?" (http://www.pbs.org/wnet/wideangle/lessons/the-peoples-court/legitimacy-through-law-in-china/4332/ (February 2010).

K. F. Lorio, "The Louisiana Civil Law Tradition: Archaic or Prophetic in the Twenty-First Century" (2002/63) *La Law Rev* 1-25.

M. Nathan Jr, "Forced Heirship: The Unheralded 'New' Disinherison Rules" (2000) *Tulane LR* 1027-1044.

M. A. Parra Lucán, "Legítimas, libertad de testar y transmisión de un patrimonio" (2009/13) *AFDUDC* 481-554.

W. Pintens, "Die Europäisierung des Erbrechts" (2001) *ZEuP* 628-648.

W. Pintens – S. Seyns, "Compulsory Portion and Solidarity Between Generations in German Law", in: C. Castelein – R. Foqué – A. Verbeke (Eds.), *Imperative Inheritance Law in a Late-Modern Society* in: European Family Law Series, No. 26 (Antwerp *et al.* 2009) 167-187.

J. M. Puig Salellas, "Notes sobre l'eventual reforma de la llegítima", in: *Materials de les III Jornades de Dret Català a Tossa. La reforma de la Compilació: el sistema successori* (Barcelona 1985) 211-224.

Á. L. Rebolledo Varela, "Problemas prácticos de la desheredación de los descendientes por malos tratos, injurias y abandono de los mayores", in: Á.L. Rebolledo Varela (Ed.), *La familia en el derecho de sucesiones: cuestiones actuales y perspectivas de futuro* (Madrid 2010) 379-462.

J. Ribot Igualada, "Comments to Art. 451-17", in: J. Egea Fernández – J. Ferrer Riba (Dirs.), *Comentari al llibre quart del Codi Civil de Catalunya, relatiu a les successions* (Barcelona 2009) 1393-1418.

A.-M. Rhodes, "Consequences of Heir's Misconduct: Moving from Rules to Discretion" (2007) *Ohio N Univ Law Rev* 975-991.

C. Rombach, "Tschechien", in: R. Süß – U. Haas (Eds.), *Erbrecht in Europa*, 2nd edn (Angelbachtal 2008) 1483-1523.

A. Röthel (Ed.), *Reformfragen des Pflichtteilsrecht* (Cologne *et al.* 2007).

V. D. Rougeau, "No Bonds but those Freely Chosen: An Obituary for the Principle of Forced Heirship in American Law" (2008/3) *Civil Law Commentaries* (http://papers.ssrn.com/sol3/papers.cfm?abstract_id=1396678).

J. C. Sonnekus, "The New Dutch Code on Succession as Evaluated Through the Eyes of a Hybrid Legal System" (2005) *ZEuP* 71-87.

R. Süß, "Kroatien", in: R. Süß – U. Haas (Eds.), *Erbrecht in Europa*, 2nd edn (Angelbachtal 2008) 935-949.

J. C. Tate, "Caregiving and the Case for Testamentary Freedom" (2008) *U. Cal. D. LR* 129-193.

T. L. Turnipseed, "Why Shouldn't I be Allowed to Leave My Property to Whomever I Choose at My Death? (Or How I Learned to Stop Worrying and Start Loving the French)" (2006) *Brandeis LJ* 737-795.

A. Van Mies de Bie, "Niederlande", in: R. Süß – U. Haas (Eds.), *Erbrecht in Europa*, 2nd edn (Angelbachtal 2008) 1049-1079.

A. Vaquer, "The Law of Successions", in: M. Bussani – F. Werro (Eds.), *European Private Law. A Handbook* (Berne *et al.* 2009) 552-582.

H. F. Zacher, "Pflichtteil und intergenerationelle Solidarität", in: A. Röthel (Ed.), *Reformfragen des Pflichtteilsrechts* (Cologne *et al.* 2007) 135-150.

R. Zimmermann, "Erbunwürdigkeit. Die Entwicklung eines Rechtsinstituts im Spiegel europäischer Kodifikationen", in: Peter Apathy *et al* (Eds.), *Festschrift für Helmut Koziol zum 70. Geburtstag* (Wien 2010) 463-511.

Bibliography Chapter 6 (Susana Navas Navarro)

K. J. Albiez Dohrmann, "Algunos instrumentos jurídicos -contractuales- para la conservación y continuidad de las empresas familiares colectivas. Su endeblez jurídica" in: F. J. Sánchez Calero – R. García Pérez (Eds.), *Protección del patrimonio familiar* (València, Tirant Lo Blanch, 2006) 216-256.

J. Alfaro Águila-Real, "Los costes de transacción", in: J. L. Iglesias Prada (Coord.), *Estudios jurídicos en Homenaje a Aurelio Menéndez*, vol. II (Madrid, 1996) 131-167.

J. M. Amat, "El relevo generacional como estímulo a la renovación estratégica en la empresa familiar" in: J. M. Amat (Ed.) *La sucesión en la empresa familiar* (Barcelona, Spanish Institute for Fiscal Studies Archives, 2004) 127-140.

M. Anderson, "Una aproximación al derecho de sucesiones inglés" (2006/3) *ADC* 1243-1281.

M. Baker – T. J. Micelli, "Land Inheritance Rules: theory and cross-cultural analysis" (2005/56) *J Organ Behav* 77-102.

S. Barbeito Roibal – E. Guillén Solórzano – M. Martínez Carballo – G. Domínguez Feijoó, "Visión europea del proceso de sucesión en la empresa familiar" (2004/2821) *Boletín económico ICE* 32-40.

A. Barrera González, *Casa, herencia, familia en la Cataluña rural* (Madrid, Alianza Universidad, 1990).

C. Bayod López, "Algunos problemas sobre invalidez, ineficacia y revocación de los pactos sucesorios en la ley aragonesa de sucesión por causa de muerte" (2005/2) *Cuadernos Lacruz Berdejo* 1-10.

J. Beckert, *Inherited Wealth*, english translation by T. Dunlap (Princeton, Princeton University Press, 2008).

B. D. Bernheim – A. Shleifer – L. H. Summers, "The Strategic Bequest Motive" (1985/93) *J Polit Econ* 1045-1056.

P. O. Bjuggren – L.G. Sund, "Strategic Decision Making in Intergenerational Succession of Small and Medium-Size Family-Owned Business" (2001/14) *Fam Bus Rev* 11-37.

E. Bosch Capdevila, *El principio nemo pro parte testatus pro parte intestatus decedere potest. Evolución y significado* (Madrid, Dykinson, 2006).

D. Bös – G. Kayser, *Der Generationenwechsel in Mittelständischen Betrieben*, IfM-Materialien Nr. 120 (Bonn, June 1996).

E. Brancós Núñez, "Els pactes successoris en el Llibre IV del Codi Civil de Catalunya" (2009/4) *RJC* 953-982.

R. H. Brockhaus, "Family Business Succession: Suggestions for Future Research" (2004/17) *Fam Bus Rev* 165-177.

S. Cámara Lapuente, "New Developments in the Spanish Law of Succession" (2007/4) *Indret* (www.indret.com).

S. Cámara Lapuente, "¿Derecho europeo de sucesiones? Un apunte", in: S. Cámara Lapuente (Ed.), *Derecho privado europeo* (Madrid, Colex, 2003) 1115-1229.

J. C. Casillas – C. Díaz – A. Vázquez, *La gestión de la empresa familiar* (Madrid, Thomson, 2005).

J. J. Castiella Rodríguez, "El testamento mancomunado, testamento exportable al Código Civil" (1993/15) *RJ Navarra* 35-53.

F. Cerdà Albero, "La empresa familiar: una noción relativa", in: Various Authors, *El Buen Gobierno de las empresas familiares* (Pamplona, Thomson/Aranzadi, 2004) 91-92.

F. Cerdà Albero, "La successió en l'empresa familiar" in: Àrea Dret Civil Universitat de Girona (Coord.), *El nou Dret successori del Codi civil de Catalunya* (Girona, Documenta, 2009) 181-206.

J. B. Davies, "Uncertain Lifetime, Consumption and Dissaving in Retirement" (1981/89) *J Polit Econ* 561-577.

E. De Hinojosa, *El régimen señorial y la cuestión agraria en Cataluña durante la Edad Media*, edited by M. Peset (Pamplona, Urgoiti, 2003).

M. J. De Waal, "A Comparative Overview", in: R. Kenneth – M. J. De Waal – R. Zimmermann (Eds.), *Exploring the Law of Succession. Studies National, Historical and Comparative*, in: Edinburgh Studies in Law, vol. 5 (Edinburg, University Press, 2007) 1-26.

P. Del Pozo Carrascosa – A. Vaquer Aloy – E. Bosch Capdevila, *Derecho civil de Cataluña. Derecho de Sucesiones* (Barcelona *et al.*, Marcial Pons, 2009).

A. Delfosse – J.-F. Peniguel, *La réforme des successions et des libéralités* (París, Litec, 2006).

J. Egea Fernández, "Comments to Arts. 431-14, 21 CC Cat", in: J. Egea Fernández – J. Ferrer Riba (Dirs.), *Comentari al llibre quart del Codi Civil de Catalunya, relatiu a les successions*, vol. II (Barcelona, Atelier, 2009) 1123-1129; 1152-1158.

J. Egea Fernández, "El nou règim jurídic de la successió contractual" (2009/1) *RJC* 9-58.

J. Egea Fernández, "Protocolo familiar y pactos sucesorios. La proyectada reforma de los heredamientos" (2007/3) *Indret* (www.indret.com).

M. A. Eisenberg, "Donative Promises" (1979/47) *Univ Chicago Law Rev* 18-60.

L. Fernández del Pozo, *El protocolo familiar. Empresa familiar y publicidad registral* (Pamplona, Thomson-Civitas, 2008).

L. Flaquer, "De la família a les polítiques familiars. Vicissituds d'un recorregut", *Papers. Revista de sociologia* (1999) 66-80.

L. Flaquer, *El destino de la familia* (Barcelona, Ariel, 1998).

J. Fuentes Ramírez, *De padres a hijos. El proceso de sucesión en la empresa familiar* (Madrid, Pirámide, 2007).

M. Gallo, "Preparación de la siguiente generación y desarrollo de la organización", in: J. M. Amat (Dir.), *La sucesión en la empresa familiar*, Colección IEF (Barcelona, 2004) 115-135.

E. García Álvarez – J. López Sintas, "El liderazgo como tema central del proceso de sucesión", in: J. M. Amat (Dir.), *La sucesión en la empresa familiar*, Colección IEF (Barcelona, 2004) 47-60.

M. P. García Rubio – M. Herrero Oviedo, "Las disposiciones generales sobre pacto sucesorio en el Libro IV del Código civil de Cataluña: apertura, innovación y alguna perplejidad", in: Àrea de Dret Civil Universitat de Girona (Coord.), *El nou Dret successori del Codi civil de Catalunya* (Girona, Documenta, 2009) 465-470.

J. R. García Vicente. "El testamento mancomunado. Razones para la derogación del artículo 669 del Código civil", in: *Derecho de sucesiones. Presente y Futuro. XII Jornadas de la Asociación de Profesores de Derecho Civil* (Murcia, Universidad de Murcia, 2006) 289-299.

E. González Bou, "Los heredamientos como forma de ordenación de la sucesión por causa de muerte de la empresa" in: M. Garrido Melero – J. M. Fugardo Estivill (Dirs.), *El patrimonio familiar, profesional y empresarial. Sus protocolos*, vol. II (Bosch, Barcelona, 2005) 733-766.

A. Gimeno Sandig, *Radiografía de la empresa familiar española. Fortalezas y riesgo* (www. fbkonline.com/es/eventos/evento_01.html).

C. Gortázar Lorente, "Derecho y empresa familiar: el protocolo y sus instrumentos de desarrollo", in: Àrea de Dret Civil Universitat de Girona (Coord.), *Nous reptes del Dret de família* (Girona, Documenta, 2005) 123-130.

J. Grima Ferrada, "Pactos entre socios familiars", in: Various Authors, *El Buen Gobierno de las Empresas Familiares* (Pamplona, Thomson/Aranzadi, 2004) 177-190.

M. Grimaldi, *Droit civil. Successions*, 6th edn (Paris, Litec, 2001).

M. Guinjoan – C. Murillo – J. Pons, *L'empresa familiar a Catalunya. Quantificació i característiques* (Generalitat de Catalunya, 2004).

S. J. Harvey, "What Can the Family Contribute to Business: Examining Contractual Relationships" (1999/12) *Fam Bus Rev* 61-72.

H. Hiram, "New Developments in UK Succession Law" (2006/10) *EJCL* (http://www.ejcl. org/103/article103-7.pdf)

Ch. Jolls – C.R. Sunstein – R.H. Thaler, "A Behavioural Approach to Law and Economics", in: C.R. Sunstein (ed.), *Behavioural Law & Economics* (Cambridge University Press, 2000) 13-59.

L. Jou Mirabent, "Los heredamientos y la transmisión del patrimonio familiar" in: M. Garrido Melero – J.M. Fugardo Estivill (Dirs.), *El patrimonio familiar, profesional y empresarial. Sus protocolos*, vol. IV (Barcelona, Bosch, 2005) 359-382.

A. Kull, "Reconsidering Gratuitous Promises" (1992/21) *J Leg Stud* 39-65.

I. Le Breton-Miller – D. Miller – L.P. Steier, "Toward an Integrative Model of Effective FOB Succession" (2004) *ET&P* 305-328.

J. J. López Burniol, "Comments to Arts. 67, 70 CS", in: L. Jou Mirabent (Ed.), *Comentarios al Código de sucesiones de Cataluña*, vol. I (Barcelona, Bosch, 1994) 327-336, 346-347.

J. J. López Burniol, "La *resurrecció* dels capítols matrimonials (L'àmbit de l'autonomia de la voluntad en els contractes reguladors de la convivència)" (Barcelona, November 1999).

M. H. Lubatkin – W. S. Schulze – Y. Ling – R. N. Dino, "The effects of parental altruism on the governance of family-managed firms" (2005/26) *J Organ Behav* 313-330.

D. Lueck – T. Miceli, "Property Law", in: A. M. Polinsky – S. Shavell (eds.), *Handbook of Law and Economics*, vol. I, Series: Handbooks in Economics, 27, 1st edn (Oxford, 2007) 183-249.

V. Magariños Blanco, "Libertad de testar" (2005) *RDP* 21-40.

J. Marsal Guillamet, in: F. Badosa Coll (Dir.) – J. Marsal (Coord.), *Manual de Dret Civil català* (Barcelona et al., Marcial Pons, 2003).

C.H. Matthews – T.W. Moore – A.S. Fialko, "Succession in the Family Firm: A Cognitive Categorization Perspective" (1999/12) *Fam Bus Rev* 159-170.

J. Mayer, *Kommentar zum BGB*, § 2265, in: O. Dittmann – W. Reimann – M. Bengel, (eds.), *Testament & Erbvertrag*, 3rd edn (Neuwied/Kriftel, Luchterhand, 2000).

D. Miller – L. Steier – I. Le Breton-Miller, "Lost in time: intergenerational succession, change and failure in family business" (2003/18) *J Bus Vent* 513-531.

S. Navas Navarro, "El pacto sucesorio de atribución particular en el Código Civil de Catalunya" (2009/1) *Indret* (www.indret.com).

Mª. L. Palazón Garrido, *La sucesión por causa de muerte en la empresa mercantil* (Valencia, Tirant Lo Blanch, 2003).

Mª. A. Parra Lucán, "Legítimas, libertad de testar y transmisión de un patrimonio" (2009/13) *AFDUDC* 481-554.

D. Parry – R. Kerridge, *The Law of Succession*, 12th edn (London, Sweet & Maxwell, 2009).

C. Paz-Ares, "El enforcement de los pactos parasociales" (2003/5) *ACiv Uría & Menéndez* 1-45 (http.//vlex.com/vid/256179).

C. Paz-Ares, "La economía política como jurisprudencia racional. Aproximación a la teoría económica del derecho" (1981/2) *ADC* 627-628.

M. Pereña Vicente, "Nuevo marco legal de los pactos sucesorios en el derecho francés" (2005/170) *RCDI* 2485-2500.

M. G. Perozek, "A Reexamination of the Strategic Bequest Motive" (1998/106) *J Polit Econ* 423-445.

M. Peset, "Propiedad y crédito agrario", in: C. Petit (Ed.), *Derecho privado y revolución burguesa* (Madrid, Marcial Pons, 1990) 172-190.

W. Pintens, "Die Europäisierung des Erbrechts" (2001/3) *ZEuP* 628-648.

R.A. Posner, *El análisis económico del derecho* (México, D. F., Fondo de cultura económica, 1998).

R. Pratdesaba i Ricart, "La successió contractual en el nou Llibre IV del Codi civil de Catalunya", in: Àrea de Dret Civil Universitat de Girona (Coord.), *El nou Dret successori del Codi civil de Catalunya* (Girona, Documenta, 2009) 151-181.

L. Puig Ferriol - E. Roca Trias, *Institucions del Dret Civil de Catalunya*, 7th edn (València, Tirant lo Blanch, 2009).

J. M. Puig Salellas, "Comments to Art. 3 CS", in: L. Jou Mirabent (Coord.), *Comentarios al Código de Sucesiones*, vol I (Barcelona, Bosch, 1994) 17-22.

M. J. Reyes López, "La Ley 7/2003, de 1 de abril, de la Sociedad Limitada Nueva Empresa y la empresa familiar" (2003/28) *ACiv.* 771-788.

J. A. Rodríguez Aparicio, "El protocolo familiar", in: Various Authors, *El Buen Gobierno de las Empresas Familiares* (Pamplona, Thomson/Aranzadi, 2004) 287-312.

I. Rodríguez Díaz, "El protocolo familiar y su publicidad: de las iniciativas comunitaria y española al Real Decreto 171/2007, de 9 de febrero, por el que se regula la publicidad de los protocolos familiares" (2007) *RDM* 1148-1160.

P. Salvador Coderch – J.J. López Burniol, "Comments to Art. 411-3 CC Cat" in: J. Egea Fernández – J. Ferrer Riba (Dirs.), *Comentari al llibre quart del Codi Civil de Catalunya, relatiu a les successions*, vol. I (Barcelona, Atelier, 2009) 68-71.

R. Sánchez Aristi, "Propuesta para una reforma del Código civil en materia de pactos sucesorios", in: *Derecho de sucesiones. Presente y Futuro. XII Jornadas de la Asociación de Profesores de Derecho Civil* (Murcia, Universidad de Murcia, 2006) 477-543.

H.- B. Schäfer – C. Ott, *Manual de análisis económico del derecho civil*, translated into Spanish by M. Von Carstenn-Lichterfelde (Madrid, Tecnos, 1991).

S. Shavell, "An Economic Analysis of Altruism and Deferred Gifts" (1991/20) *J Leg Stud* 401-421.

S. Shavell, *Foundations of economic analysis of law* (Harvard University Press, 2004).

P. Sherma – J.J. Chrisman – J.H. Chua, "Succession Planning as Planned Behaviour: Some Empirical Results" (2003/17) *Fam Bus Rev* 1-16.

E. T. Staurou – T. Kleonthous – T. Anastasiou, "Leadership Personality and Firm Culture during Hereditary Transitions in Family Firms: Model Development and Empirical Investigation" (2005/43-2) *J Small Bus Manag* 187-206.

L. P. Steier – J.J. Chrisman – J.H. Chua, "Entrepreneurial Management and Governance in Family Firms: An Introduction" (2004) *ET&P* 295-303.

P. Tedde de Lorca, "Revolución liberal y crecimiento económico en la España del siglo XIX", in: *Antiguo Régimen y liberalismo. Homenaje a Miguel Artola* (Madrid, Alianza editorial, 1994) 31-51.

R. Tena Arregui, *Costes de transacción y fe pública notarial*, Papeles de la Fundación para el análisis y los estudios sociales, No. 6 (1992).

O. Tobajas Gálvez, "El testamento mancomunado en Aragón" (2000) *ACiv.* 693-711.

J. B. Vallet de Goytisolo, *Reflexions sobre Catalunya* (Barcelona et al., Marcial Pons, 2007).

S. Van Erp, "New Developments in Succession Law" (2007/11) *EJCL* (http://www.ejcl.org).

A. Vaquer Aloy, "The Law of Successions", in: M. Bussani – F. Werro, *European Private Law: A Handbook*, vol. I (Munich et al., Sellier, 2009) 559-570.

A. Verbeke – Y.-H. Leleu, "Harmonization of the Law of Succession in Europe", in: A. Hartkamp et al. (Eds.), *Towards a European Civil Code* (The Hague, Kluwer, 1994) 335-350.

J. Vicens Vives, *Noticia de Cataluña* (Barcelona, Destino Libro, 1980).

Bibliography Chapter 7 (Roger Kerridge)

H. A. L. Fisher (Ed.), *The Collected Papers of Frederic William Maitland*, vol. I (Cambridge, 1911).

D. Hayton "By-Passing Testamentary Formalities" (1987/46) *Camb Law J* 215.

F. V. Hawkins, "On the Principles of Legal Interpretation, with Reference Especially to the Interpretation of Wills", *Papers Read before the Juridical Society (1858-1863)*, vol. II (London, 1863); later published as Appendix C to J.D. Thayer, *Preliminary Treatise on Evidence at the Common Law* (Boston, 1898).

Law Commission, *Family Law: First Report on Family Property. A New Approach* (1973/52).

Law Commission, *Family Law: Second Report on Family Property: Family Provision on Death* (1974/61).

Law Commission, *Distribution on Intestacy* (1989/187).

Law Reform Committee, Report No. 22, *The Making and Revocation of Wills*, 1980 Cmnd.7902.

F. W. Maitland, *Equity*, 2nd edn (Cambridge, 1936).

C. H. Sherrin, "Intestacy" (1987) *All ER Annual Rev* 263.

A. W. B. Simpson, *A History of the Land Law*, 2nd edn (Oxford, 1986).

J. Wigram, *The Interpretation of Wills* (London, 1831), 5th edn by C. P. Sanger (London, 1914).

Bibliography Chapter 8 (Anne Röthel)

H. G. Bamberger – H. Roth, *Kommentar zum BGB*, vol. 3, 2nd edn (Munich, Beck, 2008).

J. Beckert, "Familiäre Solidarität und die Pluralität moderner Lebensformen: Eine gesellschaftstheoretische Perspektive auf das Pflichtteilsrecht", in: A. Röthel (Ed.), *Reformfragen des Pflichtteilsrechts* (Cologne, Heymanns, 2007) 1-22.

H. Brox – W. D. Walker, *Erbrecht*, 23rd edn (Cologne, Heymanns, 2009).

B. Dauner-Lieb, "Bedarf es einer Reform des Pflichtteilrechts?" (2001) *DNotZ* 460-465.

A. Dutta, "Vor- und Nacherbschaft", in: J. Basedow – K. J. Hopt – R. Zimmermann (Eds.), *Handwörterbuch des Europäischen Privatrecht* (Tübingen, Mohr, 2009) 1735-1739.

A. Dutta, "Testamentsvollstreckung", in: J. Basedow – K. J. Hopt – R. Zimmermann (Eds.), *Handwörterbuch des Europäischen Privatrecht* (Tübingen, Mohr, 2009) 1477-1481.

U. Falk, "Zur Sittenwidrigkeit von Testamenten", in: U. Falk – H. Mohnhaupt (Eds.), *Das Bürgerliche Gesetzbuch und seine Richter* (Frankfurt Main, Klostermann, 2000) 451-494.

T. Gutmann, *Freiwilligkeit als Rechtsbegriff* (Munich, Beck, 2001).

T. Gutmann, "Der Erbe und seine Freiheit" (2004) *NJW* 2347-2349.

D. Henrich, *Testierfreiheit versus Pflichtteilsrecht* (Munich, Beck, 2000).

D. Henrich, "Familienerbrecht und Testierfreiheit im europäischen Vergleich" (2001) *DNotZ* 441-452.

R. Hüttemann – P. Rawert, "Pflichtteil und Gemeinwohl. Privilegien für gute Zwecke?", in: A. Röthel (Ed.), *Reformfragen des Pflichtteilsrechts* (Cologne, Heymanns, 2007) 73-90.

O. Karow, *Die Sittenwidrigkeit von Verfügungen von Todes wegen in historischer Sicht* (Frankfurt/ Main, Wien *et al.*, Lang, 1997).

C. Keim, "Comments to SG Dortmund, B. v. 25 September 2009" (2010) *ZEV* 56.

W. Kellenter, *Bedingte Verfügungen von Todes wegen* (Thesis Bayreuth 1989).

R. Kössinger, in: H. Nieder – R. Kössinger, *Handbuch der Testamentsgestaltung*, 3rd edn (Munich, Beck, 2008) 936 ff., 950 ff.

I. Kroppenberg, "Wer lebt, hat Recht – Lebzeitiges Rechtsdenken als Fremdkörper in der Inhaltskontrolle von Verfügungen von Todes wegen" (2006) *DNotZ* 86-105.

H. Lange – K. Kuchinke, *Erbrecht*, 5th edn (Munich, Beck, 2001).

D. Leipold, "Comments to OLG Hamm, B. v. 16 July 2009"(2009) *ZEV* 472-473

D. Leipold, "Comments to § 2074 BGB", in: *Münchener Kommentar zum BGB*, vol. 9, 5th edn (Munich, Beck, 2010).

W. Litzenburger, "Das Bedürftigentestament – Erbfolgegestaltung zu Gunsten von Langzeitarbeitslosen (Hartz-IV-Empfängern)" (2009) *ZEV* 278-281.

J. Mayer, "Comments to § 2210 BGB", in: H. G. Bamberger/H. Roth, *Kommentar zum BGB*, vol. 3, 2nd edn (Munich, Beck, 2008).

R. Meyer-Pritzl, in: *J. von Staudingers Kommentar zum BGB – Eckpfeiler des Zivilrechts* (Berlin, Sellier-de Gruyter, 2008) 1145-1189.

K. Muscheler, "Comments to OLG Schleswig-Holstein, Urteil v. 09 June 1998" (1999) *ZEV* 151-152.

K. Muscheler, "Die geplanten Änderungen im Erbrecht, Verjährungsrecht und Nachlassverfahrensrecht" (2008) *ZEV* 105-112.

K. Muscheler, *Die Haftungsordnung der Testamentsvollstreckung* (Tübingen, Mohr Siebeck, 1994).

G. Otte, "Bessere Honorierung von Pflegeleistungen – Plädoyer für eine Vermächtnislösung" (2008) *ZEV* 260-262.

G. Otte, "Comments to § 2074 BGB", in: *J. von Staudingers Kommentar zum BGB – Erbrecht, §§ 2064-2196 BGB* (Testament 1), 13th edn (revision 2003) (Berlin, Sellier – De Gruyter, 2003).

W. Reimann, "Die Reform des Erb- und Verjährungsrechtes" (2009) *FamRZ* 1633-1636.

W. Reimann, "Die rule against perpetuities im deutschen Erbrecht" (2007) *NJW* 3034-3037.

J. Ritter, *Der Konflikt zwischen einer erbrechtlichen Bindung aus erster Ehe und einer Verfügung des überlebenden Ehegatten zugunsten eines neuen Lebenspartners* (Berlin, Duncker & Humblot, 1999).

A. Röthel, *El derecho de sucesiones y la legítima en el derecho alemán*, Colección Notariado Hoy (Barcelona, Bosch, 2008) (cit. 2008a).

A. Röthel, "Was bringt die Pflichtteilsreform für Stiftungen?" (2008) *ZEV* 112-116 (cit. 2008b).

A. Röthel, "Testierfreiheit und Testiermacht" (2010/210) *AcP* 32-66 (cit. 2010a).

A. Röthel, "Erbrechtliche Wirkungsgrenzen (§§ 2109, 2210 BGB) als Intentionalitätsgarantien", in: M. Martinek – P. Rawert – B. Weitemeyer (Eds.), *Festschrift for D. Reuter* (2010), forthcoming (cit. 2010b).

A. Röthel, *Verhandlungen des 68. Deutschen Juristentages Berlin 2010*, vol. I: Gutachten – Teil A: "Ist unser Erbrecht noch zeitgemäß?" (Munich, Beck, 2010) (cit. 2010c).

K. Schmidt, "Pflichtteil und Unternehmensnachfolge – Rechtspolitische Überlegungen", in: A. Röthel (Ed.), *Reformfragen des Pflichtteilsrechts* (Cologne, Heymanns, 2007) 37-56.

G. Thielmann, *Sittenwidrige Verfügungen von Todes wegen* (Berlin, Duncker & Humblot, 1973).

P. A. Windel, "Wie ist die häusliche Pflege aus dem Nachlass zu honorieren?" (2008) *ZEV* 305-308.

R. Zimmermann, "Heres fiduciarius?", in: R. Zimmermann – R. H. Helmholtz (eds.), *Itinera Fiduciae* (Berlin, Duncker & Humblot, 1998) 267-304.

W. Zimmermann, "Comments to § 2210 BGB", in: *Münchener Kommentar zum BGB*, vol. 9, 5th edn (Munich, Beck, 2010).

Bibliography Chapter 9 (Zoltán Csehi)

L. Besenyei, "De lege ferenda gondolatok az öröklési jog köréből" [De lege ferenda reflections on the law of successions] (1998/LIII) *Acta Universitatis Szegediensis de Attila József Nominatae* 33-43.

H. Brox, *Erbrecht*, 20th edn (München, Beck, 2003).

Z. Csehi, "Das Stiftungsgeschäft im deutschen Bürgerlichen Gesetzbuch" (Magisterarbeit, Heidelberg 1991), in: Z. Csehi, *Diké kísértése* [Temptation of Dike] (Budapest 2005) 376-452.

Z. Csehi, "Coincidentia Oppositorum, avagy alapítvány és halál esetére szóló rendelkezés" [Foundation and donatio mortis causa], in: *Liber amicorum Studia Lajos Vékás dedicata* (Budapest, ELTE, 1999) 37-61.

Z. Csehi, *A magánjogi alapítvány* [The Foundation of Private Law] (Budapest 2006).

Gy. Eörsi – Gy. Gellért (Eds.), *A Polgári Törvénykönyv magyarázata* [Commentary to Civil Code], vols. I-III (Budapest 1981).

Gy. Gellér, *Az öröklési szerződés* [Contract of Inheritance] (Budapest 2001).

R. Haumann – G. Hohloch, *Handbuch des Erbrechts* (Berlin 2008).

D. Henrich, *Testierfreiheit vs. Pflichtteilsrecht* (München 2000).

D. Henrich – D. Schwab (Eds.), *Familienerbrecht und Testierfreiheit im europäischen Vergleich. Beiträge zum europäischen Familienrecht* (Bielefeld 2001) (cit. 2001a).

D. Henrich, "Familienerbrecht und Testierfreiheit im europäischen Vergleich" (2001) *DNotZ* 447 (cit. 2001b).

A. Holló – Zs. Balogh (Eds.), *Az értelmezett Alkotmány* [Constitution Interpreted] (Budapest 2005).

E. Jayme, "Europäische Menschenrechtskonvention und deutsches Nichtehelichenrecht" (19179) *NJW* 2425-2429.

U. Karpen, "Das Pflichtteilsrecht im Spannungsfeld von Einzelnem, Familie, Gesellschaft und Staat", in: A. Röthel (Ed.), *Reformfragen des Pflichtteilsrechts* (Cologne, Heymanns, 2007) 169-174.

G. Kegel, *Zur Schenkung von Todes wegen* (Opladen, Westdeutscher Verlag, 1972).

T. Kipp – H. Coing, *Erbrecht* (Tübingen, Mohr Siebeck, 1990).

D. Leopold, *Erbrecht* (Tübingen, Siehr, 2006).

D. Martiny, "Unterhalts- und erbrechtliches Teilgutachten", in: Gutachten A für den 64. Deutschen Juristentag (München 2002) 1-120.

J. Oechsler, "Pflichtteil und Unternehmensfolge von Todes wegen" (2000) *AcP* 603-626.

D. Olzen, *Erbrecht* (Berlin 2005).

K. Raffai, *A nemzetközi magánjogi közrend rétegei – különös tekintettel a közösségi és magyar jogra* [Layers of public policy of private international law with special regard to the Community law and Hungarian law] (unpublished PhD-thesis, Budapest 2009).

A. Röthel, "Zuwendungen an gemeinnützige Stiftungen und Erbrecht" in: W. Rainer Walz – L. Von Auer – T. Von Hippel (Eds.), *Spenden- und Gemeinnützigkeitsrecht in Europa* (Tübingen, Siehr, 2007) 793-811 (cit. 2007a).

A. Röthel (Ed.), *Reformfragen des Pflichtteilsrechts* (Cologne et al., Carl Heymanns, 2007) (cit. 2007b).

O. Salát, in: A. Jakab (ed.), *Az Alkotmány kommentárja* [Commentary to the Constitution], 2nd edn (Budapest 2009).

I. Sándorfalvi Pap, "Kötelesrész" [Compulsory Share], in: K. Szladits (Ed.): *Magyar magánjog* [Hungarian Private Law], vol. 6 (Öröklési jog) [Law of Succession] (Budapest 1939).

T. Schilling, *Internationaler Menschenrechtsschutz* (Tübingen, Mohr, 2004).

L. Sólyom, "Polgári jogi kérdések az Alkotmánybíróság gyakorlatában (1994)" [Civil law issues in the practice of the Constitutional Court], in: L. Sólyom, *Az alkotmánybíráskodás kezdetei Magyarországon* [The beginning of the Constitutional Jurisdiction in Hungary] (Budapest 2001) 126-140.

P. Sonnevend, in: G. Halmai – A. Tóth (Eds.), *Emberi jogok* [Human Rights] (Budapest 2003) 643-668.

L. Sőth, *Polgári Jog. Öröklési Jog. Döntvénytár 1960-1997* [Law of succession, Case Law book] (Budapest, 1997).

F. Strum, "Das Straßburger Marckx-Urteil zum Recht des nichtehelichen Kindes und seine Folgen" (1982) *FamRZ* 1150-1159.

L. Tóth, *Magyar Magánjog. Öröklési jog* [Hungarian Private Law. Law of Succession] (Debrecen 1932).

L. Vékás, "Az állampolgári tulajdonjog" [The Property Rights of the citizen], in: *Emberi jogok hazánkban* [Human Rights in Hungary] (Budapest 1988).

L. Vékás, *Öröklési jog* [Law of succession] (Budapest 1995).

M. Világhy, *Öröklési jog* [Law of succession] (Budapest 1987).

A. Weber, *Menschenrechte. Texte und Fallpraxis* (München, Selllier, 2004).

E. Weiss, "A Polgári Törvénykönyv öröklési jogi könyvének kodifikációja elé" [On the codification of the law of succession of the Civil code], in: *Magister Artis Boni et Aequi, Studia in Honorem Németh János* (Budapest 2003) 975-999.

Bibliography Chapter 10 (Andrea Fusaro)

G. Alpa – V. Zeno – Zencovich, *Italian Private Law* (Routledge, Cavendish, 2007).

G. Amadio, "La successione necessaria tra proposte di abrogazione e istanze di riforma" (2007/1) *Rivista del Notariato* 803-815.

L. Barbiera, *Le convivenze. Diritto civile nazionale e orientamenti europei* (Bari, Cacucci, 2010).

M. C. Bianca, *Diritto civile*, vol. 2, *La famiglia. Le successioni*, 4th edn (Milano, Giuffré, 2005).

M. Ciccariello, "Comments to *Cassazione civile* 6 april 2000" (2001/1) *Nuova Giurisprudenza Civile Commentata* 440

S. Delle Monache (Ed.), *Tradizione e modernità nel diritto successorio. Dagli istituti classici al patto di famiglia* (Padova, Cedam, 2007).

G. Ferrando, "Matrimonio e crisi della famiglia. Note introduttive", in: Ferrando (a cura di), *Il nuovo diritto di famiglia*, vol. I, *Matrimonio, separazione e divorzio* (Bologna, Zanichelli, 2007).

R. Frank, *Erbrecht* (München, Beck, 2007).

A. Fusaro, "Il diritto successorio inglese e il trust" (2010/5) *Notariato* 559 ff.

A. Fusaro, "L'espansione dell'autonomia privata in ambito successorio nei recenti interventi legislativi francesi ed italiani" (2009/1) *Contratto Impresa/Europa* 427 ff.

G. Gabrielli, "Tutela dei legittimari e tutela degli aventi causa dal beneficiario di donazione lesiva: una riforma attesa, ma timida" (2005) *Studium Juris* 1129 ff.

Y.- H. Leleu, *La Réserve héréditaire en droit française et en droit luxembourgeois*, in *Examen critique de la reserve successorale*, vol. II, Droit Belge (Bruxelles, Bruylant, 1997).

A. Mosca, "Comments to *Cassazione civile* 6 april 2000" (2001) *Vita notarile* 141.

A. Palazzo, *Istituti alternativi al testamento*, in: P. Perlingieri (Dir.), *Trattato di Diritto Civile* (Napoli, Edizioni Scientifiche Italiane, 2003).

M. Talamanca, *Successioni testamentarie*, in: A. Scialoja – G. Branca (Dirs.), *Commentario del codice civile* (Bologna- Roma, 1978).

C. Vallone, *Italian Family Agreements and Business Continuity* (Milano, Giuffré, 2008).

Bibliography Chapter 11 (J. Michael Milo)

B. Akkermans, *The Principle of Numerus Clausus in European Property Law* (Antwerp *et al.*, Intersentia, 2009).

C. Asser, *Het Nederlandsch Burgerlijk Wetboek, vergeleken met het Wetboek Napoleon* ('s-Gravenhage en Amsterdam, De Gebroeders van Cleef, 1838).

C. Asser – J.B.M. Vranken, *Algemeen deel* (Zwolle, W.E.J. Tjeenk Willink, 1995).

C. Asser – J. De Boer, *Personen en familierecht* 1* (Deventer, Kluwer, 2010).

C. Asser – S. Perrick, *Erfrecht en schenking* 4* (Deventer, Kluwer, 2009).

C. Asser – F.H.J Mijnssen – A.A. Van Velten – S. E. Bartels, *Zakenrecht* 5* (Deventer, Kluwer, 2008).

S.E Bartels – J.M. Milo, "Contents of Real Rights: Personal or Proprietary. A Principled History", in: S.E. Bartels – J.M. Milo, *Contents of Real Rights* (Nijmegen, Wolf Legal Publishers, 2004) 5-23.

F. Baur – R. Stürner, *Sachenrecht*, 18th edn (München, Beck, 2009).

F.E.J. Beekhoven Van den Boezem, *Onoverdraagbaarheid van vorderingen krachtens partijbeding* (Deventer, Kluwer, 2003).

A.S. De Blecourt – H.F.W.D. Fischer, *Kort begrip van het Oud-Vaderlands burgerlijk recht*, 7th edn (Groningen, Wolters Noordhoff, 1969).

F. Brandsma, "Een basterd Code Napoleon'?, Het Wetboek Napoleon ingerigt voor het Koningrijk Holland", in: J.J. Hallebeek en A.B.J. Sirks (Ed.), *Nederland in Franse schaduw. Recht en bestuur in het Koninkrijk Holland* (1806-1810) (Hilversum, Verloren, 2006) 221-247.

A. Braun, "Revocability of Mutual Wills", in: K. Reid – M. de Waal – R. Zimmermann (Eds.), *Exploring the Law of Succession. Studies National, Historical and Comparative*, in: Edinburgh Studies in Law, vol. 5 (Edinburgh, Edinburgh University Press, 2007) 208-225.

C. Castelein – R. Foqué – A. Verbeke (Eds.), *Imperative inheritance law in a late-modern society* (Antwerpen, Intersentia, 2009).

H. Coing, *Europäisches Privatrecht*, Band I (München, Beck, 1985).

J. Coren, *Observationes rerum in eodem Senatu iudicatarum* ('s-Gravenhage 1633).

M. J. De Waal, "The Social and Economic Foundations of the Law of Succession" (1997/8) *Stellenbosch LR* 162-175.

G. Diephuis, *Het Nederlandsch Burgerlijk Regt* (Groningen, J.B. Wolters, 1869-1890).

F. Du Toit, "The Impact of Social and Economic Factors on Freedom of Testation in Roman and Roman-Dutch Law" (1999/10) *Stellenbosch LR* 232-243.

J. Eggens, "Het erfrecht in het B.W. van 1838 tot heden", in: P. Scholten – E.M. Meijers, *Gedenkboek Burgerlijk Wetboek 1838-1938* (Zwolle, W.E.J. Tjeenk Willink, 1938) 425-436.

R. Feenstra, "Real rights and their classification in the 17th century: the role of Heinrich Hahn and Gerhard Feltmann" (1982) *Juridical Review* 106-120.

S.J. Fockema Andreae, *Het Oud-Nederlandsch Burgerlijk Recht* (Haarlem, De Erven F. Bohn, 1906).

P. H. M. Gerver, "Law of Succession", in: J. Chorus – P. H. Gerver – E. Hondius, *Introduction to Dutch Law*, 4th edn (Alphen aan den Rijn, Kluwer law International, 2006) 195-203.

H. Grotius, *Jurisprudence of Holland* (translation by R.W. Lee), vol. I (text) and II (commentary) (1953, reprint Aalen, Scientia Verlag 1977).

W.G. Huijgen, "Het beginsel van de testeervrijheid in het erfrecht", in: Yin-Yang (Van Mourikbundel) (Kluwer, Deventer, 2000) 85-92.

W.G. Huijgen, "Kroniek Erfrecht" (2005/7) *NTBR* 324-329.

W.G. Huijgen – J.E. Kasdorp – B.E. Reinhartz – J.W. Zwemmer, *Compendium Erfrecht* (Deventer, Kluwer, 2005).

J. Huizinga, *Herfsttij der middeleeuwen*, 7th impression (Haarlem, H.D. Tjeenk Willink, 1950).

R.W. Lee, *An Introduction to Roman Dutch Law*, 5th edn (Oxford, Clarendon Press 1953).

J. H.A. Lokin – F. Brandsma – C. Jansen, *Roman Frisian Law of the 17th and 18th century* (Berlin, Duncker & Humblot, 2003).

J.H.A. Lokin – J.M. Milo – C.H. Van Rhee, *Tweehonderd jaren codificatie van het privaatrecht in Nederland* (Groningen, Chimaera, 2010).

E.M. Meijers, *Le droit ligurien de succession en Europe occidentale* (Haarlem, Tjeenk Willink, 1928).

E.M. Meijers, "Het wetsontwerp tot wijziging der erfopvolging" (1920/2616-2619) *WPNR* 117-120; 129-132; 141-144.

E.M. Meijers, *Ontwerp voor een Nieuw Burgerlijk Wetboek. Toelichting* ('s-Gravenhage, Staatsdrukkerij- en Uitgeverijbedrijf, 1954).

M. Merlin, *Répertoire universel et raisonné de jurisprudence*, vol. 7 (Paris 1827).

J.M. Milo, *Het rechtsvergelijkende argument in de ontwikkeling van het Nederlandse vermogensrecht 1838-1940* (Antwerpen, Intersentia, 1997).

J.M. Milo – V. Sagaert, "Private Property Rights in Cultural Objects: Balancing Preservation of Cultural Objects and Certainty of Trade in Belgian and Dutch Law", in: B. Demarsin – E. Schrage – B. Tilleman – A. Verbeke (Eds.), *Art & Law* (Brugge, Die Keure, 2008) 468-491.

J. Lothrop Motley, *The rise of the Dutch Republic: a History* (London, Routledge and Sons, 1870).

P. L. Nève, "Uit de bonte berm van de juridische begrippenflora: ons 'gesloten' stelsel van beperkte rechten", in: S.C.J.J. Kortmann et al. (Eds.), *Op recht* (Zwolle, W.E.J. Tjeenk Willink 1996) 223-232.

A.J.M. Nuytinck, *A short Introduction to the New Dutch Succession Law* (Deventer, Kluwer, 2002).

A.J.M. Nuytinck, "Het gesloten stelsel van uiterste wilsbeschikkingen: Weg ermee!" (2006/6683) *WPNR* 706-709.

B.E. Reinharz, "Recent changes in the law of succession in The Netherlands", in: J.H.M. Van Erp – L.P.W. Van Vliet (Eds.) *Netherlands Reports to the Seventeenth International Congress of Comparative Law. Utrecht 2006* (Antwerpen–Oxford, Intersentia, 2006) 59-81.

J.S.L.A.W.B. Roes, *Het naaste bloed erfde het goed. De positie van de langstlevende echtgenoot in het Nederlandse erfrecht bij versterf* (Deventer, Kluwer, 2006).

J.M. Smits, *Omstreden rechtswetenschap* (Den Haag, Boom Juridische Uitgevers, 2009)

J.M. Smits, "Van partijen en derden; over interpretaties van de numerus clausus van zakelijke rechten" (1996) *GOM* 41-64.

T.H.D. Struycken, *De numerus clausus in het goederenrecht* (Deventer, Kluwer, 2007).

I. Sumner – H. Wahrendorf, *Inheritance law legislation of The Netherlands. A Translation of Book 4 of the Dutch Civil Code, Procedural Provisions and Private International Law* (Antwerp-Oxford, Intersentia, 2005).

V.J.A. Sütő, *Nieuw Vermogensrecht en rechtsvergelijking – reconstructie van een wetgevingsproces* (Den Haag, Boom Juridische Uitgevers, 2004).

Tacitus, *Germania* (New York, D. Appleton & Comp. 1869).

Gr. Van der Burgt – E.W.J. Ebben, *Erfrecht* (Deventer, Kluwer, 2004).

J.H.M. Van Erp, "The New Dutch Law of Succession", in: K. Reid – M. de Waal – R. Zimmermann (Eds.), *Exploring the Law of Succession. Studies National, Historical and Comparative*, in: Edinburgh Studies in Law, vol. 5 (Edinburgh, Edinburgh University Press, 2007) 193-207.

S. Van Leeuwen, *Rooms Hollands regt* (t'Amsterdam, Hendrik en de wed. Van Dirk Boom, 1686).

M. J. Van Mourik, "De toekomst van de legitieme portie", in: *De legitieme portie* (Deventer, Ars Notariatus-Kluwer 1995) 57-68.

M. J. Van Mourik, *Erfrecht*, 5th edn (Deventer, Kluwer, 2008).

L.P.W. Van Vliet, *Transfer of movables in German, French, English and Dutch Law* (Nijmegen, Ars Aequi 2000).

A. Verbeke, "De legitieme ontbloot of dood" (2000/3) *WPNR* 1111-1236.

L. Verstappen, "Na Wetsvoorstel 28 867 nog een Vierde tranche?" (2010/6825) *WPNR* 3-8.

J. Voet, *Commentarius ad Pandectas* (The Hague 1736).

F.C. Von Savigny, *System des heutigen Römischen Rechts*, I (Berlin, Veit & Comp., 1840).

J.C. Voorduin, *Geschiedenis en beginselen der Nederlandse wetboeken*, 2 (Utrecht 1837).

H. Warendorf – R. Thomas – I. Curry-Sumner, *The Civil Code of The Netherlands* (Alphen aan den Rijn, Kluwer Law International, 2009).

Bibliography Chapter 12 (Peter Hambro)

J. Asland, *Uskifte* (Oslo 2008).

M. Andenæs, "Arvepakt i norsk rett" (1985) *TfR* 18-79.

G. Beyer, *Wills, trusts and estates*, 4th edn (Austin 2007).

T. Frantzen, "Kan ugjenkallelighet innfortolkes i et testament?" (1996) *TfR* 85-122.

T. Frantzen, "Delegasjon av testamentsmyndighet" (1997) *TfR* 950-997.

P. Hambro, *Arveloven kommentarutgave*, 4th edn (Oslo 2007).

P. Hambro, *Avtalt Uskifte* (Oslo 2006).

P. Hambro, *Tilbakekall av testamenter* (Oslo 2010).

P. Lødrup, *Arverett*, 5th edn (Oslo 2008).

P. Lødrup – T. Sverdrup, *Familieretten*, 6th edn (Oslo 2009).

Bibliography Chapter 13 (Eric Clive)

D. Reid, "From the Cradle to the Grave: Politics, Families and Inheritance Law" (2008/12) *Edinburgh Law Review* 391-417.

L.M. Simes, "The Policy against Perpetuities" (1955/103) *Univ Penn Law Rev* 707-738.

Bibliography Chapter 14 (Suzana Kraljić)

B. Blagojević, *Nasledno pravo SFRJ sa ovratom na prava drugih država*, 5th edn (Beograd, Naučna knjiga, 1964).

S. Cigoj, *Institucije obligacij: posebni del obligacijskega prava: kontrakti in reparacije*, 3rd edn (Ljubljana, Uradni list RS, 2002).

N. Gavella, *Nasljedno pravo* (Zagreb, Informator, 1986).

M. Geč-Korošec – R. Knez – S. Kraljić, *Mednarodno zasebno pravo, drugi knjiga –posebni del* (Ljubljana, Uradni list RS, 2002).

M. Geč-Korošec – S. Kraljić, "Familienerbrecht und Testierfreiheit im slowenischen Recht", in: D. Henrich – D. Schwab (Eds.), *Familienerbrecht und Testierfreiheit im europäischen Vergleich. Beiträge zum europäischen Familienrecht* (Bielefeld, Gieseking, 2001) 273-294.

S. Kraljić, "Nujni deleži" (2005/28) *Pravna praksa* 22.

S. Kraljić, "Pogodba o dosmrtnem preživljanju" (2006/17) *Pravna praksa* 8-9.

M. Kreč – Đ. Pavić, *Komentar zakona o nasleđivanju sa sudskom praksom* (Zagreb, Narodne novine, 1964).

N. Plavšak Nina – M. Juhart – D. Jadek-Pensa – V. Kranjc – P. Grilc – A. Polajnar-Pavčnik – M. Dolenc – M. Pavčnik – R. Vrenčur – D. Možina – B. Zabel, *Obligacijski zakonik (OZ): s komentarjem* (Ljubljana, GV Založba, 2003).

V. Rijavec, *Dedovanje – procesna ureditev* (Ljubljana, Gospodarski vestnik, 1999)

A. Smole, *Zakonito in oporočno dedovanje* (Ljubljana, ČZ Uradni list SRS, 1965).

J. Šinkovec – B. Tratar, *Veliki komentar zakona o dedovanju s sodno prakso* (Ljubljana, Založniška hiša Primath, 2005).

N. Šorli, *Pregled sodne prakse in literature, Dedno pravo* (Ljubljana, Vrhovno sodišče SRS; DDU Univerzum, 1982).

K. Zupančič, *Dedovanje z uvodnimi pojasnili Prof. Dr. Karla Zupančiča*, 8th edn (Ljubljana, Uradni list RS, 2005).

K. Zupančič – V. Žnidaršič Skubic, *Dedno pravo*, 3rd edn (Ljubljana, Uradni list, 2009).

V. Žnidaršič, "Nekaj vprašanj iz dednega prava" (2000/2) *Pravna praksa* 13.

Bibliography Chapter 15 (Sergio Cámara Lapuente)

M. Aguilar Benítez de Lugo – H. Aguilar Grieder, "Orden público y sucesiones (I-II)" (2005/1984-1985) *BIMJ* 853-882; 1123-1147.

Anuario de la Dirección General de los Registros y el Notariado 2008 (Madrid, Ministerio de Justicia, 2010).

J. L. Arjona Guajardo-Fajardo, "El testamento mancomunado: reflexiones sobre su posibilidad teórica y su eventual utilidad práctica de Derecho civil común" (2008/66-67) *RJN* 9-96, 51-126.

E. Arroyo Amayuelas – D. Bondia García "¿Interpretación de testamento contraria a los derechos humanos? El caso Pla & Puncernau vs Andorra" (2004/18) *DPyC* 7-88.

E. Arroyo Amayuelas, "Pflichtteilsrecht in Spanien", in: A. Röthel (Ed.), *Reformfragen des Pflichtteilsrechts* (Cologne et al., Heymanns, 2007) 257-276.

E. Arroyo Amayuelas, "La reforma del Derecho de sucesiones y de la prescripción en Alemania" (2010/1) *Indret* (www.indret.com).

C. Asúa González, *Designación de sucesor a través de tercero* (Madrid, Tecnos, 1992).

C. Azcárraga Monzonís, "El tratamiento de las legítimas en el Derecho comparado. Su protección material y de Derecho internacional privado" (2007/43) *RJCLM* 49-86.

A. Barrio Gallardo, "Atemperar la rigidez de la legítima" (2008/21) *ArCiv* 15-41.

R. Bercovitz Rodríguez-Cano, "Comments to STS 14 september 2009" (2010/83) *CCJC* 1093-1122.

M. M. Bermejo Pumar, "La legítima (función y estructura)", in: J. F. Delgado De Miguel – M. Garrido Melero (Eds.), *Instituciones de Derecho privado*, vol. V-3, *Sucesiones: las atribuciones legales* (Cizur Menor, Civitas, 2005) 17-598.

A. L. Cabezuelo Arenas, *Diversas formas de canalización de la cautela socini* (Valencia, Tirant lo Blanch, 2002).

A. Calatayud Sierra, "Consideraciones acerca de la libertad de testar" (1995/9) *Academia Sevillana del Notariado* 241-264.

A. Calatayud Sierra, "Ley aplicable y conflictos de leyes en Derecho de sucesiones", in: M. D. Álvarez García – F. Zubiri de Salinas (eds.), *Reflexiones sobre materias de Derecho sucesorio* (Madrid, CGPJ, 2009) 33-123.

A. L. Calvo Caravaca – J. Carrascosa González, *Derecho Internacional Privado*, 8th edn (Granada, Comares, 2007).

S. Cámara Lapuente, *La fiducia sucesoria secreta* (Madrid, Dykinson, 1996).

S. Cámara Lapuente, *La exclusión testamentaria de los herederos legales* (Madrid, Civitas, 2000).

S. Cámara Lapuente, "De los fiduciarios-comisarios. Comentarios a las leyes 281-288 del Fuero

Nuevo de Navarra", in: M. Albaladejo (Ed.), *Comentarios al Código civil y Compilaciones forales* (Madrid, Edersa, 2001) 321-536.

S. Cámara Lapuente, "De los herederos de confianza. Comentarios a las leyes 289-295 del Fuero Nuevo de Navarra", in: M. Albaladejo (Ed.), *Comentarios al Código civil y Compilaciones forales* (Madrid, Edersa, 2001) 537-1078.

S. Cámara Lapuente, "¿Derecho europeo de sucesiones? Un apunte", in: S. Cámara Lapuente (Ed.), *Derecho Privado Europeo* (Madrid, Colex, 2003) 1185-1233.

S. Cámara Lapuente (2007), "New Developments in the Spanish Law of Succession" (2007/4) *Indret* (www.indret.com).

S. Cámara Lapuente, "Comments to Arts. 424-11 – 424-15 CC Cat", in: J. Egea Fernández – J. Ferrer Riba (Dirs.) *Comentari al Llibre Quart del Codi Civil de Catalunya, relatiu a les successions*, vol. I (Barcelona, Atelier, 2009) 394-447.

S. Cámara Lapuente, "Chapter 4: Spain", in: R. Zimmermann – K. Reid – M. De Waal (Eds.), *Testamentary formalities in Comparative Law* (Oxford, Oxford University Press, 2011) (in print).

M. Carballo Fidalgo, "La legítima en la Ley de 14 de junio de 2006, de Derecho Civil de Galicia", in: M. P. García Rubio (ed.), *Estudios Jurídicos en memoria del Prof. J. M. Lete del Río* (Madrid, Civitas, 2009) 139-164.

M. T. Carrancho Herrero, "Reflexión crítica de los derechos sucesorios del cónyuge viudo en el actual modelo de familia", in: J. M. Abril – M.E. Amat (Eds.), *Homenaje al profesor Lluís Puig i Ferriol* (Valencia, Tirant lo Blanch, 2006) 733-752.

A. Carrasco Perera, "Acoso y derribo de la legítima hereditaria" (2003/580) *AJA* 11-12.

E. Castellanos Ruiz, "Sucesión hereditaria", in: A. L. Calvo Caravaca – J. Carrascosa González (Eds.), *Derecho internacional privado*, 8th edn, vol. II (Granada, Comares, 2007) 283-335.

J. J. Castiella Rodríguez, "El testamento mancomunado, institución exportable al Código civil" (2001/39) *RJN* 9-38.

M. E. Cobas Cobiella, "Hacia un nuevo enfoque de las legítimas" (2006/17) *RDPat* 49-65.

E. Corral García, *Los derechos del cónyuge viudo en el Derecho civil común y autonómico* (Barcelona, Bosch, 2007).

M. Cuena Casas, "Uniones de hecho y abuso del derecho: acerca de la discriminación en contra del matrimonio" (2005/2) *La Ley* 1571-1584.

C. De Amunátegui Rodríguez, *Uniones de hecho. Una nueva visión después de la publicación de las leyes sobre parejas estables* (Valencia, Tirant lo Blanch, 2002).

F. De Castro y Bravo, "Notas sobre las limitaciones intrínsecas de la autonomía de la voluntad. La defensa de la competencia. El orden público. La protección del consumidor" (1982/4) *ADC* 987-1086 [also in: *Estudios jurídicos del prof. Federico de Castro*, vol II (CER, Madrid, 1997) 1251-1338].

P. De la Esperanza Rodríguez, "Perspectiva de la legítima. Notas para una revisión", in: *Libro Homenaje a Ildefonso Sánchez Mera*, vol. I (Madrid, CGN, 2002) 1097-1116.

I. B. De Luca, *Theatrum veritatis et justitiae, sive decisivi discursus...*, vol. X, *De fideicommissis, primogenituris, et majoratibus* (Lugduni 1696).

B. J. De Vos, "Testamentary Freedom, Despotism and Fundamental Rights: a Critical Case Study on *Drittwirkung*" (2008/5) *ERPL* 801-825.

P. Del Pozo Carrascosa – A. Vaquer Aloy – E. Bosch Capdevila, *Derecho Civil de Cataluña. Derecho de Sucesiones* (Barcelona *et al.* Marcial Pons, 2009).

J. Delgado Echeverría, "Comments to Art. 16 CC", in: J. Rams Albesa (Ed.), *Comentarios al Código civil*, vol. I (Barcelona, J. M. Bosch, 2000) 419-436.

J. Delgado Echeverría, "Una propuesta de política del Derecho en materia de sucesiones por causa de muerte. Segunda parte: objetivos de una reforma del derecho de sucesiones", in: *Derecho de sucesiones. Presente y Futuro. XII Jornadas de la Asociación de Profesores de Derecho Civil* (Murcia, Universidad de Murcia, 2006) 85-171.

A. Domínguez Luelmo, *El pago en metálico de la legítima de los descendientes* (Madrid, Tecnos, 1989).

M. Espejo Lerdo de Tejada, *La legítima en la sucesión intestada en el Código civil* (Madrid, Marcial Pons, 1996).

J. A. Fernández Campos, "La inacabada reforma de la legítima del cónyuge viudo", in: Á. Rebolledo Varela (Ed.) *La familia en el Derecho de sucesiones: cuestiones actuales y perspectivas de futuro* (Madrid, Dykinson, 2010) 263-296.

L. Fernández del Pozo, "La fiducia sucesoria. Ensayo de construcción dogmática" (1987) *RCDI* 1731-1752.

J. C. Fernández Rozas – S. Sánchez Lorenzo, *Derecho internacional privado*, 4th edn (Madrid, Civitas, 2007).

M. P. García Rubio, "La reformulación por la Ley 41/2003 de la delegación de la facultad de mejorar" (2008/1) *ADC* 57-112.

J. R. García Vicente, "El testamento mancomunado. Razones para la derogación del artículo 669 del Código civil", in: *Derecho de sucesiones. Presente y Futuro. XII Jornadas de la Asociación de Profesores de Derecho Civil* (Murcia, Universidad de Murcia, 2006) 289-298.

I. Garrote Fernández-Díez, "Sucesiones internacionales y orden público constitucional: la sucesión *mortis causa* en España cuando la ley aplicable es la de un país de tradición jurídica islámica" (2009/23) *DPyC* 149-199.

M. C. Gete-Alonso – M. Ysàs Solanes – S. Navas Navarro – J. Solé Resina, "Sucesión por causa de muerte y relaciones de convivencia", in: *Derecho de sucesiones. Presente y Futuro. XII Jornadas de la Asociación Asociación de Profesores de Derecho Civil* (Murcia, Universidad de Murcia, 2006) 305-397.

I. Gomá Lanzón, "Los derechos del cónyuge viudo", in: J. F. Delgado De Miguel – M. Garrido Melero (Eds.), *Instituciones de Derecho privado*, vol. V-3, *Sucesiones: las atribuciones legales* (Civitas, Cizur Menor, 2005) 599-943.

P. Grimalt Servera, "Los derechos legitimarios en el Derecho civil balear", in: J. M. Abril – M. E. Amat (Eds.), *Homenaje al profesor Lluís Puig i Ferriol*, vol. II (Valencia, Tirant lo Blanch, 2006) 1611-1632.

M. Herrero Oviedo, "El renacer de los pactos sucesorios", in: S. Álvarez González (Ed.), *Estudios de Derecho de familia y sucesiones (dimensiones interna e internacional)* (Santiago de Compostela, Imprenta Universitaria, 2009) 199-217.

A. M. López López, "La garantía institucional de la herencia" (1994/3) *DPyC* 29-62.

V. Magariños Blanco, "La libertad de testar" (2005/9-10) *RDP* 3-30.

J. Marsal Guillamet, "Els fills posats en condició: interpretació del testament i discriminació" (2005/2) *RJC* 477-496.

M. Martínez Martínez, "La reforma de la sucesión intestada en el Código civil", in: *Derecho de sucesiones. Presente y Futuro. XII Jornadas de la Asociación de Profesores de Derecho Civil* (Murcia, Universidad de Murcia, 2006) 438-441.

J. L. Merino Hernández, *La fiducia sucesoria en Aragón* (El Justicia, Zaragoza, 1994).

J. L. Merino Hernández, in: M. Albaladejo – S. Díaz Alabart (Eds.), *Comentarios al Código civil y a las compilaciones forales*, vol. XXXIII-1 (Madrid, Edersa, 2000) 655 ff.

J. M. Miquel González, "Legítima material y legítima formal" (2009/49) *AAMN* 493-560.

V. L. Montés Penadés, "La inesperada resurrección del Derecho *foral* valenciano" (2009/3) *El Cronista* 4-15.

J. L. Moreu Ballonga, "Aportación a la doctrina sobre la legítima aragonesa en contemplación de su futura reforma legal" (1997/1) *ADC* 97-154.

J. L. Moreu Ballonga, "El sistema legitimario en la Ley aragonesa de sucesiones", *Actas del Foro de Derecho Aragonés. XV Encuentros* (Zaragoza 2006) 149-409.

A. Nieto Alonso, "Uniones extramatrimoniales: derechos sucesorios y atribuciones *post mortem* de naturaleza familiar y social", in: Á. Rebolledo Varela (Ed.) *La familia en el Derecho de sucesiones: cuestiones actuales y perspectivas de futuro* (Madrid, Dykinson, 2010) 103-180.

A. Núñez Iglesias, *El testamento por comisario* (Madrid, Fundación Matritense del Notariado, 1991).

C. Oró Martínez, "Orden público internacional y prohibiciones para suceder de la *mudawana*: fundamento y alcance de la excepción de orden público aplicada a la sucesión de un causante marroquí [A propósito de la SAP Barcelona (sección 4ª) de 28 de octubre de 2008]" (2009/1) *Dereito* 287-304.

M. A. Parra Lucán, "Legítimas, libertad de testar y transmisión de un patrimonio" (2009/13) *AFDUDC* 481-554.

J. A. Pastor Ridruejo, "El fraude de ley en el derecho interregional español" (1966) *REDI* 40-55.

M. Pérez Escolar, *El cónyuge supérstite en la sucesión intestada* (Madrid, Dykinson, 2003).

M. Pérez Escolar, "Sucesión intestada y legítima del cónyuge supérstite en el Código civil español. Revisión de fundamentos y planteamiento de futuro" (2007/4) *ADC* 1641-1678.

C. Pinto Andrade, *Efectos patrimoniales tras la ruptura de las parejas de hecho* (Barcelona, Bosch, 2008).

L. Puig Ferriol, "Institución de heredero por fiduciario" (1964) *RJC* 13-66.

L. F. Ragel Sánchez, *La cautela gualdense o socini y el artículo 820.3º del Código civil* (Madrid, Dykinson, 2004).

A. Real Pérez, *Usufructo universal del cónyuge viudo en el Código civil* (Madrid, Montecorvo, 1988).

Á. L. Rebolledo Varela, "La actualización del Derecho sucesorio español ante los cambios sociológicos y jurídicos de la familia: conclusiones de una investigación', in: Á. Rebolledo Varela (Ed.) *La familia en el Derecho de sucesiones: cuestiones actuales y perspectivas de futuro* (Madrid, Dykinson, 2010) 23-41.

J. J. Rivas Martínez, "La delegación de la facultad de mejorar" (2007/136) *Boletín del Colegio de Registradores de España* 1629-1651.

J. J. Rivas Martínez, *Derecho de sucesiones. Común y foral*, 4th edn, vol. 2 (Madrid, Dykinson, 2009).

A. Rodríguez Yniesto, "La reforma del artículo 831 del Código Civil por Ley 41/2003: la delegación de la facultad de mejorar" (2005/55) *RJN* 169-210.

L. Rueda Esteban, "La fiducia sucesoria del artículo 831 del Código civil", in: M. Garrido Melero – L. Fugardo Estevill (Dirs.), *El patrimonio familiar, profesional y empresarial. Sus protocolos*, vol. IV (Barcelona, Bosch, 2005) 155-204.

R. Sánchez Aristi, *Dos alternativas a la sucesión testamentaria: pactos sucesorios y contratos post-mortem* (Granada, Comares, 2003).

T. Torres García, "Legítima, legitimarios y libertad de testar (síntesis de un sistema)", in: *Derecho de sucesiones. Presente y Futuro. XII Jornadas de la Asociación de Profesores de Derecho Civil* (Murcia, Universidad de Murcia, 2006) 173-227.

T. Torres García, "La legítima en el Código civil", in: S. Álvarez González (Ed.), *Estudios de Derecho de familia y sucesiones (dimensiones interna e internacional)* (Santiago de Compostela, Imprenta Universitaria, 2009) 297-321.

E. Valladares Rascón, "Por una reforma del sistema sucesorio del Código civil", in: J. M. González Porras – F. P. Méndez González (Eds.), *Libro homenaje al profesor Manuel Albaladejo García*, vol. II (Murcia, Universidad de Murcia, 2004) 4893-4902.

A. Vaquer Aloy, "Reflexiones sobre una eventual reforma de la legítima" (2007/3) *Indret* (www.indret.com).

A. Vaquer Aloy, "The Law of Successions", in: M. Bussani – F. Werro (eds.), *European Private Law: A Handbook*, vol. I (Stämpfli et al., Berne, 2009) 555-583.

M. E. Zabalo Escudero, "El fraude de ley en el Derecho interregional: comentario a la sentencia del Tribunal Supremo de 5 de abril de 1994" (1994/34) *PJ* 397-402.

A. Zoppini, *Le successioni in diritto comparato*, in: R. Sacco (Ed.) *Trattato di diritto comparato* (Torino, UTET, 2002).